A New World Order

A New World Order

ANNE-MARIE SLAUGHTER

Princeton University Press
Princeton and Oxford

Copyright © 2004 by Princeton University Press

Published by Princeton University Press, 41 William Street,

Princeton, New Jersey 08540

In the United Kingdom: Princeton University Press, 3 Market Place, Woodstock,

Oxfordshire OX20 1SY

All Rights Reserved

Fourth printing, and first paperback printing, 2005

Paperback ISBN-13: 978-0-691-12397-4

Paperback ISBN-10: 0-691-12397-7

The Library of Congress has cataloged the cloth edition of this book as follows

Slaughter, Anne-Marie.

A new world order / Anne-Marie Slaughter.

p. cm.

Includes bibliographical references and index.

ISBN 0-691-11698-9 (cl : alk. paper)

1. Globalization.   2. Intergovernmental cooperation.   3. International

law.   I. Title.

JZ1318.S59 2004

341.7—dc22   2003066413

British Library Cataloging-in-Publication Data is available

This book has been composed in Goudy

Printed on acid-free paper. ∞

pup.princeton.edu

Printed in the United States of America

10 9 8 7 6 5

For Andy

Contents

Acknowledgments

THIS BOOK HAS TAKEN A CAST OF THOUSANDS. I BEGAN WRITING IT A decade ago, in 1993. As it evolved, from article to article, and draft to draft, it absorbed the attention of sequential teams of invaluable research assistants: Mirna Adjami, Michele Beardsley, David Bosco, William Bradford, Dana Brakman, S. Chelvan, Sungjoon Cho, Cait Clarke, Aliya Haider, Sharon Kasok, Amir Licht, Neil McDonald, Anja Miller (now Manuel), Gordon Moodie, Paul Oostburg, Laura Palmer, Stephen Park, Heidi Parry, Akbar Rasulov, Donovan Rinker-Morris, Khalil Sharif, Sven Spengemann, Andrew Tulumello, Eli Wald, Stepan Wood, Scott Worden, and Patricia Yeh. Several members of this group have become scholars in their own right, writing and publishing papers that I cite, including Lore Unt and David Zaring. Special thanks go to team leaders Tim Wu and later Annecoos Wiersema and Gabriella Blum, who worked with other students to organize the research necessary for specific chapters and who took charge of plugging holes in actual drafts. I worked with them as I would with coauthors and relied on them as friends. I am grateful for their substantive comments on the manuscript as well as their invaluable organizational and research skills.

Other student contributors include the members of an extraordinary seminar on transgovernmental regulatory cooperation that I taught at Harvard Law School in the spring of 1998. Students who wrote important research papers on different dimensions of this subject, many of which are cited in chapter 1 and chapter 5, include Marne Cheek, David Knight, Kal Raustiala, Faith Teo, Jeff Walker, and Tim Wu. Marne Cheek and Kal Raustiala subsequently published versions of their papers as first-rate articles.

I also owe a debt of special gratitude to Robert Clark, former dean of the Harvard Law School, for funding many summers of book research and writing. My former colleagues at the Law School listened to numerous presentations of works in progress and offered helpful comments, as did faculty participants in legal theory workshops and international law seminars at many other law schools, including Berkeley, Chicago, Columbia, Duke, the European University Institute, Georgetown, N.Y.U., Oxford, U.C.L.A., Virginia, and Wisconsin. The searching questions and comments I received in many of these seminars have forced me to rethink and refine many issues. I am also grateful to the Carr Center for Human Rights at Harvard's Kennedy School of Government, which offered me an office and very good company for an important sabbatical year from 2000–2001.

Kal Raustiala and Michael Barnett read the entire final draft of the manuscript and offered extremely helpful comments, necessitating a substantial redraft of chapter 5. They offered vital and the moral encouragement. Thanks also to Sean Murphy, one of the reviewers for Princeton University Press and a valued colleague and friend, who made a number of very helpful suggestions, as did Lori Damrosch in a similarly detailed review. In a different vein, I am grateful to Grady Klein for translating my mental vision of a networked world order into the vibrant graphic on the cover. Jonathan Munk provided expert copyediting with a light but deft hand.

I am particularly grateful to a number of intellectual mentors, colleagues, and friends, many of whom are cited in the endnotes but who deserve separate mention here. Robert Keohane has been a tremendous personal and intellectual influence—offering me feedback, constructive criticism, and moral support every step of the way. Bob and

Joseph Nye are tremendously influential coauthors in their own right; they sowed many of the intellectual seeds that I have reaped here. They have also been great friends. Chuck Sabel provided his amazing intellectual spark and vision at various meetings over the past three years, convincing me of the potential of democratic experimentalism in ways that helped me see my own work in a new light. Ben Kingsbury is, as always, my intellectual conscience, pushing me to think through the actual consequences of my rosy visions.

Fareed Zakaria chose to publish my first version of the thesis presented here as the article "The Real New World Order" in the seventy-fifth–anniversary issue of *Foreign Affairs*. His vote of confidence in the thesis redoubled my commitment to see the project through. Finally, Abe and Toni Chayes, whose book *The New Sovereignty* is one of the most important works to be published in international law in several decades, influenced almost every page. Losing Abe several years ago hurts even more when I think that he will never be able to read this book, but Toni's steady support and confidence, as well as her lively reactions to specific parts of my work, have made it an ongoing pleasure to read and rely on their work.

To my children, Edward Moravcsik and Alexander Moravcsik, who arrived during the writing of this book and who have learned to see the laptop as their enemy, I am grateful for joy and distraction. To my parents, Ned and Anne Slaughter, I owe everything, including a particular debt for their patience while I was "finishing" my book during seven consecutive summer sojourns in Umbria. My brothers, Hoke and Bryan Slaughter, provided humor, love, and steady support. And to the lovely Sullivan sisters, Elizabeth and Katherine, who kept my children happy during those same sojourns while I typed upstairs, many thanks.

This book simply would not exist without a great editor, Ian Malcolm of Princeton University Press, who somehow convinced me to send him the manuscript in the summer of 2002 and edited it line by line, paragraph by paragraph over the ensuing year. His gentle presence and pressure were invaluable in the last rounds. Top honors, however, and the greatest debt, go to William Burke-White, my indispensable special assistant, coauthor, intellectual alter-ego, and amanuensis, and to Terry Murphy, who has worked with me on simply everything as a partner and friend for four years, and who formatted, filled, and tidied every inch of text. Without both of them, this book would never have been born.

Finally, I dedicate this book to my husband, Andrew Moravcsik. The decade of writing this book has been the first decade of our marriage. He has made it the best decade of my life, suffering and rejoicing with me through every minute. No one will be happier than he to have this finished; no one deserves greater credit for helping make it happen.

Anne-Marie Slaughter
Tuoro sul Trasimeno
July 2003

List of Abbreviations

ABA	American Bar Association
AIPO	ASEAN Inter-Parliamentary Organization
APEC	Asian-Pacific Economic Cooperation
ASEAN	Association of Southeast Asian Nations
BIS	Bank for International Settlements
BvG	German Federal Constitutional Court (*Bundesverfassungsgericht*)
CEC	Commission on Environmental Cooperation
CEELI	Central and East European Law Initiative
CICA	Conference and Interaction on Security and Confidence-building Measures in Central Asia
CICTE	Inter-American Committee against Terrorism (*Comité Interamericano Contra el Terrorismo*)
CINC	Commander in Chief
CITES	Convention on Trade in Endangered Species
COPA	Parliamentary Conference of the Americas
COSAC	Conference of the Community and European Affairs Committees
CPA	Commonwealth Parliamentary Association
CPSS	Committee on Payment and Settlement Systems

CSCE	Conference on Security and Cooperation in Europe
DOJ	Department of Justice
EC	European Community
ECHR	European Court of Human Rights
ECJ	European Court of Justice
EEC	European Economic Community
EFTA	European Free Trade Area
EMP	Euro-Mediterranean Partnership
EP	European Parliament
EPA	Environmental Protection Agency
ERISA	Employee Retirement Income Security Act
EU	European Union
FAA	Federal Aviation Authority
FAO	Food and Agriculture Organization of the United Nations
FATF	Financial Action Task Force
FBI	Federal Bureau of Investigation
FDA	Food and Drug Administration
FINCEN	Financial Crimes Enforcement Network
FIU	Financial Intelligence Unit
FOIA	Freedom of Information Act
FTC	Federal Trade Commission
GATT	General Agreement on Trade and Tariffs
GC	Global Compact
GLOBE	Global Legislators for a Balanced Environment
IAIS	International Association of Insurance Supervisors
ICC	International Criminal Court
ICCB	Interparliamentary Consultative Council of Benelux
ICN	International Competition Network
ICPAC	The International Competition Policy Advisory Committeee
ICTY	International Criminal Tribunal for the Former Yugoslavia
IDEC	International Drug Enforcement Conference
IIN	Inter-American Children's Institute (*Instituto Interamericano del Niño*)

ILA	International Law Association
ILC	ILA Committee on a Permanent International Criminal Court
IMF	International Monetary Fund
INECE	International Network for Environmental Compliance and Enforcement
IOSCO	International Organization of Securities Commissioners
IPU	Inter-Parliamentary Union
LAWASIA	Law Association for Asia and the Pacific
MOU	Memoranda of Understanding
MRA	Mutual-Recognition Agreement
NAA	North Atlantic Assembly
NAAEC	North American Agreement on Environmental Cooperation
NAFTA	North American Free Trade Agreement
NATO	North Atlantic Treaty Organization
NATO-PA	NATO Parliamentary Assembly
NCSL	National Conference of State Legislators
NGO	Nongovernmental Organization
OAS	Organization of American States
OAU	Organization of African Unity
OCSA	Organization of Supreme Courts of the Americas
OECD	Organization for Economic Cooperation and Development
OSCE	Organization for Security and Cooperation in Europe
PAEAC	Parliamentary Association for Euro-Arab Cooperation
PGA	Parliamentarians for Global Action
PROFEPA	*Procuraduría Federal de Protección al Ambiente*
SAARC	South Asian Association for Regional Cooperation
SAFTA	South Asian Free Trade Area
SAPTA	South Asian Preferential Trading Agreement
SEC	Securities and Exchange Commission
U.K.	United Kingdom
UN	United Nations

UNCITRAL   United Nations Commission on International
           Trade Law
UNEP   United Nations Environment Programme
UNPROFOR   United Nations Protection Force
U.S.   United States of America
WEU   Interparliamentary European Security and Defence
           Assembly
WHO   World Health Organization
WIPO   World Intellectual Property Organization
WTO   World Trade Organization

A New World Order

Introduction

> What is possible is not independent of what we believe to be possible. The possibility of such developments in the practical world depends upon their being grasped imaginatively by the people who make the practical world work.
> —Neil MacCormick[1]

TERRORISTS, ARMS DEALERS, MONEY LAUNDERERS, DRUG DEALERS, TRAF-fickers in women and children, and the modern pirates of intellectual property all operate through global networks.[2] So, increasingly, do governments. Networks of government officials—police investigators, financial regulators, even judges and legislators—increasingly exchange information and coordinate activity to combat global crime and address common problems on a global scale. These government networks are a key feature of world order in the twenty-first century, but they are underappreciated, undersupported, and underused to address the central problems of global governance.

Consider the examples just in the wake of September 11. The Bush administration immediately set about assembling an ad hoc coalition of states to aid in the war on terrorism. Public attention focused on military cooperation, but the networks of financial regulators working to identify and freeze terrorist assets, of law enforcement officials sharing vital information on terrorist suspects, and of intelligence operatives working to preempt the next attack have been equally important. Indeed, the leading expert in the "new security" of borders and container bombs insists that the domestic agencies responsible for customs, food safety, and regulation of all kinds must extend their reach abroad, through reorganization and much closer cooperation with their foreign counterparts.[3] And after the United States concluded that it did not have authority under international law to interdict a shipment of missiles from North Korea to Yemen, it turned to national law enforcement authorities to coordinate the extraterritorial enforcement of their national criminal laws.[4] Networked threats require a networked response.

Turning to the global economy, networks of finance ministers and central bankers have been critical players in responding to national and regional financial crises. The G-8 is as much a network of finance ministers as of heads of state; it is the finance ministers who make key decisions on how to respond to calls for debt relief for the most highly indebted countries. The finance ministers and central bankers hold separate news conferences to announce policy responses to crises such as the East Asian financial crisis in 1997 and the Russian crisis in 1998.[5] The G-20, a network specifically created to help prevent future crises, is led by the Indian finance minister and is composed of the finance ministers of twenty developed and developing countries. More broadly, the International Organization of Securities Commissioners (IOSCO) emerged in 1984. It was followed in the 1990s by the creation of the International Association of Insurance Supervisors and a network of all three of these organizations and other national and international officials responsible for financial stability around the world called the Financial Stability Forum.[6]

Beyond national security and the global economy, networks of national officials are working to improve environmental policy across borders. Within the North American Free Trade Agreement (NAFTA), U.S., Mexican, and Canadian environmental agencies have created an environmental enforcement network, which has enhanced the effectiveness of environmental regulation in all three states, particularly in

Mexico. Globally, the Environmental Protection Agency (EPA) and its Dutch equivalent have founded the International Network for Environmental Compliance and Enforcement (INECE), which offers technical assistance to environmental agencies around the world, holds global conferences at which environmental regulators learn and exchange information, and sponsors a website with training videos and other information.

Nor are regulators the only ones networking. National judges are exchanging decisions with one another through conferences, judicial organizations, and the Internet. Constitutional judges increasingly cite one another's decisions on issues from free speech to privacy rights. Indeed, Justice Anthony Kennedy of the U.S. Supreme Court cited a decision by the European Court of Justice (ECJ) in an important 2003 opinion overturning a Texas antisodomy law. Bankruptcy judges in different countries negotiate minitreaties to resolve complicated international cases; judges in transnational commercial disputes have begun to see themselves as part of a global judicial system. National judges are also interacting directly with their supranational counterparts on trade and human rights issues.

Finally, even legislators, the most naturally parochial government officials due to their direct ties to territorially rooted constituents, are reaching across borders. International parliamentary organizations have been traditionally well meaning though ineffective, but today national parliamentarians are meeting to adopt and publicize common positions on the death penalty, human rights, and environmental issues. They support one another in legislative initiatives and offer training programs and technical assistance.[7]

Each of these networks has specific aims and activities, depending on its subject area, membership, and history, but taken together, they also perform certain common functions. They expand regulatory reach, allowing national government officials to keep up with corporations, civic organizations, and criminals. They build trust and establish relationships among their participants that then create incentives to establish a good reputation and avoid a bad one. These are the conditions essential for long-term cooperation. They exchange regular information about their own activities and develop databases of best practices, or, in the judicial case, different approaches to common legal issues. They offer technical assistance and professional socialization to members from less developed nations, whether regulators, judges, or legislators.

In a world of global markets, global travel, and global information networks, of weapons of mass destruction and looming environmental disasters of global magnitude, governments must have global reach. In a world in which their ability to use their hard power is often limited, governments must be able to exploit the uses of soft power: the power of persuasion and information.[8] Similarly, in a world in which a major set of obstacles to effective global regulation is a simple inability on the part of many developing countries to translate paper rules into changes in actual behavior, governments must be able not only to negotiate treaties but also to create the capacity to comply with them.

Understood as a form of global governance, government networks meet these needs. As commercial and civic organizations have already discovered, their networked form is ideal for providing the speed and flexibility necessary to function effectively in an information age. But unlike amorphous "global policy networks" championed by UN Secretary General Kofi Annan, in which it is never clear who is exercising power on behalf of whom, these are networks composed of national government officials, either appointed by elected officials or directly elected themselves. Best of all, they can perform many of the functions of a world government—legislation, administration, and adjudication—without the form.

Understood as a foreign policy option, a world of government networks, working alongside and even within traditional international organizations, should be particularly attractive to the United States. The United States has taken the lead in insisting that many international problems have domestic roots and that they be addressed at that level—within nations rather than simply between them—but it is also coming to understand the vital need to address those problems multilaterally rather than unilaterally, for reasons of legitimacy, burden sharing, and effectiveness. As will be further discussed below, government networks could provide multilateral support for domestic government institutions in failed, weak, or transitional states. They could play an instrumental role in rebuilding a country like Iraq and in supporting and reforming government institutions in other countries that seek to avoid dictatorship and self-destruction.

Further, government networks cast a different light on U.S. power, one that is likely to engender less resentment worldwide. They engage U.S. officials of all kinds with their foreign counterparts in settings in which they have much to teach but also to learn and in which other countries can often provide powerful alternative models. In many regulatory areas, such as competition policy, environmental policy, and corporate governance, the European Union attracts as many imitators as the United States. In constitutional rights, many judges around the world have long followed U.S. Supreme Court decisions but are now looking to the South African constitutional or the Canadian supreme courts instead.

Where a U.S. regulatory, judicial, or legislative approach is dominant, it is likely to be powerful through attraction rather than coercion—exactly the kind of soft power that Joseph Nye has been exhorting the United States to use.[9] This attraction flows from expertise, integrity, competence, creativity, and generosity with time and ideas— all characteristics that U.S. regulators, judges, and legislators have exhibited with their foreign counterparts. And where the United States is not dominant, its officials can show that they are in fact willing to listen to and learn from others, something that the rest of the world seems increasingly to doubt.

Yet to see these networks as they exist, much less to imagine what they could become, requires a deeper conceptual shift. Stop imagining the international system as a system of states—unitary entities like billiard balls or black boxes—subject to rules created by international institutions that are apart from, "above" these states. Start thinking about a world of governments, with all the different institutions that perform the basic functions of governments—legislation, adjudication, implementation—interacting both with each other domestically and also with their foreign and supranational counterparts. States still exist in this world; indeed, they are crucial actors. But they are "disaggregated." They relate to each other not only through the Foreign Office, but also through regulatory, judicial, and legislative channels.

This conceptual shift lies at the heart of this book. Seeing the world through the lenses of disaggregated rather than unitary states allows leaders, policymakers, analysts, or simply concerned citizens to see features of the global political system that were previously hidden. Government networks suddenly pop up everywhere, from the Financial Action Task Force (FATF), a network of finance ministers and other financial regulators taking charge of pursuing money launderers and financers of terrorism, to the Free Trade Commission, a network of trade ministers charged with interpreting NAFTA, to a network of ministers in charge of border controls working to create a new regime of safe borders in the wake of September 11. At the same time, it is possible to disaggregate international organizations as well, to see "vertical networks" between national regulators and judges and their supranational counterparts. Examples include relations between national European courts and the ECJ or between national U.S., Mexican, and Canadian courts and NAFTA arbitral tribunals.

Equally important, these different lenses make it possible to imagine a genuinely new set of possibilities for a future world order. The building blocks of this order would not be states but parts of states: courts, regulatory agencies, ministries, legislatures. The government officials within these various institutions would participate in many different types of networks, creating links across national borders and between national and supranational institutions. The result could be a world that looks like the globe hoisted by Atlas at Rockefeller Center, crisscrossed by an increasingly dense web of networks.

This world would still include traditional international organizations, such as the United Nations and the World Trade Organization (WTO), although many of these organizations would be likely to become hosts for and sources of government networks. It would still feature states interacting as unitary states on important issues, particularly in security matters. And it would certainly still be a world in which military and economic power mattered; government networks are not likely to substitute for either armies or treasuries.

At the same time, however, a world of government networks would be a more effective and potentially more just world order than either what we have today or a world government in which a set of global in-

Atlas, by Lee Lawrie in Rockefeller Center, New York. © Ric Ergenbright/ CORBIS

stitutions perched above nation-states enforced global rules. In a networked world order, primary political authority would remain at the national level except in those cases in which national governments had explicitly delegated their authority to supranational institutions. National government officials would be increasingly enmeshed in networks of personal and institutional relations. They would each be operating both in the domestic and the international arenas, exercising their national authority to implement their transgovernmental and international obligations and representing the interests of their country while working with their foreign and supranational counterparts to disseminate and distill information, cooperate in enforcing national and international laws, harmonizing national laws and regulations, and addressing common problems.

1. THE GLOBALIZATION PARADOX: NEEDING MORE GOVERNMENT AND FEARING IT

Peoples and their governments around the world need global institutions to solve collective problems that can only be addressed on a global scale. They must be able to make and enforce global rules on a variety of subjects and through a variety of means. Further, it has become commonplace to claim that the international institutions created in the late 1940s, after a very different war and facing a host of different threats from those we face today, are outdated and inadequate to meet contemporary challenges. They must be reformed or even reinvented; new ones must be created.

Yet world government is both infeasible and undesirable. The size and scope of such a government presents an unavoidable and dangerous threat to individual liberty. Further, the diversity of the peoples to be governed makes it almost impossible to conceive of a global demos. No form of democracy within the current global repertoire seems capable of overcoming these obstacles.

This is the globalization paradox. We need more government on a global and a regional scale, but we don't want the centralization of decision-making power and coercive authority so far from the people actually to be governed. It is the paradox identified in the European Union by Renaud Dehousse and by Robert Keohane in his millennial presidential address to the American Political Science Association. The European Union has pioneered "regulation by networks," which Dehousse describes as the response to a basic dilemma in EU governance: "On the one hand, increased uniformity is certainly needed; on the other hand, greater centralization is politically inconceivable, and probably undesirable."[10] The EU alternative is the "transnational option"—the use of an organized network of national officials to ensure "that the actors in charge of the implementation of Community policies behave in a similar manner."[11]

Worldwide, Keohane argues that globalization "creates potential gains from cooperation" if institutions can be created to harness those gains;[12] however, institutions themselves are potentially oppressive.[13] The result is "the Governance Dilemma: although institutions are essential for human life, they are also dangerous."[14] The challenge facing political scientists and policymakers at the dawn of the twenty-first century is discovering how well-structured institutions could enable the world to have "a rebirth of freedom."[15]

Addressing the paradox at the global level is further complicated by the additional concern of accountability. In the 1990s the conventional reaction to the problem of "world government" was instead to champion "global governance," a much looser and less threatening concept of collective organization and regulation without coercion. A major element of global governance, in turn, has been the rise of global policy networks, celebrated for their ability to bring together all public and private actors on issues critical to the global public interest.[16]

Global policy networks, in turn, grow out of various "reinventing government" projects, both academic and practical. These projects focus on the many ways in which private actors now can and do perform government functions, from providing expertise to monitoring compliance with regulations to negotiating the substance of those regulations, both domestically and internationally. The problem, however, is ensuring that these private actors uphold the public trust.

Conservative critics have been most sensitive to this problem. Assistant Secretary of State John Bolton, while still in the private sector, argued that "it is precisely the detachment from governments that makes international civil society so troubling, at least for democracies." "Indeed," he continues, "the civil society idea actually suggests a 'corporativist' approach to international decision-making that is dramatically troubling for democratic theory because it posits 'interests' (whether NGOs or businesses) as legitimate actors along with popularly elected governments." Corporatism, in turn, at least in Mussolini's view, was the core of fascism. Hence Bolton's bottom line: "Mussolini would smile on the Forum of Civil Society. Americanists do not."[17]

Somewhat more calmly, Martin Shapiro argues that the shift from government to governance marks "a significant erosion of the boundaries separating what lies inside a government and its administration and what lies outside them."[18] The result is to advantage "experts and enthusiasts," the two groups outside government that have the greatest incentive and desire to participate in governance processes;[19] however, "while the ticket to participation in governance is knowledge and/or passion, both knowledge and passion generate perspectives that are not those of the rest of us. Few of us would actually enjoy living in a Frank Lloyd Wright house."[20] The network form, with its loose, informal, and nonhierarchical structure, only exacerbates this problem.

The governance dilemma thus becomes a tri-lemma: we need global rules without centralized power but with government actors who can be held to account through a variety of political mechanisms. These government actors can and should interact with a wide range of non-governmental organizations (NGOs), but their role in governance bears distinct and different responsibilities. They must represent all their different constituencies, at least in a democracy; corporate and civic actors may be driven by profits and passions, respectively. "Governance" must not become a cover for the blurring of these lines, even if it is both possible and necessary for these various actors to work together on common problems.

In this context, a world order based on government networks, working alongside and even in place of more traditional international institutions, holds great potential. The existence of networks of national officials is not itself new. In 1972 Francis Bator testified before Congress: "it is a central fact of foreign relations that business is carried on by the separate departments with their counterpart bureaucracies abroad, through a variety of informal as well as formal connections."[21] Two years later, in an important article that informed their later study of complex interdependence, Robert Keohane and Joseph Nye distinguished "transgovernmental" activity from the broader category of transnational activity. They defined transgovernmental relations as "sets of direct interactions among sub-units of different governments that are not controlled or closely guided by the policies of the cabinets or chief executives of those governments."[22] Moreover, government networks established for limited purposes such as postal and telecommunications have existed for almost a century.

What is new is the scale, scope, and type of transgovernmental ties. Links between government officials from two, four, or even a dozen countries have become sufficiently dense as to warrant their own organization—witness IOSCO or INECE. Government networks have developed their own identity and autonomy in specific issue areas, such as the G-7 or the G-20. They perform a wider array of functions than in the past, from collecting and distilling information on global or regional best practices to actively offering technical assistance to poorer and less experienced members. And they have spread far beyond regulators to judges and legislators.

More broadly, government networks have become recognized and semiformalized ways of doing business within loose international groupings like the Commonwealth and the Asian-Pacific Economic Cooperation (APEC). At the same time, they have become the signature form of governance for the European Union, which is itself pioneering a new form of regional collective governance that is likely to prove far more relevant to global governance than the experience of traditional federal states. Most important, they are driven by many of the multiple factors that drive the hydra-headed phenomenon of globalization itself, leading to the simple need for national officials of all kinds to communicate and negotiate across borders to do business they could once accomplish solely at home.

The point of this book is not to "discover" government networks. It is to point out their proliferation in every place we have eyes to see, if only we use the right lenses. And it is to explore their potential, highlighting their advantages and warning of their disadvantages, in constructing a world order that is better fitted to meet the challenges of the world we share.

Government networks can help address the governance tri-lemma, offering a flexible and relatively fast way to conduct the business of global governance, coordinating and even harmonizing national government action while initiating and monitoring different solutions to global problems. Yet they are decentralized and dispersed, incapable of exercising centralized coercive authority. Further, they are government actors. They can interact with a wide range of NGOs, civic and corporate, but their responsibilities and constituencies are far broader. These constituencies should be able to devise ways to hold them accountable, at least to the same extent that they are accountable for their purely domestic activity.

2. THE DISAGGREGATED STATE

Participants in the decade-long public and academic discussion of globalization have routinely focused on two major shifts: from national to global and from government to governance. They have paid far less attention to the third shift, from the unitary state to the disaggregated state.

The disaggregated state sounds vaguely Frankenstinian—a shambling, headless bureaucratic monster. In fact, it is nothing so sinister. It is simply the rising need for and capacity of different domestic government institutions to engage in activities beyond their borders, often with their foreign counterparts. It is regulators pursuing the subjects of their regulations across borders; judges negotiating minitreaties with their foreign brethren to resolve complex transnational cases; and legislators consulting on the best ways to frame and pass legislation affecting human rights or the environment.

The significance of the concept of the disaggregated state only becomes fully apparent in contrast to the unitary state, a concept that has long dominated international legal and political analysis. International lawyers and international relations theorists have always known that the entities they describe and analyze as "states" interacting with one another are in fact much more complex entities, but the fiction of a unitary will and capacity for action has worked well enough for purposes of description and prediction of outcomes in the international system. In U.S. constitutional law, for instance, the Supreme Court and the president have often had recourse to James Madison's famous pronouncement in the Federalist papers: "If we are to be one nation in any respect, it clearly ought to be in respect to other nations."[23] And in international law, the foundational premise of state sovereignty traditionally assumed that members of the international system have no right to pierce the veil of statehood.

In an international legal system premised on unitary states, the paradigmatic form of international cooperation is the multilateral international convention, negotiated over many years in various international watering holes, signed and ratified with attendant flourish and formality, and given continuing life through the efforts of an international secretariat whose members prod and assist ongoing rounds of negotiation aimed at securing compliance with obligations already undertaken and at expanding the scope and precision of existing rules.[24] The "states" participating in these negotiations are presumed to speak with one voice—a voice represented by either the head of state or the foreign minister. Any differences between the different parts of a particular government are to be worked out domestically; the analytical lens of the unitary state obscures the very existence of these different government institutions.

The result is the willful adoption of analytical blinders, allowing us to see the "international system" only in the terms that we ourselves have imposed. Compare our approach to domestic government: we know it to be an aggregate of different institutions. We call it "the government," but we can simultaneously distinguish the activities of the courts, Congress, regulatory agencies, and the White House itself. We do not choose to screen out everything except what the president does or says, or what Congress does or says, or what the Supreme Court does or says. But effectively, in the international system, we do.

Looking at the international system through the lens of unitary states leads us to focus on traditional international organizations and institutions created by and composed of formal state delegations. Conversely, however, thinking about states the way we think about domestic governments—as aggregations of distinct institutions with separate roles and capacities—provides a lens that allows us to see a new international landscape. Government networks pop up everywhere.

Horizontal government networks—links between counterpart national officials across borders—are easiest to spot. Far less frequent, but potentially very important, are vertical government networks, those between national government officials and their supranational counterparts. The prerequisite for a vertical government network is the relatively rare decision by states to delegate their sovereignty to an institution above them with real power—a court or a regulatory commission. That institution can then be the genuine counterpart existence of a national government institution. Where these vertical networks exist, as in the relations between national courts and the ECJ in the European Union, they enable the supranational institution to be maximally effective.

The first three chapters of the book describe the world as it is when viewed through the lens of disaggregated rather than unitary states. They spotlight many different types of government networks, horizontal and vertical, among government officials of every stripe. The concept of a "network" has many different definitions; I use a very broad one. The point is to capture all the different ways that individual government institutions are interacting with their counterparts either abroad or above them, alongside more traditional state-to-state interactions. For present purposes, then, a network is a pattern of regular and purposive relations among like government units working across the borders that divide countries from one another and that demarcate the "domestic" from the "international" sphere.[25]

Chapter 1 presents regulators—from central bankers to utilities commissioners—as the new diplomats. Embassies around the world have become regular hosts to regulators coming to meet with other regulators. Regulatory networks span a wide range from informal bilateral and multilateral networks to more institutionalized transgovernmental regulatory organizations such as the Basel Committee and IOSCO. The chapter distinguishes among regulatory networks that are located within traditional international organizations, those created as a result of executive agreements, and those generated spontaneously through increasingly regular contacts between specific regulators. It also identifies three broad types of networks: information networks, enforcement networks, and harmonization networks.

Chapter 2 turns to courts. Judges are perhaps the most surprising networkers, but they too are increasingly engaged with their counterparts abroad. Some of this interaction is more passive, consisting principally in learning about and citing one another's decisions. In other circumstances, judges are forming their own organizations and are actively developing principles that allow them to cooperate better in transnational litigation. They can thus be said to participate in both information and enforcement networks. Running through all these activities is a growing awareness, among both national and supranational judges, of their participation in the common enterprise of judging. The result is not a formal international legal system, but more a global community of courts.

Chapter 3 describes a parallel, although less-developed, world of legislative networks. Legislators come together within the framework of numerous international treaties and organizations and have begun to link up with one another more spontaneously to share information and coordinate activity regarding issues of common interest, such as human rights, environmental protection, and opposition to the death penalty. Legislators must inevitably respond principally to domestic constituencies, and thus benefit less from, and may even pay a price for, foreign networking. On the other hand, legislators have quite different perspectives to share with one another than those shared by regulators and judges, respectively, and are able to exercise a more direct transgovernmental influence on specific policy issues.

3. A NEW WORLD ORDER

Appreciating the extent and nature of existing government networks, both horizontal and vertical, makes it possible to envision a genuinely new world order. "World order," for these purposes, describes a system of global governance that institutionalizes cooperation and sufficiently contains conflict such that all nations and their peoples may achieve greater peace and prosperity, improve their stewardship of the earth, and reach minimum standards of human dignity. The concept of a "new world order" has been used and overused to refer to everything from George H. W. Bush's vision of a post–Cold War world to the post-9/11 geopolitical landscape. Nevertheless, I use it to describe a different conceptual framework for the actual infrastructure of world order— an order based on an intricate three-dimensional web of links between disaggregated state institutions.

Recall Atlas and his globe at Rockefeller Center. A disaggregated world order would be a world latticed by countless government networks. These would include horizontal networks and vertical networks; networks for collecting and sharing information of all kinds, for policy coordination, for enforcement cooperation, for technical assistance and training, perhaps ultimately for rule making. They would be bilateral, plurilateral, regional, or global. Taken together, they would provide the skeleton or infrastructure for global governance.

To appreciate the full implications of this vision, consider again our implicit mental maps of "the international system" or even "world order." It's a flat map, pre-Columbian, with states at the level of the land and the international system floating above them somewhere. International organizations also inhabit this floating realm—they are apart from and somehow above the states that are their members. To the extent that they are actually seen as governing the international system or establishing global order, they must constitute an international bureaucracy equivalent in form and function to the multiple domestic bureaucracies of the states "underneath" them.

In a world of government networks, by contrast, the same officials who are judging, regulating, and legislating domestically are also reaching out to their foreign counterparts to help address the governance problems that arise when national actors and issues spill beyond their borders. Global governance, from this perspective, is not a matter of regulating states the way states regulate their citizens, but rather of addressing the issues and resolving the problems that result from citizens going global—from crime to commerce to civic engagement. Even where genuinely supranational officials participate in vertical government networks—meaning judges or regulators who exercise actual sovereign authority delegated to them by a group of states—they must work very closely with their national counterparts and must harness national coercive power to be effective.

Scholars and commentators in different issue areas have begun to identify various pieces of this infrastructure. Financial regulators, for instance, are becoming accustomed to describing the new international financial architecture as a combination of networks—G-7, G-8, and G-20, the Basel Committee, and IOSCO among them—with traditional international institutions, such as the International Monetary Fund (IMF) and the World Bank. Scholars of the European Union, as noted above, are increasingly familiar with the concept of "regulation by network." Environmental activists would readily recognize some of the institutions associated with the North American Free Trade Agreement (NAFTA) as "environmental enforcement networks" composed of the environmental protection agencies of the United States, Canada, and Mexico.[26] And constitutional law scholars, human rights activists, and transnational litigators would not balk at the idea of transnational judicial networks to describe the various ways in which courts around the world are increasingly interacting with one another.

Further, different regional and political organizations around the world have already consciously adopted this form of organization. Beyond the European Union, both APEC and the Nordic System are essentially "networks of networks," organizations composed of networks of national ministers and parliamentarians. The Commonwealth has also long been structured this way, although its myriad networks of regulators, judges, and legislators have evolved more gradually over time. And the OECD is an international institution that has as its chief function the convening of different networks of national regulators to address common problems and propose model solutions.

Chapter 4 outlines a conception of a disaggregated world order based on government networks. It begins by describing the networked organizations and associations just mentioned. It then turns to the vertical dimension of a disaggregated world order, describing the more limited but critical role that could be played by networks between supranational officials and their national counterparts. The final section of the chapter turns to the relations between government networks and traditional international organizations, exploring the possibility for international organizations themselves to disaggregate into judicial, regulatory, and legislative components. The description and analysis in this chapter are equal parts fact and imagination. I outline what is, in part, and what could be. I also assume, from a normative standpoint, that a world order based on a combination of horizontal and vertical government networks, operating within and alongside future versions of our current international organizations, could be both a feasible and a desirable response to the globalization paradox.

Such a project may well be laying itself open to charges of hubris, or, at best, foolhardiness. If I attempt it, it is because I believe that politicians and policymakers wrestling daily with problems on a global scale need a structured, enduring theoretical vision toward which to strive, even if never to entirely achieve. As Neil MacCormick writes in the epigraph to this chapter, "What is possible is not independent of what we believe to be possible." To achieve a better world order, we must believe that one can exist and be willing to describe it in sufficient detail that it could actually be built.

Premises

There can, of course, be no one blueprint for world order. The proposal advanced here is part of an active and ongoing debate. In the spirit of such debate, it is important to acknowledge that the model of world order I put forward rests on a combination of descriptive and predictive empirical claims, which can be summarized in basic terms:

- The state is not the only actor in the international system, but it is still the most important actor.
- The state is not disappearing, but it is disaggregating into its component institutions, which are increasingly interacting principally with their foreign counterparts across borders.
- These institutions still represent distinct national or state interests, even as they also recognize common professional identities and substantive experience as judges, regulators, ministers, and legislators.
- Different states have evolved and will continue to evolve mechanisms for reaggregating the interests of their distinct institutions when necessary. In many circumstances, therefore, states will still interact with one another as unitary actors in more traditional ways.
- Government networks exist alongside and sometimes within more traditional international organizations.

These premises are distilled from the empirical material presented principally in the first three chapters. They specify the components and the context for the operation of both horizontal and vertical government networks. But they also specify what I am not saying. I am not arguing that a new world order of government networks will replace the existing infrastructure of international institutions, but rather complement and strengthen it. States can be disaggregated for many purposes and in many contexts and still be completely unitary actors when necessary, such as in decisions to go to war. And even their component parts still represent national interests in various ways.

Horizontal Networks

The structural core of a disaggregated world order is a set of horizontal networks among national government officials in their respective issue areas, ranging from central banking through antitrust regulation and environmental protection to law enforcement and human rights protection. These networks operate both between high-level officials directly responsive to the national political process—the ministerial level—as well as between lower level national regulators. They may be surprisingly spontaneous—informal, flexible, and of varying membership—or institutionalized within official international organizations. For instance, national finance ministers meet regularly under the auspices of the G-7 and the G-20, but also as members of the IMF Board of Governors. The extent and the kind of power they may exercise within these two forums differ in significant ways, but the basic structure of governance and the identity of the governors remains the same.

Horizontal information networks, as the name suggests, bring together regulators, judges, or legislators to exchange information and to collect and distill best practices. This information exchange can also take place through technical assistance and training programs provided by one country's officials to another. The direction of such training is not always developed country to developing country, either; it can also be from developed country to developed country, as when U.S. antitrust officials spent six months training their New Zealand counterparts.

Enforcement networks typically spring up due to the inability of government officials in one country to enforce that country's laws, either by means of a regulatory agency or through a court. But enforcement cooperation must also inevitably involve a great deal of information exchange and can also involve assistance programs of various types. Legislators can also collaborate on how to draft complementary legislation so as to avoid enforcement loopholes.

Finally, harmonization networks, which are typically authorized by treaty or executive agreement, bring regulators together to ensure that their rules in a particular substantive area conform to a common regulatory standard. Judges can also engage in the equivalent activity, but in a much more ad hoc manner. Harmonization is often politically very controversial, with critics charging that the "technical" process of achieving convergence ignores the many winners and losers in domestic publics, most of whom do not have any input into the process.

VERTICAL NETWORKS

In a disaggregated world order, horizontal government networks would be more numerous than vertical networks, but vertical networks would have a crucial role to play. Although a core principle of such an order is the importance of keeping global governance functions primarily in the hands of domestic government officials, in some circumstances states do come together the way citizens might and choose to delegate their individual governing authority to a "higher" organization—a "supranational" organization that does exist, at least conceptually, above the state. The officials of these organizations do in fact replicate the governing functions that states exercise regarding their citizens. Thus, for instance, states can truly decide that the only way to reduce tariffs or subsidies is to adopt a body of rules prohibiting them and allow an independent court or tribunal to enforce those rules. Alternatively, states can come together and give an international court the power to try war criminals—the same function that national courts perform—in circumstances in which national courts are unwilling or unable to do so.

These supranational organizations can be far more effective in performing the functions states charge them to perform if they can link up directly with national government institutions. Absent a world government, it is impossible to grant supranational officials genuine coercive power: judges on supranational tribunals cannot call in the global equivalent of federal marshals if their judgments are not obeyed; global regulators cannot impose fines and enforce them through global courts.

Their only hope of being able to marshal such authority is to harness the cooperation of their domestic counterparts—to effectively "borrow" the coercive power of domestic government officials to implement supranational rules and decisions. As discussed in chapter 2, this harnessing has been the secret of the ECJ's success in creating and enforcing a genuine European legal system within the European Union. At the global level, it can make supranational organizations more powerful and effective than many of their creators ever dreamed.

Close ties between supranational officials—judges, regulators, legislators—and their domestic government counterparts are vertical government networks. They depend on the disaggregation of the state no less than do horizontal government networks. Whereas the traditional model of international law and international courts assumed that a tribunal such as the International Court of Justice in the Hague—traditionally known as the World Court—would hand down a judgment applicable to "states," and thus up to "states" to enforce or ignore, the EU legal system devolves primary responsibility for enforcing ECJ judgments not onto EU "member-states," per se, but on to the national judges of those states. Another version of a vertical judicial network, operating on a global scale, is the jurisdictional provisions of the Rome Statute establishing an International Criminal Court (ICC).[27] Under this system, national courts are to exercise primary jurisdiction over cases involving genocide, war crimes, and crimes against humanity, but will be required to cede power to the ICC if they prove unable or unwilling to carry out a particular prosecution. Beyond judges, the European Union is also pioneering a vertical administrative network between the antitrust authority of the European Commission and national antitrust regulators that will allow the commission to charge national authorities with implementing EU rules in accordance with their particular national traditions.[28]

These vertical networks are enforcement networks. But they can also operate as harmonization networks, in the sense that they will bring national rules and supranational rules closer together. Still other vertical networks are principally information networks. The environmental ministers of NAFTA countries, for instance, benefit by working with the Commission on Environmental Cooperation (CEC), a

NAFTA supranational institution charged with gathering information on environmental enforcement policies and compiling a record of complaints of nonenforcement by private actors. This is an attempt to enhance enforcement through the provision of information. Similarly, the European Union is beginning to create Europe-level "information agencies," designed to collect and disseminate information needed by networks of national regulators.[29] Such agencies can also provide benchmarks of progress for their national counterparts against accepted global or regional standards.

Disaggregated International Organizations

Thinking about world order in terms of both horizontal and vertical government networks challenges our current concept of an "international organization." Many international organizations are primarily convening structures for horizontal networks of national officials. Others are genuinely "supranational," in the sense that they constitute an entity distinct from national governments that has a separate identity and loyalty and which exercises some measure of genuine autonomous power. For example, the Ministerial Conference of the WTO is a gathering of national trade ministers, who can only exercise power by consensus. Dispute-resolution panels of the WTO, by contrast, are composed of three independent experts charged with interpreting and enforcing the rules of the WTO against national governments.

Both of these types of international/supranational organization differ from traditional international organizations—most notably the United Nations itself—that are composed of formal delegations from each of the member states, typically headed by an ambassador serving in the capacity of permanent representative. The Organization of American States (OAS), the Organization of African Unity (OAU), and the Organization for Security and Cooperation in Europe (OSCE) all fit this model. More specialized international organizations, on the other hand, such as the International Postal Union, the World Health Organization (WHO), and the Food and Agriculture Organization, address less overtly "political" subject areas than international and regional security and have long been a forum for meetings of the relevant national ministers. Organizations such as the IMF and the World Bank are hybrid in this regard—national finance ministers and central bankers effectively run them, but they have weighted voting arrangements (like the five permanent members of the United Nations who are able to exercise a veto) that make them far more than convening structures for networks.

In a world of disaggregated states that nevertheless still act as unitary actors under some circumstances, it is important to be able to distinguish between different types of international organizations in terms both of the relevant government officials who represent their states within them and the degree and type of autonomous power they can exercise. Where international organizations have become sufficiently specialized to develop the equivalent of an executive, judicial, and even legislative branch, vertical government networks become possible. Where they are specialized in a specific issue area but exercise little or no autonomous power, they can be hosts for horizontal government networks. But when they are regional or global organizations charged with assuring peace and security, or similar very general functions, they represent an older and much more formal model of international cooperation, conducted by diplomats more than domestic government officials.

Here, then, is the structural blueprint of a new world order of government networks, complete with a set of assumptions about the nature of states and the types of international organizations those states have and will continue to create. But order must be backed by power. How can these various networks actually influence political, economic, and social outcomes to achieve substantive results? Any conception of world order must assume some set of such results. It takes structures, power, and norms to achieve them.

Global Impact

A critical piece of the puzzle is still missing. Government networks can provide the structure of a new world order, but how do we know that they actually have, or will have, any impact on addressing the problems that the world needs to solve? How do they, or will they, contribute to increasing peace and prosperity, protecting the planet and the individuals who inhabit it?

Chapter 5 takes on these questions. The first half of the chapter sets forth three ways in which government networks currently contribute to world order: (1) by creating convergence and informed divergence; (2) by improving compliance with international rules; and (3) by increasing the scope, nature, and quality of international cooperation. Kal Raustiala, a young legal scholar and political scientist, has demonstrated ways in which government networks lead to "regulatory export" of rules and practices from one country to another. The result can be sufficient policy convergence to make it possible over the longer term to conclude a more formal international agreement setting forth a common regulatory regime.[30] Soft law codes of conduct issued by transgovernmental regulatory organizations, as well as the simple dissemination of credible and authoritative information, also promote convergence. Promoting convergence, on the other hand, can also give rise to informed divergence, where a national governmental institution or the government as a whole acknowledges a prevailing standard or trend and deliberately chooses to diverge from it for reasons of national history, culture, or politics.

Government networks also improve compliance with international treaties and customary law. Vertical enforcement networks do this explicitly and directly by providing a supranational court or regulatory authority with a direct link to a national government institution that can exercise actual coercive authority on its behalf. Equally important, however, are the ways in which technical assistance flowing through horizontal networks can build regulatory or judicial capacity in states where there may be a willingness to enforce international legal obligations but the infrastructure is weak.

Finally, government networks enhance existing international cooperation by providing the mechanisms for transferring regulatory approaches that are proving increasingly successful domestically to the international arena. Most important is regulation by information, which allows regulators to move away from traditional command-and-control methods and instead provide individuals and corporations with the information and ideas they need to figure out how to improve their own performance against benchmarked standards. This approach is gaining popularity in the United States, is increasingly prevalent in the European Union, and is being tried at the United Nations. Government networks create regional and even global transmission belts for information that can readily expand to include as many nations as can usefully participate. In addition, government networks are the ideal mechanism of international cooperation on international problems that have domestic roots, as they directly engage the participation and the credibility of the individuals who must ultimately be responsible for addressing those problems.

The second half of chapter 5 turns from what is to what could be if policymakers and opinion leaders around the world began looking through the lens of the disaggregated state and decided to recognize government networks as prime mechanisms of global governance, using existing networks and creating new ones to address specific problems. First, they could harness the capacity of government networks for self-regulation, drawing on the examples of private commercial networks that succeed in enforcing "network norms" against cheating or other undesirable behavior. If government networks exist not only to address specific regulatory, judicial, and legislative problems, but also as self-consciously constituted professional associations of regulators, judges, and legislators, they should be able develop and enforce global standards of honesty, integrity, competence, and independence in performing the various functions that constitute a government.

They could socialize their members in a variety of ways that would create a perceived cost in deviating from these standards. But they could also bolster their members by enhancing the prestige of membership in a particular government network enough to give government officials who want to adhere to high professional standards ammunition against countervailing domestic forces. Just as international organizations from the European Union to the Community of Democracies have done, government networks could condition admission on meeting specified criteria designed to reinforce network norms.[31] A particular advantage of selective strengthening of individual government institutions this way is that it avoids the pernicious problem of labeling an entire state as bad or good, liberal or illiberal, tyrannical or democratic. It focuses instead on performance at a much lower level, recognizing that in any country and in any government different forces will be contending for power and privilege. It is critical to support those who are willing to practice what they preach in both their own laws and their obligations under international law.

At the same time, these networks could be empowered to provide much more technical assistance of the kind needed to build governance capacity in many countries around the world. They could be tasked with everything from developing codes of conduct to tackling specific policy problems. They could be designated interlocutors for the multitudes of nongovernmental actors, who must be engaged in global governance as they are in domestic governance. Vertical government networks could similarly be designed to implement international rules and strengthen domestic institutions in any number of ways. How well will they do? We cannot know until we try.

To take a concrete example, consider how government networks could help in the rebuilding of Iraq. A global or regional network of judges could be charged with helping to rebuild the Iraqi legal system, both through training and technical assistance and through ongoing monitoring of new Iraqi judges' compliance with the network's norms, which would incorporate standards from the UN's Basic Principles on the Independence of the Judiciary. A global or regional network of legislators could be similarly charged with helping to establish and assist a genuinely representative legislature in Iraq. And regulators and other executive officials of every stripe could help to rebuild basic government services, from policing to banking regulation. In all these cases the experts and targeted technical assistance would be readily available; the rebuilding efforts would be multilateral and sustainable; and the new Iraqi officials would have a continuing source of technical, political, and moral support.

Vertical networks can also strengthen, encourage, backstop, and trigger the better functioning of their counterpart domestic institutions. Consider again the jurisdictional scheme of the ICC. It reflects a conception of a global criminal justice system that functions above all to try to ensure that nations try their own war criminals or perpetrators of genocide or crimes against humanity. The purpose of a supranational global criminal court is to create an entire range of incentives that maximize the likelihood of those domestic trials taking place, from strengthening the hand of domestic groups who would favor such a course to reminding the domestic courts in question that the international community is monitoring their performance. In part, the aim here, as would be true of a wide variety of horizontal government networks, would be to strengthen domestic government officials as a preventive measure to head off a crisis.

Government networks that were consciously constituted as mechanisms of global governance could also acknowledge the power of discussion and argument in helping generate high-quality solutions to complex problems. For certain types of problems, vigorous discussion and debate is likely to produce the most creative and legitimate alternatives. In addition, government networks constituted in this way could harness the positive power of conflict as the foundation of lasting political and social relationships. This understanding of conflict is familiar within democratic societies; it is only within the world of diplomacy, where conflict can escalate to fatal dimensions, that conflict per se is a danger, if not an evil. Among disaggregated government institutions, national and supranational, conflict should be resolved, but not necessarily avoided. It is likely to be the long-term engine of trust.

Note that government networks, both as they exist now and as they could exist, exercise different types of power to accomplish results. They have access to traditional "hard," or coercive, power. The central role of national government officials in government networks means that when the participants make a decision that requires implementation, the power to implement already exists at the national level. The power to induce behavior through selective admission requirements is also a form of hard power. At the same time, much of the work of many horizontal government networks depends on "soft" power—the power of information, socialization, persuasion, and discussion. An effective world order needs to harness every kind of power available.

4. A JUST NEW WORLD ORDER

"World order" is not value-neutral; any actual world order will reflect the values of its architects and members. Most of these values will not be specific to particular structures or institutions operating in different issue areas. Sustainable development, for instance, is a goal or a value that may drive global environmental policy. Whether it is pursued through traditional international organizations or through a combination of horizontal and vertical government networks should not affect the goal itself.

In other circumstances, however, the choice of form may implicate substance. Some observers see government networks as promoting global technocracy—secret governance by unelected regulators and judges. Others fear that the informality and flexibility of networks is a deliberate device to make an end run around the formal constraints—representation rules, voting rules, and elaborate negotiating procedures—imposed on global governance by traditional international organizations. Absent these constraints, critics charge, powerful nations run roughshod over weaker ones. Still others, however, worry more that weak nations will be excluded from powerful government networks altogether. At the domestic level, critics charge harmonization networks with distorting domestic political processes and judicial networks through the introduction of polluting or diluting national legal traditions. Still others picture government networks as vehicles for special interests—shadowy decision-making forums to which those who are "connected" or "in the know" have access.

In response to these criticisms, I propose a set of potential solutions:

- A conceptual move to recognize all government officials as performing both a domestic and an international function. Such recognition would mean that national constituents would automatically hold them accountable for their activities both within and across borders.
- An effort to make government networks as visible as possible. Creating a common website and linking the individual websites of participants in a government network will have the paradoxical effect of making a government network real by making it virtual.
- Increasing the number and activities of legislative networks, both to monitor the activity of regulatory networks and to launch initiatives of their own.
- Using government networks as the spine of broader policy networks, including international organizations, NGOs, corporations, and

other interested actors, thereby guaranteeing wider participation in government network activities but also retaining an accountable core of government officials.

- A grab-bag of domestic political measures designed to enhance the accountability of government networks, depending on the extent to which a particular polity perceives a problem and what it decides to do about it.

None of these measures addresses the question of how members of government networks should treat each other, however, as fellow participants in, and constituents of, a world order. National and supranational officials participating in a full-fledged disaggregated world order would be accountable not only to specific national constituencies, but also to a hypothetical global polity. They would be responsible for defining and implementing "global public policy."[32] It is impossible to define the substance of that policy in the abstract. But the officials responsible should be guided by general "constitutional" norms in their relations with one another. In this context, I propose five basic principles designed to ensure an inclusive, tolerant, respectful, and decentralized world order. They include the horizontal norms of global deliberative equality, legitimate difference, and positive comity, and the vertical norms of checks and balances and subsidiarity.

Global Deliberative Equality. A global order of networks among government officials and institutions cannot work without efforts to maximize the possibilities of participation both by individuals and groups at the level of national and transnational society and by nations of all kinds at the level of the state. Absent such a principle, networks become a euphemism for clubs and a symbol of elitism and exclusion. Global deliberative equality, building on ideas developed by Michael Ignatieff, is a principle of maximum inclusion, to the extent feasible, by all relevant and affected parties in processes of transgovernmental deliberation.

Legitimate Difference. The principle of "legitimate difference" is a principle of pluralism. In contrast to the imagined uniformity that would be imposed by a central authority under an imagined and feared world government, a disaggregated world order begins from the premise of multiple ways of organizing societies and polities at the national level. Ministers, heads of state, courts, legislators, even bureaucrats all reflect national differences, flowing from distinct histories, cultural traditions, demographic and geographic necessities, and the contingencies of national fortune. Each must be prepared to recognize the validity of each other's approach, as long as all accept a core of common fundamental principles.

Positive Comity. In contrast to the traditional principle of comity as a negative principle of deference to the interests of other nations, positive comity is a principle of affirmative cooperation. As a principle of governance for transnational regulatory cooperation, it requires regulatory agencies, courts, and even legislators to substitute consultation and active assistance for unilateral action and noninterference.

Checks and Balances. All participating government institutions, national and supranational, must interact with each other in accordance with a global concept of checks and balances, whereby the distribution of power is always fluid on both the horizontal and particularly the vertical axes. The clearest example is the way in which the national courts of the European Union maintain a shifting balance of power with the ECJ, within the framework of a "cooperative relationship."

Subsidiarity. Just as the principle of checks and balances borrows from the U.S. Constitution, as translated originally from Montesquieu, the principle of subsidiarity borrows from the ideals and experiences of the European Union. It is a principle of locating governance at the lowest possible level—that closest to the individuals and groups affected by the rules and decisions adopted and enforced. Whether this level is local, regional, national, or supranational is an empirical question, dictated by considerations of practicability rather than a preordained distribution of power.

THE CHOICE AND FORMULATION OF ANY SUCH PRINCIPLES IS INEVITABLY personal and partial. The point here is that some set of constitutional principles must operate at a metalevel across all types of government networks, specifying basic ground rules for how the members of these networks treat each other and what the basic division of labor is between them. The principles I put forward reflect values of equality, tolerance, autonomy, interdependence, liberty, and self-government. These values underlie my personal conception of a just world order based on government networks, even though some of the advantages of networked governance, such as flexibility and speed, are likely to be weakened if my principles were adopted. Ultimately, however, the process both of identifying specific values and translating them into principles must be a collective one. I thus hope that the principles offered here and any competing versions will become a matter for debate among scholars, policymakers, and ultimately voters.

The disaggregation of the state is a phenomenon. Government networks are a technology of governance that are probably both cause and effect of this phenomenon. The types of power they exercise are both old and new, but are critical to their ultimate impact, as is a better understanding of the conditions most favorable to their operation. But the norms and principles that would guide their operation in a deliberately constructed disaggregated world order would be a matter of conscious public choice. They will ultimately determine whether a disaggregated world order is a world order worth having.

5. CONCLUSION: PUSHING THE PARADIGM

The mantra of this book is that the state is not disappearing; it is disaggregating. Its component institutions—regulators, judges, and even legislators—are all reaching out beyond national borders in various ways, finding that their once "domestic" jobs have a growing international dimension. As they venture into foreign territory, they encounter their foreign counterparts—regulators, judges, and legislators—and create horizontal networks, concluding memoranda of understanding to govern their relations, instituting regular meetings, and even creating their own transgovernmental organizations. They are also, although much less frequently, encountering their supranational counterparts, judge to judge, regulator to regulator, or legislator to legislator, and establishing vertical networks.

The official observers of the international scene—scholars, pundits, policymakers—cannot fully see and appreciate this phenomenon because they are handicapped by the conceptual lenses of the unitary state. Although they are accustomed to thinking of "governments" domestically—as complex conglomerates of different institutions responsible for different governance functions—they think of "states" internationally. These are purportedly unitary actors represented by the head of state and the foreign minister, represented in other countries and international organizations by professional diplomats. These representatives, in turn, purportedly articulate and pursue a single national interest.

The conception of the unitary state is a fiction, but it has been a useful fiction, allowing analysts to reduce the complexities of the international system to a relatively simple map of political, economic, and military powers interacting with one another both directly and through international organizations. But today it is a fiction that is no longer good enough for government work. It still holds for some critical activity such as decisions to go to war, to engage in a new round of trade negotiations, or to establish new international institutions to tackle specific global problems. But it hides as much as it helps.

Abandoning that fiction and making it possible to see and appreciate these networks is particularly important in a world confronting both the globalization paradox—needing more government but fearing it at the global level—and the rising importance of nonstate actors in the corporate, civic, and criminal sectors. Global governance through government networks would mean harnessing national government officials to address international problems. It would be global governance through national governments, except in circumstances in which those governments concluded that a genuine supranational institution was necessary to exercise genuine global authority. In those circumstances, which would be the exception rather than the rule, the supranational institutions would be more effective than ever before through the operation of vertical government networks.

At the same time, government networks can significantly expand the capacity of national governments to engage the host of nonstate actors who are themselves operating through networks. Networks of specific national government officials—from environmental regulators to constitutional judges—can anchor broader networks of nonstate actors pursuing global agendas of various types while still retaining a distinct governmental character and specific government responsibilities to their constituents. They can expand regulatory reach far beyond the capacity of any one national government. They can bolster and support their members in adhering to norms of good governance at home and abroad by building trust, cohesion, and common purpose among their members. They can enhance compliance with existing international agreements and deepen and broaden cooperation to create new ones.

But this is only the beginning. Push the paradigm a few steps further and imagine the possibilities. A key identifying feature of current government networks is that they are necessarily informal. Their informality flows not only from the fluidity of networks as an organizational structure, but also, and much more importantly, from the conceptual blind spot that this book seeks to repair: separate government institutions have no independent or formally recognized status in international law and politics. They exist only as part of the abstract and unitary state, aggregated together with all their fellow government institutions. Even those networks that have formalized their interactions, in the sense of establishing an organization such as the Basel Committee or the IOSCO, have no actual formal status in international law. They operate in the political equivalent of the informal economy, alongside formal international institutions.

Under existing international law, the only way to formalize networks is to negotiate an intergovernmental international organization, by treaty, and reconstitute an existing network as a committee of the organization. Thus, as explained in chapter 1, the governing committee of the IMF is the board of governors, composed mostly of members' finance ministers or central banks' governors. Alternatively, the extensive relations between the ECJ and national courts in Europe was originally structured by the Treaty of Rome, providing for national courts to refer cases involving questions of EEC law to the ECJ. Even there, however, the national courts of the individual members of the European Union have no status at international law, thus the relations that have evolved between the ECJ and the national courts and the principles governing them are still informal. So too are the many codes of best practices that are developed and disseminated by networks ranging from the G-20 to IOSCO.

In practical terms, what this informality means is, crucially, that individual government institutions cannot be subjected to specific obligations or duties under international law. Nor can they exercise specific rights. Sovereignty is possessed by the state as a whole, not by its component parts. For example, the courts that are attempting to develop a specific conception of judicial comity, as described in chapter 2, are adapting a doctrine that has traditionally applied to states as a whole to the specific needs of transjudicial relations. Overall, however, the entire world of transgovernmental relations remains largely hidden from the formal rules and foundational principles of traditional international law.

Yet suppose individual national government institutions could become bearers of the rights and responsibilities of sovereignty in the global arena. Suppose sovereignty itself could be disaggregated, that it attached to specific government institutions such as courts, regulatory agencies, and legislators or legislative committees. But as exercised by these institutions, the core characteristic of sovereignty would shift from autonomy from outside interference to the capacity to participate in transgovernmental networks of all types.[33] This concept of sovereignty as participation, or status, means that disaggregated sovereignty would empower government institutions around the world to engage with each other in networks that would strengthen them and improve their ability to perform their designated government tasks individually and collectively.

In the process, they could help rebuild states ravaged by conflict, weakened by poverty, disease, and privatization, or stalled in a transition from dictatorship to democracy. If transgovernmental organizations of judges, regulators, or legislators had formal status at the level of international law, they could adopt formal membership criteria and standards of conduct that would create many more pressure points for the global community to act upon a wayward state, but also many more incentives and sources of support for national government officials aspiring to be full members of the global community yet so often lacking capacity or political and material reinforcement in the domestic struggle against corruption or the arbitrary and often concentrated use of power. Aid, pressure, socialization, and education would no longer flow state to state, but would penetrate the state to the level of specific individuals who constitute a government and must make and implement decisions on the ground.

All these officials would also be directly subject to the obligations of treaties and other international agreements. It would not be up to "the state" to uphold human rights or protect the environment or abjure child labor or seek a peaceful resolution to conflicts. It would be up to the members of the executive branch, the judiciary, and the legislature. And in a world in which violations of international law increasingly carry individual penalties, such obligations could make themselves felt.

I explore these ideas further in the conclusion. This book is intended to help readers see and appreciate an actual world order that is emerging and to imagine what could be achieved in a world latticed by countless horizontal and vertical government networks. It would be a world of disaggregated state institutions interacting with one another alongside unitary states and unitary state organizations. The next step could be to disaggregate sovereignty itself. Only by pushing the envelope of what we assume to be natural or inherent can we hope to envision and create a genuinely new world order.

Regulators:
The New Diplomats

From my experience in these last six and half years, the minister of justice or the attorney general has become part of the international arena. When I first came into the office, not that many people came to visit. Now prime ministers and ministers of justice and security people come to visit all the time, and I am so glad to see them because they remind me of what a wonderful, wonderful institution democracy is, how hard we have to fight for it, and now how important it is that we join arms together and fight for it around the world.
—United States Attorney General Janet Reno[1]

THE BEST EVIDENCE OF THE DISAGGREGATED STATE MAY BE FOUND IN the logs of embassies around the world. The records from U.S. embassies, at least, show a steady procession of regulators visiting their foreign counterparts—from agencies and departments regulating financial markets, competition policy, environmental protection, agriculture, and all the other domains of the modern regulatory state.[2] Finances also tell the tale: foreign affairs budgets for regulatory agencies have increased dramatically across the board, even as the State Department's budget has shrunk.[3]

This disaggregation extends all the way to the top. The executive branch—"the government" in parliamentary systems—is traditionally and formally charged with the conduct of foreign policy. Where nations speak with one voice, the executive is supposed to speak for the nation and to represent it, to resolve internal differences of views and then to present a single position that reflects a consensus. In fact, chief executives—presidents and prime ministers, typically—are also networking with one another on their own behalf, achieving results in the international arena that they could not obtain by more traditional methods of negotiating and ratifying treaties. They can also reach common positions in meetings of heads of state that they can then use to strengthen their respective domestic positions back home.

Perhaps the premier network of heads of state is the G-7, the annual summit of the leaders of the most powerful economies in the world. The G-7 has no formal status as an international organization; it is simply an institutionalized relationship between a group of leaders. It has sufficient status that Boris Yeltsin was very anxious to join it as evidence that Russia was now part of the West. Since 1994 Russia has been included in the annual summit and has had full participation since 2002. It now meets as the G-8, though more restricted meetings of G-7 finance ministers have continued in parallel. In normal times the G-8 can be no more than a talking shop and a photo opportunity, but in times of crisis it provides a vehicle for prompt and decisive action. Further, as all students of bureaucracy understand, the simple fact of a meeting drives a desire to have some notable outcome, which in turn forces the "sherpas" to figure out what initiatives might be ripe for action and what actions might usefully be initiated.

The G-7 has spawned many additional "groups," each composed of the leaders of a different number of countries, leading to regularly shifting numbers (the G-34, the G-15, the G-20, which is actually the G-22 or G-19, depending on the count!). The IMF website has a helpful guide entitled "committees, groups and clubs" that describes these various networks and their current membership.[4] They are not alliances or even treaty partners. Their closest equivalent in traditional diplomacy is perhaps the "concert," as in the Concert of Europe of 1815, which brought together the traditional monarchs of Europe to create a shifting balance of power designed to keep the peace and prevent the spread of dangerous revolutionary ideas.

Below presidents and prime ministers are cabinet officials (ministers in parliamentary systems) and regulators, for our purposes defined as appointed top officials or career civil servants who possess a special expertise on a particular subject. All of these different actors are engaged in transgovernmental networking to a remarkable degree. Indeed, finance ministers, often accompanied by central bankers, form an international infrastructure of their own. They have created networks that have answered the call, substantively if not formally, for a new international financial architecture. And they have assumed equal status in many cases with heads of state, to the extent that at some G-7 meetings the finance ministers issue separate statements from the chief executives. In some cases, of course, it is the summits of chief executives that then command meetings of their various ministers to address specific problems. But in other cases it is the ministers themselves who drive the agenda.

Networking among some regulators, such as central bankers, securities commissioners, and insurance supervisors, has become so established that they now have their *own* international organizations—the Basel Committee, IOSCO Commissioners, and IAIS, among others. These organizations are transgovernmental networks that have become sufficiently formalized to warrant the title of association or organization and that have a staff and regular meetings. But they are not "inter-state" organizations; they are not formed by treaty or even executive agreement; they have no place on the landscape of the international legal system.

The role of "the executive" in foreign affairs is thus increasingly complex and differentiated. It includes a variety of diverse actors networking with their foreign counterparts for different reasons. Nevertheless, for present purposes I will treat them all together as participants in executive transgovernmental networks. Taken together, they engage in a wide array of activities that either traditionally did not take place at all or were much more the province of professional diplomats.

Today readers of the popular press could be excused for thinking that diplomacy is conducted by everyone *but* the diplomats.

This is not strictly fair, of course. Foreign ministers and foreign ministries—the State Department in the United States—still play an active and often critical role in a host of areas from conflict resolution to human rights policy. Indeed, the very idea of diplomacy, with its intimations of nuance, tact, and care, implies a type of state-to-state relation that is delicate and even precarious—far from the mundane details of regulatory cooperation or even economic interdependence. For such matters, diplomats remain essential.

Further, in some cases foreign ministers have their own networks, as they must to counter networks of finance ministers or defense ministers.[5] In other cases, as in a number of the examples below, the executive networks arise within more traditional international organizations—organizations created by treaties negotiated by foreign ministers and heads of state acting as representatives of unitary states. In short, the point here is not that the secretary of state is unimportant. It is just that she has to share an increasingly crowded stage.

Neither is the point to identify and trace the *causes* of the growing plethora of executive-branch participants in foreign policy, or at least international affairs. These are many and complex; indeed, they are the subject of a considerable literature in political science. Writing in the 1970s, Keohane and Nye identified transgovernmental coalitions as one of the hallmarks of "complex interdependence."[6] Complex interdependence, as an overall description of relations among nations, has only increased with the waves of globalization since the 1990s. Businesses that cross borders must be regulated across borders. More precisely, the increasingly transnational nature of services and the recognition of the extraterritorial dimension of domestic regulation mean that regulators often simply cannot do their job without cooperating with one another.

Other causes are political and organizational. Politically, two hallmarks of modern industrialized society are specialization and regulation. The result? Legions of regulators with specialized expertise—expertise that often guarantees a measure of deference from judges, legislators, and fellow regulators.[7] At the same time, at least in the

United States, the rising political attractiveness of "presidential administration" has led the president and his men and women to rule increasingly by executive orders, followed up by agency initiatives.[8] Indeed, in many ways the rise and growing ambition of head-of-state networks appear motivated by the sort of complaints about traditional international negotiations that U.S. presidents make about Byzantine dealings with a refractory Congress. Finally, governments are reflecting a broader organizational trend, much noted in recent years among corporations and NGOs, away from hierarchical structures to networked structures. Governments, in many ways, have just been keeping up organizationally with the societies they govern.

In section 1, I will review a number of the factors that have focused attention on executive transgovernmental networks, but without claiming that they are entirely new and without attempting to duplicate the work of political scientists in pinpointing the causes of their most modern manifestations. For present purposes, it is more important to identify and describe government networks than to explain them, and, above all, to understand how they are changing the present and future of global governance. To that end, section 2 examines the different places that executive transgovernmental networks can be found, both within international organizations and without. It also highlights the pioneering nature of EU governance, which is heavily dependent on networks of both ministers and regulators.

Section 3 sets forth what these networks actually do: exchanging information; coordinating policy; cooperating on enforcement issues; collecting and distilling best practices; exporting particular regulatory forms; bolstering their members in domestic bureaucratic politics; and transmitting information about their members' reputations. These networks and their activities are not necessarily way-stations on the road to more formal organizations; they are themselves an organizational form of global governance. Moreover, the types of governance functions they can perform—and those they cannot—are also not necessarily imitations of "real" governance, but rather a distinctive type of governance that may be more appropriate for the global level.

1. A NEW PHENOMENON?

Is executive transgovernmentalism really new? As previously mentioned, Francis Bator's 1972 testimony before Congress pointed to the increasing complexity of connections undergirding the setting and implementation of foreign policy,[9] while already in 1974 Keohane and Nye were able to identify transgovernmental activity as a separate sphere of action within the wider range of transnational activities.[10] Their principal interest in doing so was to identify the various ways in which transgovernmental politics, as well as transnational politics, could help international organizations to play an important role in world politics.[11] Along the way, they identified different types of transgovernmental activity (among them policy coordination and coalition building), specified the conditions under which transgovernmental networks are most likely to form, and specified different types of interactions between international organizations and transgovernmental networks.

Keohane and Nye excluded heads of state from their analysis on the grounds that it would be odd to regard "a head-of-state meeting, at which new initiatives that deviate from established policy are taken, as an example of transgovernmental politics."[12] Fifteen years later, however, Robert Putnam developed the idea of the "two-level game," whereby heads of state manipulate international policy to enhance their strength domestically and take advantage of domestic politics to strengthen their hands in international negotiation. The central insight of two-level–game analysis is that these games are separate but interrelated because "each national political leader appears at both game boards."[13] The result, at the international level, is that executives have more room to "pursue [their] own conception[s] of the national interest."[14]

Not only do presidents and other heads of state operate autonomously, they often do so in order to improve their own domestic standing and that of their counterparts. In the logic of the two-level game, executives are aware that they can expect more frequent and more favorable international agreements if their negotiating partners have strong domestic standing, as any agreements reached at the international game-board are then more likely to be ratified at the domestic board. Therefore, each negotiator at the international level "has a strong interest in the popularity of his opposite number."[15] For example, Yasser Arafat's frequent visits to the Clinton White House can be interpreted as efforts to improve Arafat's domestic standing to give him greater room to conclude a comprehensive peace settlement.

Two-level–game analysis made it easier to identify head-of-state networks as part of the larger set of executive transgovernmental networks. At the same time, events of the 1990s cast a new light on the entire phenomenon of transgovernmentalism, which was embedded within the larger resurgence of transnational action of all types. As the bipolar state system of the Cold War disappeared and nonstate, substate, and supranational actors rode the tide of globalization, pundits and many scholars began heralding the era of complex, multilevel, global governance, tied together by networks.[16]

Early on, Peter Haas explored the role and power of "epistemic communities," which he defined as networks "of professionals with recognized expertise and competence in a particular domain and an authoritative claim to policy-relevant knowledge within that domain or issue-area."[17] Later work absorbed the insights about the power of shared learning and knowledge production generated by the literature on epistemic communities but focused on more concrete and observable organizational forms. A number of convergent factors focused growing attention on the more specific phenomenon of executive transgovernmental networks, particularly among regulators.

First were observable changes in the organization and activities of national financial regulators. Under the auspices of the BIS the central-bank governors of the G-10 countries created the Basel Committee on Banking Supervision in 1974. It is now composed of the representatives of thirteen central banks that regulate the world's largest banking markets.[18] Between 1975 and 1992 it issued the Basel Concordat, with several sets of subsequent amendments, to enhance cooperation between regulators of multinational banks by dividing specified tasks between home-country and host-country regulators. In 1988 the Basel Committee issued a set of capital adequacy standards to be adopted as the new regulatory standard by all member countries, which had a sharp impact on the availability of credit in the world's most important economies.[19] IOSCO emerged in 1984, followed in the 1990s by the creation of IAIS and then a network of all three of these organizations and other national and international officials responsible for financial stability around the world called the Financial Stability Forum.[20] As a number of scholars point out, these "organizations" do not fit the model of an organization held either by international lawyers or political scientists: they are not composed of states and constituted by treaty; they do not have legal standing; they have no headquarters.[21] According to Sol Picciotto, however, they "form part of a more general shift from 'government' to 'governance,' involving the delegation or transfer of public functions to particularized bodies, operating on the basis of professional or scientific techniques."[22]

A second major impetus for the study of transgovernmental regulatory networks has been the emergence of a new multilayered regulatory system, concentrated among OECD countries.[23] The governments of these countries have had to respond to deepening economic and financial integration and increasing interdependence by developing strategies for regulatory cooperation and rapprochement. Ongoing regulatory cooperation, in turn, is the foundation for a transgovernmental network. As an OECD study concluded in 1994, however, the new forms of governance necessary to make regulatory cooperation work cannot simply follow function. They must instead be managed within a principled framework designed not only to improve their effectiveness and the quality of their output, but also to "protect democratic processes."[24]

Third, the most concentrated site for multilevel governance, and particularly transgovernmental regulatory interactions, is the European Union itself. In the wake of the completion of the single market in 1992, the European Union has emerged as a regulatory state, exercising power through rule making rather than taxing and spending.[25] In response to the challenges of trying to harmonize or at least reconcile the regulations of its diverse and growing membership, the European Union has developed a system of regulation by networks, located in the EU Council of Ministers and closely connected to the complex process of "comitology" that surrounds council decision making.[26] The question now confronting a growing number of legal scholars and political theorists is how decision making by networks of national regulators fits with varying national models of European democracy.[27]

Fourth is the emergence of a system of transatlantic governance to help foster and manage the increasingly dense web of transatlantic economic cooperation.[28] David Vogel, for example, points out that "[a]s the regulatory competence of the EU has expanded, so have both formal and information discussions between regulatory officials in Washington and Brussels. These officials now regularly monitor and exchange information about each other's proposals and policies, especially those likely to affect bilateral trade."[29] Although transatlantic regulatory relations may seem only a subset of the larger multilayered regulatory system just discussed, they take place within the framework of specific initiatives launched by heads of state. As described by Mark Pollack and Gregory Shaffer, transatlantic governance involves cooperation at the intergovernmental level, the transgovernmental level, and the transnational level.[30] The evolution of transatlantic relations over the course of the 1990s has thus spawned complicated questions concerning the interrelationship and relative importance of these three levels.[31]

Finally, executive transgovernmental networks play an important role in several recent and still actively debated theories of why states comply with international rules. Abram and Antonia Chayes and Harold Koh have emphasized the importance of regular interaction, dialogue, and "jawboning" among networks of government officials at both the international and transnational levels.[32] Both theories penetrate the traditional black box of the state to focus on the activities of specific government institutions and officials.

So are they new? Does it matter? Government officials have been linking up with their counterparts for a long time to get the actual business of foreign affairs done. But the scope and substance of that business has expanded; the range and intensity of transgovernmental ties have increased and in many cases become institutionalized; the advantages of transgovernmentalism have become more prominent while the disadvantages of many more formal international institutions have become clearer. Perhaps most important, as the line between "national" and "international" affairs blurs, national officials find that they need to negotiate across borders to do business they could once accomplish solely at home. In sum, even if not new, government networks are increasingly noteworthy.

2. WHERE ARE THEY?

Where are these networks of executive-branch officials? In some familiar places and some new ones. It is possible to identify three types of networks, each arising and operating in a different context. First are those networks of executive officials that develop within established international organizations. Second are networks of officials that develop under the umbrella of an agreement negotiated by heads of state. And third are the networks that have attracted the most attention over the past decade—networks of national regulators that develop outside any formal framework. These networks arise spontaneously from a need to work together to address common problems; in some cases members interact sufficiently autonomously to require the institutionalization of their activities in their own transgovernmental regulatory organizations.[33] These three types are interlinked in many ways: some may seem such a standard part of the international furniture as to be beneath notice, while others compete directly with actual or possible international organizations.

Government Networks within International Organizations

National government officials have always networked within international organizations. After the fanfare of signing the treaty and actually creating the organization, the heads of state go home and leave the task of actually getting on with the business of the organization to national government officials from whatever sector of government is involved. Indeed, depending on the subject area, they often play a role in the creation of the institution—U.S. Assistant Secretary of the Treasury Harry Dexter White was certainly present at Bretton Woods.[34] But certainly once an institution has been established, whether to regulate international labor, the environment, health, crime, or the sprawling and increasingly untidy global markets, it will fall to the national ministries or agencies in the relevant sector to work with the nascent international secretariat officially charged to represent the organization's interests.

Keohane and Nye describe networks of government ministers within international organizations as emblematic of the "club model" of international institutions.[35] Within a particular intergovernmental institution established by treaty, "cabinet ministers or the equivalent, working in the same issue-area, initially from a relatively small number of relatively rich countries, got together to make rules. Trade ministers dominated GATT; finance ministers ran the IMF; defense and foreign ministers met at NATO; central bankers at the Bank for International Settlements (BIS)."[36] This mode of operation was very efficient for participating governments because the relatively small and like-minded number of ministers involved came to form a negotiating "club" in which they reached agreements and then reported them to national legislatures and publics.[37]

The OECD is the quintessential host of transgovernmental regulatory networks, as well as a catalyst for their creation. Its primary function, at least in recent decades, has been to convene government officials in specific fields to figure out the best ways to fix a common economic or regulatory problem and sometimes to promulgate a model code for its solution.[38] As discussed above, the EU Council of Ministers operates the same way, although council members exercise actual decision-making power. Finally, in some cases, the secretariat of an international institution deliberately encourages the formation of a network of officials from specific governments to act as a negotiating vanguard in developing new rules ultimately designed to apply to all members.[39]

Government Networks within the Framework of an Executive Agreement

The second type of transgovernmental network is more striking as a form of governance, in that it emerges outside formal international institutions. Nevertheless, the members of these networks operate within a framework agreed on at least by the heads of their respective governments. A prime recent example are transatlantic transgovernmental interactions specifically authorized and encouraged by executive agreement. Pollack and Shaffer chronicle a series of executive agreements between the President of the United States and the president of the EU Commission to foster increased cooperation, including the Transatlantic Declaration of 1990, the New Transatlantic Agenda of 1995 (with a joint U.S.–EU Action Plan attached), and the Transatlantic Economic Partnership agreement of 1998.[40] Each of these agreements spurred ad hoc meetings between lower-level officials, as well as among businesses and environmental and consumer groups, to address common problems. Many of these networks of lower-level officials were emerging anyway, for functional reasons, but they undoubtedly received a boost from agreements at the top.

Another example is the web of transgovernmental networks among financial officials that have emerged as the pragmatic answer to calls for "a new financial architecture for the twenty-first century" in the wake of the Russian and East Asian financial crises of 1997 and 1998.[41] Notwithstanding a wide range of proposals from academics and policymakers, including one for a global central bank,[42] what actually emerged was a set of financial reform proposals from the G-22 that were subsequently endorsed by the G-7 (now the G-8).[43] The United States pushed for the formation of the G-22 in 1997 to create a transgovernmental network of officials from both developed and developing countries, largely to counter the Eurocentric bias of the G-7, the Basel Committee, and the IMF's "interim committee," which is itself a group of finance ministers.[44] The East Asian countries most affected were happy to leave the details of financial reform to the G-22, in lieu of any grander vision.[45] And a number of the more sweeping reform proposals advanced suggested the formation of still other networks—a G-16 or a G-15.[46]

The actual work done within these networks—making policy recommendations, new sets of standards, model codes—is done by finance ministers, securities regulators, central bankers, and other officials responsible for national economic policy. But they are convened and approved by heads of state, often simply through informal agreement or joint communiqué. In fact, when the G-7 issued a statement on global economic reform in October 1998, the statement itself was issued by finance ministers and central bank governors, accompanied by a parallel statement from heads of government.[47]

Spontaneous Government Networks: Agencies on the Loose?

In 1974, Keohane and Nye wondered "whether the common interests of central bankers in a stable currency system have been implemented as fully by transgovernmental contacts as they might have been."[48] Today, by contrast, the transgovernmental regulatory networks that have spurred the greatest concern are those that have emerged outside formal intergovernmental agreements, whether treaties or executive agreements. The Basel Committee is the leading suspect. The image of national regulators coming together of their own volition and regularizing their interactions either as a network or a networked organization raises the specter of agencies on the loose, unrestrained by democratic accountability.

Some of these networks—like the Basel Committee, IOSCO, and the INECE—have actually institutionalized themselves as transgovernmental regulatory organizations. The founding and designated members of these organizations are domestic agencies, or even subnational agencies such as provincial or state regulators. The organizations themselves tend to operate with a minimum or physical and legal infrastructure; most lack a foundational treaty, and operate under only a few agreed upon objectives or bylaws. Nothing they do purports to be legally binding on the members, and there typically are few or no mechanisms for formal enforcement or implementation. Rather, these functions are left to the members themselves.

Others are the head-of-state networks like the G-7 or G-8 or the others that meet initially and then trigger the formation of other executive networks. From a cynical point of view, chief executives may simply want to be seen to be doing something in response to various international crises splashed across the front pages. But it seems equally likely that they actually want to do something—to decide on and implement policies without the delays and complications of formal intergovernmental diplomacy. They may well be seeking to circumvent their own legislatures and the governments of countries with whom they did not think they could reach agreement, but less for the purposes of exclusion than of speed and effectiveness.

Still other networks result from agreements between domestic regulatory agencies of two or more nations. The last few decades have witnessed the emergence of a vast network of such agreements effectively institutionalizing channels of regulatory cooperation between specific countries. These agreements embrace principles that can be implemented by the regulators themselves; they do not need further approval by national legislators. Widespread use of Memoranda of Understanding (MOUs) and even less formal initiatives has sped the growth of transgovernmental interaction exponentially, in contrast to the lethargic pace at which traditional treaty negotiations proceed. Further, while these agreements are most commonly bilateral, they may also evolve into plurilateral arrangements, offering greater scope but less formality than traditional transgovernmental organizations.[49]

Financial regulatory networks are an example of such spontaneous networks created by agreements among domestic agencies. The Financial Crimes Enforcement Network (FINCEN) is a "means of bringing people and information together to fight the complex problem of money laundering" through "information sharing among law enforcement agencies and its other partners in the regulatory and financial communities."[50] FINCEN's International Coordination Group includes domestic regulators in a variety of states and provides "knowledge, policy recommendations, and staff support for international anti-money laundering efforts."[51] Similarly, the Egmont Group is a "worldwide network of Financial Intelligence Units" (FIUs) that serves as a "forum for FIUs around the world to improve support to their respective governments in the fight against financial crimes."[52] Egmont includes sixty-nine member countries from all parts of the world.[53]

Putting It All Together: Pioneering New Forms of Regional and Global Organization

Collections of different types of these networks can themselves constitute a new form of international organization. I discuss these "networks of networks" more extensively in chapter 4, but offer a brief overview here. APEC was driven initially by meetings of heads of state, which then devolved to regular meetings of finance ministers and other economic regulators, and then ultimately to meetings of parliamentarians, as described in chapter 3. Its formal title as an "organization" is a "cooperation," essentially a term for institutionalized cooperation through regular meetings of different types of transgovernmental officials—first from the executive branch, then later judges and legislators.

Similarly, the birth of a new organization entitled the Conference and Interaction on Confidence-building Measures in Central Asia (CICA) was a meeting of the heads of states of the member-countries, together with representatives from various observer-states and participating international organizations.[54] Organizations entitled "conferences," like the original Conference on Security and Cooperation in Europe (CSCE), are initially created as forums for transgovernmental networks, led by heads of state. Over time, as with CSCE becoming the Organization for Security and Cooperation in Europe (OSCE), they may ripen into more traditional organizations. But they need not.

The most highly developed and innovative transgovernmental system is the European Union. Legal scholar Renaud Dehousse describes a basic paradox in EU governance: "increased uniformity is certainly needed; [but] greater centralization is politically inconceivable, and probably undesirable."[55] The response is regulation by networks—networks of national officials.[56] The question now confronting a growing number of legal scholars and political theorists is how decision making by these networks fits with varying national models of European democracy.

The European Union itself sits within a broader set of regulatory networks among OECD countries. OECD officials see all OECD member states, including the United States, all EU members, Japan, and now South Korea and Mexico, as participating in a multilayered regulatory system.[57] The infrastructure of this system is government networks.

Put these all together and the world becomes a world of concentric circles of regulatory networks, although with different centers. Fred Bergsten has explicitly called for global financial governance by "concentric network of largely informal groups to manage international economic and monetary affairs; a core G-2 comprising the United States and Europe; a G-3 including Japan; the existing G-7, G-10, and G-22 to engage the next tier of countries."[58] Alternatively, it is quite possible to envision global governance by government networks as radiating outward from the European Union itself, which is pioneering a way for states to govern themselves collectively without giving up their identity as separate and still largely sovereign states. Still another vision, given APEC and the growth of transgovernmental networks in NAFTA, is of concentric circles of government networks spreading from various regions in the world. The relative density of these circles in different regions is likely to reflect a host of different factors: relative homogeneity of political systems; degree of trust among government officials; degree of economic development; degree of economic interdependence, shading into genuine economic integration; and relative willingness of national governments specifically to delegate government functions beyond their borders to networks of national officials.

3. WHAT DO THEY DO?

So what exactly do government networks do? Their members talk a lot. Indeed, in one category of networks, talking is the primary activity. These are information networks, created and sustained by the valuable exchange of ideas, techniques, experiences, and problems. In many ways these networks create the equivalent of collective memory and collective brainstorming over time. In a second category of networks, talk leads to action—direct aid in enforcing specific regulations against specific subjects. These are enforcement networks, which also encompass training and technical-assistance programs of developed-country regulators for their counterparts in developing countries in order to build the recipients' capacity to enforce their own domestic regulations. A third category comprises harmonization networks—networks that, to facilitate trade, provide the infrastructure for complicated technical negotiations aimed at harmonizing one nation's laws and regulations with another's. Harmonizing distinctive national laws can have significant policy implications, which makes harmonization networks suspect for those concerned about democratic input into the regulatory process.

These three types of networks have overlapping functions—harmonization and enforcement networks also exchange information and offer assistance; information networks can also make common policy for their members under certain circumstances. Nevertheless, this basic categorization helps us think about what functions government networks perform and what impact they have, a subject for chapter 5. The typology applies to vertical as well as horizontal networks, although as yet very few vertical regulatory networks exist. It also applies to networks of judges and legislators as well regulators.

Information Networks

The glue of any transgovernmental network is the exchange of information and ideas. Put a group of environmental regulators, central bankers, or utilities commissioners in a room and they will begin talking about different techniques of regulation, commiserating about common problems, and brainstorming new approaches. To take one example, from an annual conference of utilities regulators from around the world, one participant is reported as carrying two notebooks. One notebook is used to write down ideas stemming from the meeting, the other simply to write down information learned about current techniques of utilities regulation. In this regard, meetings of national government officials are no different from professional conferences in myriad other professions. As an hour in any big convention hotel will attest, participants go to panels on new developments and techniques in their profession, hold roundtable discussions sharing experiences, and network furiously in the lobbies.

Link government officials across the internet and their networks become more durable—by virtue of being virtual. They exchange data of
different types, organization charts and policies, and lessons learned
from specific experiences. Indeed, antitrust regulators are in such constant informal communication that one observer has concluded from
interviews with these regulators that "[p]hone, email, and fax are the
primary mode of contemporary international regulatory diplomacy."[59]

Some information exchanges are more purposeful. For instance, the
EPA and its Mexican counterpart, PROFEPA, have exchanged information on their respective policies for assessing monetary penalties in
enforcement cases, on administrative enforcement procedure, on the
development of programs for criminal environmental enforcement,
and more. They have also exchanged statistics on enforcement activities and accomplishments. In doing so, they were able to identify differing methodologies and capabilities for enforcement activities.[60] Further, the Commission on Environmental Cooperation and its standing
North American Working Group on Environmental Enforcement and
Compliance Cooperation, consisting of regulators from the United
States, Mexico, and Canada, regularly convenes meetings and workshops to exchange information on cross-border pollution issues.[61]

Not surprisingly, information exchange through transgovernmental
networks is particularly important among agencies that engage in the
business of gathering information. Following the September 11 attack
on the United States, American intelligence agencies called for enhanced intelligence cooperation to combat international terrorism.
According to press reports, this call may have led to diplomatic break-
throughs and long-term global realignments through the sharing of
information between countries that previously "did not talk to one
another."[62]

In addition to exchanging information, information networks often
actively collect and distill information about how their members do
business. The standard product of this distillation is a code of "best
practices," meaning a set of the best possible means for achieving a desired result identified by any members of the network at a given point
in time.[63] The Basel Committee, IOSCO, and financial regulators
around the world have all issued codes of best practices on everything

from how to regulate securities markets to how to prevent money laundering. Indeed, IOSCO has even issued a set of principles for concluding MOUs, which is essentially a set of best practices for transgovernmental networking. One example of such a code is the Basel Committee's *Core Principles for Effective Banking Supervision*, released in 1997. Distilled from the practices and policies of member states, it "provides a comprehensive blueprint for an effective [financial] supervisory system."[64]

Participants in information networks can also actively cooperate in uncovering new information of value to all members. Again in the area of securities regulation, IOSCO has led to coordination of research among members to try to respond to new regulatory challenges posed by globalization. Similarly, the FATF, created by the G-7 in 1989, has tried to fulfill its mission of reducing money laundering by promoting standards designed to provide countries with a blueprint for the establishment and implementation of anti-money-laundering laws and programs. In addition, law enforcement officials from the FATF countries meet each year to exchange information on significant money-laundering cases and operations. These annual "Typologies" exercises are important opportunities for operational experts to identify and describe current money-laundering trends and effective countermeasures.[65]

Equally important is the information that participants in a network exchange about each other—concerning competence, quality, integrity, and professionalism. Once a network is established, it essentially becomes a conduit for information about members' reputations—even if they didn't have or care about their reputations beforehand. Having and caring about a reputation among one's peers is a very powerful tool of professional socialization—in the profession of governance no less than in the private or nonprofit sector. To the extent that the bond between members of a network is that they face common challenges and responsibilities, they are likely to strengthen norms of professionalism. It is likely that evident violations of those norms would quickly be transmitted across the network, raising the cost of those violations.

Giandomenico Majone refers to such networks within the European Union as "bearers of reputation," observing that they "facilitate the development of behavioral standards and working practices that create shared expectations and enhance the effectiveness of the social mechanisms of reputational enforcement."[66] For example, the European Agency for the Evaluation of Medicinal Products "works closely with the corresponding national authorities," linking together national agencies that have an incentive "to maintain their reputation in the eyes of the other members of the network."[67]

Reputation is particularly important to the extent that specific government networks themselves embody a system of regulation by information, in which power flows not from coercive capacity but from an ability to exercise influence through knowledge and persuasion.[68] The EU has pioneered this type of regulation through networks of national regulators operating within the framework of Brussels-based governance. Here more than ever, success in exercising this kind of power requires an agency to establish its credibility and professional reputation.[69]

Enforcement Networks

A second type of network focuses primarily on enhancing cooperation among national regulators to enforce existing national laws and rules. As the subjects they regulate—from criminals to corporations—move across borders, they must expand their regulatory reach by initiating contact with their foreign counterparts. In some cases, as with antitrust networks between the United States and the European Union, the exchange of confidential information is authorized by Congress. In other cases, these networks have just evolved. In many instances they overlap with information networks, but they engage in sufficiently specialized kinds of activity to merit separate discussion.

SHARING INTELLIGENCE IN SPECIFIC CASES

Not surprisingly, enforcement networks are densest among those government officials whose job is actually law enforcement: police officers, customs officials, drug agents, and prosecutors. The best example is Interpol, or the International Police Organization. Interpol has a General Secretariat that offers exchange of information through an automated search facility operating twenty-four hours a day in four languages, issues international "wanted" notices, distributes international publications and updates, convenes international conferences and symposia on policing matters, offers forensic services, and makes specialist analysts available for assistance and support of local police efforts.[70] With a membership of 179 police agencies from different countries, it is the second largest international organization after the United Nations, which makes it all the more remarkable that it was not founded by a treaty and does not belong within any other international political body.[71]

Other examples include the EU criminal enforcement network, known as Trevi, which was initially created in 1976 as a forum to exchange information regarding terrorism. It was later expanded to deal with international organized crime and public order. At the highest level, Trevi is run by ministers who are responsible for internal security matters in their own member-states. The European Union also has a criminal enforcement network (EMP) with twelve Middle Eastern countries.[72] Two additional groups—the Dublin Group and the Pompidou Group—provide the auspices for antidrug cooperation between the European Union, the United States, and several other states. And in the Western Hemisphere, the annual International Drug Enforcement Conference (IDEC) brings together upper-level drug law–enforcement officials from South, Central, and North America, as well as the Caribbean, to share drug-related intelligence and develop operational strategies that can be used against international drug traffickers.

Moving away from pure criminal law, the U.S. International Antitrust Enforcement Assistance Act of 1994 authorizes the antitrust division of the Justice Department to "provide assistance to foreign authorities regarding possible violation of the foreign antitrust laws . . . if U.S. authorities are confident that the foreign authorities will reciprocate."[73] The United States and the European Union now cooperate directly on many cases of mutual interest, to the extent, in the words of one observer, that they have come "to redefine their roles as members of a transatlantic community of professionals dealing with common problems."[74]

At a very concrete level, enforcement cooperation is exactly the sharing of information and the collaborative development of specific enforcement strategies in individual cases. The next step is cooperating in strategic priority setting and targeting, as well as in taking measures to promote citizen compliance with the relevant laws and to monitor that compliance. Measures to promote compliance in turn can lead to consultation on the provisions of the law in the first place. Yet all of these activities will come to naught if some members of the network do not have sufficient capacity—buildings, computers, personnel, training—actually to engage in enforcement activity. All the will and cooperation in the world cannot compensate for lack of capacity. One of the principal activities of enforcement networks thus becomes capacity-building through technical assistance and training.

CAPACITY BUILDING
When the official U.S. foreign aid budget is tallied, it does not include technical assistance from the SEC, the EPA, the Justice Department, or the Treasury Department. Yet all of these parts of the U.S. government provide growing amounts of such assistance to their counterparts around the world. During fiscal year 2002, the SEC provided training to over five hundred officials from eighty-seven countries.[75] The EPA offers twenty-three courses to train foreign regulators and environmental officials.[76] These agencies are working to build regulatory capacity in countries with poorly developed or weak legal systems—capacity to enforce not only national regulations, but also international and foreign law when necessary. The aim is not altruism. It results from the recognition that a global regulatory system based on transgovernmental networks is only as strong as its weakest link.

Consider. Each year the SEC hosts "major training program[s] for foreign securities regulators" which, by 2000, had trained over 1,260 regulators from more than one hundred countries.[77] The United States has trained all of Mexico's environmental regulators. And in the area of competition policy, for example, Spencer Weber Waller notes that "the rest of the world looks to the United States as one of the most important sources of learning about competition law."[78] Similarly other countries and international networks themselves engage in such training processes. Through the biannual International Conference of Banking Supervisors, the Basel Committee itself provides training and assistance to regulators around the world.[79] Through the Emerging Markets Committee, IOSCO offers "training programs for the staff of members" and facilitates the "exchange of information and transfer of technology and expertise."[80]

Technical assistance can extend beyond training to actual help with establishing a regulatory office. Mexican environmental regulatory cooperation with the EPA led to the creation of PROFEPA, a largely U.S.-trained environmental enforcement office.[81] The SEC has concluded MOUs with many foreign securities regulators not only to create a framework for cooperation, but also to provide technical assistance that seeks to establish mini-SECs abroad.[82] If a foreign authority does not have sufficient power under its domestic law to replicate the SEC's principal features, then the SEC generally requests it to obtain legislation to enable it to do so. Again, the aim is to create a counterpart node in the transgovernmental network. In other examples, the International Criminal Investigative Training Assistance Program of the U.S. Department of Justice has as its watchword: "Building Law Enforcement Institutions Worldwide."[83] Assistance from the Pentagon also helps build actual military infrastructure in other countries.

Training and capacity building, like simple information exchange, is a two-way street. Even as the EPA was trying to train their Mexican counterparts to replicate the EPA in Mexico, Mexican officials were training EPA officials as well—teaching them about Mexican practices and policies.[84] Further, they help instill a sense of professional community among all concerned. In April 1998 the FBI informed the U.S. Senate of its growing cooperation with Central European countries and republics of the former Soviet Union. In particular, the bureau stressed the importance of training foreign law enforcement officers through the FBI's National Academy program, which helps build "cop-to-cop relationships not only between law enforcement from the United States and participating countries, but also between officers from participating countries themselves."[85]

Harmonization Networks

Many of the most powerful transgovernmental networks are a product of harmonization agreements. Generally acting within the framework of a trade agreement, often with a specific legislative mandate, regulators may work together to harmonize regulatory standards, such as product-safety standards, with the overt aim of achieving efficiency.[86] Critics of harmonization, led by the U.S. advocacy group Public Citizen, charge that these harmonization initiatives often result in quiet changes to domestic regulation in ways that cannot be justified solely by efficiency gains.[87] Behind the facade of technical adjustments for improved coordination of regulations and uniformity of standards lie subtle adjustments in levels of consumer, environmental, and social protection of all kinds—or so it is argued. Harmonization efforts thus demonstrate the complex interrelationship between formal international agreements, transgovernmental interaction, and domestic regulation—a relationship that may often produce unintended consequences.

Harmonization involves "the adoption of an international standard that adjusts the regulatory standards or procedures of two or more countries until they are the same."[88] Harmonization is often required by trade agreements such as NAFTA and the WTO, resulting in harmonization networks of countries moving toward a single standard. The process is currently underway on issues ranging from public health and food safety to consumer, worker and environmental protection policies.[89] More specifically, the Agreement on Technical Barriers to Trade obligates the United States to "use international standards . . . as a basis for technical regulation."[90] Similarly, "U.S. and EC regulators are informally cooperating in the writing of international aviation standards," even in the absence of a harmonization or mutual-recognition agreement by trade negotiators.[91]

A less demanding alternative to harmonization is mutual recognition by two countries of each other's regulatory standards and decisions on specific cases. Mutual-recognition agreements (MRAs) are widely used in the EU; in effect, country A agrees to substitute country B's regulatory apparatus for its own with regard to products and services originating in country B. This step automatically connects the regulators in both countries. Beyond the European Union, MRAs have emerged between the United States and the European Union, now linking the regulators in all fifteen (soon to be twenty-five) EU members to their U.S. counterparts.

Harmonization processes and MRAs can provide valuable cover in domestic bureaucratic battles. According to Kalypso Nicolaïdis, an expert on these types of negotiations, "regulators from both sides who have been talking to one another under the aegis of technical cooperation can enter into a transnational alliance and jointly resist capture of 'their' issue by the trade community."[92] She offers as an example the FAA's ability to keep aviation standards out of trade negotiations by collaborating with other aviation regulators.[93] Similarly, the FDA reached an MRA with its foreign counterparts that essentially allowed it "to delegate its foreign inspections to foreign bodies," a move that allowed it to husband scarce resources and helped preserve its regulatory autonomy and possibly its very existence.[94] Such bureaucratic bolstering is exactly the type of effect about which public interest groups such as Public Citizen worry, although they probably would not object to strengthening the hand of environmentalists and aviation regulators against trade officials!

Overall, the difference between beneficial bolstering and worrisome collusion is likely to be in the eye of the beholder. In some situations it is quite possible that the bolstering process works not to advance special interests, but rather to support clean government against corrupt government and professional practices against openly politicized processes. On the other hand, Spencer Weber Waller makes the point that in antitrust matters a community of international scholars, lawyers, and competition officials have "learned to think, speak, and write about competition issues in a similar way" through their participation in "bilateral and multilateral discussions, national and international bar associations, common conferences, and specialized publications."[95] He concludes that this community has become an interest group itself, seeking "to improve its power, prestige, jurisdiction, and resources in competition with other bureaucratic and nongovernmental interest groups."[96]

But is the emergence of transgovernmental networks of different types of regulators operating as their own interest groups a good or bad thing? When the U.S. Department of Justice proposes the creation of a Global Competition Network as a forum for countries to "formulate and develop consensus on proposals for procedural and substantive convergence of antitrust enforcement," it is not surprising that many corporations and commentators might find reason to worry—depending on the ideas and principles around which the members of such a network are likely to converge.[97] But then what of INECE, founded by Dutch and the American environmental regulators? Suppose that network produces convergence around higher environmental standards worldwide?

Chapter 6 takes on these questions directly. It should be evident that they cannot be answered categorically on one side or the other. But harmonization networks, real or perceived, often raise hackles. They may be networks explicitly charged with harmonizing a specific area of law or regulation, or, more broadly, information and enforcement networks that simply begin to generate convergence around a set of common ideas, approaches, and principles. What they do, or what they are thought to do, matters increasingly to an increasing number of people.

4. CONCLUSION

When the Pakistani army staged a coup in October 1999, the Clinton administration sent a stern protest to the new, self-appointed ruler, General Pervez Musharraf. A nuclear-capable, unstable nation had plunged into fresh turmoil, and Washington waited anxiously: How would Musharraf respond? When the general finally placed his call, it was not to President Clinton, Secretary of State Madeleine K. Albright, Defense Secretary William S. Cohen, or the U.S. ambassador in Islamabad. Instead, Musharraf telephoned Gen. Anthony C. Zinni of the U.S. Marines, who happened to be sitting with Cohen at an airfield in Egypt.

American generals and admirals, emissaries of the world's strongest military for fifty years, have long exercised independent influence abroad, jockeying with diplomats and intelligence agencies to shape U.S. foreign policy. But the swelling institution of the CINC has shifted this balance during the 1990s. Sheer budgetary prowess is one reason. Another is that the nature of post–Cold War U.S. military engagements, emphasizing peacekeeping and nation building, has steadily pushed the uniformed CINCs into expanded diplomatic and political roles.[98]

Transgovernmentalism in the executive branch is well established. Executive-branch officials have long been charged with implementing international agreements within their domain of expertise; they also formed "clubs" within various international organizations. More recently, however, chief executives, top ministers, and independent regulators have all reached out specifically to their foreign counterparts for a wide variety of purposes. Some of the resulting networks have become sufficiently institutionalized as to become transgovernmental regulatory organizations. This relative formalization resulted not from any actual international negotiations but simply from sufficiently regular meetings that the participating regulators decided to constitute themselves an organization. Other regulatory networks are much looser, consisting of webs of bilateral and plurilateral agreements between specific regulatory agencies cemented by MOUs.

Heads of state and top ministers, most frequently economic ministers, have done the same thing, although their networks are not dubbed organizations but rather "groups," as in the G-7, the G-8, the G-20. These are essentially institutionalized summits of the officials involved. They have played an important role in responding to financial and political crises such as the East Asian financial crisis, the Russian financial crisis, and more recently problems of terrorists and states sponsoring terrorism purchasing nuclear and other deadly materials in the former Soviet Union. The G-20 is also engaged in longer-term examination of how to reshape the international financial architecture to include the concerns of developing-country economies.

These various networks, crisscrossing one another in different regional and global configurations, fall into three broad categories of activity. In information networks, participants exchange information on
common problems and actual and potential solutions. They collect information on various national regulatory practices and distill them into
codes of best practices, which they then disseminate with the special
imprimatur of a transgovernmental organization—benefiting not only
from combined technical expertise, but also from the ability to change
and amend these practices as new information, which also includes information about each other's reputation for probity and competence, is
received.

In enforcement networks, members help each other enforce national laws by exchanging information and actively assisting one another in tracking down criminals, monopolists and unfair competitors,
polluters, and other violators of the web of national and international
regulations. Some members, from the advanced industrial democracies,
consciously export their structure, organization, and mode of operation
through technical assistance and training in developing countries.
Replicating these basic features then makes enforcement cooperation
that much easier. It also builds governance capacity in many countries.

Finally, harmonization networks allow their members to engage in
the ongoing, often highly detailed work of making national laws in a
particular regulatory area consistent with one another. These networks
are generally authorized by some international agreement between the
participating countries. But the work of harmonization by networks of
regulators entrusts many important choices to technical expertise and
can allow network members to bolster one another in domestic bureaucratic struggles. Such bolstering could mean the privileging of a
technocratic over a democratic policy outcome, but it could also mean
supporting an independent regulatory voice against corrupt political
pressure.

In all these areas, regulators genuinely are the new diplomats—on
the front lines of issues that were once the exclusive preserve of domestic policy, but that now cannot be resolved by national authorities
alone. These regulators must often work side by side with the "old
diplomats," the highly trained members of national foreign services

who must tackle delicate issues of statecraft. But the world of ambassadors in diplomatic dress presenting their nations' views to one another on a select set of security and economic issues is gone.

Many readers will not be surprised by this assertion. We have grown accustomed to a world in which finance ministers issue their own communiqués. But what few foreign policy observers realize is that the same embassy logs that are recording the visits of regulators networking with their national counterparts are also increasingly recording the visits of judges. Judicial networks, which I will examine the next chapter, have developed differently from regulatory networks, but comprise a distinctive and increasingly important world of their own.

Judges: Constructing a Global Legal System

The greater use of foreign material affords another source, another tool for the construction of better judgments. . . . The greater use of foreign materials by courts and counsel in all countries can, I think, only enhance their effectiveness and sophistication.
—Canadian Supreme Court Justice G.V. La Forest[1]

GLOBALIZATION IS GENERALLY THOUGHT OF IN TERMS OF CORPORATIONS more than courts, global markets more than global justice. Yet judges around the world are talking to one another: exchanging opinions, meeting face to face in seminars and judicial organizations, and even negotiating with one another over the outcome of specific cases. The Federal Judicial Conference established a Committee on International Judicial Relations in 1993 to conduct a wide variety of exchanges and training programs with foreign courts. The U.S. Supreme Court has regular summits with its counterpart in the European Union, the ECJ; it has also visited the House of Lords, the German Federal Constitutional Court, the French Conseil d'Etat, the Indian Supreme Court, and the Mexican Supreme Court. Beyond the United States, to take only one recent example, the United Nations Environment Programme (UNEP) and the INECE—itself a regulators network—organized a Global Judges Symposium in conjunction with the UN Conference on Sustainable Development in Johannesburg. The symposium brought together over one hundred of the world's most senior judges from over eighty countries to discuss improving the adoption and implementation of environment-related laws.

One result of this judicial globalization is an increasingly global constitutional jurisprudence, in which courts are referring to each other's decisions on issues ranging from free speech to privacy rights to the death penalty. To cite a recent example from our own Supreme Court, Justice Stephen Breyer recently cited cases from Zimbabwe, India, South Africa, and Canada, most of which in turn cite one another.[2] A Canadian supreme court justice, noting this phenomenon, observes that unlike past legal borrowings across borders, judges are now engaged not in passive reception of foreign decisions, but in active and ongoing dialogue.[3] She chides the United States Supreme Court for lagging behind, but in recent speeches Justices Sandra Day O'Connor and Stephen Breyer have urged American lawyers to know and cite more foreign and international law in their arguments and briefs to U.S. courts.[4] And Chief Justice William Rehnquist now urges all U.S. judges to participate in international judicial exchanges, on the ground that it is "important for judges and legal communities of different nations to exchange views, share information and learn to better understand one another and our legal systems."[5]

This growing judicial interaction is not only transnational. Judges are also forging relationships with their regional and international counterparts. Constitutional courts frequently cite the European Court of Human Rights alongside the decisions of foreign courts, not only within Europe but also around the world. Opportunities to build such "vertical" relationships can only increase; a wave of new international courts and tribunals has followed in the wake of economic globalization.[6] For instance, both NAFTA and the Rome Statute establishing an international criminal court envision direct relationships between national and international tribunals. These relationships are likely to have important consequences far beyond the intentions of their creators. To take the most prominent example, the catalyst for the creation and implementation of the EU legal system was a set of relationships developed between the ECJ and lower national courts in EU member states, relationships largely unanticipated by the diplomats negotiating the Treaty of Rome.

Another set of examples of direct and at least quasi-autonomous judicial interaction comes from the realm of private litigation. In a breach-of-contract case in 1983, Lord Denning observed that he was faced with a situation in which "one [court] or another must give way. I wish that we could sit together to discuss it."[7] Twenty years later courts *are* sitting together to discuss it, at least virtually. Judges are increasingly entering into various forms of "international judicial negotiation."[8] In transnational bankruptcy disputes, for instance, national courts are concluding "Cross-Border Insolvency Cooperation Protocols," which are essentially minitreaties setting forth each side's role in resolving the dispute. More generally, at least in the United States, judges are beginning to develop a distinct doctrine of "judicial comity": a set of principles designed to guide courts in giving deference to foreign courts as a matter of respect owed judges by judges, rather than of the more general respect owed by one nation to another.

Taken together, these wide-ranging examples represent the gradual construction of a global legal system. It is a far different kind of system than has traditionally been envisaged by international lawyers. That vision has always assumed a global legal hierarchy, with a world supreme court such as the International Court of Justice resolving disputes between states and pronouncing on rules of international law that would then be applied by national courts around the world.[9] What is in fact emerging is messier and much more complex. It is a system composed of both horizontal and vertical networks of national and international judges, usually arising from jurisdiction over a common area of the law or a particular region of the world. The judges who are participating in these networks are motivated not out of respect for international law per se, or even out of any conscious desire to build a global system. They are instead driven by a host of more prosaic concerns, such as judicial politics, the demands of a heavy caseload, and the new impact of international rules on national litigants.

What these judges share above all is the recognition of one another as participants in a common judicial enterprise. They see each other not only as servants and representatives of a particular government or polity, but also as fellow members of a profession that transcends national borders. They face common substantive and institutional problems; they learn from one another's experience and reasoning. They cooperate directly to resolve specific disputes. And they conceive of themselves as capable of independent action in both the international and domestic realms. Indeed, a 1993 resolution by the French Institute of International Law calls upon national courts to become independent actors in the international arena and to apply international norms impartially, without deferring to their governments.[10]

The system these judges are creating is better described as a community of courts than as a centralized hierarchy.[11] Nevertheless, it is emerging as a community with identifiable organizing principles. Recognition and elaboration of these principles is critical to understanding the full scope, implications, and potential of the examples set forth in this chapter. They include, first, a rough conception of checks and balances, both vertical and horizontal. In the most developed set of vertical networks, the EU legal system, neither national nor international tribunals hold the definitive upper hand. Horizontally as well, national courts remain acutely conscious of their prerogatives as representatives of independent and interdependent sovereigns, even as they recognize the need for cooperation and even deference to one another.

Second, and relatedly, is a principle of positive conflict, in which judges do not shy from arguing with one another, even acrimoniously, yet do not fear a fundamental rupture in their relations. In this sense, judges are drawing on a domestic understanding of transjudicial relations rather than a diplomatic one. Conflict in domestic politics is to be expected and even embraced; conflict in traditional unitary state diplomacy is to be avoided or quickly resolved.

Third is a principle of pluralism and legitimate difference, whereby judges acknowledge the validity of a wide variety of different approaches to the same legal problem. This pluralism is not unbounded, however. It operates within a framework of common fundamental values, such as recognition of the necessity of judicial independence and basic due process.

Fourth, and finally, is acceptance of the value of persuasive, rather than coercive, authority. Judges from different legal systems acknowledge the possibility of learning from one another based on relative experience with a particular set of issues and on the quality of reasoning in specific decisions.

This chapter sets forth five different categories of judicial interaction: constitutional cross-fertilization, the construction of a global community of human rights law, relations between national courts and the ECJ, private transnational litigation, and face-to-face meetings among judges around the world. The contexts are very different, involving both vertical relations between national and international tribunals and horizontal relations across national borders. Each category is itself the subject of an extensive literature analyzing its causes and consequences within the specific framework of constitutional law, human rights law, EU law, and transnational litigation.

Taken together, however, these categories reveal a larger whole; a world in which courts interact quasi-autonomously with other courts—national and international. They create information networks, enforcement networks, and at least nascent harmonization networks. Their interactions fulfill specific needs and reflect the predilections of specific judges, yet at the same time reveal larger patterns and principles. The result is a growing and overlapping set of vertical and horizontal networks that together establish at least the beginnings of a global legal system.

1. CONSTITUTIONAL CROSS-FERTILIZATION

Consider the following statement by former Chief Justice Smith of the Norwegian Supreme Court: "The Supreme Court has to an increasing degree taken part in international collaboration among the highest courts. It is a natural obligation that, in so far as we have the capacity, we should take part in European and international debate and mutual interaction. We should especially contribute to the ongoing debate on the courts' position on international human rights."[12] More generally, he notes, "it is the duty of national courts—and especially of the highest court in a small country—to introduce new legal ideas from the outside world into national judicial decisions."[13]

Chief Justice Rehnquist would certainly not go this far, although as discussed below, several of his associate justices are beginning to sound precisely this theme. Yet high court judges—judges with constitutional jurisdiction, whether or not they serve on courts limited to constitutional cases—are engaging in a growing dialogue with their counterparts around the world on the issues that arise before them. They conduct this dialogue through mutual citation and increasingly direct interactions, often electronically. In the process, as Norway's former chief justice suggests, they both contribute to a nascent global jurisprudence on particular issues and improve the quality of their particular national decisions, sometimes by importing ideas from abroad and sometimes by resisting them, insisting on an idiosyncratic national approach for specific cultural, historical, or political reasons. Further, they are remarkably self-conscious about what they are doing, engaging in open debates about the uses and abuses of "persuasive authority" from fellow courts in other countries. The results are striking and new, if not in form, then certainly in import.

In the words of Justice Claire L'Heureux-Dubé of the Canadian Supreme Court, "More and more courts, particularly within the common law world, are looking to the judgments of other jurisdictions, particularly when making decisions on human rights issues. Deciding on applicable legal principles and solutions increasingly involves a consideration of the approaches that have been adopted with regard to similar legal problems elsewhere."[14] From England comes confirmation from Lord Brown-Wilkinson, citing comments by "several senior members of the British judiciary" on their increased willingness "to accord persuasive authority to the constitutional values of other democratic nations when dealing with ambiguous statutory or common law provisions that impact upon civil liberties issues."[15] The new South African Constitution requires the South African Constitutional Court to "consider international law" and permits it to consult foreign law in its human rights decisions;[16] in a landmark opinion holding the death penalty unconstitutional, the Court cited decisions of the U.S. Supreme Court, the Canadian Supreme Court, the German Constitutional Court, the Indian Supreme Court, the Hungarian Constitutional Court, and the Tanzanian Court of Appeal.[17] More systematically, scholars have documented the use of comparative material by constitutional courts in Israel, Australia, South Africa, Canada, India, New Zealand, Zimbabwe, and Ireland.[18]

What's New?

But is such cross-fertilization really new? It is a well-recognized phenomenon among imperial powers and their colonies.[19] It is well established in the Commonwealth.[20] Plenty of evidence of borrowing from English law can be also found in nineteenth-century U.S. federal reports. In this century, the traffic has largely flowed in the other direction; since 1945 recent constitutional courts around the world, frequently established either by the United States or on the model of the U.S. Supreme Court, have borrowed heavily from U.S. Supreme Court jurisprudence.[21] Thus it is difficult to show from existing data that the use of comparative materials in constitutional adjudication has in fact increased.[22]

On the other hand, many participating judges and a number of observers think today's constitutional cross-fertilization is new in important ways.[23] They point to a number of distinctive features: the identity of the participants, the interactive dimension of the process, the motives for transnational borrowings, and the self-conscious construction of a global judicial community. For Justice O'Connor, what is new is the world itself, or at least the professional need to know it. She asks: "Why does information about international law matter so much? Why should judges and lawyers who are concerned about the intricacies of ERISA, the Americans with Disabilities Act, and the Bankruptcy Code care about issues of foreign law and international law?" She answers: "The reason, of course, is globalization. No institution of government can afford now to ignore the rest of the world."[24]

Justice O'Connor's argument is functional: globalization means that judges in different countries will have to decide more and more cases involving issues governed by international or foreign law. They must thus familiarize themselves with those bodies of law, just as they must know the general dimensions of different areas of American law. Such functional demand can drive technological supply, but in this case the extraordinary increase in information availability through the Internet has likely itself also become a driver of judicial globalization. The two principal electronic legal databases, Lexis-Nexis and Westlaw, now include legislation and decisions from the European Union, the United Kingdom, Australia, Hong Kong, Russia, Mexico, Ireland, New Zealand, Singapore, and Canada.[25] Access to these foreign sources has expanded primarily in the last decade.

Yet if the constitutional cross-fertilization we are witnessing were only a function of globalization and the information revolution, it would at best be a change of degree but not of kind. A third set of factors driving this phenomenon is political. The European Commission for Democracy through Law (the Venice Commission) operates a website called CODICES, in addition to a paper Bulletin on Constitutional Case-Law, which regularly collects and digests the decisions of constitutional courts and courts of equivalent jurisdiction around the world. CODICES has liaisons in over fifty countries; it not only offers a précis of each case in the database but also makes it possible to search the entire database by keyword or phrase to allow researchers to find out quickly what courts in many different countries have said on a particular issue.[26]

The expressed purpose of CODICES is instructive. It is "to allow judges and constitutional law specialists in the academic world to be informed quickly about the most important judgments" in constitutional law.[27] But the underlying reason is explicitly political: to build democracy through law. According to the CODICES website, "The exchange of information and ideas among old and new democracies in the field of judge-made law is of vital importance. Such an exchange and such cooperation, it is hoped, will not only be of benefit to the newly established constitutional jurisdictions of Central and Eastern Europe, but will also enrich the case-law of the existing courts in Western Europe and North America."[28] The aim is to strengthen the new constitutional courts in the fledgling democracies and facilitate convergence of constitutional law across Europe.

Across the Pacific, LawAsia is a form of regional bar association, composed of different kinds of legal associations across the region as well as individual lawyers, law firms, and corporations. It publishes law bulletins and offers many different venues for its members to come together and exchange information and ideas. Its primary goal as a professional association has been to offer networking opportunities for its members, but a secondary goal, made quite explicit, includes promoting the rule of law through: "disseminating knowledge of the law of members' countries"; "promoting the efficient working of the legal systems of members' countries"; and "promoting development of the law and uniformity where appropriate."[29] Other goals refer to the promotion of human rights and the administration of justice throughout the region.

On the demand side, many commentators note the impact of the end of the Cold War and the resulting emergence of many fledgling democracies with new constitutional courts seeking to emulate their more established counterparts. A flood of foundation and government funding for judicial seminars, training programs, and educational materials under the banner of "rule of law" programs helped provide personal contacts and intellectual opportunities for these new judges.[30] Frederick Schauer points out, however, that in countries seeking to cast off an imperialist past, be it colonial or communist, it is likely to be particularly important to establish an indigenous constitution, including a set of human rights protections.[31] Borrowing constitutional ideas is thus likely to be politically more problematic than borrowing a bankruptcy code.[32]

Individual courts are often thus quite particular about when they borrow and from whom. Schauer argues that governments that want to demonstrate their membership in a particular political, legal, and cultural community are likely to encourage borrowing from members of that community.[33] In this regard, consider again the provision in the new South African Constitution requiring the constitutional court to look abroad. The clear message, from a state emerging from pariah status during the years of apartheid, is a desire to be part of a global legal community and to make the consistency of South African constitutional law with the law of other leading liberal democratic legal systems explicit. For the South African Constitutional Court itself, becoming part of a global judicial conversation has become a badge of legitimacy.

The identity of the most influential "lender" or "donor" courts in recent years is equally striking. The South African Constitutional Court and the Canadian Supreme Court have both been highly influential, apparently more so than the U.S. Supreme Court and other older and more established constitutional courts.[34] In part, their influence may spring from the simple fact that they are *not* American, thus rendering their reasoning more politically palatable to domestic audiences in an era of extraordinary U.S. military, political, economic, and cultural power and accompanying resentments.[35] But equally if not more important is the ability of these courts themselves to capture and crystallize the work of their fellow constitutional judges around the world. Schauer argues that the "ideas and constitutionalists of Canada have been disproportionately influential" in part because "Canada, unlike the United States, is seen as reflecting an emerging international consensus rather than existing as an outlier."[36]

Canada and South Africa—one old democracy and one new—with two new constitutional courts (the Canadian Supreme Court has existed since the mid-nineteenth century but the new Canadian Constitution was only enacted in 1982; the South African Constitutional Court was created in 1994), each looking around the world and canvassing the opinions of its fellow constitutional courts and each disproportionately influential as a result. Here is the most dramatic difference with past patterns of legal transplantation or cross-fertilization. According to Canadian Justice L'Heureux-Dubé, the most important break with the past is that "the process of international influences has changed from *reception* to *dialogue*. Judges no longer simply *receive* the cases of other jurisdictions and then apply them or modify them for their own jurisdiction."[37] Instead, appellate judges around the world are engaging in self-conscious conversation.[38]

This *awareness* of constitutional cross-fertilization on a global scale—an awareness of who is citing whom among the judges them-

selves and a concomitant pride in a cosmopolitan judicial outlook—
creates an incentive to be both lender and borrower. Indeed, the Tai-
wanese Constitutional Court has translated large portions of its case
law into English and made them available on its website to ensure that
it is part of this global dialogue.[39] Further, constitutional judges in many
different countries, including the United States, are actively and
openly discussing the legitimacy of this phenomenon. It is one thing to
borrow to fill a gap or even build a foundation, as courts in fledgling
states or newly decolonized countries have long had to do. It is another
to have a domestic legal system developed enough to be able to decide
the case in question, but nevertheless to search out how foreign judges
have responded to a comparable case. The point is less to borrow than
to benefit from comparative deliberation.

It is to this debate that we now turn. First, is it legitimate for a judge
to consult foreign case law to help him or her decide a case? A judge
can take this step in the privacy of chambers, without ever revealing
the actual process of decision on the outcome of a particular case. But
in common law legal systems, we require judges to provide an explicit
account of that process in a written opinion, by citing previous cases
that support the conclusion reached and distinguishing previous cases
that do not. Indeed, when those previous cases have been decided by
the same court or by a higher court in the same legal system, they are
binding as precedent, at least in common law systems. In this context,
the question of drawing on and actually citing foreign cases becomes
one of the legitimacy of "persuasive authority."

The Rise of Persuasive Authority

Where should individual courts draw a line between the requirements
of their own legal systems and the resources of others? According to
Justice O'Connor, speaking at the American Society of International
Law, "Although international law and the law of other nations are
rarely binding upon our decisions in U.S. courts, conclusions reached
by other countries and by the international community should at times
constitute persuasive authority in American courts. This is sometimes

called 'transjudicialism.' "[40] Her colleagues are sharply divided on this point. In *Knight v. Florida*—the recent decision rejecting the plaintiff's application to have his case heard by the Court in which Justice Breyer reviewed a number of foreign precedents in his dissenting opinion— Justice Clarence Thomas observed tartly: "Were there any support [for the defendant's argument] in our own jurisprudence, it would be unnecessary for proponents of the claim to rely on the European Court of Human Rights, the Supreme Court of Zimbabwe, the Supreme Court of India, or the Privy Council."[41] For his part, Justice Breyer retorted that although the views of the foreign authorities are not binding, the "[w]illingness to consider foreign judicial views in comparable cases is not surprising in a nation that from its birth has given a 'decent respect to the opinions of mankind.' "[42]

This exchange between Justice Thomas and Justice Breyer is only one sally in an ongoing tussle. Justice Antonin Scalia took a strong stand on this issue in 1988. When confronted with evidence of how other countries view the death penalty, he wrote that "[w]e must not forget that it is the Constitution for the United States that we are expounding."[43] Almost a decade later, Justice Breyer joined the issue directly, albeit in dissent. He admitted that "we are interpreting our own constitution, not that of other nations and there may be relevant political and structural differences" between foreign legal systems and the U.S. system. Nonetheless, he observed that "their experience may . . . cast an empirical light on the consequences of different solutions to a common legal problem."[44] Unconvinced, Justice Scalia reaffirmed his position, insisting that "such comparative analysis [is] inappropriate to the task of interpreting a constitution, though it was of course quite relevant to the task of writing one."[45]

For her part, Justice Ruth Bader Ginsburg, writing about the motives behind and deficiencies in U.S. affirmative action programs, notes India's experience with affirmative action, including a decision by the Indian Supreme Court imposing a *ceiling* on the number of positions that can be reserved for disadvantaged citizens. "In the area of human rights," she observes, "experience in one nation or region may inspire or inform other nations or regions."[46] She notes that the Indian Supreme Court has considered U.S. precedents, but that the "same readiness to look beyond one's own shores has not marked the decisions of the court on which I serve." At a later speech on the same subject, however, she argued that "change is in the wind,"[47] reviewing the efforts of Justice O'Connor and noting that Justice Breyer pins his hopes on the wired classroom, which will "permit U.S., Canadian, French, German, or Indian professors to 'team teach' classes held simultaneously in different nations."[48] The results will later be felt in courts.

For judges favoring the use of persuasive authority, looking abroad simply helps them do a better job at home, in the sense that they can approach a particular problem more creatively or with greater insight. Foreign decisions are persuasive because they offer new information and perspectives that may cast an issue in a different and more tractable light.[49] Breyer again, from *Knight v. Florida*: "In these cases, the foreign courts I have mentioned have considered roughly comparable questions under roughly comparable legal standards. Each court has held or assumed that those standards permit application of the death penalty itself. Consequently, I believe their view [*sic*] are useful even though not binding."[50] Compare Justice Albie Sachs of the South African Constitutional Court, who writes: "If I draw on statements by certain United States Supreme Court Justices, I do so not because I treat their decisions as precedents to be applied in our Courts, but because their *dicta* articulate in an elegant and helpful manner problems which face any modern court dealing with what has loosely been called church/state relations. Thus, though drawn from another legal culture, they express values and dilemmas in a way which I find most helpful in elucidating the meaning of our own constitutional text."[51]

Justice Ginsburg offers yet another formulation of the same rationale, noting that just as the problems of "irrational prejudice and rank discrimination" are global, all societies can usefully learn from one another about various solutions.[52] And Justice Shirley Abrahamson, Chief Justice of the Wisconsin Supreme Court and an intellectual leader among state judges, points out that U.S. state court judges automatically canvass the case law of sister states for ideas and perspectives on the issues before them, yet shrink automatically from looking at case law even from so near a geographic and cultural neighbor as Canada[53]

"We are already comparatists," she writes. "We just don't think of ourselves that way."[54]

Where judges do cite foreign decisions as persuasive authority and are persuaded to the point of actual convergence of decisions on certain issues, constitutional cross-fertilization begins to evolve into something deeper, resembling an emerging global jurisprudence. Shirley Abrahamson again: "When courts from around the world have written well-reasoned and provocative opinions in support of a position at odds with our familiar American views, we would do well to read carefully and take notes."[55] This simple desire to look around the world for good ideas, rather than "some judges being 'givers' of law while others are 'receivers,'" reflects a spirit of genuine transjudicial deliberation within a newly self-conscious transnational community.[56]

An Emerging Global Jurisprudence

Increasing cross-fertilization of ideas and precedents among constitutional judges around the world is gradually giving rise to increasingly visible international consensus on various issues—a consensus that, in turn, carries its own compelling weight. Thus, for instance, former Chief Justice Smith of Norway notes the need "to weigh the advantages of international legal unity in various legal areas against the need to protect the legal foundation of national and local cultures."[57] More broadly, in hypothesizing the reasons for specific patterns of legal transplantation, Schauer argues that "ideas that are seen as close to an emerging international consensus are likely to be more influential internationally."[58]

Justice Abrahamson offers an illustration of how such a consensus has emerged on the question of the definition of informed consent to a medical procedure. She notes that "courts . . . around the world have struggled to balance the values integral to the doctrine: individual autonomy vs. efficient administration of justice and health care systems."[59] The U.S. Supreme Court has a clear precedent establishing a particular standard for informed consent, resting on the conception of the "prudent patient." Outside the United States, however, the German Constitutional Court, an Australian appellate court, and Canadian appellate courts have all concluded, after considering the U.S. Supreme Court's views, that the prudent-patient standard does not go far enough and instead adopted a subjective standard that inquires precisely into whether an individual patient understood the risks of the specific medical procedure he or she was being asked to undergo.[60] Justice Breyer offers another example. The cases that he cites in his dissent in *Knight v. Florida* cite each other in coming to roughly the same result on the impermissibility of executing a convicted criminal after extraordinary delay, lasting as long as twenty years.[61]

In many cases, however, judges are more likely to reach consensus on the relevant cases from courts around the world when consulting on a particular issue than on a particular answer or position. As former Chief Justice Smith notes, although individual judges may put a value on international uniformity, they must also take into account a range of specifically national considerations that are as likely to lead them to deviate from the decisions of their fellow judges as to conform. In this sense, the emergence of a global jurisprudence refers more to the existence of active dialogue among the world's judges based on a limited number of precedents on any particular issue. No one answer is the right one; the principles of pluralism and legitimate difference again prevail. Nevertheless, failure to participate in this dialogue can sharply diminish the influence of any individual national court.[62]

2. TOWARD A GLOBAL COMMUNITY OF HUMAN RIGHTS LAW

To the extent that pockets of global jurisprudence are emerging, they are most likely to involve issues of basic human rights. Courts may well feel a particular common bond with one another in adjudicating human rights cases, however, because such cases engage a core judicial function in many countries around the world. They ask courts to protect individuals against abuses of state power, requiring them to determine the appropriate level of protection in light of a complex matrix of historical, cultural, and political needs and expectations. Actual decisions must be highly individualized.[63] But the process of sifting and balancing rights, powers, and privileges certainly crosses borders.

Further, these basic human rights issues are not only regulated by national constitutions, but also by international human rights treaties. The interpretation and application of each of these treaties typically falls to an international tribunal, generally established by the treaty itself. When these tribunals join the mix of national constitutional courts, the result is a genuinely global community of courts and law.

The international tribunal most frequently cited is the European Court of Human Rights (ECHR). The European Convention on Human Rights sets forth a substantive catalogue of human rights and creates an intricate enforcement mechanism to permit individuals and groups to file complaints against their national governments. The treaty now compels all state signatories to recognize this right of petition and the compulsory jurisdiction of the ECHR.[64]

Like the ECJ, discussed below, the ECHR has succeeded in transforming an empty docket into a teeming one. It has declared its principal text, the European Convention, a "constitutional instrument of European public order in the field of human rights" and has successfully established itself as the exclusive interpreter of the Convention's provisions.[65] And it has begun to witness its rulings change the shape of domestic law, through legislative revision and administrative decree as well as judicial decision.[66] It has also had an impact on national courts, launching a genuine vertical dialogue between national judges and ECHR judges.[67]

Even more remarkably, the ECHR has become a source of authoritative pronouncements on human rights law for national courts that are not directly subject to its authority, either because its role as interpreter of the European Convention has not been recognized as a matter of domestic law, or, much more strikingly, because the national court's state is not a party to the European Convention in the first place. The South African Supreme Court also cited ECHR decisions in its decision finding the death penalty unconstitutional under the South African Constitution.[68] The Supreme Court of Zimbabwe similarly cited ECHR decisions to support its determination that corporal punishment of an adult constitutes cruel and unusual punishment and that corporal punishment of a juvenile is unconstitutional;[69] the Israeli High Court of Justice turned to the ECHR decision in *Ireland v. United Kingdom* to determine that some interrogation methods employed by the Internal Security Agency were tainted by an "inhumane and degrading" treatment and therefore forbidden;[70] the British Privy Council, sitting as the Constitutional Court of Jamaica, relied on the ECHR's decision in *Soering v. United Kingdom* (as well as a decision by the UN Human Rights Committee) to commute a Jamaican death penalty to life in prison.[71] J. G. Merrills has also documented numerous instances in which the reasoning and interpretative methodologies first developed by the ECHR were later accepted by the Inter-American Court of Human Rights and the UN Human Rights Committee.[72] Reviewing these cases, one commentator has described the ECHR as a "sort of world court of human rights," whose judgments are increasingly quoted by national courts and accepted by them.[73]

What is striking, of course, is that the ECHR has no formal authority over these courts. Its decisions have only persuasive authority—the weight accorded them out of respect for their legitimacy, care, and quality by judges worldwide engaged in a common enterprise of protecting human rights. Commentators have adduced various explanations for this phenomenon, including the dictates of domestic or international law,[74] the increased publication and hence availability of human rights decisions,[75] and a growing sense that other countries are taking human rights treaties seriously, a sense enhanced by the explicitly universal rhetoric surrounding human rights law.[76]

The Supreme Court of Norway has a particularly interesting perspective, even within Europe. Writing in 1998, former Chief Justice Smith observed that the European Convention of Human Rights, "as applied by the Strasbourg Court, is on the verge of becoming an essential supplement to our traditional right to review legislation."[77] He noted that the rights protected in the Convention are more explicit than those enumerated in the Norwegian Constitution, and that the relative priority of national and international rules remains unclear. The Norwegian Court has moved, however, from simply determining that Norwegian legislation is not contrary to the Convention to introducing the ECHR's decisions, "together with [its] dynamic interpretation of the Convention," as "important legal sources in reaching its own decisions."[78] He argued further that it is impossible to establish clear priority of one body of rules over another; in some cases the international rules take precedence but that in other cases the court has reached the limit in applying human rights provisions in its decisions "without their having greater support in existing legislation."[79]

Here is a system of vertical checks and balances. National courts respect and interact with a supranational tribunal, but only to a point. When a developing international rule, as promulgated by a supranational tribunal, moves too far out of line with a prevailing domestic democratic consensus, the national courts will not follow. This system is most developed and refined within the European Union, to which we now turn.

3. THE ROLE OF NATIONAL COURTS IN THE CONSTRUCTION OF THE EUROPEAN COMMUNITY LEGAL SYSTEM

The legal system of the European Community, now the European Union, was built through the decisions of lower national courts to send cases up to the ECJ. These lower courts regarded the ECJ not as a supreme court, but as a supranational court, often bypassing their own supreme courts and at least in tacit opposition to the views of the executive branch in their respective countries.[80] The ECJ in turn, took the opportunity to lay the foundation of what it originally called "a new legal order," in which the Treaty of Rome and much legislation passed in Brussels was "directly effective" ("self-executing" in U.S. terms) and thus able to be invoked by individuals in national courts.[81] The result was to empower individual litigants and lower national courts to hold government (executive and legislative branches) to their international commitments.

Higher national courts, particularly constitutional courts, ultimately realized that their power was being eroded and fought back. The result is what the German Constitutional Court has called a "cooperative re-lationship" between the ECJ and national high courts. This is a rela-tionship defined court to court and based explicitly on both entities re-spective competencies in domestic and international law.

A new generation of scholarship has focused on the motives driving the national courts to ally themselves with the ECJ, noting substantial variation in the willingness both of different courts within the same country and of courts in different countries to send references to the ECJ and to abide by the resulting judgments. What is most striking about these findings is the extent to which specific national courts acted independently not only of other national courts, but also of the executive and legislative branches of their respective governments.[82] For example, a lower German financial court insisted on following an ECJ judgment in the face of strong opposition not only from a higher financial court, but also from the German government.[83] The French Court of Cassation accepted the supremacy of EU law, following the dictate of the ECJ, even in the face of threats from the French legisla-ture to strip its jurisdiction amid age-old charges of "gouvernement par juges."[84] British courts overturned the sacrosanct doctrine of parlia-mentary sovereignty and issued an injunction blocking the effect of a British law pending judicial review at the European level.[85]

Such judicial action might be unremarkable in the domestic con-text. Particularly in the early days of the construction of the European Community, however, steps toward further integrating the Treaty of Rome were considered foreign policy decisions to be made by the exec-utive on the basis of calculations of relative advantage and disad-vantage among competing member states. How then to explain why national courts did not line up behind the executive and await instruc-tions? The motives of these various national courts were multiple: a de-sire for "empowerment";[86] competition with other courts for relative prestige and power;[87] a particular view of the law that could be achieved by following EC precedents over national precedent;[88] or the desire to advantage, or at least not to disadvantage, a particular constituency of litigants.[89]

Many observers might discount the experience of national courts in the European Union either as a sui generis phenomenon or as more analogous to the experience of state courts in the early decades of the United States than to that of contemporary courts worldwide. It is certainly possible that the European Union is an emerging federal state, but federalism is currently out of fashion among member governments. More important for the argument advanced here, a federalist vision of the Union has been rejected by leading national courts, which see themselves as still interacting with a supranational rather than a federal tribunal. Together with the ECJ, they have constructed a European legal system that is a potential model for relations between national and international courts worldwide.

The German Federal Constitutional Court (*Bundesverfassungsgericht*, or BvG) in particular has a long history of engaging and challenging the ECJ as a co-equal rather than a superior court.[90] In its recent decision in *Brunner v. The European Union Treaty*[91]—a case that challenged the constitutionality of the Treaty of Maastricht—the BvG explicitly proposed a "cooperative relationship" with the ECJ, by which the BvG would establish a threshold of constitutional guarantees and the ECJ would adjudicate the application of these and additional guarantees on a case-by-case basis.[92] Within this relationship, both courts are to ensure that both Union law and national law are properly respected by the government institutions most directly within their jurisdiction and to acknowledge their "mutual influence" on one another.[93]

The BvG has been the most outspoken and perhaps the most assertive in its relations with the ECJ, but it is not alone, garnering support from the Italian, French, and Belgian high courts in more subtle guises.[94] The tug of war between the ECJ and all national courts, both high and low, will continue, even as their relations and their jurisprudence become increasingly intertwined. But just as the BvG declared the European Union to be not a "confederation" but a "community of states,"[95] so too is its legal system best characterized as a community of courts. Within this community, each court is a check on the other, but not a decisive one; the courts assert their respective claims through a dialogue of incremental decisions signaling opposition or cooperation. It is a dialogue of constitutionalism within a recognizably traditional

framework of international law, a framework that can be adopted and adapted by courts around the world.[96]

4. JUDICIAL COOPERATION AND CONFLICT IN TRANSNATIONAL LITIGATION

The global economy creates global litigation. When products can have their components manufactured in three different countries, be assembled in a fourth, and marketed and distributed in five or six others, the number of potential forums for resolving disputes multiplies rapidly, leading litigants to battle as fiercely over jurisdiction and choice of forum as over the merits of the case. Such battles have long been the stuff of private international law; they have also fueled the growth of international commercial arbitration.

Today, however, the question facing judges around the world, in the words of Judge, now Justice, Stephen Breyer, is how to "help the world's legal systems work together, in harmony, rather than at cross purposes."[97] Even more boldly, Judge Guido Calabresi of the U.S. Court of Appeals for the Second Circuit interpreted a U.S. discovery statute as follows: the U.S. statute contemplates international cooperation, and "such cooperation pre-supposes an ongoing dialogue between the adjudicative bodies of the world community."[98] This is an extraordinary vision. This "[d]ialogue between the adjudicative bodies of the world community" does not distinguish between U.S. courts, French courts, German courts, Japanese courts, and associated international tribunals. It simply imagines courts—adjudicative bodies of a single world community—resolving disputes, interpreting and applying the law as best they can. It is a vision of a global legal system, established not by the World Court in The Hague, but by national courts working together around the world.

Transjudicial relations within this system are not always harmonious, however. On the contrary, judges are engaging one another more directly and more familiarly, in ways that can create opportunities for both cooperation and conflict. This combination of active col-

laboration and vigorous conflict marks a move from comity among what Justice Breyer called the "world's legal systems," in which judges view one another as operating in equal but distinct legal spheres, to the presumption of an integrated system. This presumption, in turn, rests on a conception of a single global economy in which borders are increasingly irrelevant and an accompanying legal system in which litigants can choose among multiple forums to resolve a dispute. Paradoxically, however, whereas a presumption of a world of separate sovereigns mandates courtesy and periodic deference between them, the presumption of an integrated system takes mutual respect for granted and focuses instead on how well that system works. It is a shift that is likely to result in more dialogue but *less* deference.

The growth of judicial cooperation in transnational litigation is enabled and characterized by three important developments. First, courts are adapting the general notion of international comity, or the comity of nations, to fit the specific needs of courts. The result is the emergence of a narrower doctrine of judicial comity. Second, often as a concomitant of this process, judges are necessarily evaluating the independence and quality of fellow judges of other nations. Third, judges are actually negotiating with one another to determine which national court should take control over which part of multinational lawsuits.

Judicial Cooperation and Conflict: The Emergence of "Judicial Comity"

The "comity of nations" is a venerable legal and political concept. In its best-known judicial formulation, it means the respect owed to the laws and acts of other nations by virtue of common membership in the international system—a presumption of recognition that is something more than courtesy but less than obligation.[99] Courts have invoked it in many different contexts and with many different meanings, to justify everything from deference to the executive branch in decisions touching on foreign relations to the enforcement of foreign judgments.[100] It arises regularly in the growing number of suits in which courts must decide where the suit should be heard, at home or abroad. More con-

cretely, they must decide whether to enforce the provisions of an initial contract between two business litigants selecting a particular forum to hear their disputes; which forum will be most convenient in terms of gathering evidence, minimizing travel of litigants and witnesses, and maximizing the judge's knowledge of the applicable law; and how to decide which litigation should go forward in cases where the plaintiff has sued the defendant in one country and the defendant has sued the plaintiff in another over the same disputes. As courts grapple with these issues, they are developing a more specific and nuanced conception of judicial comity.[101]

Judicial comity provides the framework and the ground rules for a global dialogue among judges in the context of specific cases. It has four distinct strands. First is a respect for foreign courts qua courts, rather than simply as the face of a foreign government, and hence for their ability to resolve disputes and interpret and apply the law honestly and competently.[102] Second is the related recognition that courts in different nations are entitled to their fair share of disputes—both as co-equals in the global task of judging and as the instruments of a strong "local interest in having localized controversies decided at home."[103] Third is a distinctive emphasis on individual rights and the judicial role in protecting them.[104] Fourth, although seemingly paradoxically, is a greater willingness to clash with other courts when necessary, as an inherent part of engaging as equals in a common enterprise.

To illustrate the ways in which the general idea of the comity of nations translates into a more specific judicial context, it is helpful to examine how U.S. courts are handling situations when a litigant who is a defendant before them in a U.S. suit suddenly turns around and brings essentially the same suit in reverse in a foreign court. Should both cases be allowed to go forward, on the same facts but before different judges and within different legal systems? Or should the litigants be compelled to proceed in only one forum?

The U.S. Court of Appeals for the Fifth Circuit recently addressed this issue, in a case in which an American manufacturer of athletic shoes sued its Japanese distributor in U.S. court for breach of contract.[105] The Japanese company had agreed to the U.S. forum in the distributorship agreement. The two sides proceeded with the litigation, requesting documents from one another and deposing witnesses. After six months, the Japanese company suddenly brought a parallel suit in Japanese court, accusing the American company of breach of contract. The American company then asked the U.S. court to issue an antisuit injunction, barring the Japanese company from proceeding with the suit in the Japanese court.

In the suit, the circuit court, applying a liberal standard of comity, concluded that the Japanese suit would be "an absurd duplication of effort" and that the Japanese litigant sought primarily to harass the U.S. litigant and delay resolution of the suit.[106] As for comity, the court held that comity concerns were satisfied absent a demonstration that the antisuit injunction would pose an actual threat to relations between the United States and Japan. Unless specific evidence of such a threat could be produced, the court declined "to require a district court to genuflect before a vague and omnipotent notion of comity every time that it must decide whether to enjoin a foreign action."[107] This judgment stopped the Japanese suit, not because the Japanese court has to enforce the U.S. ruling, but because if the Japanese litigant had proceeded with its suit in Japan, it would be violating the U.S. court's order and subject to fines or even an automatic judgment against it in the U.S. suit.

What is at stake here, underneath the legal jargon, is a decision. Should the court begin from a presumption of difference and diplomatic prerogative, in which blocking a suit from proceeding in a foreign legal system is automatically deemed an affront to the nation as a whole? Or should the court presume a fundamental identity of transnational judicial interests in resolving suits as quickly and efficiently as possible? If the goal is to resolve suits as quickly as possible, then the Japanese court should not be offended by interference with its jurisdiction through the issuance of an antisuit injunction by a U.S. court; it should instead share the same concern regarding duplication of effort and harassment of individual litigants, in this case the U.S. plaintiff.

The U.S. Court of Appeals for the Seventh Circuit has gone the farthest in breaking down the barriers between foreign and domestic legal systems in this area of the law. Judge Richard Posner argues that the emergence of what is "increasingly . . . one world" suggests that domestic rules for "limiting duplicative litigation" should also apply abroad.[108] He thus insists that instead of deferring to an abstract notion of comity, courts should require "some empirical flesh on the theoretical skeleton" and insist on actual evidence of harm to bilateral relations.[109] Without an explicit indication of such harm from the State Department or the Foreign Ministry of the country involved, the court is free to proceed as it determines in the best interests of justice.[110]

Many observers, both in this country and abroad, will hear this claim as a power play—an assertion that foreign courts should now receive as little deference as state courts and hence that U.S. federal courts are now free to insist on exclusive jurisdiction over all transnational cases with a link to the United States. Indeed, the majority of commentators on judicial comity have argued that comity court to court requires more deference rather than less on reciprocity grounds.[111] This reasoning suggests that the same U.S. courts that are willing to block foreign litigation would not be willing to let foreign courts take over cases that could equally have been brought in the United States.

It is certainly true that U.S. judges have not shied from conflict with their foreign brethren. In the same case in which Judge Calabresi wrote so glowingly of judicial dialogue, the dissenting member of the panel accused him of blatant interference with the French legal system.[112] In another example, Judge Richard Owen of the Southern District of New York squared off with a Hong Kong judge over an insider trading case. In refusing to defer jurisdiction to the Hong Kong court, Judge Owen declared: "I am not going to do this. I'm an American judge and this is an American agency and I will keep jurisdiction and I will direct payment into court."[113] In his paraphrase, the defendant in the New York case was arguing for litigating in Hong Kong on the ground that "out here in Hong Kong they practically give you a medal for doing this kind of thing."[114] For his part, Judge Gordon Cruden in Hong Kong observed that "this court will always take whatever effective steps are legally available to it under Hong Kong law, to deal with illegal or morally reprehensible commercial conduct. . . . Where a conflict of laws situation does arise . . . the dispute should be approached in a spirit of judicial comity rather than judicial competitiveness."[115] Similarly, in a case discussed further below, Judge Posner overrode a protest from the French Insurance Commission, which denounced a U.S. district court's characterization of a French commercial court as "insulting."[116]

Paradoxical as it may seem, however, the willingness to weather conflict reflects the certainty of ongoing interaction. The proof is an equal readiness on the part of U.S. courts espousing the liberal standard of comity to enjoin U.S. proceedings in favor of foreign proceedings where the balance of equities tips toward the foreign court.[117] Thus, the clear message of the Fifth Circuit's reasoning in the suit between the U.S. plaintiff and the Japanese defendant is that if the Japanese litigant had sued first in Japan and the case had proceeded there, the U.S. litigant would have been guilty of imposing an undue burden on both the courts and the Japanese litigant if it had subsequently sued in the United States. Staying litigation in such cases in favor of a foreign court is a natural extension of the U.S. Supreme Court's decision in 1972 that U.S. litigants could no longer expect a guarantee of being able to sue in the United States if they were engaged in transnational business and had contracted to have disputes heard in a foreign forum.[118] It explicitly rejected the "parochial concept that all disputes must be resolved under our laws and in our courts."[119]

Judges elsewhere in the world are perhaps less assertive than their U.S. brethren, but many are beginning to recognize their obligations to a community of litigants beyond the borders of their home jurisdiction. In the words of Canadian Supreme Court Justice Gérard La Forest, explaining a decision to apply foreign rather than forum law: "The court takes jurisdiction not to administer local law, but for the convenience of litigants, with a view to responding to modern mobility and the needs of a world or national economic order."[120] More generally, courts in the United States, Australia, Japan, Switzerland, and Quebec are all moving toward a position of upholding the law of the place of the accident, with various exceptions for situations in which litigants can be shown to have had a more significant relationship or a closer connection with another forum.[121] In a related development, British courts have moved strikingly over the past two decades from the position that all plaintiffs should be entitled to litigate in British court "as of right," regardless of links between the parties, the litigation, and a foreign forum,[122] to the view that a stay should be granted in favor of a foreign forum if the defendant can show that the foreign forum is more suitable "for the interests of all the parties and the ends of justice."[123]

The significance of this shift is that courts are beginning to recognize that in many cases one "natural" or "most appropriate" forum exists among the courts of the world, rather than automatically asserting jurisdiction over litigants who happen to have chosen a particular court to sue in or who are citizens of the court's own country. Any move toward cooperation in finding "the natural forum" must rest, however, on a prior recognition by all the courts involved that multiple forums are possible. Further, it assumes that these forums are roughly equivalent and that the appropriate forum can be identified on the basis of specifically judicial rather than conventional national interests: the "interests of all the parties," a recognition of the needs of individual litigants, and the "end of justice," the special province of judges.

Judges Judging Judges

This conception of an integrated global legal system has two characteristics: (1) litigants move relatively freely across borders, carrying their disputes with them and choosing a particular national forum subject to judicial review of that choice; and (2) judges defer to or reject their foreign counterparts for reasons of efficiency, fairness, or the "ends of justice" rather than of sovereign prerogatives. These traits lead to judges judging judges. In the case discussed above in which Judge Posner upheld a stay of litigation before a French tribunal, he ultimately concluded that the Commercial Court of Lille, "although called a court, . . . is actually a panel of arbitrators, composed of businessmen who devote part time to arbitrating."[124] After reviewing an affidavit from a French legal expert, which the district court had also credited, Posner concluded that this tribunal could not handle the documentary burden of massive insurance litigation and would not be able to hear live witnesses.

Judge Posner was aware of the seeming offensiveness of his conclusions, admitting that "at first glance the action of an American judge in

enjoining what is practically an arm of the French state . . . from litigating a suit on a French insurance policy in a French court may seem
an extraordinary breach of international comity."[125] Nevertheless, and
even in the face of expostulations from the French Insurance Commission, Posner insisted that the U.S. courts were not questioning the
competence of their French counterparts, only their "capacity relative
to a U.S. District court to resolve this particular dispute."[126]

To prove his point, Posner was quite willing to entertain the possibility of a reverse situation, in which the French courts would be better
equipped to adjudicate than the relevant U.S. tribunal. He noted that
the U.S. has arbitral bodies overseeing, for example, railroad cases
where the "French have courts staffed by professional judges." Thus, he
continued, "We can imagine a mirror-image case in which a French
court was asked to enjoin an American firm from proceeding in the
National Railroad Adjustment Board because that board was not
equipped to do justice between the parties in the particular circumstances of the dispute."[127] Again, what is most striking is Posner's willingness to equate French government entities with their U.S. counterparts simply as official institutions with a job to do, but with the
corollary result of being willing to accord them *less* deference rather
than more. Similarly, his analysis assumes that "professional judges"
share the same basic characteristics the world over, at least as compared to arbitrators, regardless of nationality or specific legal training.
Those common standards of professionalism once again afford a basis
for mutual evaluation.

Posner's evaluation of the French commercial court is a particularly
bold example of what lawyers generally call "adequate forum analysis."
Inquiry into the adequacy of the foreign forum is a standard component
of judicial analysis not only in cases involving parallel litigation in a
domestic and a foreign forum, but also in any case in which a litigant
seeks either the transfer of a case to a foreign forum or the enforcement
of a foreign judgment. The opposing litigant in turn will often argue
that the foreign forum is "inadequate," on grounds ranging from corruption to diminished opportunities to get access to necessary documents and witnesses. Even a brief review of adequate forum decisions
by U.S. courts reveals patterns of larger significance: the establishment

or recognition of a minimum standard of international justice and a willingness to evaluate foreign tribunals on the same criteria as domestic tribunals. These two trends sometimes point in opposite directions, but make sense in the context of the construction of a global community of law.

Consider the following determinations. U.S. courts have found that a Chilean court was an inadequate forum due to lack of judicial independence under the military junta;[128] that an Iranian court was an inadequate forum due to presumed bias against Americans;[129] and that a Romanian judgment was unenforceable because it was not achieved "under a system of jurisprudence likely to secure an impartial administration of justice."[130] On the other hand, U.S. courts have quickly rejected assertions that the Israeli or the French judicial systems were inadequate, holding that it would be completely inappropriate for a U.S. judge to speculate "that his Israeli colleagues would violate their oaths of office,"[131] and that "comity as well as common knowledge preclude our characterizing the French judicial system as any less fair than our own."[132] Similarly, in *The Bremen v. Zapata*, the Supreme Court readily assured itself that "the courts of England meet the standards of neutrality and long experience in admiralty litigation."[133]

Contrary to appearances, however, adequate forum determinations do not depend on first-world versus third-world status. Determinations of outright bias or other corruption are relatively rare.[134] Most of the hard questions are instead litigated in the context of foreign legal systems that function less efficiently than the U.S. system or that present a very different procedural system. Some of these cases involve foreign plaintiffs seeking to take advantage of the plaintiff-friendly features of the U.S. legal system when suing U.S.-based multinational corporations investing in their countries, leaving the U.S. defendant in the awkward position of arguing that a U.S. court is not a convenient forum and seeking to have the case transferred back to the plaintiff's country.[135] In these cases the real issue for the court typically has more to do with the politics of allowing a foreign plaintiff to benefit from the U.S. tort system and the ethics of global corporate accountability than the adequacy of the foreign forum.[136] Other cases involve claims that the foreign legal system in question permits far more limited discovery than the U.S. system,[137] does not allow contingency fees,[138] lacks a jury system,[139] denies the recovery of punitive damages,[140] or caps damage recoveries altogether.[141] Determinations of the adequacy of the foreign forum in these cases vary, but are based on the court's assessment of the legitimate expectations of the individual litigant rather than the quality of the foreign legal system as a whole.

Overall, these cases reflect the same deep paradox identified above. Where courts begin from a presumption of difference, an abstract insistence on "separate but equal" embedded in formal notions of sovereignty, only big differences matter. Procedural variations of various kinds, such as differences in discovery, the presence or absence of contingency fees, or differences in the role of the judge, are part of the normal variation in legal systems that litigants must expect when they venture across borders. Only if a foreign legal system can be shown to violate a minimum standard of transnational justice, through overt bias, systemic corruption, or denial of basic due process, will a U.S. court allow a litigant to escape the bonds of contract or place and choose a U.S. court instead.

By contrast, where courts begin from a presumption of identity, then they scrutinize each other according to the same criteria that they would apply to other domestic tribunals in the same circumstances. And as in the domestic context, seemingly small differences can matter a great deal, depending on the configuration of each case. Thus the assumption that the foreign legal system is not separate and entitled to sovereign deference, but is rather part of an emerging transnational litigation space in which litigants move freely and choose different national courts to resolve their disputes can result in greater short-term conflict in the service of deeper long-term cooperation.

Judicial Negotiation

In some cases, transjudicial dialogue becomes interjudicial negotiation. This practice is highly developed in cases of global bankruptcies, where judges increasingly communicate directly with one another with or without an international treaty or guidelines to ensure a cooperative and efficient distribution of assets. Governments have left these matters up to courts; courts have responded by creating their own regimes. Two commentators describe these court-to-court agreements, which have come to be known as "Cross-Border Insolvency Cooperation Protocols," as "essentially case-specific, private international insolvency treaties."[142] As of the late 1990s, courts had negotiated these Protocols in seven major global insolvency proceedings.[143] The first was the bankruptcy of Maxwell Communications Corporation, an English holding company with more than four hundred subsidiaries worldwide. It filed for Chapter 11 bankruptcy in the Southern District of New York and entered insolvency proceedings in the United Kingdom simultaneously. To determine what laws and procedures to apply in the reorganization, judges in both countries appointed administrators or liquidators, who engaged in extensive discussions and ultimately reached an agreement setting forth procedures and assigning responsibility for the liquidation. This minitreaty was then memorialized by an "Order and Protocol" approved and adopted by the two courts within two weeks of each other.[144]

As the number and complexity of international bankruptcies grow, bankruptcy courts since Maxwell have continued to extend and improve these agreements, often working with practitioners, to coordinate insolvency proceedings in multiple jurisdictions as smoothly as possible.[145] The proceedings in the Nakash case, involving a U.S. debtor and a defunct Israeli bank, are particularly interesting, as they involved relations between common law and civil law courts.[146] In this context the U.S. and the Israeli courts adopted a protocol that specifically provided for cooperation between the courts as well as between the parties, including a Preamble setting forth the goal, among others, of "honoring . . . the integrity of the Courts of the United States and the State of Israel."[147] The U.S. judge approving the Protocol explicitly mentioned the importance of a "bridge" between courts to enable both sides to understand each other's goals; once a framework for cooperation has been established "the tensions then become more common tensions and [c]ourts then can with more facility either get in or get out of each other's way but understand exactly what is happening."[148] The Israeli judge concurred, noting that the "representatives of the two courts are meant to cooperate, according to the authority given to each within its territorial boundaries."[149]

Observers of such transjudicial cooperation typically emphasize that it has flourished in the absence of a treaty, as a matter of necessity for courts faced with global assets and no guidance from national and international law. The intense debates among bankruptcy scholars over the virtues of a universal versus a territorial system—whether distribution of assets should be centralized globally or should proceed state by state wherever assets are located—reflects the desire to supplant such ad hoc judicial agreements with a rationalized global framework established by treaty. Lore Unt, a young bankruptcy scholar, sees transjudicial cooperation as a system of its own, however, arguing that "a decentralized system of courts applying evolving legal standards on a case-by-case basis is the most workable system for developing legal international insolvency cooperation."[150]

5. MEETING FACE TO FACE

Judges are also meeting face to face. Justice O'Connor has led several delegations of Supreme Court justices to meet with their counterparts in France, Germany, England, and India. More recently, two "summits" between the U.S. Supreme Court and the ECJ have occurred. In 1998 Justices O'Connor, Breyer, Ginsburg, and Kennedy went to Luxembourg; they had both private meetings and several public sessions with their European counterparts and sat in on an ECJ hearing. In April 2000 several members of the ECJ came to Washington for a second meeting with Supreme Court justices.[151] Most recently, Chief Justice Rehnquist led a delegation that included Justice Breyer on a "judicial exchange" to Mexico, on the invitation of Chief Justice Genaro David Góngora Pimentel of the Mexican Supreme Court. A Mexican judicial delegation had visited Washington in 1999. In Rehnquist's words:

> The exchange consisted of a series of meetings where we spoke about topics as varied as the Judicial Branch and the press, and judicial educa-

tion. But as is common in these types of meetings, the real value of these reciprocal visits is in establishing face-to-face contact with judges in another country who, despite the differences between our judicial systems, face many of the same problems faced by federal judges in the United States.[152]

Judges in other parts of the world have increasingly institutionalized such exchanges. Beginning in the early 1980s, judges from the constitutional courts in Western European countries began meeting every two or three years and publishing their proceedings.[153] Supreme court justices in the Americas have taken one step further, establishing the Organization of Supreme Courts of the Americas (OCSA). At a conference of representatives of the Supreme Courts of twenty-five countries of the Western Hemisphere in October 1995, delegates approved a charter for the organization with the stated aims of promoting and strengthening "judicial independence and the rule of law among the members, as well as the proper constitutional treatment of the judiciary as a fundamental branch of the state."[154] These objectives are to be achieved through activities such as the provision of "a permanent link" between national judicial systems and various educational and technical assistance systems "designed to promote international judicial cooperation in the hemisphere."[155] More recently the organization has been tasked with the "creation of a Center for Exchange of Information on Judicial Matters."[156]

Common law countries have similarly institutionalized their biannual meetings in order to promote face-to-face contact and dialogue among the judiciaries of these countries who operate in similar legal systems.[157] The First Worldwide Common Law Judiciary Conference was sponsored by the Judiciary Leadership Development Council, a nonprofit organization located in Washington D.C. whose goal is to encourage judicial education through seminars and conferences. The purpose of the conference, according to Judge A. Paul Cotter of the U.S. Nuclear Regulatory Commission, was to bring together common law judges to discuss common problems, mutual interests, and recent developments: "A pragmatic judge-to-judge exchange of information on, and analyses of, particular elements of their respective courts, law, and procedures will enable the participants to take home immediate, practical benefits both for themselves individually and for their respective courts."[158] In yet another region, judges from Estonia, Latvia, and Lithuania have formed the Association of Judges of the Baltic States.[159]

Less formal meetings have been sponsored by various aid agencies and nongovernmental organizations and organizations such as the London-based human rights organization InterRights. Similarly, LAWASIA, with its Secretariat in Australia, fosters judicial exchange through annual meetings of its Judicial Section.[160] The ABA Central and Eastern European Law Initiative (CEELI) periodically sends American judges to various Central and Eastern European countries to assist with law reform, codification efforts, and judicial training.[161] Closer to home, the Washington-based Center for Democracy has sponsored four conferences to date involving courts of "ultimate appeal" of Central and Eastern Europe and the new independent states, a grouping of countries that fits the criteria for both regionality and similarity.[162]

Law schools have also played an important role. New York University Law School's Center for International Studies and Institute of Judicial Administration hosted a major conference of judges from both national and international tribunals in February 1995 under the auspices of N.Y.U.'s Global Law School Program.[163] Similarly, Harvard Law School hosted part of the Anglo-American Exchange.[164] For its part, Yale Law School has established a seminar for members of constitutional courts from around the globe to meet annually as a means of promoting intellectual exchange among the judges.[165] The participants in these seminars exchange precedents and personal experiences, creating judicial networks that are powerful channels for continuing cross-fertilization.[166] Likewise, academic and public institutions also contribute to the international exchange of judicial ideas through the compilation of websites through which courts can access information regarding the activities of national and supranational courts and tribunals from around the world.[167]

Perhaps the clearest illustration that judicial globalization is here to stay is the formation of an actual "foreign policy" arm of the U.S. federal judiciary. As noted in the introduction to this chapter, Chief Justice Rehnquist and the U.S. Judicial Conference created the Committee on International Judicial Relations, first chaired by Judge Michael Mihm of the Illinois District Court. According to Judge Mihm, the purpose of the committee is to "coordinate the federal judiciary's relationship with foreign judiciaries and with official and unofficial agencies and organizations interested in international judicial relations and the establishment and expansion of the rule of law and administration of justice.[168] The committee now issues a weekly bulletin, the contents of which are a remarkable documentation of judicial globalization and global judicial networks. In any given week, readers might encounter Russian judges on a whistle-stop tour of cities across the U.S., Turkish jurists learning from a judge in Maryland, or a U.S. district court judge meeting with colleagues in Ecuador.[169]

All these visits and exchanges and seminars have multiple functions. They certainly serve to educate and to cross-fertilize. They broaden the perspectives of the participating judges. Indeed, Justice Breyer reports that he returned from a trip to India, in which he had the opportunity of observing an Indian mediation program, wondering "if we, in the United States, did not have something to learn from the cross-disciplinary, problem-based approach."[170] But perhaps most important, they socialize their members as participants in a common global judicial enterprise. That awareness is important for convincing judges to try to uphold global norms of judicial independence and integrity in countries and at times when those are under assault.

At one seminar for judges from international tribunals around the world, an African judge recounted a meeting with the beleaguered chief justice of the Zimbabwean Supreme Court, who had been under direct attack, including physical threats, from the government of Robert Mugabe. The chief justice had been receiving letters and faxes of support from fellow judges all over the world, many of whom had met him through the kinds of judicial networks described here. At this particular meeting, he said that the greatest value of all these meetings and communications was the reminder: "I am not alone."[171]

6. CONCLUSION

The judicial networks described in this chapter fit the general categories of information networks, enforcement networks, and harmonization networks. The networks of national constitutional courts are explicitly focused on the provision and exchange of information and ideas. To the extent that they stimulate actual convergence of positions through the emergence of a global jurisprudence in any one area—through cross-fertilization of national constitutional law and/or the decisions of international human rights tribunals—they shade into harmonization networks, although the process of harmonization/convergence is quite different than in the regulatory context. Networks of courts in transnational litigation, by contrast, are essentially enforcement networks. They arise in the wake of efforts by one or more litigants to enforce a body of law in different national courts. As transnational disputes grow more and more complex, it is increasingly the courts themselves who must cooperate to resolve them most efficiently and effectively.

The vertical judicial networks described above also fit these categories. The relationships between the ECJ and national European courts are enforcement networks, as are the relationships between the European Court of Human Rights and national courts. Relations between NAFTA tribunals and national courts in Mexico, Canada, and the United States fall into the category of nascent enforcement networks. On the other hand, relations between the European Court of Human Rights and constitutional courts outside Europe are information networks that once again may become harmonization networks.

What is most striking about the world of judicial networks, however, is how they all fit together. Talk of a "global legal system" sounds ambitious, if not fanciful. It conjures images of a global supreme court with satellites in every region and country, with national courts carefully tied in. In fact, however, the system described here is loosely composed of horizontal and vertical networks of national and supranational judges. It is closer in some ways to a global "community of courts," in the sense that judges around the world interact with one another aware of their membership and participation in a common enterprise—regardless of their actual status as state, national, regional, or international judges.

Some judicial networks are formal and structured, such as the treaty-based relationship between the supranational judges of the ECJ and national courts at every level. Vertical relations between NAFTA arbitration panels and U.S. national courts have similar roots in NAFTA itself, but as in the European Union, the actual shape and strength of these relations will almost certainly be a function of the actions and interactions of the judges themselves. So, too, with the degree of deference and reference that national courts are willing to pay to the rulings of regional human rights courts, such as the European Court of Human Rights, the Inter-American Court of Human Rights, and the new African Court of Human Rights, all of which must judge the judgments of national courts against global and regional codes of human rights.

Many other networks, both horizontal and vertical, are far looser. They are tied together not only by the awareness of foreign courts and decisions, but active transjudicial dialogue on common problems ranging from privacy to the death penalty. The tracks of these discussions become actual law in different jurisdictions, in the sense that the courts actually cite each other in the ultimate decisions. The citations, however, are only persuasive rather than precedential authority—a national judge, or an international one, cannot be bound to follow a foreign decision, only persuaded of its value in helping him or her sort through a knotty legal problem. In addition, the psychological impact is considerable, leading constitutional judges to feel part of a larger judicial community, an awareness strengthened by face-to-face meetings.

At a more workaday level, judges handling transnational commercial disputes are coming gradually to think of themselves as different points on a spectrum of possibilities for litigating the same underlying disputes, disputes that are themselves an inevitable byproduct of a globalizing economy, rather than as separate, self-contained spheres entitled to treat all cases before them as unique and arising uniquely under their national legal system. Here again, the long-term impact is less legal than psychological. Viewed from a traditional perspective of difference, all states are formally equal and functionally identical; each duplicates the same governance functions within a self-contained and largely impenetrable sphere. Each state handles its own affairs with a minimum of interference; conflict is to be avoided because its consequences are unpredictable. Yet viewed from a perspective of identity, in which courts in different countries are engaged in the same enterprise of judging and resolving disputes that themselves cross many borders, the focus shifts from the dispute-resolvers to the disputes themselves, to the common values that all judges share in guaranteeing litigant rights while also safeguarding an efficient and effective system.

The familiarity generated by regular interaction within this category of disputes does not breed contempt and indeed raises the tolerance for conflict, precisely because the regular relations and knowledge of one another provides assurance that conflict will not escalate or rupture the underlying relationship. Consider the scope for conflict within a family consistent with the maintenance of close relations, as compared to the enforced politeness between strangers. Thus the hallmarks of the emergence of a global commercial judicial system, paradoxically, are often noisy and even outraged claims and counterclaims about the sacred right to litigate in a particular national jurisdiction.

In sum, judges around the world are coming together in various ways that are achieving many of the goals of a formal global legal system: the cross-fertilization of legal cultures in general and solutions to specific legal problems in particular; the strengthening of a set of universal norms regarding judicial independence and the rule of law (however broadly defined); the awareness of judges in every country and at every level of participation in a common judicial enterprise; and the increasing ability for transnational disputes to be resolved either in one forum or in several forums that are coordinating with one another. Even more important, however, judges are in many ways creating their own version of such a system, a bottom-up version driven by their recognition of the plurality of national, regional, and international legal systems and their own duties of fidelity to such systems. Even when they are interacting with one another within the framework of a treaty or national statutes, their relations are shaped by a deep respect for each other's competences and the ultimate need, in a world of law, to rely on reason rather than force.

How else to build a world under law? The disaggregation of global judicial relations is rooted in the pluralism of multiple legal systems but driven by the expression of a deeper common identity. Dialogue is prized over uniformity; debate and reasoned divergence over adherence. So it must be, because global legal authority, except in areas such as cases governed by public international law and specifically committed to the International Court of Justice in the Hague for resolution or more specialized areas such as the law of the sea, does not exist. Transjudicial networks, animated largely by persuasive authority, personal contacts, and peripatetic litigants, are likely to be as close as we can come.

Legislators: Lagging Behind

A gap increasingly separates transgovernmental cooperation from domestic debate. . . . The result is a mutual
democratic deficit, with publics mistrusting the multilateral deals that their governments strike behind closed
doors in foreign countries.
—Lord William Wallace, foreign policy spokesman for the
Liberal Party in the House of Lords[1]

LORD WALLACE'S PERCEPTION OF A DEMOCRATIC DEFICIT REGARDING
transgovernmental activity is widely shared. Legislators are seen to be
lagging behind. The voice of the people—province by province, country by country, region by region, is much softer and less likely to be
heard than the voice of the regulators, the judges, the ministers and
heads of state.

One response has been a call for a global parliament.[2] Far more
likely, and from my point of view far more desirable, would be the creation of networks of legislators to match the networks of ministers, regulators, and judges described in the last two chapters. These networks
do exist, often in surprising places, and are growing. But they are less

common, and have less impact, than other transgovernmental networks for a variety of reasons.

First, at least in democratic political systems, the legislature's function is to represent as much as it is to regulate, meaning that legislators are most directly tied to territorially defined policies. In this sense, it could be said that remaining resolutely "national," or even parochial, is their job. Even when they focus on international issues, it is generally through the prism of domestic interests rather than through an independent interest in foreign policy, much less global governance. To ensure their reelection, legislators must demonstrate concern and action in their voters' areas of interest, and must ceaselessly lobby for their constituency's share of the national pie. To the vast majority of these constituencies, international cooperation usually takes a low priority.

Second, the high turnover among legislators, whose terms in office are typically short, gives them little incentive to invest in long-term relationships with their foreign counterparts, who themselves will be likely to change frequently—and this disincentive is in addition to the usual shifting priorities and commitments based on political affiliation. Generally, in democratic regimes, legislators will serve less time in their official capacities than judges or bureaucrats. Third, parliamentarians by definition lack the specialized technical expertise and disengagement from popular politics that have played such a large role in bolstering judicial and regulatory networks. Domestic challenges vary greatly among nations; leadership and parliamentarianism take different forms, and neither is commonly considered a "profession" or "expertise" other than in the practice of democracy itself.

Finally, regulatory networks are highly issue-specific and are composed of members with largely the same professional training and socialization. They are thus generally able to operate through simpler decision-making procedures, typically by consensus. Parliamentarians, on the other hand, tend to deal with a wide array of issues and interests.[3] Different parliaments are also organized differently in terms of committee structures and the allocation of power among individual legislators. It is thus harder to identify natural "counterparts," as in the regulatory area, such as finance committees, foreign relations committees, or justice and home affairs committees. As a result, individual legislators are more likely to come together across borders based on common party affiliation or a common interest in a particular set of issues, such as the environment or human rights, rather than on a common and enduring position in the political power structure.

Given all these disincentives, the wonder is perhaps that legislative networks exist at all. And yet they do, within international organizations, independently, at the regional level, and in a variety of professional associations. In some cases it is possible to discern legislators genuinely finding their voice on the international stage, injecting new and different elements into politics and policies formerly controlled almost exclusively by the executive branch of different governments. They are inventing and legitimizing themselves as they go along, within organizations such as NATO, the OSCE, and, most notably, the European Union. They are also gradually organizing as a counterbalance to the forces of free trade and economic integration, as they realize the extent to which some of these ideologies cut across national borders and enhance executive power. And they play a growing role in democratization efforts, providing not only technical assistance to young parliaments but also the crucial sense of belonging in a larger global or regional club.

Reading through some of the examples in this chapter, it is hard not to begin envisioning networks of legislators forming and demanding a formal voice in the affairs of the WTO, the IMF, NAFTA, or indeed the United Nations itself. It is also possible to imagine any number of bilateral and plurilateral initiatives to establish ongoing contacts between legislators, at least as long as particular political parties are in power in the relevant countries. These networks should in many cases parallel various kinds of executive and regulatory networks.

At the same time, it is also apparent that many existing regional "parliaments" or "assemblies" are quite ineffective—the kind of entities that spread skepticism about international law or institutions of any kind. At a deeper level, it is not actually clear what "effectiveness" should mean in this context. What should regional or global legislative networks be doing, and how will we know when they are doing it successfully? Scholars such as Bruce Ackerman argue that parliamentarians, with a mandate that is clearly distinct from those of regulators and administrators, are well equipped to elaborate basic values.[4] A recent "summit" of heads of parliaments designed to denounce the death penalty offers some support for this idea. But parliamentarians are also supposed to reflect and represent deep divisions in basic values—divisions of the sort that can drive elections. These divisions are even deeper in the international context.

How else, if at all, should legislative networks exercise power? By drawing up model legislation to serve as templates for national drafters? By responding to the reports and pronouncements of various executive and regulatory networks? By trying to develop transgovernmental methods of monitoring the activity of other transgovernmental networks, as legislative committees monitor agencies in the United States? By trying directly to check the power of networks of chief executives, which may be operating in part to circumvent the power of domestic legislators?

Some of these possibilities seem unlikely at best, silly at worst, but before complaining of "democratic deficits," or more specifically, of "lagging legislators," it is important to think through what transgovernmental legislative networks can and should do. The first step, therefore, is to understand what they are already doing.

The first section below sets forth a number of ways in which legislators are networking with one another on specific political issues, whether within or without existing international organizations. The second discusses the wide array of legislative networks, including actual regional parliaments, that exist both to express and advance regional identity and also to counteract or at least slow down a variety of forces pushing regional economic integration. Finally, the third section turns to the ways in which legislators are bolstering fellow legislators around the world, through the professionalization of democratic representation and the socialization and support of individual representatives.

1. LEGISLATORS FINDING THEIR VOICE ON THE WORLD STAGE

The traditional way for legislators to express themselves in foreign affairs is by trying to keep members of the executive—the ministers or head of state—on a short leash. Some contemporary political scientists argue that at least in the United States that system is working well; Congress is actually calling many of the shots in foreign affairs.[5] The examples below, however, suggest that many legislators are not content with this traditional role—they are seeking ways to exercise power and influence directly on the international stage. They are networking with one another to enhance their collective voice both inside international organizations and independently.

Legislative Networks within International Organizations

As with regulatory networks, national legislators periodically find themselves working together within the context of international organizations. By and large, their task within these organizations is to define an effective role for themselves as elected representatives in an environment traditionally dominated by diplomats, civil servants, or political appointees. They are succeeding in unexpected ways, perhaps most surprisingly in security organizations such as NATO or the OSCE, where the subject matter purportedly requires a high degree of specialized knowledge and an ability to withstand or ignore popular pressures. Other organizations are more hospitable from the outset. To the extent that these organizations include the harmonization and convergence of law and policy among their member states, legislative networks within them have growing influence.

Networking in NATO
In the case of NATO, the NATO Parliamentary Assembly (NATO-PA) provides a communication link between partner countries. Composed of parliamentarians from the member countries of the alliance, the assembly's objectives include strengthening understanding and developing solidarity among member countries, encouraging member countries to take into account NATO viewpoints when drafting national legislation, and acting as a link between alliance parliaments and NATO authorities.[6]

The NATO treaty has no explicit mention of a parliamentary assembly. A formal recognition of such an assembly would have required amending the Washington treaty, which some of the governments and parliaments wish to avoid. Thus, the NATO-PA has long operated as a separate entity from NATO, although embodying its fundamental mission and maintaining close working relationships with it. It was the recognition of the growing involvement of the NATO-PA in the oversight and operation of the organization that brought the assembly in 1998 to change its name from the North Atlantic Assembly (NAA) to the NATO Parliamentary Assembly.[7] Nevertheless, it has real influence on NATO policies. Its committees—including Civilian Affairs, Defense and Security, Economic, Political, Scientific and Technical—draft policy recommendations on areas ranging from the Bosnian crisis to setting human rights standards to reform of the Euro-Atlantic security relationship.[8] NATO itself, composed of its national delegations typically headed by ambassadors, has subsequently adopted many of these recommendations.[9]

NETWORKING IN THE ORGANIZATION FOR SECURITY AND COOPERATION IN EUROPE (OSCE)

The OSCE's Parliamentary Assembly was established in Madrid in 1991, amid heated debate over its organization and the very necessity of its existence. Today, the assembly brings together over three hundred parliamentarians representing fifty-five OSCE participating states. The assembly's objectives are to facilitate interparliamentary dialogue, assess the implementation of OSCE objectives by participating states, support democratic institutions in participating states, and contribute to the development of OSCE institutional structures and of relations and co-operation between existing OSCE institutions.

The assembly has had to fight hard to establish its legitimacy within the framework of the OSCE. While it has performed functions such as providing neutral observers to Russia's first post-Soviet parliamentary elections, and suggested the need for a major modification of the OSCE's functions, the assembly has consistently demanded more influence within the OSCE. Although its 1994 session also included discussion of substantive issues such as Turkey's relations with the Kurdish minority, Greece's unilateral trade embargo on Macedonia and the UNPROFOR mission in Bosnia, ultimately the assembly's primary concern seemed to be whether any of its resolutions would be heard or acted upon at all.

Since 1994, the assembly has gained both legitimacy and support from the OSCE as well as its member-states. The assembly's members now consistently monitor elections in both Eastern Europe and the former Soviet Union. In the spring of 1998, an assembly member pronounced the Ukrainian election less than "free and fair," and subsequently drew criticism from Ukrainian officials who were keen to have the assembly approve their electoral process.[10] Another observers' mission set out to monitor the elections in Russia in March 2000. The assembly's website claims, probably correctly, that because parliamentarians are themselves directly elected public officials, their observations carry considerable weight with local and international media.[11]

Technically, the assembly is geared to allow for maximum participation and collaboration. It meets annually, in the beginning of July, at which time most national parliaments are not in session, so as to allow key members to participate. The product of each such annual session is a Final Declaration, as well as resolutions and recommendations that are submitted to the OSCE Ministerial Council, the OSCE Chairperson-in-Office, and the national parliaments of the OSCE participating States.

Recent annual sessions of the assembly have produced important resolutions, including an appeal to the OSCE Council of Foreign Ministers to discuss the drafting of a European Security Charter, which should become "the backbone of the (European) security system for the 21st century."[12] In July 2000, the assembly issued a Final Declaration dealing with situations in North Caucasus, Southeastern Europe, Belarus, and Moldova. Observers of the session saw it as a promising sign of a renewed, stronger, and welcome involvement of the OSCE in the security problems in these areas.[13]

Following the 9/11 attack on the United States, the Standing Committee of Heads of Delegation of the Assembly convened for a special meeting in Sintra, Portugal, to condemn all terrorist actions and recommend that the OSCE participating states agree on a definition of terrorism and elaborate on global strategies for fighting terrorism. The assembly called upon the participating states to adopt appropriate legislative measures and cooperate with one another in combating terrorism. The assembly also urged the governments to address the issue of international terrorism at the OSCE Ministerial Council later in the year.[14]

LEGISLATIVE NETWORKS WITHIN ASEAN

Parliamentary cooperation takes place in other regions as well, perhaps most notably in Asia. In 1977, Southeast Asian nations, under the auspices of the Association of Southeast Asian Nations (ASEAN), a regional security and economic organization, created the ASEAN Inter-Parliamentary Organization (AIPO). Participants in the AIPO General Assembly consist of members of the ASEAN parliamentary delegations and observer groups, with a maximum of fifteen delegates from each AIPO member's parliament.

The justifications for the creation of AIPO were both democratization and popularization: a close network of ASEAN legislators would enhance democratic participation by the people of these countries, thereby strengthening the ties between the people themselves, and between the peoples and the organization.[15]

AIPO has undertaken a number of concrete initiatives that have served primarily to educate national legislators, interest groups, and individual constituents as to what is taking place in neighboring countries. Thus, for instance, AIPO indexed all national laws that relate to the ASEAN Free Trade Area in order to make them readily available and transparent to the business community.[16] Similarly, it created an electronic bulletin-board system to enable individual members of various parliaments to correspond directly with their counterparts in other states.[17]

AIPO members have also tried to use the collective power of the organization to pressure their governments on specific issues, most notably the devastation wrought by the East Asian financial crisis in 1997. The parliamentarians called on their governments to step up cooperation among financial markets to avoid further turmoil. They also held a meeting in the Philippines and adopted a number of specific measures to help redress the crisis, although it is not clear what impact these measures actually had.[18]

Like its European counterparts, AIPO currently plays a largely consultative role. It has had to build its own legitimacy and influence. It has done so largely through the power of information and socialization. Its ability to collect and then distill information has made it a credible source of legislative initiatives. Further, it has been able to welcome parliamentarians from new ASEAN members, such as Vietnam and even Myanmar. AIPO members also engage in ongoing dialogue with observer delegations of parliamentarians from countries such as China, Australia, Canada, New Zealand, Russia, and the European Parliament.[19] Again, however, it is very difficult to track the actual impact of these various activities in terms of new legislation proposed or individual government officials bolstered.

—

THE NETWORKS AMONG LEGISLATORS IN EACH OF THESE THREE ORGANIzations create opportunities for parliamentarians to play an active role in international or at least regional security policy. In the two European cases, they have had to fight to make their voices heard, and have gradually insisted on playing a more direct role in the organization's mission. AIPO has been less effective, or at least its effectiveness is harder to track. It has chosen to work more through links to existing national parliaments—functioning to collect and disseminate information and lending its authority to model legislation in the form of resolutions. IOSCO functions this way on the regulatory side, as described in chapter 1, but its model legislation is aimed at an enduring audience of securities commissioners who often have a direct professional interest in getting it passed in their home legislatures.

Independent Legislative Networks

In June 2001 fifteen heads of European and non-European parliaments came together in Strasbourg, on the premises of the European Parliament, in the first Global Conference Against the Death Penalty.[20] Aside from the heads of the Council of Europe and the European Parliament, the signatories on the appeal for the abolition of the death penalty included representatives from Belgium, Chile, Ivory Coast, Greece, Spain, France, Cambodia, Italy, Malta, The Netherlands, Austria, Portugal, and Ukraine. Fifteen other countries sent telegrams of support for the appeal. Pursuant to the appeal, the Assembly of the Council of Europe adopted a resolution requiring Japan and the United States to impose a moratorium on executions without delay and to take steps to abolish the death penalty. It also warned that it would question the continuing observer status of Japan and the United States with the council should no significant progress be made by 1 January 2003.[21]

This meeting caused considerable controversy. Of particular surprise, at least to media commentators, was that parliamentarians should take such an initiative in their official capacities—as the heads of national parliaments rather than as individual politicians. Here is an example of a spontaneous legislative network, sparked by depth of conviction about a specific political issue. It is characteristic in this regard of spontaneous or at least independent legislative networks; they are typically driven by commitment to a particular political issue, or set of issues, or at least a specific political ideology or philosophy.

The U.S. Congress–Russian Duma Study Group

When Newt Gingrich was Speaker of the House, he was convinced that parliamentary networks would give domestic legislators a new role in foreign policy. In 1996 he sent a letter to his Russian counterpart, Gennady Seleznyov, to create a forum made up of members of U.S. and Russian legislatures to discuss issues of defense, foreign policy, energy, and the environment on a regular basis. The result was the U.S. Congress–Russian Duma Study Group. Formation of the group was prompted by a belief that the relationship between the United States and Russia had for too long been focused on the executive level, a state of affairs that made it necessary to redevelop ties with each change in administration.[22]

Gingrich hoped that the group would meet informally twice a year.[23] Curt Weldon, representative from Pennsylvania and a member of the National Security Committee, was chosen to head the U.S. membership in the study group, which met for the first time in November 1997.[24] In June 2000, members of the two parliaments suggested a joint effort by their respective governments to develop and deploy a strategic missile defense system.[25] Representative Weldon made it clear that the Clinton administration did not necessarily welcome independent parliamentary contacts, complaining that "[m]any in Congress have been advocating cooperation with Russia for several years now, but have been ignored by the Clinton-Gore Administration."[26]

During the Clinton administration, Vice President Al Gore established a special commission with Viktor Chernomyrdin, prime minister of Russia. The commission created a special channel to advance not only common political objectives but also to enhance each politician's political position at home.[27] In this context, it is not particularly surprising to see one of the most important U.S. legislators of the opposite political party attempt to build his own bridges. To level the political playing field, it was necessary not only to reach beyond national borders but also to a different branch of the foreign government. Executive transgovernmentalism was thus in this case met and matched by a legislative counterpart.

Since 2001, the Congress-Duma study group has continued its efforts to foster "closer relations" between the two legislatures to "help address key bilateral issues, across a wide range of substantive issues."[28] Meetings in 2002 and 2003 in Moscow and Washington have discussed topics including "developing a US-Russia partnership in the areas of trade and energy,"[29] as well as countering international terrorism.[30]

The Parliamentary Association for Euro-Arab Cooperation (PAEAC)

The Parliamentary Association for Euro-Arab Cooperation (PAEAC) was founded in Brussels in 1974 by parliamentarians from the then nine countries of the European Community to improve relations between the two regions. Its main objectives are the promotion of peace in the Middle East and the strengthening of political, economic and cultural cooperation between Europe and the Arab world.

PAEAC consists of six hundred members from eighteen different national parliaments, including members of European national parliaments, the European Parliament, and the Parliamentary Assembly of the Council of Europe. It confers with and attempts to influence the European Union as well as individual Arab governments, organizes Euro-Arab working groups consisting of Arab ambassadors to the European Union and members of the European Parliament, and holds observer status with the Inter-Parliamentary Union (IPU) and the UN Economic and Social Council. PAEAC holds an annual Euro-Arab Dialogue in conjunction with the Arab Inter-Parliamentary Union.

In its 1998 meeting in Damascus, the dialogue led to a series of recommendations and resolutions on a range of subjects, varying from the Middle East peace process (including a series of condemnations of Israel and an expression of regret over the "lack of consistency of the U.S. as sponsor of the peace process in its dealing with the Israeli government"), the need for a dialogue with the Libyan government to resolve the Lockerbie case and the need to reexamine the sanctions imposed on Libya, the effects of the embargo imposed on Iraq on its civilian population, the effect of the sanctions on Sudan on its civilian population, terrorism in Algeria, terrorism in general, economic liberalization of the Arab world, cultural cooperation and cultural values. The participants also expressed their support for a full membership of Palestine in the IPU.[31]

ADVOCACY GROUPS FOR LEGISLATORS: THE IPU AND THE PGA

These newer initiatives exist alongside much older and more institutionalized parliamentary networks, but of a somewhat different character. The Parliamentarians for Global Action (PGA) and the IPU are long-standing fixtures on the international scene, but they have often seemed extracurricular, more like nongovernmental than transgovernmental organizations. They have provided forums in which national parliamentarians could come together on specific issues of concern, not merely alternative channels for official business. On the other hand, some of their more recent activities have brought legislators together to circumvent roadblocks that other branches of the same governments could not overcome.

The oldest parliamentary network is the IPU, founded in 1889 and headquartered in Geneva. Its objectives include working for peace and international cooperation, strengthening and developing representative assemblies, and improving working methods of parliamentary institutions. The group of 135 member parliaments submits resolutions to represented assemblies on matters including disarmament, drug trafficking, environmental and agricultural development, and international security, and lobbies for their implementation.[32] Initiatives undertaken by the IPU have been rather varied in scope. In 1926, the IPU began work with the International Association of Penal Law to create a permanent international criminal court.[33] In 1988, it passed a resolution supporting self-determination for Puerto Rico.[34] In 1995, the IPU passed a motion proposed by New Zealand, calling on France and China to abide by a voluntary ban on nuclear testing.[35]

IPU meetings have provided valuable communication opportunities for parliamentarians, who in some cases have been able to break deadlocks privately where their governments have failed to communicate. Much of the groundwork for the Dayton accord was initiated by Croatian, Bosnian, and Serbian deputies at IPU meetings.[36] Interestingly, in July 1996 the IPU signed an agreement with the United Nations, formalizing a cooperative relationship between the two organizations and facilitating the initiation of joint projects. Part of the purpose of this agreement, at least in the eyes of some UN delegates, was to help build support for the United Nations among national parliaments,[37] whereas, from the perspective of the parliamentarians, it is equally likely this agreement will provide channels of communication to the United Nations independent of, or at least supplementary to, the official country delegation, which is staffed by fairly entrenched bureaucracy.

Americans are most likely to think of the PGA as the Professional Golfers' Association. In fact, Parliamentarians for Global Action is a nonpartisan advocacy group composed of parliamentarians from seventy countries.[38] The organization conducts policy studies and organizes trips, in something of a "Jimmy Carter–style" diplomacy.[39] For example, the parliamentarians organized a trip of forty politicians from nineteen countries to Haiti in 1993 to help guarantee the safety of pro-Aristide legislators.[40] Unfortunately, the military government then in power refused to guarantee the safety of the parliamentarians, who ultimately did not attend.[41] The PGA also has a policy component; it issued formal comments to the United Nations on the establishment of a war-crimes tribunal for Yugoslavia.[42] It has also organized a number of influential conferences concerning the establishment of the International Criminal Court, including "An Informal Parliamentary Assembly for the International Criminal Court and the Promotion of the Rule of Law" held in Ottawa in November 2002.[43]

PGA has also been particularly active in addressing environmental issues. Parallel to the World Summit on Sustainable Development in Johannesburg in August 2002, PGA organized the Parliamentary Workshop on Clean Air and Clean Water, which included more than 1,300 parliamentarians from 105 countries.[44] The workshop provided parliamentarians with "the legal and technological tools necessary to make concrete improvements in air and water quality on a national and regional level."[45] The World Bank has recently observed that "parliamentarians are playing an increasingly important role in environmental decision making" due to the "development . . . of democratically elected legislatures in most African countries . . . and the move towards democratization of the environmental decision making process."[46] The PGA is now turning its attention in this area to renewable-energy policy, with a series of conferences scheduled throughout 2003 and 2004.[47]

By its own account, the PGA offers a chance for legislators from small and medium-sized states that do not have strong political, military, or economic leverage to exercise group diplomacy in order to make decisive contributions to world policy.[48] Two recent examples of this kind of work are the PGA's assistance to Canada in promoting the International Convention to Ban Landmines and its role in promoting the creation of the permanent International Criminal Court. It offers a network of 1,300 legislators from around the world. Then again, although the power and influence of PGA policy resolutions and activity is unquestionably enhanced because its members are parliamentarians and hence, by definition, skilled politicians and respected individuals in their countries, these members do not exercise their official governmental power through the PGA in the way that regulatory or even judicial networks do. It allows individual legislators to amplify their voice on issues they care about, but does not enhance the power of legislatures per se relative to other branches of government in the international sphere.

⟶

THESE FOUR EXAMPLES, AS DIVERSE AS THEY ARE, ILLUSTRATE SOME OF the potential of, but also the obstacles to, effective transgovernmental legislative networking. On the one hand, it is quite possible that several decades of regular relations between Arab and European parliamentarians through PAEAC has had an impact on the way many European politicians view security and economic issues in the Middle East. Similarly, it is possible that a continuation of U.S.-Russian legislative contacts or a replication of similar bilateral legislative networks with other countries could affect the political balance of power in relations between the countries in question by providing alternative channels of information and influence—particularly, again, in presidential systems. On the other hand, it is highly unlikely that the threat of loss of observer status at the Council of Europe Parliamentary Assembly will shift the attitude of U.S. and Japanese legislators on the death penalty. And for all the support given the International Criminal Court by the PGA and the IPU, they are unlikely to have much effect on shifting legislative attitudes in countries opposed to the court, most notably the United States—at least in the short term.

Parliaments are almost by definition divided: by party, by politics, by region, by ideology, by power. Individual parliamentarians may band together across borders on issues that they care about; powerful legislators with a different agenda than their presidents may form useful alliances. But parliamentarians are politicians responsible to constituents. They cannot rely on the professional consensus that so often provides the glue for regulatory and even judicial networks. That glue must instead come from a common mission, as discussed below in the context of regional integration efforts, or from an effort to support one another across borders as parliamentarians.

2. LEGISLATIVE NETWORKS AS CATALYSTS AND CORRECTIVES FOR REGIONAL INTEGRATION

Parliamentarians have been considerably more active in regional politics than in global politics, often leading the way toward greater regional cooperation and even integration. Where they have lagged behind, they have later filled an important role as a democratic corrective to technocratic control of economic integration. In both cases, the most effective voices have been national legislators speaking and acting in a dual capacity—as the representatives of their national constituents and as the articulators and implementors of a larger regional vision.

The Catalysts

One of the oldest networked government systems is the Nordic System, which was originally driven entirely by legislators. Today those pioneers have imitators in South Asia, the Baltics, and, less successfully, Latin America. The motives driving the formation and flourishing of these networks vary, but they include a strong affirmation of regional identity as well as a desire to work together on common regional problems.

THE NORDIC COUNCIL

The Nordic Council formed in 1952 as a forum for interparliamentary cooperation. The national parliamentarians of the five different Nordic countries, as well as three independent regions (Greenland, Iceland, and the Faroe Islands), came together to cooperate on legal, social, cultural, and financial matters, as well as on specific initiatives concerning transportation and the environment. More recently, they have expanded their goals to include foreign policy and security matters. The council holds a general meeting every year with additional meetings on selected issues. It conducts continuous work on policy issues through five committees and four political party groups.

In its fiftieth anniversary session in 2002, the council addressed issues including the freedom of movement within the Nordic area, trafficking of women for the sex trade, sustainable development, immigration policy, and general labor and tax issues.[49] As discussed further in chapter 4, over time the parliamentarians' meetings led to cooperation among the executive branches of these countries as well—designated "intergovernmental" rather than "interparliamentarian"—through the medium of regular meetings among different councils of ministers.

INTERPARLIAMENTARY CONSULTATIVE COUNCIL OF BENELUX (ICCB)
Founded by Belgium, Luxembourg, and the Netherlands in 1955, the Interparliamentary Consultative Council of Benelux (ICCB) makes recommendations to the member-governments on a wide range of mutually relevant issues, in particular economic and cultural integration, foreign policy, and legal harmonization. The council is composed of forty-nine members designated by their national parliaments. Since 1985 the council has been increasingly charged with overseeing the application of the Schengen agreements on the free movement of people and goods among a number of EU countries.[50] This mandate flows from a broader recognition of the council's long and proven experience in the field of interparliamentary cooperation.

THE SOUTH ASIAN ASSOCIATION FOR REGIONAL
COOPERATION (SAARC)
Founded in 1985, the South Asian Association for Regional Cooperation (SAARC) consists of parliamentarians from India, Bangladesh, Bhutan, the Maldives, Nepal, Sri Lanka, and Pakistan. Their mandate is to address regional questions of economic development, population, and the general quality of life. Under SAARC's auspices, a Preferential Trading Arrangement (SAPTA) has been established and negotiations are continuing on the reduction of tariffs and other impediments to a freer flow of trade within the region. Negotiations are also proceeding towards the establishment of a South Asian Free Trade Area (SAFTA).

SAARC has adopted conventions on the suppression of terrorism as well as on narcotic drugs and psychotropic substances, and is finalizing additional conventions on trafficking of women and protection of children.[51] In 1992 it established a training center to combat tuberculosis in the region.[52] And at its annual conference in 1997, it passed recommendations to relax visa restrictions and to exchange data through e-mail on the Internet to keep all parliamentarians in the region posted about the latest developments in each other's parliaments.[53]

THE BALTIC PARLIAMENTARY ASSEMBLY

Shortly after gaining independence from the Soviet Union, the Baltic states of Latvia, Lithuania, and Estonia began taking steps to create cooperative arrangements, beginning with a Baltic trade agreement and customs union, joint production of farm equipment, and construction of a highway from Helsinki through Russia. The states also established the Baltic parliamentary assembly, modeled on the Nordic and Benelux examples.[54] Among its activities today, the Baltic Assembly encourages cooperation in harmonizing the legislation of all three countries in conformity with EU requirements, works to improve border facilities and border crossing-points, and coordinates foreign policy.[55] It is also cooperating with other regional assemblies: it signed a cooperation agreement with the ICCB in 1994;[56] authorized its presidium to lobby for a merger with the Nordic Council in 2001;[57] meets jointly with the Nordic Council;[58] and, also in 2001, joined with parliamentarians from the ICCB and the Nordic Council to hold a symposium on climate change in Brussels.

OTHER REGIONAL ASSEMBLIES

It is frankly hard to find a region of the globe without some kind of parliamentary assembly, but the ones I've described are the most active and influential. Others include: the Latin American Parliament, founded in 1964 and consisting of ten representatives each from twenty-two nations; the African Parliamentary Union, founded in 1976 and encompassing thirty-five African parliaments; the Arab Inter-Parliamentary Union, founded in 1974 and comprising eighteen parliaments and legislative assemblies; and the Parliament of the Andean Group, created on 25 October 1979 and consisting of Bolivia, Colombia, Ecuador, Peru, and Venezuela.[59] All these organizations, like those above, promote regional cooperation and even integration, and add the voice of parliamentarians to regional politics otherwise conducted through more bureaucratic bodies, such as the OAS and the OAU.

The problem with these other assemblies, quite frankly, is relative ineffectiveness. All are worthy organizations with worthy goals—and they do some valuable work in professional socialization and training, discussed below—but they have little impact on world or even regional affairs. Their problem may be the relative power of the legislative and the executive branches in the member-countries; the design of the institutions themselves; the lack of homogeneity and common interests among the member-countries; or a combination of all three. Whatever the reason, participants exercise little official power and rarely find themselves in situations where they can use the mechanisms of soft power—information exchange, deliberation, persuasion—with much impact.

The Correctives

The other type of regional parliament, led by the European Parliament (EP), which is the parliament of the European Union, has gained power as a reaction to a perceived "democracy deficit," arising from the number of EU decisions made without input from elected representatives. The question for Europe—a question likely to be repeated soon in other regions—is whether more democracy at the regional level means more input from a separate regional parliament or from networks of national parliamentarians. To match the other government networks described in chapters 1 and 2, the answer seems obvious: national parliamentarians must create similar networks.

THE EUROPEAN PARLIAMENT AND ITS NETWORKS
The European Parliament is in some ways a world of its own. It is an independent legislative body established as one of the governing institutions of the European Union; further, it is composed not of national parliamentarians, but of directly elected representatives. Originally, the Treaty of Rome, which established the European Economic Com-

munity (EEC) in 1957, gave the EP only a consultative role in Community decision making. Subsequent treaties and important rulings by the ECJ have extended the EP's autonomy as an institutional actor within the European system, so that the Parliament and the Council of Ministers now share power in a substantial number of areas. Especially in recent years, the EP has been much more influential than the looser regional assemblies described above.

Notwithstanding this increased power for parliamentarians at the European level, discussions of the "democratic deficit" within the European Union in the 1990s still focus on input from national parliamentarians. Shirley Williams, ever an advocate of legislative power, pointed out in 1991 that "most national parliaments have until recently lacked effective mechanisms linking them to the EP. They have been suspicious of attempts by the EP to demand greater powers and have been unwilling to work closely with it in establishing a joint structure of parliamentary accountability."[60] She proposed holding occasional "assizes," consisting of specialized parliamentary commissions from national parliaments and the EP, to address specific policy areas in depth.[61]

The powers that be did not see fit to follow her advice. The European Union, however, is gradually constructing something similar: a set of vertical legislative networks between a genuine supranational parliament and its national counterparts, similar to its vertical judicial networks, although less formal and powerful. In 1989, for example, the EP created a body to bring together the committees of national parliaments that specialized in European affairs—the awkwardly named Conference of the Community and European Affairs Committees of the Parliaments of the European Union (COSAC). COSAC convenes twice a year; it has discussed subjects such as internal security and the environment and has done a lot of work on the role of national parliaments in EU decision making. Partly as a result of this activity, the Treaty of Amsterdam in 1997 included a special Protocol requiring the EP to share information and consult with national parliaments on pending EP legislation.[62]

In sum, the past decade has witnessed many initiatives in EU parliamentary relations that have important implications for other parts of the world. Directly elected legislative assemblies at the regional level may yet have a valuable role to play in the world. Similar bodies on a global scale may also have a future, though it is hard now to imagine any that would be taken seriously. Even at the regional level, however, a directly elected assembly cannot substitute for national parliaments. It is likely to be effective only to the extent that it succeeds in networking with national parliamentarians and helping serve as a catalyst for their interactions with one another.

THE PARLIAMENTARY CONFERENCE OF THE AMERICAS

The Parliamentary Conference of the Americas held its inaugural conference in Quebec City, Canada, in September 1997. Four hundred parliamentarians from 28 countries attended and were joined by nearly 400 observers from intergovernmental organizations, research institutes, and entrepreneurial and union groups. Organized by the National Assembly of Quebec, the conference was convened to enable parliamentarians to discuss the impact of increasing economic integration and the role of parliamentarians in the process. The conference organizers hoped that it would lead to more extensive and continued interparliamentary relations throughout the Americas.[63] The Closing Declaration of the conference dealt with issues including encouragement of democratic ideals, human rights, free trade, and employment, improvement in education and job training, and social security and health policies.[64]

The participants of the conference also agreed to create a Follow-up Committee to examine the establishment of a permanent inter-American parliamentary dialogue. In May 1999, the committee agreed on the general principles for establishing a permanent, yet flexible and effective, parliamentary forum. Today, the conference is the Parliamentary Confederation of the Americas (COPA), composed of a general assembly, an executive committee, and a general secretariat.[65]

—

UNLIKE THE ASSEMBLIES THAT GREW UP LARGELY AS CATALYSTS FOR regional integration—situations in which legislators took the initiative in reaching out to one another to help address common regional problems—the national legislators in this second category have been much more driven by the perceived need to catch up with "governments," meaning chief executives, their ministers, and their regulators, all of whom are pursuing the goals of free trade and economic integration faster than many legislative constituencies want. Other examples include a standing committee of national parliamentarians from countries in the European Free Trade Area (EFTA) comprising countries that once chose not to be members of the European Union but that are now more likely to be candidate members, that is designed to ensure meaningful parliamentary input on all matters of economic integration, and an Assembly of Caribbean Community Parliamentarians aimed at democratizing the process of Caribbean integration. Regardless of their different forms, they are networks of national legislators talking back— "correcting" the course of regional integration more than catalyzing it.

3. HELPING LEGISLATORS "DO THEIR WORK BETTER"

A final function of most legislative networks today is helping their members be better legislators. They provide their participants with professional and technical support, advice, and resources, thereby working to professionalize legislators and to help build parliamentarianism as an acquired skill or expertise rather than as a mere political tool. Supplying legislators with specialized expertise not only assists them in their day-to-day activities as parliamentarians, but also promotes their status as an international elite. This professionalism also establishes a common language for the parliamentary job, which in itself helps cut across countries to make cooperation easier—rather like the functional expertise that facilitates cooperation among regulators.

Within the United States, such cooperation among state legislators is well established. The National Conference of State Legislators (NCSL) is a nonprofit organization funded by the fifty state legislatures.[66] NCSL trains state legislators, sponsors information exchanges and biannual conferences, and supports at least ten different professional staff organizations for shared learning and professional development for state legislative staff at all levels. It also maintains a Southern Africa Task Force, which "seeks opportunities to assist the developing democratic governments in southern Africa through election observation, technical assistance to the national legislatures and hosting delegations in their state capitols."[67]

Beyond national borders, more than technical assistance is at stake. Professional associations are essentially clubs; clubs that can both extend and withdraw membership. For legislators in transitional countries facing pressure of various kinds at home, bolstering from the outside may be very important. For legislators excluded or expelled from the club, conversely, the sting is much like that South African officials felt when excluded from international associations over the decades of apartheid. The IPU, discussed above, has deliberately sought to use its wide base to support weaker parliaments, such as those in Haiti, South Africa, and Cambodia.[68]

Virtually all of the regional assemblies or parliamentary organizations just described offer training programs and at least moral support for their fellow parliamentarians. The African Parliamentary Union, for instance, organizes information and training seminars for parliamentarians across the continent and extends technical assistance to specific parliaments.[69] The best example, however, is probably the Commonwealth Parliamentary Association (CPA), which was founded in 1911 and now includes 142 national, state, provincial, and territorial parliaments. The CPA acts as an all-purpose reference center for Commonwealth parliaments, as well as sponsoring exchanges by delegations and individual members. To build parliamentary professionalism, members of the CPA have formulated a model training manual for parliamentary staff and are actively looking for new ways to improve the actual legislative and constituent-service skills of their members.

Newt Gingrich sought to achieve a similar goal by creating the Twenty-First Century International Legislators Network, launched in 1996 and sponsored by the U.S. Congressional Institute. Gingrich explicitly sought to encourage not only bilateral legislative networks, described above, but also a global web of legislators. The purpose of the network was precisely to help legislators and parliamentarians around the world "do their work better"[70]—by collecting information and enabling legislators to exchange views on leadership and problem-solving techniques in the public sector. The website is now defunct, however. Even when it was in operation, many legislators from other countries may have suspected a hidden substantive agenda behind the project, one tied to the expansion of U.S. power. To allay such suspicions, members of the U.S. Congress would probably fare better if they partnered with selected foreign counterparts from Europe, Asia, Africa, and Latin America to establish a global legislators' network.

Helping legislators around the world "do their work better" is a worthy goal. But this focus comes at the expense of the common substantive focus that helps strengthen networks of judges or regulators. Any strength in numbers that a legislative network might otherwise have is diminished by its inability to speak authoritatively on particular subjects other than the value of democratic representation itself. By contrast, PGA has increased its influence by bringing its members together around core substantive issues such as sustainable development, human rights, and democratization while simultaneously providing professional support and development.[71] Still another approach is to tie professional training and bolstering to a regional political agenda, such that the network of parliamentarians can at least claim to represent the voters of a particular region.

4. CONCLUSION

A growing number of legislators around the world are finding their voices in the international arena. They lag behind judges and various members of the executive branch for a variety of reasons, ranging from constituents' suspicion of foreign "junkets" to their own inability to stay in office long enough to develop enduring relationships with their foreign counterparts.[72] Given these disincentives, it is striking to see the number and variety of legislative networks that nevertheless have formed. The different contexts in which they are growing shed light on the motives behind them and thus which are most likely to prosper.

First, legislators are creating international networks of representatives elected nationally in order to counter or at least complement the existing networks of national officials, from generals to trade promoters. In security organizations such as NATO and the OSCE, legislators have constituted themselves as "assemblies" and insisted first on consultation regarding institutional policies and then increasingly on a more direct role in institutional affairs. Recall the role of the OSCE parliamentarians in monitoring elections in member-states, such as Ukraine and Russia, and providing a "parliament to parliament" stamp of approval. As security itself becomes more broadly defined, expanding to include the vitality of democratic institutions, legislators should find it easier to carve out a constructive role for themselves within organizations traditionally run by foreign ministers and generals.

The growing role of legislative networks is even clearer in trade organizations, where the catalyst for their participation is clear. As free trade rules and even deeper economic integration take hold, its distributional—read political—effects begin to bite. Whether it's the standardization of sausages in the European Union or the perceived weakening of labor and environmental protections in NAFTA, legislators—or at least their constituents—decide that they have been circumvented. Cries of "democratic deficit" quickly lead to hand wringing over how to enhance the voice of the people in a chorus of technocrats and powerful interest groups. Less combatively, economic integration ultimately requires legislative harmonization or at least mutual recognition, processes that must ultimately involve lawmakers themselves. In both cases, elected representatives are likely to come to the rescue.

The interesting question is how precisely to restructure international organizations to create a genuine role for legislators, and how to structure legislative networks for maximum influence and effectiveness. Two possible models come to mind. On the one hand, it is possible to imagine various international organizations as essentially collections of complementary networks of different types of national officials: executive, judicial, and legislative. Thus, for instance, just as the European Union operates with alternating councils of national ministers for different issue areas, staffed with networks of supporting national bureaucrats and interwoven with both horizontal and vertical networks of national and supranational judges, it could have a legislative assembly of national parliamentarians rather than a directly elected parliament. (It is actually working on both.)

Alternatively, legislators could work within networks designed not to play a direct role in international organizations, but rather to enhance the ability of legislators working within national parliaments to monitor and regulate the activity of executive-branch officials engaged in international work. In other words, parliamentary committees responsible for trade, the environment, immigration—for any issue— would network with counterparts in other nations to better understand the issues before them and to counterbalance the claims that bureaucrats and regulators make on the same issue. When coupled with a specific substantive agenda, these networks would also be likely to bolster legislators in a particular nation against a power-hungry executive.

The second source of legislative networks is an independent desire on the part of specific legislators to interact with their foreign counterparts for political purposes. These networks have at least begun bilaterally and are well-established regionally and globally. Examples include the U.S. Congress-Russian Duma Study Group, PAEAC, and longstanding organizations such as the IPU and PGA. Networks such as the PGA often unite legislators around specific issue areas about which they have particularly strong interests, giving them a louder voice on the world stage and the technical resources to make policy at home. Parliamentarians have also been catalysts for regional cooperation in areas such as Scandinavia, the Baltics, and South Asia.

On closer examination, however, a number of these networks seem more like nongovernmental than transgovernmental organizations. They are frameworks for like-minded legislators to voice their support regionally or globally for specific political issues, such as nuclear arms control or a permanent international criminal court. Given the deeply political nature of a parliamentarian's job, this is perhaps not surprising. But this is quite a different function from actually coming together in an official capacity to address common problems, as in the U.S.-Russian example or the Nordic or Baltic assemblies. These examples thus shed some light on what makes a transgovernmental network truly transgovernmental. It is not just ties between like government officials across borders, but rather links, even if informal ones, between government *institutions* in their performance of their official functions. Here legislators do indeed lag behind.

The third impetus for legislative networks is the desire to strengthen parliamentarianism as a profession—a global profession. Many of the existing legislative networks within international organizations or at the regional level provide technical assistance and training to fledgling legislators often in transitional democracies. They also exercise collective judgment to support legislators under threat and to denounce the political actors who threaten them. The International Legislators' Network, founded by Newt Gingrich, has these activities as its principal focus—to strengthen democracy around the world by strengthening the capacities of elected representatives in every nation that has them. In theory, as with judges, creating a global web of legislators should help to assure individual parliamentarians under siege in specific countries that they are not alone. It is not yet clear, however, that such a project can succeed when divorced from a substantive or regional agenda.

Overall, however, these assessments of different types of legislative networks beg a more fundamental question: what exactly should legislative networks be doing as part of a larger conception of global governance in a disaggregated world order? How should they be constituted: through already existing international organizations or through independent dedicated networks? Should they be composed of members of existing parliaments, or should they be generally elected as delegates to these networks, as in the EP? And what measures should we use to evaluate their success? Given that most are unlikely to have direct decision-making power—although the EP is a notable exception—how, then, is one to measure the power of consultation, deliberation, socialization, and information-exchange?

The answers to these questions cannot emerge from a study of legislative networks in isolation. They require a much more comprehensive conception of what global governance through government networks should look like. Legislative, judicial, and regulatory networks, both horizontal and vertical, must all fit together. They must also coexist with traditional international organizations. Putting all those pieces together is the task of the next chapter.

FOUR

A Disaggregated World Order

On our increasingly small and interconnected planet . . .
global problems cannot be solved within any one nation-
state. They call for collective and collaborative action—
something that the nations of the world have never been
good at. . . . The current international system is simply
not effective enough—or fast enough—to solve these
problems.
—Jean-François Rischard, Vice President for Europe,
   World Bank[1]

RECALL ATLAS AND HIS GLOBE AT ROCKEFELLER CENTER. A DISAGGRE-
gated world order would be a world latticed by countless government
networks. In form, these networks would include both horizontal and
vertical networks. In function, they would include networks for collecting and sharing information of all kinds, enforcement cooperation,
technical assistance and training, as well as policy coordination and
rule harmonization. In scope, they would be bilateral, plurilateral, regional, and global.

The defining feature of government networks is that they are composed of government officials and institutions—either national to national, in horizontal networks, or national to supranational, in vertical networks. Yet they coexist and increasingly interact with networks of nongovernmental actors, both from the private and nonprofit sectors. Similarly, members of government networks interact with one another informally, at least in the eyes of the law and traditional diplomacy of the international system. Yet their networks exist alongside and within formal international organizations.

The first three chapters documented the disaggregation of the state and emergence of regulatory, judicial, and legislative government networks. The job of this chapter is to assume that those existing networks form the foundation of a full-scale disaggregated world order and to identify the additional elements necessary to bring such an order into being. It will require the integration of existing networks: essentially the creation of networks of networks. It will require the addition of more vertical government networks. And it will require the reinvention of many existing traditional international organizations.

The first section of this chapter thus describes existing international entities that are themselves networks of networks. Like the transgovernmental regulatory organizations described in chapter 1—IOSCO or the Basel Committee—these entities range from well-established, permanent entities such as the Commonwealth or APEC to more fluid arrangements such as the Financial Stability Forum, a network of networks of financial regulators. These examples illuminate what a networked order can look like, based on regional, historic, or functional ties.

The second section turns to the vertical dimension of a networked world order, which is far less developed in actual practice than the horizontal dimension. Vertical government networks pierce the shell of state sovereignty by making individual government institutions—courts, regulatory agencies, or even legislators—responsible for the implementation of rules created by a supranational institution. Under international law, these rules bind the state as a whole; traditionally, it has been up to the state to pass the necessary domestic legislation that would allow for implementation. Vertical government networks make it possible for a supranational court, regulatory entity, or parliament to create a relationship with its national counterparts to make those rules directly enforceable.

The coercive power of vertical networks is much greater than that of horizontal networks; it is thus not surprising that they are much harder to find. Ultimately, however, they have a critical role to play in making selected international agreements as effective as possible. The trick for the architects of these networks (which could be the participating national and supranational government institutions themselves) will be to strike the right balance between national and supranational functions and responsibilities. We turn to a brief case study of one such effort: the detailed negotiations on how national courts and a supranational tribunal should relate to one another in the context of the International Criminal Court (ICC).

The third section examines the relations between government networks and traditional international organizations. These two worlds are closely interconnected. International organizations can help existing government networks work better; they can also foster the creation of new government networks. Conversely, the growth of government networks can give rise to new international organizations and offer a blueprint for the reinvention of old ones.

Taken as a whole, this chapter is equal parts fact and imagination. To grasp fully the concept of a disaggregated world order—a world order in which horizontal and vertical networks are the principal structures—we must move back and forth between actual and hypothetical, between what we see now and what we can envision in the future. The architecture of world order, however imperfect and even ineffective at times, does not fall from the sky. It is a deeply human creation motivated by human aspiration. That aspiration, in turn, is motivated by a vision of what is possible as much as what is desirable.

A world in which horizontal and vertical government networks comprise different types of government institutions (regulatory, judicial, legislative), perform different functions (information exchange, enforcement cooperation, harmonization, technical assistance and training), have different members, have different degrees of formality, and coexist in different ways with international organizations is a messy world indeed. It may seem impossibly complex. But the underlying concept is simple. It is a world in which the basic elements of gover-nance—making rules, implementing rules, enforcing rules and resolv-ing disputes arising under the rules—are carried out by networks of the government institutions, national and supranational, responsible for performing those functions.

The model for this world order in many ways is the European Union. Networks of government ministers exercise the most important powers in the European Union at the European level; networks of national judges exchange ideas and cooperate in resolving Europe-wide dis-putes; networks of national parliamentarians are emerging to monitor the European activities of the networks of ministers. At the same time, the European Union has genuine supranational institutions—a court, a commission, a parliament—that exercise genuine governmental au-thority and that increasingly enforce their authority through vertical networks with their national counterparts. Indeed, it is really the ge-nius of the European Union, and the reason that it is such an extraor-dinary model for other regions of the world, that it is much more a transgovernmental than a federal system. Individual EU members can maintain the distinctive character and autonomy of their national in-stitutions, while at the same time reaping the benefits of collective gov-ernance through government networks.

Yet the world differs from the European Union in critical ways. EU members share a common region, history, culture, as well as political and economic ideologies. These factors all reinforce the founding com-mitment of the EU treaties toward: "an ever closer union."[2] This com-mitment provides both impetus and cover for government networks within the European Union. They are explicitly charged with cooper-ation, harmonization, and enforcement of national and EU laws. And they operate with a high degree of trust in one another—trust strength-ened by the knowledge that they will be interacting with one another for a very long time to come.

Global networks, by contrast, must often operate with much lower levels of trust and homogeneity among their members. Members also often lack the security and direction provided by an overarching, treaty-based framework spelling out long-term political and economic commitments. Their membership itself is much more variable, depending on the type of government institutions participating and the substantive subjects at issue. And, again, they coexist and interact with traditional international organizations much more than EU networks do. For all these reasons, global governance through government networks is its own distinct phenomenon.

1. THE HORIZONTAL DIMENSION: NETWORKS OF NETWORKS

The best way to integrate the various government networks described in the first three chapters into a more recognizable structure of world order is to create networks of networks. Such integration can occur between networks in different geographic regions. Thus, for instance, the CPA, discussed in chapter 3, has sought to extend its influence beyond the geographic boundaries of the Commonwealth by maintaining an ongoing dialogue with European parliaments on various matters. Various regional assemblies, which are themselves networks of national legislators, have also sought to network with each other.

Alternatively, regulatory or judicial networks with a particular substantive focus can network with one another to address a particular problem or set of problems. Two prominent examples of this approach are the Financial Stability Forum, mentioned in chapter 1, and the Year 2000 Network. The Financial Stability Forum was originally established in 1996 as the "Joint Forum on Financial Conglomerates," a joint venture between the Basel Committee, IOSCO, and IAIS. It is composed of senior bank, insurance, and securities supervisors from thirteen countries, with the EU Commission attending in an observer capacity.[3] In 1995, in a prior, even less formal incarnation, the "Tripartite Group," it issued a discussion paper on the supervision of financial conglomerates.[4] It has subsequently prepared a number of papers for consideration by its three parent organizations on subjects such as capital adequacy principles and a framework and principles for supervisory information sharing.[5]

The Basel Committee, the BIS Committee on Payment and Settlement Systems (CPSS), IOSCO, and IAIS also created the Year 2000

Network. The G-7 finance ministers welcomed the formation of the council; the BIS provided its secretariat. Its mission was to encourage the development of coordinated national strategies to address the Year 2000 problem, including the development of a global databank of contacts in individual countries covering a wide range of actors in both the private and public sectors; the issuance of policy papers on specific Year 2000 issues; and the provision of supervisory guidance for assessing Year 2000 preparations by financial institutions. It focused its attention directly on both private and public actors in the global financial supervisory community.[6]

What is absolutely striking about this council was the speed and sophistication with which it organized itself. It was a functional network, addressed to the solution of a specific but very important problem. It exercised no actual authority; its principal functions were coordination and information sharing. Nevertheless, it was able to marshal key figures worldwide to create synergies and enhance their individual reach in addressing the problem. It offered recommendations to national authorities and provided them with the informational tools to act on those recommendations. And all of this within the span of barely six months.[7] It is difficult to imagine the global community doing anything that fast or that effectively through the traditional machinery of international negotiations or even through traditional international institutions.

In addition to these spontaneous networks of networks, a number of existing international organizations—or, more accurately, associations—operate through networks of national ministers, regulators, judges, and, in some cases, legislators. Prominent examples include the Commonwealth, the Nordic System, APEC, and the OECD. Each of these entities is fundamentally a collection of government networks facilitated by a supranational secretariat with only informational power.

These organizations would be regarded as quite weak in traditional terms—weak in ways that could only be remedied by strengthening the supranational dimension and creating a separate set of officials with loyalty only to the organization and with as much independent power as possible. But from the perspective of a disaggregated world order, these entities are pioneering a different form of international organization, one that relies on horizontal relations among national government officials playing the same roles and performing the same functions; on the power of information, deliberation, socialization, and exclusion; and on a limited supranational entity that serves as a handmaiden to the national officials rather than as a competitor. Each of the institutions described below differs in significant ways, but each offers a glimpse of a what a horizontal world order based on networks of networks of national officials could—and in some ways does—look like.

The Commonwealth

Consider the following passage from Lord David Howell, former chairman of the British House of Commons' all-party Committee on Foreign Affairs:

> [In the post–Cold War world,] the Commonwealth is emerging as much the most appropriate and effective type of international organization in existence. Its character, as a vast network of bodies, both official and unofficial, with global reach and stretching across all the regions, makes it distinctly superior to supranational institutions in addressing global problems, and the best model for future combinations and linkages between states, between agencies of the state and between nationally based groups and organizations of many kinds with global concerns.[8]

Lord Howell contrasts the transgovernmental networks of the Commonwealth to international institutions like the UN or the WTO, preferring the transgovernmental approach. My own view, as discussed later on, is that both types of institutions are necessary, and indeed complement each other, in an effective global governance system. Taken together, the different Commonwealth organizations, encompassing 54 countries, together with their 202 nongovernmental counterparts, reveal the "biochemistry of transgovernmentalism—the new international system in action."[9] It is precisely the "informal but really useful ties" that networks provide that can, for example, "meet both Chinese sensitivities and Hong Kong needs."[10] Finally, the Commonwealth has been "pioneering new forms of partnership between nation-state governments on practical development matters."[11]

The Commonwealth is a forum for multiple policy-development meetings at the transgovernmental and transnational levels, involving heads of governments, finance ministers, education ministers, parliamentarians, and judges, who meet with their counterparts from other Commonwealth countries.[12] The Commonwealth has a secretariat, based in London, which facilitates these various meetings.[13] The Commonwealth has also pioneered the use of a subgroup of ministers as a policy-making or implementation task force. In October 1991, the Commonwealth Heads of Government adopted the Harare Declaration, a statement of principles by which they affirmed their commitment to good governance, democracy, and human rights. A Ministerial Action Group, composed of the foreign ministers from eight countries, plus an additional two from particular regions as necessary, "deal[s] with serious or persistent violations of the principles contained in that Declaration."[14] In its early years the action group did not, in truth, accomplish much beyond monitoring progress toward the restoration of democracy in countries such as Nigeria and Sierra Leone, but the possibilities for more decisive action certainly exist.[15]

In 1995, the Foreign Affairs Committee of the House of Commons found that the British government had underestimated the enormous value of the "Commonwealth network," recommending that the "government should both bilaterally and through the [Commonwealth] Secretariat seek to extend the role of the Commonwealth network in the field of intergovernmental policy matters."[16] The committee urged the governments of all Commonwealth countries to make greater use of the annual meeting of Commonwealth finance ministers, particularly to launch development and debt-relief initiatives, but also to "share new ideas and good practice Commonwealth-wide." Overall, "[f]rom being a 'club' of countries all too ready both to criticize and make demands on the former imperial power, the Commonwealth is rapidly metamorphosing into a network with quite different interests and ambitions."[17] Of particular value is the way in which the Commonwealth spawns both governmental and nongovernmental networks, many of which then work together.

The Nordic System

A little-known example of government networks as a governance structure is the Nordic System, which originally emerged from the Nordic Council, the forum for interparliamentary cooperation described in the last chapter. Two decades after the creation of legislative networks among Nordic parliamentarians, the ministers of the five participating countries (and three independent regions) came together in 1971 to create the Nordic Council of Ministers. This is the designated forum for "intergovernmental" cooperation, meaning cooperation among members of the executive rather than the legislative branches of the Nordic countries.[18] Ministers of all different portfolios, including education, the environment, and health, hold regular meetings.

What do these meetings accomplish? They launch a wide range of initiatives and programs, amounting to the work of a regional legislature. A committee of parliamentarians considers proposals developed by the council of ministers and may send them for consultation and comments by individuals and organizations in the five societies. A plenary session of the council can then adopt or reject the proposal based on a committee recommendation. If the proposal is adopted, the council will send it directly to the five Nordic governments for implementation, which will in turn require adoption by each national parliament.[19] The Nordic Council's agenda for November 2000 included proposed measures on refugee policy, trade, education, and information technology.[20] The work of preparing all these measures falls to networks of national officials linked under the auspices of the Council of Ministers' Cooperation Committee.[21]

This system has several striking features. First, it is a system that performs many of the functions of a regional government with only a skeletal supranational bureaucracy. The officials who run it are overwhelmingly national officials, from the executive and legislative branches. Second, the system shows a successful mixture of formal and informal structures. As the council itself observes: "Cross-border networking is customary and co-operation works smoothly with a minimum of formal restrictions. But many of the opportunities the Nordic citizens have for working together are based on formal agreements between the Nordic governments."[22] Third, the system has multiple democratic safeguards. Supranational bureaucracy is kept to a minimum. The individual Nordic parliaments appoint the members of the Nordic Council from among their own number. In addition, as noted above, national parliaments must separately approve any measure formally approved by the Nordic Council.

Such checks are undoubtedly frustrating to the officials within the Nordic System; they resemble that inbuilt friction that Justice Brandeis famously identified as one of the intentional features of the U.S. Constitution.[23] The Nordic System has accordingly lost—or forfeited—control over some issues to overlapping institutions with "real authority," such as the European Union and NATO.[24] Yet on the larger issue of where power should be located—at the national or the supranational level—the jury is still out. It is quite likely that the European Union will increasingly evolve toward the Nordic System, particularly regarding interparliamentary cooperation. After all, and as was described in chapter 3, the Baltic states have been quick to follow the Nordic example.

Asia-Pacific Economic Cooperation (APEC)

Perhaps the loosest system of government networks, and one very deliberately maintained as such, is the Asia-Pacific Economic Cooperation (APEC). APEC began in 1989 as an "informal Ministerial-level dialogue group."[25] In 1993, the participants added an "annual informal Economic Leaders' meeting," consisting of the heads of state or government of the member-economies.[26] By 2001, APEC had expanded to include regular ministerial meetings of ministers from every sector, including education, energy, environment, finance, human resources development, science and technology, telecommunication and information technology, trade, transportation, and women.[27] The participating ministers have also established committees to pursue specific initiatives, which in turn have spawned subcommittees and work groups. Finally, to institutionalize participation from the private sector, particularly business, the APEC economic leaders established the Business

Advisory Council—a permanent council composed of up to three senior business people from each member-economy.[28]

APEC has thus generated an institutionalized transgovernmental bureaucracy, but informality remains its hallmark, in the sense that the networks all operate by consensus, through meetings, information exchange, commissioning reports and proposals, and setting target goals, which they then monitor. APEC members have strongly resisted any efforts to "legalize" their operations, such as by adopting a convention establishing APEC as a formal legal organization with binding commitments of various kinds.[29] They resolutely reject any notion of a teleological progression from informal to formal; from soft law to hard law; or from consensus among national ministers to supranational weighted voting. In an era in which many Western governments are beginning to understand the domestic political costs of tying themselves to a supranational mast, maintaining maximum flexibility with regard to domestic constituencies while nevertheless institutionalizing international cooperation may prove a very valuable model.[30]

A second and related hallmark of APEC is its determination to maintain the reins of power at the national level. The goal adopted by APEC economic leaders in 1994 is nothing less than the creation of a common market for trade and investment in the Asia-Pacific region by 2010 for developed member-economies and 2020 for developing economies.[31] This project is vast in scope, given that APEC includes twenty-one members around the Pacific Rim, including all the NAFTA countries, many of the Latin American countries on the Pacific, Australia, New Zealand, Japan, China, Vietnam, and South Korea.[32] Yet the institutional framework for achieving this goal remains almost entirely within networks of national ministers. APEC ministers created a secretariat in 1993, but solely to serve as "the central link and core support mechanism for the APEC process."[33] In practice, the secretariat provides coordination, technical, and advisory support to member-economies and APEC forums, as well as performing a project management role for over two-hundred APEC-funded projects.[34]

A third striking feature is the degree of disaggregation exhibited by the APEC networks. APEC distinguishes between "leaders" and "ministers."[35] Leaders frequently endorse, encourage, or "welcome" decisions and initiatives undertaken by ministers.[36] They also "instruct" or "direct" the ministers to undertake specific initiatives, as would be expected in traditional diplomacy. Overall, this dimension of APEC fits with the distinction drawn between heads of state and finance ministers in the G-20, discussed in chapter 2.

Fourth, APEC is notable for its deliberate efforts to reach beyond government actors. As a self-conscious economic forum, its aim has been primarily to reach out to the business world. Such efforts are not likely to satisfy global groups complaining of a massive democracy deficit; nevertheless, APEC ministers have managed to institutionalize input from leaders in the private sector in ways that few other networks have. It is not simply, as in the Commonwealth, that the government networks exist alongside a wealth of civil society and corporate networks, but that they have recognized and regularized and important channels of interaction.

Finally, APEC has pioneered a mode of governance that consists primarily in assessing current practices of member-states, benchmarking them, and adopting individualized national plans for improvement. As a forum with no coercive power or even supranational decision-making procedures, APEC must depend on collective goal setting and voluntary compliance. The principal method by which APEC as an institution encourages members to achieve collective goals is the adoption of "electronic–Individual Action plans," described as "the basic road maps by which each APEC member charts its progress toward the goals of trade and investment liberalization."[37] This approach heralds an important advance in the use of information for the promotion of self-governance within a collective framework.

The Organization for Economic Cooperation and Development (OECD)

The Organization for Economic Cooperation and Development (OECD) is essentially an intergovernmental organization that has evolved from its original mission to administer the Marshall Plan to a framework for convening networks of national ministers of thirty coun-

`tries to share information, conduct studies, and produce model codes.[38] Some members of the OECD secretariat have reportedly felt that the OECD could only become a powerful international organization by developing formal rule-making capacity—in other words, by moving from a transgovernmental organization to a more traditional formal international organization. In fact, however, its experience with more formal negotiation and proposed rule making has been largely mixed; the proposed treaty on anticorruption measures was well received, but the effort to draft a treaty governing foreign investment blew up in the face of strenuous opposition from developing countries and NGOs.[39]

From the perspective of a networked world order, the OECD's current structure and function are well adapted to address many contemporary global problems. Its Principles of Corporate Governance (adopted in May 1999) and Guidelines for Multinational Enterprises (revised in June 2000), for example, are used to gauge public policy in developing countries and have become criteria taken into account in country assessments by the World Bank.[40] It is not hard to imagine further codes and sets of principles on issues of concern to countries well beyond the OECD membership, all of which could be inclusively arrived at and flexibly drafted to provide benchmarks of behavior without the difficulties and complexities of formal legal obligations.

—

ALL OF THESE EXAMPLES HAVE DIFFERENT ORIGINS AND DIFFERENT purposes. Some, like the Commonwealth, are only now evolving into organizations with an explicit governance component. Others, like APEC, are inventing themselves as they go along. But each demonstrates that it is possible to aggregate individual networks of government officials into a larger system, or, indeed, for a formal intergovernmental organization to devolve into a framework for different networks.

The Commonwealth, the Nordic System, and APEC are all founded on specific ties between member-countries, ties of regional geography or of history, language and culture. The OECD originally had such a regional focus, but has evolved beyond geography to economic criteria, becoming the organization open to countries that have attained a certain level of economic development. More generally, its focus on economic development and regulation allow it to be characterized as a functional organization more than a geographic or historic one.

Even with networked networks, however, the creation of a genuinely global networked order will mean considerable expansion of many existing functional networks to include a much wider range of countries. Indeed, Lord Howell commends the Commonwealth model over that of the OECD precisely because the OECD "lacks an obvious and centrally valuable feature of the Commonwealth—namely, its scope for bringing together and giving a common voice to both richer and poorer, developed and developing societies."[41] The OECD tries to constitute networks of ministers from less-developed countries to offer reactions and advice on the various codes it is developing, but it still suffers from the perception that it is a "rich-country" club.[42]

Canadian Finance Minister Paul Martin, in his capacity as chair of the G-20, specifically praised the G-20 for its relative inclusiveness: "What makes [the G-20] unique is the fact that it brings together a cross-section of national economies at different stages of economic maturity, thereby providing the diversity needed to address the wide range of human needs."[43] Yet the G-20 has certainly not replaced the G-8, nor even been invited to meet and consult with the G-8 on a regular basis. How inclusive specific networks can be will ultimately depend in part on their particular functions. Information networks are likely to have the farthest reach; enforcement networks next; and harmonization networks the narrowest compass. But even given these constraints, more needs to be done in virtually every regulatory sector.

2. THE VERTICAL DIMENSION

The organizations just described demonstrate the potential substantive and geographic range of a networked world order. But they also demonstrate the potential weakness of such an order. Even accepting that these organizations may be much stronger and more effective than a traditional hierarchical view of such organizations would suggest, they remain considerably weaker than organizations like the European Union or the WTO. The European Union and the WTO have, at least in the popular perception, "real power"—meaning coercive power. Such power contains a paradox, however. It is these organizations that are the most sought after for membership. They are the clubs that non-members want to get into. Their effectiveness is directly related to their exclusivity and hence their power both of implementation and of attraction.

Here is also the paradox of government networks. In their horizontal form, they are looser and less coercive—even aspirationally—than other forms of international organization. They thus guarantee that power remains principally in the hands of nation-states through their national officials. But in their vertical form, government networks can be the critical ingredient that gives a supranational organization real power. The possibility of direct relations between a supranational court and national courts, or between a supranational regulatory agency and its domestic equivalent, pierces the shell of state sovereignty and creates a channel whereby supranational officials can harness the coercive power of national officials.[44]*

A disaggregated world order would include vertical as well as horizontal government networks. Given a presumed aspiration to avoid world government, the power of vertical government networks should be used sparingly. In some cases, however, governments will in fact choose to delegate some functions to an independent organization, whether to solve a collective action problem, tie their hands, or compensate for their own domestic incapacity or the incapacity of other countries. When they do so choose, they will want the organization to actually work. They will thus either establish a vertical network directly or create the structural conditions for the emergence of one.

For instance, when the members of the European Union wanted to create a single market, the members of the General Agreement on Trade and Tariffs (GATT) wanted to resolve disputes amongst themselves on a legal basis, or the members of the NAFTA wanted to ensure

---

*A note on definitions is in order, specifically concerning my usage of the terms "international" and "supranational." Each term has many different definitions, but as used here, "international" or "intergovernmental" refers to relations between sovereign states acting as unitary actors. "Supranational" refers to an entity "above" states. For further discussion, see note 44.

that investors from one country have recourse against the government of another for illegal discrimination, they transferred a measure of their sovereignty to a supranational court or arbitral tribunal, empowering the judges or arbitrators to make legally binding decisions with which the parties to the dispute in question are expected to comply. Similarly, when the members of a human rights convention—whether European, Latin American, or global—wanted to "give it teeth," they created a protocol whereby members who sign on agree that their nationals can sue them before a supranational tribunal.

It is also possible, however, for governments to get more than they may have bargained for. The direct interaction of a supranational institution and a national government institution pierces the shell of sovereignty that formally defines the state as a unitary actor in the international system. It penetrates the domestic political system, working to command or persuade not the government as a whole, but rather one government institution that has power with regard to other government institutions according to the rules of the domestic political game. Conversely, of course, recourse to the supranational institution becomes part of the arsenal of tools and strategies that domestic political institutions deploy against each other.

Recall the discussion of the ECJ and its relations with national courts in chapter 1. The ECJ essentially built its own power base in the European Union by interacting directly with national courts, cultivating relationships with national judges in order to encourage them to send up cases involving European law directly to it. Lower national courts quickly saw the advantage in using this option as a means of bypassing higher national courts in cases in which the lower national court likely had a different view of the law than did the higher court. And when the ECJ handed down its decisions back to the referring national court, that court could enforce the decision through the coercive force of the national legal system.

The other examples we have seen are less well developed, but nevertheless support the overall concept of how vertical networks work. The European Court of Human Rights, for instance, has also developed relationships not only with national courts—both inside and outside Europe—but also with other national government institutions, such as human rights commissions and even legislatures, that use its judgments to bolster their positions in domestic politics. The EP is developing direct relationships with national legislators, which should ultimately strengthen its position against the executive and even the judicial branches of the European Union.

Still other examples demonstrate the other side of vertical networks: the ways in which national institutions can *limit* the power of supranational institutions in an ongoing relationship of checks and balances. Just as the lower courts of many EU members found a potential ally in the ECJ, many high courts saw a rival. They pushed back, exerting their considerable power, to define the respective limits of European and national law. This same dynamic is developing in both NAFTA and even the WTO. In NAFTA, losing litigants at the supranational level are challenging the decisions of NAFTA arbitral tribunals in national courts.[45]

Such cases make the courts and tribunals in the two legal systems, national and supranational, much more aware of each other and more wary about treading too much on each other's toes. Supranational tribunals in both NAFTA and the WTO must ultimately often review the work of national courts in deciding whether or not a particular national legal arrangement violates the provisions of NAFTA or GATT. Conversely, national courts will increasingly look to the decisions of these supranational tribunals as helpful, even if not definitive, interpretations of the relevant treaty. As these entities at different legal levels try to define the boundaries of their respective competences and occasionally jockey for position, they will be developing a direct relationship with one another that over the long term will make it more difficult for the participating member-states in any of these treaty organizations to ignore or avoid the law that they purported to create.

Given the potential power of vertical government networks, the architects of the next generation of international institutions should focus on how best to structure the relations between a supranational entity and its domestic counterpart. Assuming, once again, that the goal is in fact to make the institution in question maximally effective, then it will be critical to ensure that any supranational institutions—those entitled to exercise independent power above the state—be able to interact directly with their national counterparts. At the same time, however, it is equally important to ensure that the national institution retains enough power in the relationship to be able to more than hold its own. The story of the evolving jurisdictional provisions of the ICC reflects an ongoing attempt to get this balance right.

From Primacy to Complementarity in the International Criminal Court (ICC)

After decades of inaction following the Nuremberg trials, the international community eventually found both the will and the occasion to pursue perpetrators of genocide, serious war crimes, and crimes against humanity.[46] In 1993, the UN Security Council passed Resolution 827 creating an international tribunal to punish war crimes in the former Yugoslavia.[47] Under Article 9 of Resolution 827, the tribunal, known as the International Criminal Tribunal for the Former Yugoslavia (ICTY), has concurrent jurisdiction with national courts to prosecute persons for serious violations of international humanitarian law. Further, the international court has primacy over national courts and may at any stage of a criminal proceeding formally request that a national court defer to the competence of the tribunal.[48]

In plain English, this provision means that the tribunal can "cut in," taking over a case from a national court that otherwise can properly hear the case. The first criminal defendant brought before the tribunal quickly challenged this provision. Justice Antonio Cassese wrote an Appeals Chamber opinion justifying this primacy on the grounds that the national courts involved in the case had accepted the tribunal's jurisdiction outright and that national courts in general were increasingly willing to accept human rights as an international body of law properly decided outside of national courts.[49] Commentators were not so sure, except in the specific case of a supranational tribunal serving as a transitional court for a country so divided or shattered as to be unable to run its own legal system.[50]

This issue came to a head in the years of negotiations over the establishment of a permanent international criminal court.[51] Many international law groups, NGOs, and the first two prosecutors of the tribunal, Richard Goldstone and Louise Arbour, argued strenuously for maintaining primary jurisdiction at the supranational level.[52] On the other side, the United States and many other countries, joined by various national law groups, argued for "complementarity"—the principle that primary jurisdiction be vested in national courts with the ICC exercising "complementary" jurisdiction in the event of a clear failure or inability of national courts to conduct their own trials.[53] The question of complementarity versus primacy became one of the most contentious issues in the entire ICC debate, but ultimately the Rome Statute, concluded in July 1999 and signed by 160 countries, established a complementary jurisdictional structure.

Article 17 of the Rome Statute provides that national courts have primary jurisdiction—meaning that it is up to them to prosecute war criminals or perpetrators of genocide or crimes against humanity over whom they would otherwise have jurisdiction, unless they are "unwilling or unable" genuinely to do their job. Being "unwilling or unable" includes situations in which the executive branch of the state in question is unwilling to carry out the prosecution. If the prosecutor of the ICC determines that a member-state is unwilling or unable to prosecute or try a case—a determination subject to review by a panel of the ICC itself—then, and only then, will the ICC itself be able to take jurisdiction of the case.

The negotiators got it right. Now that the ICC has actually come into being, following the ratification of the Rome Statute by over sixty of the signatory states, it will take years of litigation to establish precisely what "unable or unwilling" actually means, thereby establishing the precise parameters of ICC jurisdiction in relation to national courts. Nevertheless, for several reasons the provision for complementarity is a milestone not only for international law but also for a disaggregated world order. First, it recognizes national government institutions as a first choice to exercise power and responsibility even in the design of an international system of governance. This acceptance, however grudging, is a radical departure for most international lawyers and diplomats, who are accustomed to operating on the international plane as something apart from and presumably superior to the particularities and prejudices of domestic institutions. In addition to signaling a major psychological shift, it also has considerable implications for the allocation of resources. To take the most prominent example, this type of thinking might have led the United Nations to spend the millions of dollars it has poured into the International Criminal Tribunal for Rwanda—sitting in Arusha, Tanzania—into the reconstruction of the domestic Rwandan legal system.

Second, and equally important, the ICC will become a stronger and more effective supranational institution due to its relationship with national courts around the world. In the best scenario, this relationship will become a full-fledged partnership, in which national courts look to ICC decisions for guidance in handling the substance of complex cases involving relatively new and quickly evolving areas of international criminal law.[54] In addition, the *potential* for an ICC move to take over a particular case may expand a domestic court or prosecutor's room for maneuver in a difficult and incendiary domestic political climate.

The ICC may also engage in direct conflict with some domestic courts, particularly those controlled by executive branches or otherwise undermined by years of neglect and disparagement. Even in these cases, however, the evolution of international criminal law will be greatly strengthened by the interaction of a supranational tribunal with national courts in a give and take over many years: defining jurisdictional boundaries, exchanging opinions on substantive law, and mixing national and international legal traditions. And the ICC itself will benefit from an institutional design that would penetrate the surface of the fictional unitary state, giving it a direct interlocutor within domestic government. It will never face the situation of the ICJ, in which it issues decisions binding on states, conglomerates of politicians, diplomats, and bureaucrats, and hopes that they see fit to comply.

Beyond Courts

The ability to improve the performance of both domestic and supranational institutions by linking like units of government together is not limited to courts. The EU Commission has recently moved to establish similar domestic-supranational relationships in the antitrust arena. In early 2001, it announced a new initiative to devolve primary responsibility for enforcing EU antitrust law to national competition authorities.[55] Under the previous system, corporations contemplating a merger or other activity that could be deemed anticompetitive had to seek approval directly from Commission. Under the new system, they must notify their national competition authorities, which are directed to apply EU law. The decisions of those authorities are in turn reviewed in the first instance by national courts, which also apply EU law. The commission thus now has a direct relationship with national competition regulators.

Both the motives for this rule and its likely results are instructive. Due to the increasing volume of antitrust rules and regulations at the EU level, the commission is no longer able to carry out all monitoring and enforcement responsibilities itself. At the same time, the interrelationship between national competition law and EU competition law has grown increasingly complex. The commission thus has in mind harnessing national antitrust authorities as its agents in interpreting and enforcing EU law. The result, however, is much more likely to be an equal partnership, as national authorities exert counterpressure in the same way that national constitutional courts have defined the respective limits of EU and national jurisdiction against the ECJ.

It is possible to imagine similar arrangements in NAFTA or even the WTO, as well as in a future global environmental regime. In situations in which states have collectively decided that a genuinely supranational institution is needed, it will be possible to make that institution more effective than ever before by forging structural links between it and its national counterparts. At the same time, however, states have the option of ensuring that primary power remains in the hands of national authorities, with supranational entities playing a subsidiary role. And even where supranational authorities have primary authority, their national counterparts will inevitably exert a healthy check upon their power.

3. GOVERNMENT NETWORKS AND TRADITIONAL INTERNATIONAL ORGANIZATIONS: INTERCONNECTED WORLDS

Government networks, both horizontal and vertical, are necessarily informal because separate government institutions have no formal standing in the international system or under international law. In layman's language, lack of formal standing essentially means that these institutions don't exist in the eyes of the law, so that they cannot possibly create institutions that do. Even when central bankers, securities commissioners, or antitrust officials seek to regularize their relations by actually creating their own organizations, those organizations exist in an informal sector alongside the formal sector of international organizations composed of states interacting as unitary actors.

This formal sector will not disappear, nor should it. States will continue to come together as unitary actors and engage in treaty making and institution building with all the pomp and solemnity of traditional diplomacy. The interesting question is how these formal unitary state relations coexist and/or conflict with relations among parts of states in the informal sector, along both the horizontal and the vertical dimensions of a disaggregated world order.

Government networks can exist both within and alongside formal organizations in a wide variety of modes, although some of these may require the reinvention, or at least the reconceptualization, of existing international organizations. First, governments acting as unitary actors can conclude treaties and establish international institutions that in turn create and host government networks; indeed, as we have just seen, some are nothing more than a framework for government networks. Finance ministers come together as the members of the all-important Board of Governors of the IMF; organizations such as the European Union, the Nordic Council, NAFTA, and the Commonwealth create councils of ministers in different issue areas; organizations such as NATO and the OSCE create legislative networks to focus on specific mandates. This top-down creation of government networks allows states to preserve more of their sovereignty than they otherwise might in creating a supranational organization, ensuring that the actual fleshing out of what states have committed to remains in national hands.

Second, states coming together to conclude treaties and other types of international agreements that mandate substantial change at the domestic political and legal levels can trigger the formation of government networks as an inevitable part of the implementation of these agreements. Third, particular types of international organizations—secretariats, commissions, or even agencies—can evolve or be created largely to facilitate the work of horizontal government networks by collecting and disseminating needed information and performing other coordinating functions. In some cases, particularly in Europe, it is the preexisting government network that is exerting the pressure to create the more formal organization at the supranational level, rather than an international organization pressuring for a government network.

Finally, the creation of a government network within a traditional international organization, such as the formation of a negotiating network among ministers from particular countries in the World Intellectual Property Organization (WIPO), can breathe new life and power into the international organization itself.[56] Indeed, international organizations can reinvent themselves, or be reinvented by their member states, as collections of government networks. This section describes the efforts of the Organization of American States (OAS) in that direction.

Taken all together, these examples demonstrate a complex world of links between the informal and the formal governance sectors. Transgovernmentalism and intergovernmentalism can flourish side by side, each shaping the other in a variety of ways. A disaggregated world order would have to include both.

Creating Government Networks from the Top Down

A recent example from North America illustrates the way in which states can deliberately create a government network. Canada, the United States, and Mexico, acting within the framework of NAFTA, signed a separate North American Agreement on Environmental Cooperation (NAAEC).[57] The NAAEC institutionalized, merged, and expanded preexisting bilateral environmental cooperation and enforcement agreements between the United States and Mexico, on the one hand, and the United States and Canada, on the other.[58] The major breakthrough of the NAAEC was the creation of the North American Commission for Environmental Cooperation (CEC), a trilateral institution "that conducts cooperative enforcement activities and promotes effective enforcement of each nation's environmental laws."[59]

The CEC is a trilateral government network of North American environmental ministers, together with a secretariat and a joint public advisory committee.[60] Its function is to improve the level of environmental protection and compliance with existing international laws and treaties by pressuring each member-state to enforce its own environmental laws and regulations effectively.[61] Furthermore, this obligation to enforce its environmental laws is upheld by the possibility of sanctions,[62] a first for an international environmental agreement.[63] Since the NAAEC's inception, the three parties have defined their goals and enforcement mechanisms more precisely. In 1995, for example, the CEC council members set up the standing environmental enforcement network discussed extensively in chapter 1.[64]

Certain characteristics of the NAAEC prove the novelty and potential efficacy of such a top-down transgovernmental network. First, it respects law enforcement as a key element of national sovereignty, thereby preserving and enhancing national implementation of goals set by the international agreement. Second, created as a side-agreement to NAFTA, the NAAEC benefits from the institutional legitimacy of NAFTA. It is a stated function of the CEC to cooperate with the NAFTA Free Trade Commission, itself a network of the three North American trade ministers.[65] If this cooperation were to emerge in such a way as to integrate trade policy and environmental policy across all three countries, then NAFTA itself would begin operating more through integrated horizontal government networks, in addition to nascent vertical networks between NAFTA tribunals and national courts.

Triggering Government Networks

A second way in which supranational or international organizations may bring transgovernmental networks into being is by adopting ambitious substantive agendas with no formal institutional means of accomplishing them. In cases in which a body of legal rules has emerged at the supranational level, they must be implemented. Where the negotiating states have failed to design and bring to life an implementing structure, national officials must fill the breach. Suppose, by analogy, that Congress passed a new set of federal laws without creating new federal agencies to implement them. The only option would be for the relevant state officials to create their own implementation structure—through networks.

Once again, NAFTA and the European Union both provide useful examples. In the case of NAFTA, Alan Swann describes a process of "juridification," by which he means the transformation of political commitments into legal obligations.[66] Without any supranational bureaucracy, the commitment made by the states participating in NAFTA not only to open their markets, but equally importantly, to enforce their domestic laws, "necessarily forces a wide range of national bureaucracies to work together in the day to day running of the system. It not only brings together national trade authorities but labor, transportation and agriculture departments, securities, banking and other regulators of financial services, anti-trust authorities and more."[67]

Regarding the European Union, in many ways the phenomenon of supranational lawmaking requiring national implementation through government networks is the hallmark of the EU method of integration. The effort to harmonize national laws within the European Community (EC) involves the passage of regulations at the Community level but depends on national authorities for their implementation.[68] The EU legislative process, involving its council, commission, and parliament, issues directives that set forth Community objectives. National authorities must then implement the goals of these directives into their national laws.[69] This process is "slow and cumbersome."[70] But as scholars like Renaud Dehousse point out, it is in many ways the secret of the

European Union's success. It permits collective action at the supranational level while nevertheless leaving enormous power and discretion in the hands of the national regulatory authorities.[71]

These national regulatory authorities, in turn, must devise their own ways of working together. As Dehousse describes it, the alternative that has emerged in the European Union is the "transnational option"—the use of an organized network of national officials of member-states to ensure "that the actors in charge of the implementation of Community policies behave in a similar manner."[72] In other words, government networks.

Facilitating the Work of Government Networks

A third important way in which international and transgovernmental—formal and informal—elements of world order may be closely linked is through the facilitation of the work of government networks by international or regional "information agencies."[73] The principal and stated purpose of such entities is to make networks run more smoothly and efficiently and to respond to the needs of their members. Thus, for instance, as demonstrated in chapter 3, the parliamentary assembly of ASEAN, AIPO, works primarily through the provision of information and the development of model legislation for use by its member parliaments. The Technical Committee of IOSCO, the Secretariat of the Convention on Trade in Endangered Species (CITES), and the Secretariat of the Commonwealth all perform similar functions. The relations between these information agencies and the networks of national government officials they serve are not "vertical" government networks. The agencies themselves have no independent governing authority. They are not counterparts to national government officials, but rather handmaidens. They are not harnessing national government officials to enforce supranational law, but providing national government officials with the information they need to coordinate and enforce national law.

Many secretariats, commissions, and other entities that I have lumped together here under the category "information agencies" are created as part of a traditional international treaty-making process, whereby the parties to a treaty conclude the document and establish a secretariat to administer it. The CITES Secretariat is a classic example. It cooperates closely with several other international environmental organizations (International Union for the Conservation of Nature, The World Wide Fund for Nature, and the TRAFFIC network) in collecting and disseminating information through a variety of reports on how well member-states are complying with their treaty obligations. The existence of a secretariat or similar entity can then become a focal point for government networks of national officials concerned with the particular subject of the treaty—trade or environment or intellectual property; alternatively, the secretariat, like some regional parliamentary groups, can choose to orient its activities toward helping national officials.

But another way that information agencies get created is from the bottom up, demonstrating again the close intertwining of the informal world of government networks and the formal world of international institutions. We just saw how nation-states coming together and committing to international obligations that require extensive domestic implementation can trigger the formation of government networks to fulfill these obligations. Conversely, however, the resulting efforts of these networks to harmonize national laws or coordinate policy can ultimately require and indeed trigger the creation of an information agency at the international level to facilitate their work.

Turn back to the European Union, where the "EU method" of legislating at the supranational level but implementing at the national level requires the formation of government networks. Renaud Dehousse's identification of the resulting regulation by network thus refers to the functional need for mid-level officials from national ministries in different issue areas to exchange information with one another and with both commission officials and private actors. Dehousse casts upon these networks a far more favorable eye than many of his fellow EU observers. Even for him, however,

> *ad hoc* meetings of national officials, no matter how frequent, are not enough to bring about a true "community of views," let alone a "com-

munity of action." Partnership must be structured by common rules, which lay down the rights and duties of all members. Equally important, the network itself must be given some stability, which generally implies the setting-up of a structure which will manage the interaction among network members.[74]

European regulatory agencies fulfill this function. Eight new agencies were created at the European level between 1990 and 1997 as a way of facilitating further harmonization. Four of these—the European Environmental Agency, the Lisbon Drug Monitoring Centre, the European Agency for Health and Safety at Work, and the European Agency for the Evaluation of Medicinal Products—are best described as "information agencies."[75] Their job is to collect, coordinate, and disseminate information needed by policymakers. They lack decision-making authority, much less coercive enforcement power.

Dehousse and fellow EU scholar Giandomenico Majone both describe these agencies as easy to underestimate though actually likely to play an important and powerful role. Majone sees them as the quintessential example of regulation by information. Their power will lie not in their coercive apparatus but in their ability to exercise influence through "knowledge and persuasion."[76] He notes a general disenchantment with the "efficacy of [command-and-control] policy instruments," undermined by factors from increasingly porous national borders to the growing complexity of public policy.[77] "Modes of regulation based on information and persuasion" are perceived to be more flexible, responsive, and effective.[78] To be successful in this environment, an information agency needs to establish its credibility and professional reputation.[79]

Dehousse also sees the European information agencies as network creators and coordinators.[80] "Their primary aim is to run networks of national administrations which come into play in the implementation of Community policies."[81] They accomplish this function by setting up a "permanent technical and administrative secretariat," which tries not only to collect and disseminate necessary information but also to encourage "horizontal cross-fertilization" among counterpart national officials.[82] From a more dynamic perspective, it appears that the emergence of transgovernmental networks through the EU method has given rise to the need for a central node, which in turn helps spur more coordinated and effective transgovernmental action.

Reforming and Reinventing International Organizations

At least to their critics, international organizations all too often look like monolithic behemoths. Kofi Annan repeatedly reminds his audiences that as Secretary General he is a spokesman for the United Nations and exercises limited powers on behalf of the secretariat, but in the end his power depends almost entirely on the will of the member-states.[83] The United Nations is, instead, an enormously complex and often conflicting set of member-states, departments, agencies, and officials. More generally, international organizations are increasingly differentiated in terms of the types of functions performed within them and by them. Their component parts link up to national government officials and institutions in transgovernmental networks. Further, they often bring these networks into being and facilitate their operation.

Understanding international organizations in this way, however, requires rethinking, even reinventing, them. Most important, to the extent that they are shells for hosting transgovernmental networks, as in the Keohane and Nye "club model," the purported egalitarianism of their creation and membership may have to extend to their internal governance structures. Keohane and Nye argue forcefully that closed clubs have lost their legitimacy.[84] Opening them up requires many different measures, but one of the most obvious is making sure that a wider range of relevant government officials are genuinely represented, not simply at the ambassadorial, but also at the working, level.

Second, recognizing the actuality and the potential of transgovernmental networks for carrying out a host of critical functions—from the collection and dissemination of information to policy coordination to implementation and enforcement—relieves international organizations of the burden of trying to take on all the functions of government in a particular issue area. Instead of trying to replicate the job of their national counterparts, supranational agencies can simply supplement them in a variety of helpful ways. For example, in the debate over whether the WTO should expand to include rules governing competition policy, the issue has hitherto been framed in terms of a supranational organization, the WTO, versus transgovernmental networks of antitrust officials. A better approach would be to figure out how a quite limited supranational entity could help facilitate and improve the operation of existing transgovernmental networks among officials from a number of different countries.[85]

Third, government networks can revitalize existing international organizations. The best example may be the World Intellectual Property Organization (WIPO); in this case, the efforts of countries vitally concerned about intellectual property issues have led to the creation of a partial network of intellectual property officials, which was then vaulted into the vanguard of efforts at global governance in this area. This revitalization was particularly important because the WTO had been increasingly encroaching on the regulation of intellectual property issues, threatening to sideline WIPO completely.[86]

Another example of revitalization—tending toward reinvention—is the OAS. The OAS fits the definition of a "traditional" international organization: it is based on a treaty and composed of formal delegations from its member-governments headed by ambassadors. Its essence as an organization is the meeting and taking of decisions by these diplomatic delegations as an explicitly international, intergovernmental entity charged with the governance of security, prosperity, and development in the region.[87] It traditionally operates quite apart from domestic government officials within member-countries.

Yet the OAS has also created networks of ministerial or bureaucratic officials within the context of seven "specialized organizations," including the areas of terrorism, child development, women's issues, geography and history, indigenous rights, and agriculture.[88] The Inter-American Committee against Terrorism (CICTE), for example, is staffed by members of "competent national authorities" in this field. Its objectives are, inter alia, the exchange of information, the formulation of proposals to assist member-states in drafting antiterrorist legislation, the enhancement of border cooperation, and the development of training programs. The committee began to operate in 1999, but has been strengthened in response to the events of September 11, 2001.

Another example is the Inter-American Children's Institute (IIN), led by a "Directing Council" composed of national bureaucrats from ministries involved with child development. The directing council meets annually to develop policy and monitor implementation of its proposals. It receives input from the Pan-American Child Congress, a body composed of ministers, secretaries of state, or their delegates, which meets every four years to "promote an exchange of experience and knowledge among the peoples of the Americas" with regard to children's issues.

The remaining five organizations or commissions are modeled on a similar approach. They generally involve a "board" composed of ministerial-level representatives or senior bureaucrats who meet regularly to develop policies, pass resolutions, or adopt codes of best practices. The board is often coupled with an executive or oversight organ, and, in more complex subject areas like agriculture, a directorate that can provide technical support and implementation assistance. The key objective is to help domestic government officials do their jobs better by learning from each other and undertaking some initiatives collectively in response to global or regional challenges.

＿

IN SUM, THE PARALLEL WORLDS OF TRANSGOVERNMENTAL NETWORKS and more traditional international organizations are interconnected in many ways. Indeed, in some areas they can be said to be increasingly dependent on one another. The ability to use government networks as the working machinery of a formal international treaty or convention—as with NAFTA and its side-agreements—provides a guarantee of continuing respect for national sovereignty in the implementation of international commitments. This guarantee is likely to be politically reassuring to many domestic publics; it is also likely to keep coercive power in the hands of those officials who can use it most democratically and effectively.

In other areas national governments may bring government networks into being almost unwittingly, by passing the equivalent of unfounded mandates at the international level. The more that international commitments require the harmonization or other adjustment of domestic law, the coordination of domestic policy, or cooperation in domestic enforcement efforts, the more they will require government networks to make them work. Finally, from the other side, many government networks are likely to find that they need some more centralized organization to facilitate their own activities. These "information agencies" have no independent governing authority. But they exist in the international rather than the transgovernmental realm.

Kal Raustiala, among others, has argued persuasively that transgovernmentalism can be a complement to intergovernmentalism. He focuses on the ways in which government networks can trigger policy convergence, provide avenues of cooperation where the consensus for an international agreement does not yet exist, and build government capacity to comply with formal international obligations. These are all important consequences of government networks, as explored more fully in the next chapter. Yet as the examples above demonstrate, government networks and traditional international organizations are intertwined in many other ways.

4. CONCLUSION

We have moved in this chapter from individual examples of government networks to an actual vision of a disaggregated world order. The core of this vision is a concept of an international order in which the principal actors are not states, but parts of states; not international organizations, but parts of international organizations. Those parts, either national or supranational, that perform the same governance function—legislation, execution, adjudication—link up with one another around the world. Were we truly architects of world order, able to start from the beginning, it would seem to make sense to begin with the functions necessary for establishing world order and then creating the forms to follow. In practice, however, we are imposing an ideal type on a messy reality. To achieve a disaggregated world order based on the world that now exists requires understanding how all the myriad horizontal networks that already exist and that are likely to emerge can fit together; how vertical networks play a critical, albeit more limited role; and how the informal sector of government networks intersects with the formal sector of traditional international organizations.

The first step is to understand how horizontal networks can become networks of networks. These can be assembled ad hoc to address a specific problem or established on a long-term basis within the framework of an intergovernmental organization or association. Government networks already span every region in the globe, linking the majority of the world's countries in one way or another; from the Commonwealth to the Nordic System to APEC, from the European Union to NAFTA. Regardless of the external, differentiating shell, the principal mode of governance in all these institutions is the same in being conducted through networks of counterpart national officials.

Vertical networks are less frequent and more potent. They link national government officials with their supranational counterparts in those cases in which states acting as unitary actors have agreed to delegate part of their sovereignty to an institution operating at the global or regional level. These institutions, or at least some of the officials in them, have autonomous governing power akin, at least formally, to their national counterparts. The most prominent examples are the judges on the ECJ, the European Court of Human Rights, or the WTO Appellate Body.

These institutions, like the Pope, have no legions at their disposal. What they do have, however, at least in some cases, is the capacity to develop direct relationships with their national counterparts, who can then exercise coercive power on their behalf. Conversely, however, these national officials will defend their own turf and competences in ways that ensure a "cooperative" rather than a hierarchical vertical relationship. The net effect, where states either choose to enable the formation of these vertical networks or simply create institutional structures that facilitate them, is that government networks can either provide an informal alternative to traditional international organizations or mechanisms to make those traditional organizations more effective than ever before.

The informal sector of government networks coexists with the formal sector of traditional international organizations in a number of ways. International organizations can host government networks, in the sense that many of the governing committees in organizations like the IMF, the WTO, or the WHO are composed of national finance ministers, trade ministers, or health ministers. More recently, however, states entering into treaties and creating accompanying organizations can also create government networks directly, institutionalizing links that already exist between counterpart national officials or creating new ones by constituting entities such as the CEC of NAFTA, which is simply composed of the environmental ministers from all three NAFTA countries.

Another way that national governments can create government networks from the top down rather than the bottom up is to force or trigger their formation by undertaking international obligations that have an enormous impact domestically without providing authority or creating capacity for their implementation at the international or regional level. That is left to national officials themselves to figure out, which then requires them to work together. NAFTA and, above all, the European Union specialize in this approach.

Finally, government networks themselves can bring international organizations into being, creating "information agencies" that will facilitate and streamline their work. Many international secretariats already essentially perform this function, providing a crucial information resource for national officials and often acting as a go-between between nongovernmental institutions that collect information on the implementation and effectiveness of international obligations and the government officials responsible for implementation. Yet new information agencies are being created, this time from the bottom up as the participants in government networks figure out what they need to work better.

The result can be a different conception of international organizations themselves, as part of a changing global landscape. Imagine a global governance system principally composed of horizontal government networks of counterpart national officials, working on their own behalf or to implement formal international obligations undertaken by their national states acting in a unitary capacity. Many, if not most, of the international organizations dotting this landscape, regardless of form or title, are in substance largely facilitative "information agencies"; their job is to collect, distill, and disseminate information needed by network participants and to help the networks coordinate their work.

The networked structures described here, and the political processes within them, map a world order without world government. The inevitable question, however, is what makes such a world order hang together?[89] Without coercion, where is power? If President Jackson could say, even of John Marshall, chief justice of the United States, "he has made his decision, now let him enforce it," what hope is there for international tribunals?[90] Or secretariats? Or indeed networks? Without even the filament of legal obligation, how to tie all these structures together into fabrics of substance? How can the participants in them hope to do anything more than talk?

The next chapter examines the actual impact of government networks on the basic problems of world order—problems of peace, prosperity, and the protection of the planet. It analyzes not only what government networks can accomplish, but also the precise mechanisms by which they achieve specific results. At the same time, just as this chapter describes both the foundation of a disaggregated world order and the additional elements needed to bring it into being, chapter 5 explores both what government networks can do now and what they could do in the future, if they were self-consciously created and used as primary mechanisms of global governance.

FIVE

An Effective World Order

[T]here is a separate and critical need for programs like this one—programs devoted to the real nitty gritty of law enforcement against international cartels, where front-line enforcers can meet one another and try to solve common practical problems.
—Former Assistant Attorney General Joel Klein, commenting on an international workshop for antitrust regulators[1]

A DISAGGREGATED WORLD ORDER, IN WHICH NATIONAL GOVERNMENT institutions rather than unitary states are the primary actors, would be a networked world order, a globe covered by an increasingly dense lattice of horizontal and vertical government networks. Yet how exactly would these networks create and maintain world order? How, in short, can they help us solve the world's problems?

Recall the definition of world order put forward in the Introduction: a system of global governance that institutionalizes cooperation and contains conflict sufficiently to allow all nations and their peoples to achieve greater peace, prosperity, stewardship of the earth, and minimum standards of human dignity. Describing the structure of this order is not enough. We must understand how all these networks achieve specific outcomes, how they actually conduct the business of global governance.

I will answer these questions in two parts: what government networks are already doing to strengthen world order and what they *could* do if they were self-consciously constituted and strengthened as mechanisms of global governance. I will take as a given the point made in the Introduction and previous chapters about the ability of government networks to solve the globalization paradox (by expanding our global governance capacity without centralizing policy-making power), as well as their general virtues of speed, flexibility, inclusiveness, ability to cut across different jurisdictions, and sustained focus on a specific set of problems. These features have led a number of European scholars, most focused on the European Union, to conclude more categorically that networks are an optimal form for policymaking in general, superior either to hierarchies or markets.[2] My purpose here, however, is to catalogue the more specific ways in which government networks respond to global problems and could do so even more creatively and effectively in the future.

In both halves of the chapter, it will be useful to recall and distinguish among the three broad categories of government networks described in chapters 1–3: information networks, enforcement networks, and harmonization networks. Each can solve different problems, although in practice their activities overlap considerably. Harmonization networks contribute to world order by allowing nations to standardize their laws and regulations in areas where they have determined that it will advance their common interests in trade, environmental regulation, communications, protecting public health, or any number of other areas. (Many do not see this as an unalloyed good, to say the least, but bear with me.) Enforcement networks, again as the name suggests, contribute to world order by helping nations enforce law they have individually or collectively determined to serve the public good.

Information networks are a bit harder to peg. Scholars tend to assume automatically that more information is better, for a whole host of reasons, but in a world of information overload, that proposition is increasingly debatable. Further, politicians may be more concerned with the source of particular information—from within a particular polity, constituted by the people of a specific nation, or from abroad—as more important than the content. Model legislation, codes of best practices, even judicial decisions developed by or passed along through government networks may actually be problematic. From another perspective, how can the mere provision of information, assuming that it is indeed valuable and helpful information, actually contribute to world order? What are the precise mechanisms by which all the talking and information exchange that is the lifeblood of many government networks translate into concrete action?

A second point to bear in mind throughout the chapter is that in cataloguing actual outcomes of government network activities, I am necessarily describing the exercise of different kinds of power. Transgovernmental networks, both horizontal and vertical, establish order through a variety of different types of power. Understanding the different mechanisms of impact requires appreciating these different types of power.

Power can generally be classified as either "hard" or "soft." As defined by Joseph Nye, hard power is "command power that can be used to induce others to change their position."[3] It works through both carrots and sticks—rewards and threats. Soft power, by contrast, flows from the ability to convince others that they want what you want. It is exercised through setting agendas and holding up examples that other nations seek to follow. "It co-opts people rather than coerces them."[4] Soft power is no less "powerful" than hard power. It is simply a different kind of power.

Part of the genius of government networks is that they marry soft with hard power. The power within the networks themselves—among different national regulators or judges, or between a supranational court or parliament and a national court or parliament—is soft. Even when, as in a vertical network, the supranational entity has formal legal authority over its national counterpart, it has no actual means of enforcing the obligation. Instead, it must use everything from expertise to endearments: information, persuasion, socialization. Once convinced of a particular path of action or the wisdom of a particular result, however, the national government officials operating in both horizontal and vertical networks possess hard power to make things happen—as much hard power as they possess within their own domestic political systems.

At the same time, government networks are pioneering various forms of soft power. The power of information is particularly important in an age of information overload, when credibility becomes critical.[5] Government networks possess particular credibility through their capacity to collect, distill, and disseminate information from and to all their members on a regional or global scale. As the boundaries for information collection spread ever wider, the authority of an entity that, for example, promises a survey of multiple countries and a carefully considered code of best practices increases by the minute.

In the first section, I analyze the current impact of government networks on world order in three categories: convergence, compliance, and cooperation. In a wide variety of ways, government networks promote convergence of national laws and regulations—not simply through harmonization networks, which are expressly charged with this task, but through information networks. Kal Raustiala argues that this convergence often creates possibilities for deeper cooperation through more formal international agreements. Government networks also foster compliance with existing treaties and other international agreements, not only through vertical and horizontal enforcement networks, which, again, often exist for this express purpose, but also through information networks.

Finally, government networks can improve the quality and depth of cooperation across nations. They can increase the number of nations cooperating in any particular regime and the scope of that regime across issues. Equally important, they can improve the effectiveness of the solutions adopted in two ways. First, information networks are ideally adapted to address a whole set of national and global problems that are more amenable to regulation by information, dialogue, and collective learning than by traditional command-and-control techniques. Simply providing information to individuals and organizations permits self-knowledge, which is the heart of self-regulation. Self-regulation in a collective context means setting standards collectively and pooling information in ways that can help all participants. It is the Weight Watchers model of global governance.[6]

Second, government networks are uniquely capable of addressing the many global problems that flow from domestic sources. To the extent that problems ranging from support for terrorism to destruction of the environment result from a failure of domestic government in different ways in different countries—dictatorship, severe and systematic human rights abuses, corruption, poverty so severe it prevents the building of even a basic government infrastructure, or a lack of capacity to implement technical solutions, to name only a few—the solutions must be implemented at the level of domestic government officials. The current international system assumes that nations will come together as unitary states and agree on the solutions, then turn to their domestic political processes to figure out how to translate those solutions into actual action. Government networks, by contrast, involve those officials in formulating the solution from the beginning, and can apply pressure or offer support directly to ensure implementation.

In the second section I move from what exists, however patchily in places, to a vision of what could be. I emphasize the capacity of government networks to regulate themselves. By making reputation matter, socializing their members, and developing clear criteria for initial and continuing membership, they could develop and support the implementation of "network norms" that would strengthen the integrity and competence of all their members. Government networks could also instill habits of multilateral discussion and argument in their members to maximize their ability to formulate informed, innovative, and legitimate solutions to common problems. Third, they are likely to be sites of positive conflict, conflict that will in the long term strengthen trust and habits of compromise among network members.

Two final caveats. It is impossible to support these various claims of impact systematically. The number and range of government networks described in the first four chapters—with different members, different purposes, different geographic reach, different structure (horizontal versus vertical), and different modes of operation—mean that the best I can hope for is to generalize from clusters of examples. Other scholars and practitioners will have to test and elaborate specific claims with specific networks. Further, in this chapter I do not review the various critiques of whether in fact convergence, in particular, and to a lesser extent compliance and cooperation, enhance world order or stifle diversity in the service of hegemony; that will be adressed in chapter 6.

1. WHAT GOVERNMENT NETWORKS DO NOW

Raustiala's study of government networks among securities, antitrust, and environmental regulators leads him to conclude that networks promote regulatory export from stronger to weaker states.[7] This transfer of rules, practices, and whole institutional structures, in turn, "promotes policy convergence among states," an effect that he attributes to special characteristics of government networks and to the role of "network effects," a concept developed by economists to explain the impact of private commercial networks.[8] Raustiala also finds that networks permit cooperation that would not otherwise be possible, and that they can build capacity in weak states that allows them to comply more readily with international obligations.[9] (The process of capacity building in the regulatory context was discussed in chapter 1, and, with regard to parliaments, in chapter 3.)

I adapt these findings somewhat in the first half of this chapter. I discuss the present impact of government networks in terms of convergence, but also informed divergence of national rules, principles, and judicial decisions around the world. The second section addresses improved compliance with international agreements not only through capacity building, but also through vertical networks. The third section argues that government networks improve cooperation due not only to network effects, but also to the availability of new regulatory approaches through government networks that are particularly suitable for addressing a host of global problems.

Creating Convergence and Informed Divergence

Harmonization networks exist primarily to create compliance. Enforcement networks encourage convergence to the extent that they facilitate cooperative enforcement. Information networks promote convergence through technical assistance and training, depending on how they are created and who their most powerful members are. Indeed, some regulatory information networks have an explicit agenda of convergence on one particular regulatory model. At the same time, however, those who would export—not only regulators, but also judges—may also find themselves importing regulatory styles and techniques, as they learn from those they train. Those who are purportedly on the receiving end may also choose to continue to diverge from the model being purveyed, but do so self-consciously, with an appreciation of their own reasons.

Regulatory Export

Raustiala offers a number of examples of regulatory export in the securities, environmental, and antitrust areas. According to one securities regulator he interviewed, a prime outcome of SEC networking is the dissemination of "the 'regulatory gospel' of US securities law," including: "strict insider trading rules, mandatory registration with a governmental agency of public securities issues; a mandatory disclosure system; issuer liability regarding registration statements and offering documents; broad antifraud provisions; and government oversight of brokers, dealers, exchanges, etc."[10] This outcome is precisely what the SEC intended and hoped for when it began reaching out to foreign agencies in the early 1980s. Former SEC Commissioner Bevis Longstreth argued explicitly, "The trick will be to encourage the securities regulators of the other major trading nations to develop systems that provide protections to investors substantially similar to those provided in this country."[11]

The many MOUs that the SEC has concluded with foreign securities regulators create frameworks for cooperation and provide technical assistance that deliberately seeks to transplant features of U.S. securities regulation abroad.[12] If a foreign authority does not have sufficient power under its domestic law to replicate these features, then the SEC generally requests it to obtain legislation to enable it to do so. This practice is explicitly recommended in IOSCO's Report on Principles for Memoranda of Understanding.[13] In addition, each year the SEC hosts the International Institute for Securities Market Development and the International Institute for Securities Enforcement and Market Oversight, which train hundreds of securities regulators from around the world.[14] Not surprisingly, this training "provides grounding in the basic principles and approaches employed by the SEC."[15]

In the environmental arena, the U.S. Environmental Protection Agency has engaged in many of the same activities as the SEC, both bilaterally and through the International Network for Environmental Compliance and Enforcement (INECE), which was founded in 1997 and plays a similar role to IOSCO. The EPA offers over twenty courses for foreign regulators on a wide range of issues regarding the running of an environmental protection agency and the enforcement of international, national, and local environmental laws and regulations.[16] In Raustiala's words, "Courses such as these essentially provide a handbook—'environmental regulation in a nutshell'—that is closely tied to U.S. practice."[17] These training programs also showcase environmental technologies developed by U.S. firms, another way of fostering convergence between U.S. and foreign modes of environmental protection.[18]

The EPA founded INECE with the Dutch environmental protection agency; U.S. and Dutch environmental regulators had been working together since the mid-1980s, when the Dutch sought technical assistance from their U.S. counterparts. They jointly organized a series of conferences in the early 1990s, which were attended by scores of foreign regulators.[19] INECE now maintains a website that features training videos, sets of enforcement principles, and regular newsletters.[20] Closer to home, as discussed in chapter 1, the United States has effectively extended the network technique that it uses domestically to strengthen state and local enforcement of environmental laws to Mexico. The Southern Environmental Enforcement Network, one of four regional associations of state and federal environmental enforcement agencies that work with the EPA in building domestic enforcement capacity in the United States, has provided training courses for the new Mexican environmental protection agency (PROFEPA), which was itself modeled on the EPA.[21]

Antitrust law and policy has long been a U.S. preserve, at least in the sense that the U.S. has had stronger antitrust laws than other countries and has actively sought to enforce them extraterritorially, generally in the face of stiff opposition.[22] In recent decades the tide has begun to turn. The European Union has generally accepted and even embraced U.S. principles and modes of enforcement, although it now means that the EU commission is enforcing EU antitrust law against U.S. companies—as in the EU Commission's high-profile rejection of a proposed merger between Honeywell and General Electric.[23] Indeed, Spencer Weber Waller argued in 1997 that "the rest of the world looks to the United States as one of the most important sources of learning about competition law. Foreign legislators considering antitrust legislation often turn to the United States enforcement agencies and the American Bar for comments on the best path to choose."[24] The International Competition Policy Advisory Committee (ICPAC) to the Attorney General and Assistant Attorney General for Antitrust confirms this trend.[25]

Scholars have documented training and technical assistance programs by the Antitrust Division of the Department of Justice (DOJ) and the Federal Trade Commission (FTC) like those developed by the SEC and the EPA.[26] Of particular interest are programs under which U.S. antitrust regulators have been stationed abroad for months and even years—in countries from Poland to New Zealand. An ongoing Competition Law and Policy roundtable sponsored by the OECD has also been an important forum for sharing expertise and problem solving, as has been the annual Fordham Law School Conference on International Antitrust Law and Policy. Indeed, the ICPAC reports its hope "that the United States will be able to build on the prevailing climate favoring international antitrust enforcement cooperation by sharing its recent experiences with foreign authorities in informal fora," giving as examples the Fordham conference and the DOJ's own International Cartel Enforcement Workshop in 1999.[27]

U.S. antitrust authorities have explicitly pushed a transgovernmental network approach to global antitrust regulation as an alternative to periodic efforts by other countries to push for a multilateral treaty regulating competition policy. These efforts have repeatedly stalled, although WTO members did agree at Doha, Qatar, in 2001 to begin negotiations on a common framework for regulating competition. At the same time, a senior Bush administration official proposed the creation of an International Competition Network, a forum for countries to "formulate and develop consensus on proposals for procedural and substantive convergence in antitrust enforcement."[28] The network "provide[s] competition authorities with a specialized yet informal venue for maintaining regular contacts and addressing practical competition concerns."[29] The network's members include regulatory authorities from more than sixty-five states; its first conference was held in September 2002 in Naples, Italy and its second in June 2003 in Merida, Mexico.[30] Initial topics of discussion included "the merger review process in the multi-jurisdictional context, and the advocacy role and activities of competition authorities."[31]

The United States has historically favored the network approach precisely because it has differed substantially with many other countries, including some of its most important trading partners, on the need for and the substance of a vigorous antitrust policy, and thus has had much to lose in multilateral negotiations. Strikingly, however, existing networks are beginning to produce convergence around other models as well. The EU approach to competition policy has won out in Eastern Europe.[32] And, according to an American Bar Association Report, "[c]lusters of nations are tending to adopt one or another of the different models," citing as examples Mexican convergence toward the United States; the laws of Argentina, Brazil, Chile, Colombia, and Venezuela combining aspects of U.S. and EU law; the laws of countries across Europe converging on the EU model; and the laws of smaller Asian trading nations converging on Japanese and Korean models.[33]

What is clear from these three cases is that U.S. regulatory agencies offer technical assistance and training to their foreign counterparts to make their own jobs easier, in the sense that strong foreign authorities with compatible securities, environmental, and antitrust regimes will effectively extend the reach of U.S. regulators. It also seems clear that if foreign regulators are being trained by U.S. regulators, their practices and procedures are likely to reflect how the United States does things. What is not clear, however, is the extent to which U.S. regulators actually succeed in establishing themselves as the dominant model around which other regulators converge. Raustiala argues that the degree of convergence on any particular regulatory model in a subject area is most likely to reflect the "concentration of regulatory power"— in other words, how dominant a specific regulatory agency is in a regional or global arena.[34] The SEC is clearly the dominant securities regulator worldwide; the Antitrust Division of the DOJ is certainly a force but faces increasingly strong competition from the EU Commission; and the EPA is a relative latecomer to environmental regulation in comparison to many of its European counterparts.

Another factor that appears to affect the degree and type of convergence that occurs is the role of would-be regulatory "importers," as well as exporters. In each of the three cases discussed above, U.S. agencies were flooded with requests for training and technical assistance from countries all around the world, developing and developed.[35] Many of these countries were setting up regulatory systems from scratch and were actively looking for an effective and legitimate model. Requests for assistance from such countries may be motivated by a keen awareness of the global distribution of military and economic power, but it is also true that regulators in countries with the most powerful economies have had the most experience with domestic regulation in areas like securities and antitrust efforts and have thus had the most opportunity to develop genuine expertise. Even accepting that technocracy is rarely apolitical, a favorite point made by opponents of "technical" harmonization, it surely must be possible to build an objectively "better" mousetrap in some cases, or to develop codes of genuinely "best" practices.

Even for countries with relatively developed regulatory frameworks of their own, however, convergence to some general model through a network may pay off. Raustiala borrows from the economic theory of "network effects" to demonstrate that, as with a network of telephones or computers, each participant in a regulatory network derives greater benefits from the network as the network expands. Government networks "are characterized by extensive sharing of information, coordinating enforcement efforts, and joint policymaking activities. These activities plausibly exhibit network effects: the more regulatory agencies that participate in coordinating and reciprocating enforcement efforts, for example, the better off are all the other agencies."[36] It follows that both "powerful and weak jurisdictions" have an incentive to join regulatory networks and "engage in the export and import of regulatory frameworks."[37]

In fact, however, we still do not have good empirical evidence on the actual degree of convergence among all countries or even a group of countries in any of these areas, much less the extent to which this convergence has actually resulted from network activity. Such evidence would have to be painstakingly gathered country by country and accompanied by detailed research on the causes of any convergence found. But if technical expertise and network effects are driving a process of global regulatory convergence, then the learning that goes on through government networks should be a two-way street. Regulators from all countries should be able to recognize better approaches when they see them—just as some U.S. judges have begun to do when they encounter a foreign decision that seems to be a more sensible resolution of a particular legal issue. Conversely, they still should be able to diverge from a dominant regulatory model on the basis of a reasoned analysis as to why their nation's economic, political, or cultural circumstances differ.

Distilling and Disseminating Credible Information

Convergence through regulatory export assumes a deliberate effort to create convergence, whether successful or not. An even simpler way to understand the power of government networks in promoting convergence is through their role as distillers and disseminators of credible information in a world of information overload. Too much information translates into what Keohane and Nye call "the paradox of plenty. A plenitude of information leads to a poverty of attention."[38] The deluge of facts and opinions through phone, fax, e-mail, and the Internet, not to mention more traditional print and other media sources, is simply overwhelming. As a result, sources that can command attention gain power.

Keohane and Nye note the importance of "[e]ditors, filters, interpreters, and cue-givers," as well as "evaluators" in distilling power from the plentitude of information.[39] "Brand names and the ability to bestow an international seal of approval will become more important" in determining which sources of information are utilized.[40] In short, the ability to provide credible information and an accompanying reputation for credibility become sources of soft power. Many NGO networks establish credibility by creating a community of like-minded professionals who can frame a particular issue, create knowledge around it, and set the agenda for how to pursue it. Government networks can do the same thing.

What better source on how to run a securities system, regulate commercial banks, protect the environment, pursue different types of criminals, safeguard human rights or foster business competition than networks of government officials from around the world charged with precisely those functions? These government networks understand themselves to be in the business of collecting, distilling, and disseminating information—precisely the "editing" or "filtering" role that is such a crucial source of soft power.

The Hard Impact of Soft Law

Government networks often distill and disseminate information in a particular form that enhances its impact—as a code of best practices, model legislation, or a set of governing principles. Packaged this way, these exhortations become a version of soft law. Whereas traditional international lawmaking has come in the form of hard law—treaties and other international agreements—soft law, provided in the form of international guidance and nonlegal instruments, is emerging as an equally powerful, if not more powerful, form of regulation.

Andres Rigo, former general counsel of the World Bank, documents the extraordinary impact of the World Bank in areas including procurement policy, environmental protection, foreign investment, and international waterways.[41] In each of these cases, Rigo traces substantial harmonization or convergence among national laws, harmonization that is not part of the World Bank's official mission but that nevertheless frequently results from World Bank activity. The engine of such change is not hard law of any kind, but rather soft law in the form of principles, guidelines, codes, standards, and best practices.

Where states seek to create new legal rules and policies in the face of a dearth of local knowledge and expertise, they often seek to borrow from other states or internationally renowned experts. The World Bank is an obvious source from which to borrow. In the procurement arena, for example, the World Bank long ago developed a set of guidelines on procurement for its own internal use. Over time, it supplemented these guidelines with a set of standard bidding practices, both of which were adopted as part of every World Bank loan agreement. Bank officials built on their expertise in this area in advising UNCITRAL, the UN Commission on International Trade Law, on its model procurement law, which has subsequently served as a model for over twenty countries in drafting national legislation. Regional development banks have also followed the World Bank's procurement practices.[42] In short, through soft law a new international standard was set, which states now borrow and apply domestically.

In environmental regulation, the World Bank issued an internal operation manual in 1984 collecting all the various instructions issued by the office of environmental affairs. Although these instructions were generally geared to specific countries and situations, the manual contained a more general set of policy principles, such as prohibitions on financing projects that "cause severe or irreversible environmental deterioration, displace people, or seriously disadvantage certain vulnerable groups without mitigation measures."[43] Rigo documents the ways in which both the "requirement and the process of environmental assessments has found its way into the national legislation of many countries," again through multiple channels. Some of these channels, such as conditions attached to various projects funded by the World Bank or provisions developed by it and subsequently adopted in international conventions, are not particularly surprising.[44] In other cases, however, the World Bank's influence has been felt through simple acts, such as the publication of a handbook on pollution prevention or promulgation of a policy referring to Food and Agriculture Organization of the United Nations (FAO) guidelines on packaging, storage, and labeling of pesticides.[45] Countries seeking to implement new rules have found the implementation of such guidelines into national law to be a cost-effective means of determining and complying with international standards.

In developing these policies for its own purposes, the World Bank has been increasingly aware of the need to consult a wide range of interested groups both within countries and in international civil society. The result is a brokered set of guidelines that tend to be all the more effective as models for being more representative. In the investment context, World Bank officials surveyed bilateral investment treaties, multilateral instruments, national legislation, arbitral awards, and international law literature. They also consulted widely with "the executive directors of the World Bank, interested countries, intergovernmental organizations, business groups and international legal associations."[46] The resulting guidelines, after review by the Development Committee, were recommended to member-states of the World Bank as "acceptable international standards which complement applicable treaties."[47]

These results should not be particularly surprising. They buttress Keohane and Nye's analysis of the value of credible information. Even more valuable is a distillation and evaluation of information from many different sources, wrapped up in a neat package with an official imprimatur. Recommended rules and practices compiled by a global body of securities regulators or environmental officials offer a focal point for convergence. Equally important, they offer a kind of safe harbor for officials the world over looking for guidance and besieged with consultants, who need not only to make a choice but to be able to defend it to their superiors. In that sense, they are quite similar to the "rolling best practices" rules identified by Michael Dorf and Charles Sabel. Within a culture of democratic experimentalism, states ensure efficiency and compliance with international standards by borrowing the then-existing best practices from other states or international actors.[48]

Critics who castigate government networks for being mere "talking shops" radically underestimate the power of this kind of activity. As Rigo explains:

> The enormous increase in transnational activities as a result of global-
> ization highlights the legislative void at the international level. The ac-
> tivities described . . . respond, sometimes unconventionally, to the need
> to fill this gap. Traditional means of treaty making are too cumbersome
> for the tasks at hand and too time consuming. There may also not be
> the need for full agreement in all the details that a treaty requires, but
> simpler and more expeditious means to provide guidance may be
> sufficient.[49]

In the examples cited above, then, the World Bank provides guidance,
saves transaction costs, and offers the luxury of security. The value of
such guidance rises concomitantly with both uncertainty and complexity, circumstances likely to arise more and more frequently in a
world of complex rules and technical regulations.

The guidance that organizations such as the World Bank provide is
often informal. As Rigo's study shows, it may come "in the form of
guidelines on which to base advice, inspire legislation or future treaties
(Guidelines on Foreign Investment), or in the form of benchmarks
against which to measure existing legislation (financial standards) or of
an acceptable practice in the absence of regulatory instruments (Pollution Abatement and Prevention Handbook)."[50] Rigo himself, following
Wolfgang Reinicke, sees his examples as incipient "cross-national
structures of public interest from which global public policy is emerging."[51] The effect is as great as, or greater than, the impact of many
"harder" rules and conventions designed to provide global uniformity
by reshaping international law.

Informed Divergence

When states diverge, either in regulatory standards, legislative prohibitions, or legal doctrines, they can do so fortuitously or deliberately.
Most divergence is a function of cultural, historical, or political differences, or of simple path-dependence over time—meaning that one nation chose one kind of typewriter keyboard and another chose another
and those choices then dictated different typewriters, computers, per-

sonal desk assistants, and so forth, but divergence can also be deliberate and informed. When a nation has the option of harmonizing its rule or standard or decision to converge with other nations but *chooses not to*, it is making a statement about the uniqueness of its national tradition or the intensity of its political preferences.

It is easiest to see this phenomenon in the judicial arena. Take free speech, for instance. The United States offers more protection to freedom of speech than any other nation in its constitutional peer group. That is a historical and cultural artifact shaped over centuries by Supreme Court decisions interpreting the First Amendment and building on one another. Suppose that in attending a conference of constitutional judges from around the world, U.S. judges become aware of just how far out of line they are with prevailing doctrine in other countries. They might discover, for instance, that their fellow constitutional judges from different countries, having consulted one another's decisions, virtually all agree that hate speech constitutes an exception to a liberal constitutional right of freedom of speech and should not be permitted.

Suppose further that the next First Amendment case before the U.S. Supreme Court involves hate speech. In the Court's opinion, the justices openly discuss the prevailing trends in global constitutional jurisprudence and announce that under U.S. constitutional precedents, they have decided to continue to permit hate speech as a necessary concomitant, however deplorable, of freedom of speech. They might justify their decision on the grounds that they are U.S. judges bound by a distinct legal and political tradition. Alternatively, they might declare that the U.S. historical and cultural trajectory has been sufficiently distinct from that of other nations as to warrant a different understanding of what freedom of speech must mean. Or they might invoke the specific text of the U.S. Constitution as opposed to the texts of other constitutions.

Any of these options would be informed divergence, a deliberate decision to pursue an explicitly idiosyncratic path in the face of global trends in the other direction. It is equally possible to imagine legislators or regulators being made aware of the divergence between their laws or rules and those of a substantial number of other countries and nevertheless concluding to prize and preserve their differences on historical, cultural, political, economic, social, religious, or any other distinctive national grounds. What is critical is that the same forces pushing *toward* convergence—the forces of regulatory export, technical assistance, distilled information, and soft law—can also result in informed divergence. They permit any subset of national officials, or indeed all three branches of a national government, to decide deliberately to affirm their difference.

Improving Compliance

In addition to fostering convergence of national laws and regulations, government networks also improve compliance with international law. Indeed, vertical government networks exist essentially for that purpose, to use personal relationships to harness the power of national government institutions in the service of their counterpart supranational institutions. This approach strengthens compliance by backing enforcement efforts with genuine coercive authority—at least as much as is typically exercised by a domestic court or regulatory agency. A second way to strengthen compliance is to improve the capacity of a government to comply where the spirit is willing but the infrastructure is weak. Here the training and technical assistance provided through horizontal government networks does double-duty, not only making foreign regulators better partners for the enforcement of national laws, but also better able to comply with their own international obligations.[52]

Enforcement: Harnessing the Power of National Government Institutions

Describing and praising the G-20, Canadian Finance Minister Paul Martin writes:

> Because it brings together finance ministers and central bank governors, the G-20 closely reflects the fiscal and monetary capacities of national

governments and the realities of national economies. This provides a practical link between the objectives of international development and the national institutions that are crucial to bringing them to reality.[53]

He contrasts the G-20 with the public international financial institutions, such as the IMF and the World Bank, noting that they "remain at the heart of global economic development and stability."[54] Nevertheless,

> it is important to recognize the natural limits to what can be achieved by the international institutions acting alone. The IMF, for example, can recommend policies. It can hold out financial assistance as an incentive to get governments to accept its advice. And it can withhold its financial support if that advice is not taken. *But it is national governments that exercise the sovereign right to implement those policies, and who must answer to their populations for the consequences.*[55]

The same principle operated in the construction of the EU's legal system, although it was never overtly recognized. The ECJ was empowered to hand down decisions on European law, including decisions regarding the distribution of powers among EU institutions, between EU and national institutions, and on the rights of individuals vis-à-vis their governments in matters falling within EU jurisdiction, but the ECJ had no direct enforcement power. It was up to the national courts, which retained the de facto sovereign right to implement the ECJ's decisions.

A third example of harnessing national governmental power is the coordinated efforts of national parliamentarians to pass legislation promoting environmental protection or human rights, as discussed in chapter 3. The adoption of international conventions or the evolution of customary international law on the environment or human rights involves a two-step process of implementation. National parliaments must first ratify the conventions their executive branches have concluded. Next, they must decide whether to pass specific implementing legislation, which they often fail to do. By contrast, where transgovernmental legislative networks succeed in coordinating action, the result is a plethora of similar national laws that are automatically enforceable.

In all these examples, the key players are national government officials who exercise the same array of coercive and persuasive powers on behalf of transgovernmental decisions that they do domestically. They can coerce, cajole, fine, order, regulate, legislate, horse-trade, bully, or use whatever other methods that produce results within their political system. They are not subject to coercion at the transgovernmental level; on the contrary, they are likely to perceive themselves as choosing a specific course of action freely and deliberately. Yet having decided, for whatever reasons, to adopt a particular code of best practices, to coordinate policy in a particular way, to accept the decision of a supranational tribunal, or even simply to join what seems to be an emerging international consensus on a particular issue, they can implement that decision within the limits of their own domestic power.

Capacity Building

Building the basic capacity to govern in countries that often lack sufficient material and human resources to pass, implement, and apply laws effectively is itself an important and valuable consequence of government networks. Regulatory, judicial, and legislative networks all engage in capacity building directly, through training and technical assistance programs, and indirectly, through their provision of information, coordinated policy solutions, and moral support to their members. In effect, government networks communicate to their members everywhere the message that the Zimbabwean chief justice understood when he was under siege: "you are not alone."

Building domestic governance capacity obviously improves the prospect for compliance with domestic law. It is likely to have an equal impact on prospects for compliance with international law. Abram and Antonia Chayes have developed a "managerial theory" of compliance with international rules that locates problems of noncompliance as much in lack of capacity to comply as in lack of will.[56] They reject a "criminal law" model of international order, based on the threat of external sanctions, insisting instead that actors in the international system have a "propensity to comply."[57] The task of maximizing compliance with a given set of international rules is thus a task more of management than enforcement, ensuring that all parties know what is expected of them, that they have the capacity to comply, and that they receive the necessary assistance.

Chayes and Chayes argue that lack of capacity is a particular problem regarding compliance with complex international regulatory regimes, requiring nations not simply to refrain from certain actions—such as shooting at ships on the high seas or harming another nation's diplomats—but rather to take positive steps to cut back on the production of ozone or carbon levels, to improve health standards, to reduce tariffs or corruption or poaching. Such efforts require both administrative resources and information—precisely what many governments lack and what government networks can help to supply. Further, as Raustiala reminds us, the managerial theory assumes that "a successful compliance management process is explicitly cooperative and interactive," features that also characterize government networks.[58]

Raustiala reviews several other reigning theories of why nations do or do not comply with international law—theories about the role of transnational legal process and the legitimacy of the international norms or rules—and finds that they also predict a positive role for government networks in enhancing compliance.[59] Further, "by facilitating the export of ideas, technologies, and procedures," government networks help spread "extra-legal cooperative forces" that convince states that it is in their best interests to comply with a particular legal regime.[60] Overall, by harnessing hard power, building compliance capacity, and diffusing ideas and technologies around the world, government networks are likely to strengthen the rule of international law in ways long demanded and expected of traditional international institutions.

Enhancing Cooperation

To understand the full impact of government networks, it is necessary to understand how the information revolution is changing the nature of government at home and the problems governments face abroad.

Keohane and Nye are wise and right to warn against assuming that traditional resource-based power no longer matters; that technology has created a brave new world that will operate according to a brave new politics.[61] Nevertheless, in some very deep ways, the availability and cheapness of information is changing the way government works: the kind of power it possesses and the way it exercises that power.

Instead of deciding how individuals should behave, ordering them to behave that way, and then monitoring whether they obey, governments are learning how to provide valuable and credible information that will let individuals regulate themselves within a basic framework of standards. Giandomenico Majone, who pioneered the concept of the European Union as a "regulatory state,"[62] explains that whereas direct regulation relies on a variety of command-and-control techniques such as orders and prohibitions,[63] regulation by information attempts "to change behaviour indirectly, either by changing the structure of incentives of the different policy actors, or by supplying the same actors with suitable information."[64] Having access to credible information can change the calculations and choices that different actors make.

Regulation by information is government by soft power. By changing the information available to others, you convince them that they want what you want—the very definition of soft power. Majone agrees with Keohane and Nye, however, that the key is access to *credible* information. The core role of the state thus shifts from enforcer to provider and guarantor of the quality of the available information.

In the international arena, where government must become governance precisely because of the absence of any centralized authority to exercise command-and-control power, regulation by information is very promising. It holds out the simultaneous prospect of the effective exercise of power without hierarchy and of maximum diversity within a basic framework of uniformity. If governments can provide information to help individuals regulate themselves, then government networks can collect and share not only the information provided, but also the solutions adopted. The network provides and guarantees the quality of information, possibly through a secretariat or information agency that facilitates the collection and transmission of information along the network.

A principal reason that governments are experimenting with regulation by information domestically is their perception that problems and contexts are changing faster than centralized authorities could ever respond. They also seek to empower active citizen participation in addressing issues requiring regulation of some sort, although not necessarily formal legal rules. Cooperation across borders on a whole host of old and new issues in the coming decades will similarly have to address fast-changing circumstances and an astonishing array of contexts, as well as the need for active citizen participation in as many of the world's countries as possible. The availability of government networks will enhance the likelihood and quality of that cooperation.

Regulation by information is an idea gaining currency in many different political systems simultaneously. This section examines examples from the European Union, NAFTA, and the United Nations. The EU example involves horizontal regulatory networks and supranational information agencies; the NAFTA example illustrates a vertical network operating through the provision of information; and the UN example engages private corporations in a collective learning forum.

European Information Agencies

Within the EU, the shift from direct regulation to regulation by information is part of a "radical rethinking of the way in which norms are elaborated and applied."[65] Even the EU Commission has had to recognize that the straightforward model of regulation as "the elaboration of norms by legislators followed by their application by administrators or judges" is inadequate in the face of uncertain and complex public policy issues, particularly those involving risk regulation. The response has been what the European Union dubs "co-regulation"—the simultaneous decentralization of regulatory authority, so as to shift more power to regulators within the EU member-states, and the creation of a new generation of specialized administrative agencies at the supranational level.[66]

In the previous chapter, these agencies were discussed within the context of examples of how an international organization could help facilitate the work of government networks; that is, through provision of a structure within which networks of national officials can operate most effectively.[67] The decentralization of regulatory authority to national officials increases the need to ensure minimum uniformity among them—hence the value of a network. The network can and does emerge on an ad hoc basis, but the existence of a supranational agency charged with its coordination strengthens it immeasurably. Thus, according to the commission, the eight new agencies created at the European level between 1990 and 1997 have broadened the existing government network to include parallel networks of private actors, "with the aim of establishing a 'community of views.' "[68] Creating these broader networks has resulted in "wider ownership of the policies in question" and has thereby achieved "better compliance, even where the detailed rules are non-binding."[69]

How, then, does this activity relate to regulation by information? To ensure that the European agencies do not usurp too much power from their national counterparts, "their powers are limited and their primary role is the collection of data and the provision of information."[70] The collection and dissemination of information, in turn, is the force that animates the networks and helps ensure a degree of common understanding and uniformity of interpretation.[71]

The link back to credibility here is interesting. To be effective, the European agencies must be credible, an attribute that they can only safeguard by being as independent as possible and by pursuing a role as coordinator and honest broker among the national authorities. At the same time, the national authorities need to establish credibility as independent regulators with their publics. This means a potential three-way flow of information: among the members of a particular government network, facilitated by the information agency; from the government network upward to policymakers at the European level; and downward to interested members of national publics.[72]

The NAFTA Commission on Environmental Cooperation

To the extent that credibility is based on expertise, it is also undermined by claims of insulation and isolation from a broader public. This is the continuing conundrum of administrative law: how to assure both independent judgment and adequate consideration of legitimate political concerns. Majone and Dehousse, addressing this problem in the context of European agencies, emphasize the need to "integrate expert and social judgment throughout the regulatory process."[73] The EU Commission agrees, stressing the importance of bringing the widest possible range of stakeholders into the process, including the weak and disorganized.[74]

Crossing the ocean, NAFTA has inaugurated a novel dispute-resolution mechanism based entirely on the concept of mobilizing the public by informing them. That is the explicit charge of the Commission on Environmental Cooperation (CEC), established under the North American Agreement on Environmental Cooperation (NAAEC) (a side agreement to NAFTA).[75] Under its terms, Canada, the United States and Mexico granted private parties, including NGOs, the power to bring complaints before the CEC against one of the three states for failure to enforce its environmental laws.[76] The secretariat of the CEC decides whether the complaint is sufficiently credible to justify the preparation of a "factual record." If the secretariat decides that it is, the environmental ministers of all three states (known collectively as the "council") must vote whether to proceed.[77]

If these ministers do vote to authorize preparation of a factual record, the secretariat can not only solicit information from both the plaintiffs and the defending state concerning the charges, but can also develop the record by getting information from outside experts about the strength and nature of the allegations.[78] Neither the secretariat nor the council can actually reach a legal conclusion as to whether the defending state is failing to enforce its environmental laws; however, the council must vote whether to accept the factual record and make it public.[79] Making it public invites increased public participation in the enforcement process; the record, along with numerous supporting documents, becomes a strong weapon for NGOs to use in mobilizing domestic public opinion in favor of stronger domestic enforcement.[80]

This process is so new that it is not yet clear how well it works; many environmental NGOs seek a more traditional model of enforcement "with teeth." This preference assumes that coercive enforcement still works best, in which case a dispute-resolution model limited to providing information can only be a pale imitation of the real thing. If, however, officials increasingly regulate by information, then a key is to disseminate information to as many relevant parties as possible when disputes arise. Such information should then get fed back into the political process in ways that will change the incentives of noncompliant parties.

THE UN GLOBAL COMPACT

The European Union's shift to regulation-by-network and by information and the NAAEC's dispute-resolution process still operate on a static model. Both still assume that the information that is actually provided through an EU agency or the CEC Secretariat is collected at one point by a disinterested party and then provided to interested parties at a second point. This model does not allow for the possibility that the regulated parties themselves may be the most valuable source of information and that the most valuable information will continue to change in the face of changing problems and experimental solutions.[81]

The EU Commission alludes to this possibility by identifying several key issues to take into account in designing and reforming institutional arrangements: First is "the importance of reflexivity or the ongoing questioning of assumptions, assessments of risks, etc."[82] Second is "the need to achieve a contextualised approach to the regulatory process."[83] And third is "the utility of a vision of the regulatory process as a process of collective learning."[84] As an EU White Paper explains, "structured and open [information] networks should form a scientific referee-system to support EU policy making."[85] Such networks of information are flexible and responsive to changing conditions. Even so, it is the commission itself that is to publish the information provided by these networks.

The concept of regulation as a highly flexible process of collective learning through dialogue is precisely what animates the United Nation's new effort to improve corporate behavior around the world through partnership with UN agencies and officials. The Global Compact brings companies together with UN organizations, international labor organizations, NGOs, and other parties to foster partnerships and to build "a more inclusive and equitable global marketplace."[86] It aims, in the words of Secretary General Kofi Annan, to contribute to the emergence of "'shared values and principles, which give a human face to the global market.'"[87]

Surprisingly, however, the Global Compact does not attempt to set forth a code of conduct and to monitor corporate compliance. On the contrary, the compact itself is not an agreement to comply with anything, but rather to supply information. According to one of the Global Compact's chief architects, "The core of its change model is a learning forum. Companies submit case studies of what they have done to translate their commitment to the GC principles into concrete corporate practices. This occasions a dialogue among GC participants from all sectors—the UN, labor and civil society organizations."[88]

The dialogue, in turn, is supposed to generate "broader, consensus-based definitions of what constitutes good practices than any of the parties could achieve through unilateral declarations."[89] The practices identified, along with illustrative case studies, are then made available both to members of the Global Compact and to the broader public through an "on-line learning bank."[90]

If it works as designed, the Global Compact will be a model of collective learning in action. "The hope and expectation is that through the power of dialogue, transparency, advocacy and competition good practices will help drive out bad ones."[91] The deep assumption here is that the simple provision of information will trigger a powerfully dynamic process. This is governance by dialogue. Posting information will invite a response, either from another corporation or from an NGO; the original speaker may then seek to justify itself, opening itself to persuasion by seeking to persuade; the effort by multiple speakers to demonstrate the relative value of their particular practices will then produce healthy competition and beneficial new ideas.

This model once again assumes that some practices are in fact better than others in terms of trying both to make a profit and live up to collectively shared goals and values. The idea of actually learning rests on a belief that these often conflicting objectives can be reconciled in innovative ways when backed by a sincere commitment to try. Other underlying assumptions are hackneyed but true: that multiple minds are better than one and that experience is the best teacher. Based on these beliefs and assumptions, the hope is that providing information and subjecting it to debate, deliberation, and dialogue will yield valuable lessons and new solutions.

Finally, the concept of a "learning forum" abolishes hierarchy in the learning process. It is the antithesis of the notion of experts handing down their carefully acquired and husbanded knowledge to a mass audience and thus moves beyond the EU model. Each participant in the process bears equal responsibility for teaching and learning. Within the Global Compact, the United Nations has retained a university center to "facilitate" the debate, but not actually to teach or regulate the content and flow of information. The facilitators will at most distill the lessons generated by the participants.

If this entire process is understood as a substitute for traditional command-and-control regulation, then what is most striking is the apparent disappearance or dispersal of governmental authority. Government does not lay down rules or monitor their enforcement; it neither teaches nor learns. What it does is bring the network into being, constructing and animating a forum for dialogue and collective learning. Then it steps back and lets the process run.

⟶

IN ALL THESE CASES — INFORMATION AGENCIES, EMPOWERING POLITICAL pressure groups by informing them, a learning forum—regulation through information establishes a very different relationship between the regulator and the regulated, one less of command than of facilitation. Through, for example, "benchmarking" and "rolling–best practices rulemaking," regulators can create "the infrastructure of decentralized learning."[92] Dorf and Sabel argue that benchmarking "leads to the discovery of unsuspected goals and indicates the guiding principles and related kinds of means for obtaining them."[93]

Best practices are never static; they are instead subject to constant improvement through experimentation. The mode of analysis here is deeply pragmatic, meaning a complete acceptance of the "pervasiveness of unintended consequences" and "the impossibility of defining first principles that survive the effort to realize them."[94] In layman's language, we learn through doing and communicate the lessons we've learned on a rolling basis. We must plunge into a fast-changing information environment and recognize an ongoing dialectic between collective uncertainty and collective experience. In the end, we must rely on our own dynamic capacity for learning and self-improvement.

Individuals can organize themselves in multiple networks or even communities to solve problems for themselves and for the larger society. These networks or problem-solving groups are not directly connected to the "government" or the "state," but they can nevertheless compile and accumulate knowledge, develop their problem-solving capacity, and work out norms to regulate their behavior. The importance of this activity is increasing, precisely because the traditional separation between the formulation and application of rules is being dissolved by technology, a development that is in turn undermining "a shared common knowledge basis of practical experience."[95] Instead, public and private actors are coming together to develop new ways of "decision-making under conditions of complexity."[96]

Participants in these multiple, parallel networks, both domestic and transnational, face a continuous stream of problems and require a continuous stream of knowledge both about each other and about their counterparts in other networks. They are in "permanent, polyarchic dis-equilibrium," which they are seeking to overcome through solving problems and pooling information.[97] The state's function is to manage these processes, rather than to regulate behavior directly. It must help empower individuals to solve their own problems within their own structures, to facilitate and enrich direct deliberative dialogue. It must also devise norms and enforcement mechanisms for assuring the widest possible participation within each network, consistent with its effectiveness.[98]

Taken together, these ideas add up to a new conception of democracy, of what self-government actually means. It is a horizontal conception of government, resting on the empirical fact of mushrooming private governance regimes in which individuals, groups, and corporate entities in domestic and transnational society generate the rules, norms, and principles they are prepared to live by. It is a conception in which uncertainty and unintended consequences are facts of life, facts that individuals can face without relying on a higher authority. They have the necessary resources within themselves and with each other. They only need to be empowered to draw on them.

2. WHAT GOVERNMENT NETWORKS COULD DO

In this part I turn to the world of what could be and imagine a brave new world, or at least the hope of one. Suppose that heads of state, prime ministers, regulators, judges, legislators, pundits, and scholars everywhere embraced the concept of government networks as prescription rather than description and sought actively to create and use them as instruments of global governance. Suppose that the participants in existing and new networks were much more self-conscious about their role in the larger architecture of world order.

In such a world, government networks would not only produce convergence and informed divergence, improve compliance with international rules, and enhance international cooperation through regulation by information. They would also regulate themselves in ways that would deliberately improve the governing performance of both actual and potential members; create forums for multilateral discussion and argument by all their members; and create opportunities to harness the positive rather than the negative power of conflict.

Inducing and Enforcing Compliance with Network Norms

One of the most promising dimensions of government networks is their capacity for self-regulation and for socialization and support of their members. They exist currently to help their members—regulators, judges, and legislators—by providing access to needed information and exposure to new ideas, facilitating cooperation in enforcement and dispute-resolution, and providing a forum for harmonization of law and regulations. They could, however, become far more effective at regulating themselves, developing "network norms" designed to strengthen domestic governance capacity and competence. In particular, they could do much more to instill and champion norms of honesty, integrity, independence, and responsiveness and to bolster those members who face domestic resistance in enforcing those norms.

A Propensity for Self-Regulation

Government networks have specific properties that are highly conducive to self-regulation. First, they are conduits for information, not only about regulating, judging, and legislating, but about the individual regulators, judges, and legislators who make up their membership. That means, as discussed in chapter 1, that they can be "bearers of reputation"—they can broadcast accounts of a particular member's actions and create a context in which it matters. Majone argues that the credibility of each member of a network is enhanced because each member must safeguard its reputation within the network and it can only do so by adhering to common norms. Outside observers understand how these pressures to conform act as safeguards and hence will accord the network participant greater legitimacy.[99]

Similarly, Amitai Aviram has identified a set of features of private networks—of corporations and individual merchants—that make reputation matter.[100] Other members of a network will know whether a particular member has defaulted on its commitments; they can choose to switch their business to another network member; the defaulting member can be sanctioned by a central "control mechanism"; and in extreme cases the defaulting member can be excluded from the network.[101] To some extent, these features depend on the anonymity of markets—a buyer can switch to another seller as long as the same goods are on offer; a seller can switch to another buyer as long as the money is good. Further, exclusion from a commercial network means being denied an economic opportunity.

In government networks, by contrast, although network members will quickly come to learn of one another's reputation for competence and trustworthiness, a bad reputation carries social and professional opprobrium rather than any direct sanction. It is not clear, at least in information and harmonization networks, how one member would "switch its business" to a member with a better reputation. In enforcement networks, it might be possible for a government official from one country to decide not to cooperate in enforcement efforts with officials from another country due to their bad reputation, but often it is countries with corrupt or ineffective governments that most need bolstering to make global enforcement efforts credible.

On the other hand, as with a private network, it might well be possible for network members to decide to block access to important information collected by the network to members caught violating network norms. Further, to the extent collaborating on common problems and developing codes of best practices is done through committees composed of a subset of network members, a good reputation can be an important criterion for selection to serve on these committees. And if a central "control mechanism" exists, like an information agency, it could suspend service to some members for breaking network rules.

But what would those rules be? How can government networks regulate themselves in ways that will strengthen world order? They can constitute themselves not only as networks devoted to specific substantive activities, but also, and simultaneously, as professional associations of regulators, judges, legislators, and even heads of state and ministers dedicated to upholding the norms and ideals of their profession. They can cultivate the concept of governance as a profession, exercised through legislation, regulation, enforcement, provision of services, and dispute resolution. Like a bar association for lawyers or a medical association for doctors, a network of judges or legislators or regulators will provide both a focus of substantive learning and information exchange and a source of education in, and enforcement of, professional ethics.

It is not hard to imagine some general professional norms that government networks could inculcate in their members. Honesty, for instance. They could pledge adherence to agreed international standards of clean government, such as those set forth in the OECD Anti-Bribery Convention, which has now been signed and ratified by thirty-five countries.[102] They could agree to ongoing monitoring by NGOs such as Transparency International. A second general norm could be equal treatment of all citizens, regardless of family connections or social status. A third could be a concept of professional integrity that would require of judges and regulators a degree of independence from the political process and of legislators independence from electoral machines.

These are general ideals of public service in virtually all countries; each branch of government would also develop more specific professional standards tailored to the profession of judging, legislating, and regulating different subjects, from securities to the environment. Indeed, in some cases such standards already exist, such as the UN Basic Principles on the Independence of the Judiciary and the UN Basic Principles on the Role of Lawyers, and are monitored by the International Commission of Jurists.[103] Individual government networks could promulgate these norms as standards for the profession and ensure that a reputation either for upholding them, on the one hand, or violating them, on the other, would have genuine consequences, either in terms of denial of membership benefits or loss of standing in network affairs. Better still, as discussed in the next section, network members could work to ingrain these standards in all their members through a general process of professional socialization.

Socialization

Socialization is a complex and varied phenomenon, rich enough to merit its own discipline of sociology. But for our purposes a layman's definition will do. A socialized individual may want something intensely, but will not seek it if doing so would contravene prevailing social norms and result in social opprobrium. Alternatively, socialization may be so strong that it directly conditions an individual's interests and identity. In such cases, however, its effect will more likely be unconscious.[104]

Socialization can operate within government networks in a number of ways.[105] One of the most interesting is the phenomenon of inducing compliance with collectively generated rules through small, close-knit groups.[106] Many legal scholars have identified this phenomenon in the domestic context—most notably Robert Ellickson in *Order Without Law*.[107] Sheep farmers, diamond merchants, and sumo wrestlers are all able to establish and enforce a collective set of norms outside any formal legal framework.[108]

Mancur Olson identified the logic of this phenomenon as part of the logic of collective action. Small groups are particularly well suited to overcoming the problems of collective action because the benefits of providing collective goods are likely to exceed the costs and because they can use "social pressure and social incentives" to induce compliance with whatever norms they adopt.[109] Any member of a garden club, a charity committee, or a gang can testify to the power of these forces. Such incentives, in turn, are most powerful when they are *selective*—when "the recalcitrant individual can be ostracized, and the cooperative individual can be invited into the center of the charmed circle."[110]

These types of incentives operate primarily in groups small enough that the members can know each other personally and have face-to-face contact.[111] They are even stronger when the groups are relatively homogeneous in terms of values.[112] Ellickson focuses less on the size of the group than the degree of cohesion, predicting for "close-knit groups" greater norm-compliance and ability to act for the maximum benefit of the group as a whole.[113] The members of these groups may be acting simply out of self-interest, wanting to be a member of the group and fearing expulsion for deviation as well as expecting praise for compliance. Alternatively, as predicted by mainstream socialization theory, members may internalize group norms.[114]

"Many international government networks have the descriptive characteristics identified as key to group solidarity: repeated, frequent interaction; shared values; small size; and opportunities for informal sanctions or rewards."[115] They thus have the potential, in Timothy Wu's phrase, to create "order without international law."[116] Many members of networks who reflect self-consciously on their meetings with fellow government officials across borders emphasize the importance of personal relationships, the building of trust and a sense of common enterprise, as well as the awareness of each other's activities and the value of regular meetings.

The Basel Committee, most obviously, operates this way, deliberately keeping its membership small and selective. The central bankers who created it specified that members could send no more than two representatives each—a central banker with responsibilities for foreign exchange and another appropriate banking supervisor.[117] They have highly homogeneous beliefs about the need for stability in the world banking system and how to maintain it. They meet four times a year in Basel. They have no means of actually making their agreements binding other than mutual monitoring and peer pressure, which they exert freely.[118]

Other networks are either small enough to operate this way or contain subgroups within them. IOSCO, for instance, has open membership. Yet it makes key decisions through the President's Committee and the Executive Committee, consisting of only nineteen members.[119] On the other hand, the Basel Committee, while tightly restricting full membership, invites nonmember central bankers from other countries to participate in collective deliberations through larger biannual conferences and ongoing contacts.[120] Groups like the G-20, which has ranged from 22 to 34 members before cutting back to 20, are also small enough to socialize their members if they meet on a regular and structured basis.

Selective Membership

Commercial networks and small groups both rely on the power of exclusion as a way of enforcing compliance with their self-generated norms. Aviram points out that "exclusion from a network may result in exclusion from the entire line of business; this is a very powerful sanction, rivaling the government's in effectiveness."[121] He notes further, however, that suspension may be even more effective than exclusion, as it avoids a situation in which the party to be excluded concludes that it has nothing left to lose.[122] Similarly, the literature on socialization through small groups, as just noted, emphasizes the value of selectivity, allowing a defaulting member to be "ostracized."

Exclusion and even suspension of this type is likely to be less effective in government networks, for the simple reason that representatives of different countries are reluctant actually to censure one another. Examples of this phenomenon in traditional international institutions are legion; it is precisely the reason that it is so hard to mobilize an international institution to condemn a member's actions. Principles of sovereign respect, live and let live, and reciprocity, meaning fear of retaliation, all militate against censure and sanction. States have hesitated even to sue one other in an international legal forum expressly established to hear and resolve inter-state disputes.[123] Part of the point of government networks is to move away from the formalities and courtesies of traditional diplomacy and toward recognition of common professional interests and standards. Even so, it is hard to imagine a group of regulators, judges, or legislators blithely expelling one of their members for corruption or bias or simple incompetence.

A more promising strategy is to recognize that government networks can be sources of status for their members, which means that potential members can be induced to regulate their behavior by the prospect of inclusion. The power to control admission to membership in any particular regime or "club" is a powerful weapon. States that would join the European Union, for instance, face a long list of demands, including specific types of market regulation, or deregulation, and systems of safeguards for human rights, including the protection of ethnic minorities. The OECD, NATO, the Council of Europe, the OAU, and the OAS all impose increasingly stiff membership requirements. Even the Commonwealth stipulated that Cameroon must meet certain human rights benchmarks as a condition of membership, as "admission to the commonwealth" constitutes a form of "implicit endorsement" of the government.[124]

Indeed, Abram and Antonia Chayes argue that governments actively seek to join international regulatory regimes that impose real constraints on their freedom of action as an indication of status. To maintain this status, governments will work hard to remain members in good standing.[125] The international regulatory regimes that Chayes and Chayes describe are formal, treaty-based regimes composed of unitary states. Nevertheless, the logic of their argument applies even more forcefully to individual government officials, who are likely to be the direct recipients of the benefit conferred.[126]

Consider the following examples. The current G-20 started as the

G-22, quickly expanded to the G-33 due to the insistence of a number of countries that their ministers be included, and was finally cut back to the G-20.[127] Russia fought to be included in the G-7, making it the G-8, although finance ministers still meet as the G-7 alongside formal G-8 meetings.[128] It appears that the general desire for national prestige is driving inclusion of specific ministers in these groups, but the desire of individual ministers to be included could also lead them to pressure their governments. And in either case, if one of the conditions of membership was evidence that the prospective member his or herself—regulator, judge, or legislator—met specified standards of behavior, the individual would have a strong incentive to meet these standards and the government as a whole would have an incentive to help, or at least not to hinder.

In other networks the current system is effectively automatic admission followed by exhortation to comply with network norms. The Organization of Supreme Courts of the Americas strongly endorses norms of judicial independence among its members. The Commonwealth Magistrates and Judges Association does the same, providing its members with moral support and examples of the professional norms they collectively espouse. In an effort to support judicial independence throughout the Commonwealth, particularly in the face of executive interference in some member-states, the association has issued the Latimer House Guidelines for the Commonwealth on Parliamentary Supremacy and Judicial Independence.[129] Lord Howell also argues that the Commonwealth spreads practices of good governance by power of example.[130] Unfortunately, as any parent knows, it's not so easy.

Again, however, suppose that to gain admission a country's legislators, regulators, or judges had to meet specified criteria and that if they could not immediately, they would become candidate members for a period of time, similar to EU candidate members or NATO's partners for peace. Other network members could serve as both trainers and monitors, bolstering individual government officials in the performance of their jobs. Even the presence of network members could help in certain circumstances: Justice Richard Goldstone recounts that South African judges under apartheid were more inclined to assert their independence from the government in the presence at their trials of judicial observers from the American Bar Association.[131]

Further, if countries had to jump through these hoops to gain admission for their officials to these networks, they might also be more inclined to respect the obligation then incumbent on those officials to live up to network norms while members. Networks could also develop a disciplinary system providing for suspension of membership for severe and demonstrable infractions. Such a system would only have impact, however, if the value of membership, through status as much as services provided, were already clear.

A major advantage of inducing compliance with norms of good governance through selective admission and discipline of individuals members of government networks is the ability to target specific government institutions either for reform or reinforcement, regardless of how their fellow government institutions are behaving. This exercise of such targeted power holds the possibility of helping transitional states stabilize and democratize by offering inducements and applying pressure to some of their institutions, such as particular regulatory agencies or the executive, while bolstering others, like the courts. It avoids the pernicious problem of labeling an entire state "liberal," or "illiberal," or "democratic," or "undemocratic," or even "rogue" or "pariah." Many citizens comprise a state, and many institutions a government. All desire inclusion and dislike exclusion, and each can be individually subject to this power as circumstances warrant.

Generating Reasoned Solutions to Complex Problems

Government networks that are self-consciously constituted as mechanisms of global governance can inculcate habits of discussion as part of a collective decision-making process. Networks that enforce network norms through the mechanisms just discussed will create favorable conditions for the emergence of a reasoned consensus on many problems. This process will produce better-quality decisions than are likely to result from interest-based bargaining, adherence to prevailing political, economic, or social norms, or acquiescence to the will of the most powerful state or states.

James Fearon argues that any group of people can have at least six reasons to want "to discuss matters before making a collective decision."[132] To paraphrase his account, discussion in a group decision-making context can allow everyone involved: (1) to make a decision based on more information both about one another's preferences and about the likely consequences of different decisions; (2) to pool their brainpower and think their way through a problem and brainstorm solutions that no one member of the group could do on her own; (3) to ensure that all of the solutions on the table satisfy basic criteria of public over private interest;[133] (4) to get members of the group to "buy in" to the solution ultimately adopted; (5) to spur the public engagement and hence civic virtues of group members; and (6) to engage each individual's inherent human ability "to compare and assess different reasons" for action,[134] which itself will make the decision taken more legitimate.[135]

Fearon does not claim that these outcomes will result from every discussion. On the contrary, he is careful to identify a number of underlying conditions. For instance, members of a group are only likely to reveal private information about their own preferences in a discussion when they perceive themselves to have largely convergent or at least nonconflicting interests.[136] And group discussion is only likely to overcome the "bounded rationality" of any one individual if the problem on the table is sufficiently complex that pooling both knowledge and creativity is likely to result in a better solution. Similarly, the claim that discussion can result in more public-spirited solutions than would otherwise obtain assumes that "the people in question have the motivation, or can be motivated, not to appear selfish or self-interested."[137] Finally, the claim that discussion will help legitimate the decision ultimately taken depends on two assumptions: that consensus is more likely to emerge than dissensus, on average, and that the overall culture or context is one "where people associate fair procedure with having the opportunity to have their say."[138]

If we assume that government networks are constituted as professional associations, where the profession involved is judging or legislating or making and implementing regulations; that their members subscribe to basic standards of professional competence and ethics; and officials who do not measure up to these standards are not admitted, then the conditions specified for fruitful discussion should obtain. To begin with, we can assume that members' interests are convergent enough that they will reveal their actual preferences, as well as share information about the background or consequences of various decision options on the table. We can also assume that they come together to grapple with extremely complex problems.

Further, a common core of professionalism should motivate members of government networks not to appear overtly selfish or self-interested in front of their professional peers. Imagine, for instance, the Supreme Court justices of the United States and the judges of the European Court of Justice meeting to discuss a problem of transatlantic judicial comity. It is difficult to imagine judges on either side saying, in Fearon's words, " 'We don't care what anyone else gets; we just want more for ourselves.' "[139] Finally, although the participants in government networks come from many different cultures with many different assumptions about the sources of legitimacy, it is not unreasonable to assume that where the basis of their association is public governance, fair procedure must include an opportunity to be heard.

If Fearon favors discussion, German social scientist Thomas Risse recommends argument. "Let's Argue!" is the title of an article in which he makes the case for argument as a mode of "truth-seeking" that permits actors in the international realm, as in domestic affairs, to achieve desired outcomes through "communicative action."[140] Instead of a lowest–common denominator solution, in which all parties calculate their interests and how best to pursue them in a particular negotiation, or a norm-driven outcome, in which all parties figure out what is appropriate behavior given the rules or norms governing a particular context, deliberation and argument hold open the possibility that one or more parties will be persuaded to define their interests differently or to pursue them differently based on new information, new ideas, and new points of view.[141]

Imagine a group of teenagers in which the oldest and the most sophisticated member of the group lights up a cigarette and offers her pack around to other members. If the other teenagers are "rational calculators" following a "logic of consequentialism," then each one should calculate whether the future risk of dying is greater than the present benefit of looking cool.[142] If the other teenagers are socialized actors following a "logic of appropriateness," which way they decide should depend on prevailing social norms—whether ads featuring famous models with cigarettes in their ears have turned the tide against Joe Camel.[143] Yet according to Risse, if the teenagers are "reasoners," they will pursue a "logic of arguing,"[144] whereby they will seek "a mutual understanding based on reasoned consensus."[145] They will collectively discuss what each member of the group knows about the long-term risks of smoking, perhaps including examples of relatives or friends who have died of cancer; they will invoke celebrity role models who do and who do not smoke; they will argue about what they think is and is not cool.

The debate may be heated, with different members expressing strongly conflicting views, but the outcome, in this model, should reflect the side of the argument that ultimately has the most reasons in its favor. Thus, on the side of smoking, some famous people still smoke and some people still think it is cool. On the side against, smoking causes cancer; many famous people do not smoke; it is smelly and dirty and dumb-looking. The reasoned consensus? Don't smoke.

Risse recognizes that "[n]on-hierarchical and networklike international institutions characterized by a high density of informal interactions" are most likely to produce a reasoned consensus.[146] Equally important are situations in which participants in these networks are uncertain of their interests or relatively ignorant about the problems they face.[147] Recall the constitutional judges exchanging decisions and debating different approaches to human rights problems that they all face in various forms, or the finance ministers trying to develop a code of core principles to guide the reconstruction of shattered national financial systems in the wake of the East Asian financial crisis of 1998, or the environmental regulators in INECE seeking to find common policies to address communal environmental problems.[148] These are all settings in which both discussion and argument are likely to elicit information, proposed solutions, and contending justifications that will help produce a reasoned and legitimate consensus.

These are also settings in which differences of material power are minimized.[149] The idealized version of this world is one in which the "better argument" prevails, regardless of who makes it. In reality, such an ideal is elusive, to say the least. Differences of power almost always matter at some level. Nevertheless, just as the Canadian and the South African constitutional courts have proved more influential than the U.S. Supreme Court on many human rights issues, officials searching for solutions may be less concerned with the source of an argument than with the merits of the argument itself.

Traditionally powerful actors may find themselves surprised and even entrapped by this dynamic. They may start out intending to use rhetoric, to persuade others to follow their desired course while remaining impervious to changing their own minds. Yet elementary psychology teaches that those who would persuade others of their views are likely to be most effective when they appear equally willing to be persuaded of their listeners' positions. Adopting such a psychological posture, even if intended as a ruse, is likely to open both minds and ears.

Risse provides a number of examples from the human rights arena in which powerful government officials seeking to deny human rights abuses have gradually shifted positions through extensive dialogue with human rights NGOs, in which declared acceptance of human rights norms has gradually become real acceptance.[150] The same dynamic is likely to operate regarding the acceptance of professional norms in a variety of government networks.

For scholars such as Lani Guinier, the potential for such a two-way exchange is the essence of "power with" rather than "power over"; a model of power that holds enormous potential for creative synergies and growth.[151] From "power over" to "power with" is precisely the transformation from hierarchy to network, from hard power to soft power. Guinier's ideal is that in wrestling to solve common problems, parties do not have to find solutions that rest on preexisting distributions of power, but can find answers that give new powers to all of them.

A final important dimension of this kind of power is its dynamism. Harking back to the concept of embracing uncertainty by continually experimenting and assessing the results, it becomes apparent that the very tentativeness and informality of "rolling codes of best practices" enhance their persuasiveness. Results are rarely fixed for long; they are instead presented and debated as the latest best answer. A network of policymakers or regulators or judges thus becomes a rolling forum for "communicative action," generating ideas and prototypes that persuade only until a better one comes along.

So what does all this mean for world order? Government networks that encourage and even require multilateral discussion prior to all decisions taken are likely to produce more creative, more reasoned, and more legitimate solutions to many of the problems that members face. Many problems will not be suitable for resolution in these forums: problems involving vital national security interests, for instance, or touching on issues of high domestic political sensitivity. Others will, however: problems ranging from how best to balance the competing constitutional demands of liberty and order; of how best to regulate online sales of securities over the Internet; of how to mesh antiterrorism legislation to minimize loopholes but maximize national autonomy, among others. In many of these cases, no one solution may prove "the best" for all nations involved, but a set of preferred possibilities can likely be identified. And even in those cases where contending interests are too strong to allow a reasoned outcome, present conflict can be transformed into the stuff of future compromise.

Harnessing the Positive Power of Conflict

Within government networks, conflict—meaning the nonforcible clash of interests—need not be a source of separation or a struggle for lasting and definite dominance. Rather, it can be an engine of increased trust and ultimately cooperation. It is positive conflict. To say it is positive does not mean that it is pretty or pleasant; it is still conflict. Yet in government networks that are self-consciously constituted as mechanisms of global governance, that induce and enforce compliance with norms of good governance particular to the network through socialization and selective membership, and that impose requirements of collective discussion as part of decision-making processes, the effects of conflict can be positive over the long term, helping to strengthen the networks themselves as structures of world order.

The very notion of positive conflict may seem an oxymoron, but conflict in many domestic societies is seen as the motor of positive change, as the engine of economic growth in the form of competition, and as the lifeblood of politics. Conflict in the international arena, by contrast, is worrisome because of the possibility, however distant, that it could escalate into military conflict and the perception that, on a zero-sum world, conflict will reduce overall welfare. Conflict between states has thus traditionally been a problem to be avoided, mitigated, and solved.

Here, then, is the paradox. Writing about "social conflicts as pillars of democratic market societies," Albert Hirschman underlines a point made by the German sociologist Helmut Dubiel: "social conflicts themselves produce the valuable ties that hold modern democratic societies together and lend them the strength and cohesion they need."[152] Hirschman reviews the long intellectual history of this idea, arguing that, due to its paradoxical power, it is "reinvented with considerable regularity" in literatures ranging from political philosophy to development studies.[153]

The same point can also be made closer to home. Quarrels among family members are often sharper than disputes among friends, precisely because the depth of the relationship, and thus the diminished likelihood of serious consequences, is taken for granted. The same paradox arises. Conflict can be most intense between individuals who are closest to one another and who have myriad ties to cushion the blows, as well as between those who are furthest apart and have no other affiliating ties or even a guarantee that they will see one another again. It is in the center of the distribution, among those who have only some ties, that actors will most likely seek to avoid conflict and its untempered dangers.

If conflict can be positive, however, it can also obviously still be deeply negative. It can destroy social and political relationships as well as deepen and improve them. Thus the task, as Hirschman presents it, is to move beyond identification of the phenomenon of positive conflict to an understanding of the conditions under which conflict is more likely to act as a "glue [rather than] a solvent."[154] He claims that learning to "muddle through" a "steady diet" of conflicts in "pluralist market societies" is more likely to be productive.[155] The conflicts typical of these societies, in his view, have three basic characteristics:

- They occur with considerable frequency and take on a great variety of shapes.
- They are predominantly of the divisible type and therefore lend themselves to compromise and to the art of bargaining.
- As a result of these two features, the compromises reached never give rise to the idea or the illusion that they represent definitive solutions.[156]

Conflicts of the "divisible type" refer to conflicts that are essentially distributive, "conflicts over getting more or less" of something, as opposed to nondivisible "either/or" conflicts "that are characteristic of societies split among rival ethnic, linguistic, or religious lines."[157]

The types of conflicts observable within government networks generally seem to fit the "divisible" description. Consider, for instance, the various conflicts described in chapter 2 among national courts and between national courts and supranational courts. National courts from different countries frequently quarrel over which court should have jurisdiction over a transnational dispute, or which law should apply. Frequently the solution is to allow both courts to proceed with litigation of some or all of the issues in dispute and to allow the litigants to race to judgment. Alternatively, in relations between European national courts and the ECJ, the balance of power is constantly shifting depending on which side is more assertive over a period of time or a series of cases. In both contexts the relationship is best described as an ongoing tug of war rather than a search for definitive solutions.

In the regulatory arena, to take one prominent example, conflict between U.S. and EU regulators often makes headlines. The fight over approval of a proposed merger between Honeywell and General Electric, granted in the United States and then denied by the EU Commission, put antitrust regulators at direct loggerheads. Yet as the *New York Times* pointed out in an editorial on the case, the prominence of the conflict should not be allowed to obscure the remarkable "record of co-operative relationship[s] on regulation" between European Union and United States antitrust regulators.[158] And in none of these areas, even where cooperation is spottier with fewer tangible results, does conflict suggest a broader rupture of relations.

Such empirical examples are anecdotal, though numerous. More systematic research is required, but we should expect to find empirical confirmation of the predominance of positive conflict in government networks precisely because of the preconditions that make such networks work in the first place. As discussed in chapter 1, network relations depend on "reputation, trust, reciprocity and mutual interdependence."[159] Positive conflict can be understood as the corollary of these characteristics. Trust, interdependence, and reciprocity do not guarantee harmony, defined as an absence of conflict, but they do facilitate cooperation, which means resolving conflict in a positive way.[160] Mutual adjustment does not happen spontaneously; it is a result of conflict. It follows that in a form of governance, networks, that depends on these characteristics, it is reasonable to assume that all conflict is positive conflict.

Yet what in fact does it *mean* to treat conflict as positive? How do we actually understand conflict as a force for cohesion rather than disruption, at least over the long term? Here it is helpful to draw on insights from the legal process school in American law.[161] An emphasis on legal process, rather than the decisions and rules generated by that process, sees law as a tool more for managing conflict than resolving it.

Projecting some of the precepts of the legal process school into the international arena, Abram and Antonia Chayes depict compliance with international regulatory agreements as a process of "managing" the problems that face countries seeking to comply with their obligations against various odds.[162] Yet if law successfully manages conflicts, then repeated conflicts should actually strengthen the legal order. The process of managing each conflict will build strong transnational relationships, which in turn will generate the principles that ripen into law.[163]

This next step is captured by Robert Cover's concept of a "jurisgenerative process."[164] The procedures and substantive principles developed over the course of repeated conflicts among the same or successive actors take on precedential weight, both through learning processes and the pragmatic necessity of building on experience. As they become increasingly refined, these procedures and principles are increasingly likely to be codified in informal and increasingly formal ways. Indeed, Harold Koh captures many of these features in his concept of transnational legal process, although he does not specify the underlying conditions that make it work.[165]

A final dimension of positive conflict within transgovernmental networks is the power of conflict to generate information. A frequent source of conflict between regulatory officials from different countries is a failure to understand or to appreciate sufficiently the political constraints under which all regulators must operate. Thus, for instance, in the fights between the European Union and the United States over issues such as the importation of bananas or hormone-treated beef, the trade officials on the frontlines of the conflict are likely often to be in agreements about the applicable legal rules or the optimal course of action. Their views are, however, quite likely to be overruled in the domestic political process by powerful domestic interest groups. In this context, a public conflict can clarify the positions of *all* the parties to the dispute, giving each side a better understanding of the actual room for maneuver in the strictly regulatory realm. Such public airings can help the regulators themselves understand their counterparts as individuals acting in good faith, but often under constraints beyond their control.

Understanding conflict as a positive force does not mean that it should not be resolved. On the contrary, the process of resolving a conflict is what generates its positive effects. What this understanding of conflict *does* mean is that conflict should not necessarily be avoided or suppressed as a dangerous dimension of relations between states. Within a disaggregated world order, conflict is an inevitable and natural part of transgovernmental relations, with all the attendant bumpiness and unpleasantness that recognition entails. Cooperation, understood as a process of mutual adjustment in the pursuit of common goals, would be impossible without it.

3. CONCLUSION

How do government networks contribute to world order? How do they institutionalize cooperation and contain conflict sufficiently to allow all nations and their peoples to achieve greater peace, prosperity, stewardship of the earth, and minimum standards of human dignity? In a variety of actual and potential ways.

Government networks promote convergence of national law, regulations, and institutions in ways that facilitate the movement of people, goods, and money across borders; that assure a high and increasingly uniform level of protection of legal rights; and that guarantee the cross-fertilization of ideas and approaches to common governance problems. That cross-fertilization, in turn, may in some cases produce competition among competing standards. It also makes possible informed divergence, where national regulators, legislators, or judges deliberately proclaim and preserve a national law, rule, principle, or tradition in the face of countervailing global trends.

Government networks also strengthen compliance with international rules and norms, both through vertical enforcement and information networks and by building governance capacity in countries that have the will but not the means to comply. Those international rules and norms are themselves efforts to achieve goals that will serve the peoples of all nations and the planet they inhabit; government networks allow them to penetrate directly into the domestic political sphere. Finally, government networks make it possible for national government officials of all kinds and from every nation to regulate by information, permitting nations to adopt cooperative regulatory solutions that are much better suited to rapidly changing problems and the need for decentralized solutions. They empower national government officials to empower the people they serve, giving them the information they need to help themselves from a global or regional database.

If we embraced government networks as the architecture of a new world order, coexisting with and even inside traditional international institutions, they could be even more effective. They could become self-regulating networks, each with the mission of inducing and compelling its members to behave in accordance with "network norms" that would reflect the highest standards of professional integrity and competence for judges, regulators, legislators, ministers, and heads of state. The networks would create a context in which reputation matters; they would also condition initial and continuing membership in good standing on adherence to the norms.

At the same time, these networks, designed to double as professional associations for government officials, would bolster their members under pressure to depart from those norms by other branches of their governments, such as a court or a legislature in its efforts to resist political pressures from the executive branch. Alternatively, in cases of post-conflict reconstruction, these networks could help rebuild a country's institutions—judges helping judges, legislators helping legislators, regulators helping regulators with help that is not simply technical assistance and training, but ongoing participation in a network of fellow government professionals with strong professional norms. Seeing states and aiding them as aggregations of different government institutions, at least for some purposes, will also help prevent labeling them inaccurately and potentially unfairly as illiberal, rogue, pariah, or simply failed. It is specific government officials and institutions that make the decisions that may merit these labels, not the state as a whole.

Finally, government networks designed as structures of global governance would harness the power of discussion, debate, and even heated conflict. Within a government network in which members had achieved a degree of professional homogeneity, at least, members should interact with sufficient trust and confidence in their underlying common interests to benefit from the fruits of vigorous discussion and argument as part of a collective decision-making process. Discussion under these conditions helps maximize the information available to the decision makers, generate new and better solutions than would be available to any one member acting alone, and improve the legitimacy and likelihood of implementing the decision taken. Further, even where discussion produces protracted conflict, over time the resulting compromise, or even the decision simply to live with the disagreement, becomes an engine of greater trust.

Government networks use both hard and soft power. They can harness the coercive power of national government officials, but they also operate through information, socialization, persuasion, deliberation, and debate. They have as much power at their disposal as many national governments do and more power than many international institutions. They are also self-propelling in ways that reach out to the institutions of all states, regardless of the divisions imposed by more traditional power, cultural, or ideological relations.

What is still missing from this order, however, is norms. Power without norms is both dangerous and useless. It is dangerous because of the risk of abuse. It is useless because it lacks purpose. The answer in both cases is to harness power and to constrain it through norms. The international order established by formal international law and international institutions operates according to many norms, established and promulgated through written texts and solemn declarations.

The informal order of global government networks operates largely without norms, or, at least, without explicit norms. To many, it also seems like a secret, technocratic, unaccountable, and exclusive order. The more power government networks exercise and the more effective they can be, the more worrisome their flaws. We turn now to the dark side of a networked world order, or at least the perceived dark side, and to an array of potential solutions.

SIX

A Just World Order

Only governments bear the political imprimatur that is
bestowed by political accountability. Neither multinational corporations nor international bureaucracies are
a substitute. Addressing the most complex challenges
posed by globalization requires the direct accountability
carried by the representatives of sovereign nations.
—Paul Martin, Prime Minister of Canada, former Canadian
    Finance Minister and Chair of the G-20[1]

A SEARCH FOR THE ARCHITECTS OF WORLD ORDER IS A POGO-LIKE QUEST:
they are us. No hypothetical leaders or experts sit outside the world on
some Archimedean platform, able to design and implement new global
structures. Rather, heads of state, ministers, judges, legislators, heads of
international organizations, civic and corporate leaders, professors, and
pundits all make the choices and participate in the processes that design a blueprint of world order at any given moment and give it continually evolving substance.

Chapter 4 outlined the structure of a disaggregated world order
based on horizontal and vertical government networks coexisting with

traditional international organizations. Chapter 5 described the mechanisms by which these networks can establish an effective world order—in their current form and in a reconstituted or newly constituted and much more self-conscious form. Yet it is up to all of us to determine the actual substance of the outcomes that such a world order achieves and the ideals that it promotes. A feasible and effective world order is not necessarily a desirable one. It must also be a just world order—or as just as human aspiration and capacity can make it.

Many of the descriptions and visions put forward in the previous chapters resonate more with the liberalism of progress than that of fear.[2] I have focused more on what could go right than what could go wrong. Indeed, the very concept of "a new world order" has an inevitably utopian ring, but other observers of existing government networks, as well as critics of what they could become, have pointed out plenty of problems. This chapter tries to address those problems. In addition, I advance a set of my own prescriptions aimed at ensuring that a networked world order is as inclusive, tolerant, respectful, and decentralized as possible.

1. PROBLEMS WITH GOVERNMENT NETWORKS

Critiques of government networks come from many different directions. Some are based on perception more than fact; some apply to certain kinds of government networks more than others. Thus, for instance, fears that harmonization networks are circumventing democratic input into rule making, discussed below, do not seem to have much bearing on information networks of regulators, judges, or legislators. More surprisingly, perhaps, even information networks have their detractors. Each of these different categories, of course, also holds many different networks, with different members and activities. Thus a grounded, systematic critique of "government networks" in general, or any specific category of networks, is difficult to mount at this stage.

A frequent and easy charge is "lack of accountability." Yet this claim highlights another difficulty with criticisms of government networks, and with figuring out how to respond to those criticisms. Accountability to whom? (Even assuming we know what "accountability" means in these circumstances.) Government networks are largely composed of national government officials, interacting either with each other, or, less frequently, with their supranational counterparts. Those national officials are responsible to national constituencies for their domestic, and, as we shall see, their transgovernmental activities. At the same time, taken all together, government networks constitute a global governance system, which must somehow be accountable to the global community as a whole, comprising both states and individuals whose collective interests stem from a common humanity. Yet what may be desirable from a national point of view in terms of serving a particular set of interests may be highly problematic from a global point of view; conversely, positing and serving "global" interests can undercut or contravene specific national interests. In the listing of specific problems to follow, several have both a global and a national dimension.

We will return to these issues after discussing specific problems that have been raised by critics, but a final caveat is in order. Always present, whether explicit or not, is the problem of power. From a national perspective, the subtext of many critiques is the ways in which expanding the ambit of governance processes beyond national borders—even processes of gathering information and brainstorming about problems—changes a particular domestic political balance of power. From a global perspective, the perennial and unavoidable problem is stark asymmetries of power among different nations. It is worth remembering at the outset, however, that these problems are by no means limited to government networks. Those who would keep domestic borders hermetically sealed must contend with the far larger phenomenon of globalization. And those who would equalize the distribution of power across nations must grapple with the tremendous asymmetries built into our current world order, from the existence of permanent members on the UN Security Council to weighted voting in the IMF and the World Bank.

A Global Technocracy

Perhaps the most frequent charge against government networks is that they are networks of technocrats—unelected regulators and judges who share a common functional outlook on the world but who do not respond to the social, economic, and political concerns of ordinary citizens. Antonio Perez, for instance, accuses government networks of adopting "Platonic Guardianship as a mode of transnational governance," an open "move toward technocratic elitism."[3] The affinity and even solidarity felt among central bankers, securities regulators, antitrust officials, environmental regulators, and judges, in this view, socialize them to believe that deeply political trade-offs are value-neutral choices based on "objective" expertise. To allow these officials to come together off-shore, free from the usual mandated intrusions of public representatives and private interest groups in their decision-making process, is to allow them to escape politics.

A related concern is a lack of transparency, generally. According to Philip Alston, the rise of government networks "suggests a move away from arenas of relative transparency into the back rooms and the bypassing of the national political arenas to which the United States and other proponents of the importance of healthy democratic institutions attach so much importance."[4] Sol Picciotto agrees: "A chronic lack of legitimacy plagues direct international contacts at the sub-state level among national officials and administrators."[5] He attributes this lack of legitimacy to the informality and confidentiality of such contacts, precisely the attributes that make them so attractive to the participants.[6]

The most frequent example of alleged global technocracy at work is the Basel Committee's adoption and enforcement of capital adequacy requirements (the Basel Capital Accords) among its members. Some experts have argued that these requirements ultimately contributed to a global recession.[7] Jonathan Macey argues that the Accords were an effort by the regulators themselves to "protect their autonomy in the face of international competition," and that, for the Japanese in particular, they "represented a hands-tying strategy" that allowed "the Japanese bureaucrats . . . to collude with bureaucrats from other countries in order to obtain more discretionary regulatory authority."[8] Yet central bankers are supposed to be domestically independent in many political systems; they are deliberately insulated from the direct political process. Indeed, as with courts, being perceived as "political" undermines, rather than bolsters, their legitimacy. Why, in an increasingly global economy, should they be more politically constrained when coordinating policy with their foreign counterparts?

In any event, a subsequent effort to adopt similar regulations by the Basel Committee failed, as did efforts to adopt common securities regulations by the IOSCO Technical Committee. Overall, fears of an international cabal of some kind, secretly meeting and making rules, are hard to sustain on the facts. On the other hand, one of the intentions of this study is to point out ways in which some government networks could at least potentially exercise an actual rule-making capacity such that the rules they make would be directly enforceable by the members of the network themselves, without any other domestic or global political input. Concerns about unchecked technocratic rule-making authority could thus be more justified in the future.

The standard response to concerns about technocracy is to increase transparency. Yet transparency can make the network even more accessible to sectoral interest pressures, leading to 'overpoliticization' in the form of distorted representation of specific domestic or international preferences. At the same time, government networks can pose the problem of not knowing enough about who is making decisions and when they are being made to have meaningful input into them. As Joseph Weiler observes with regard to charges of a democracy deficit within the European Union, "Transparency and access to documents are often invoked as a possible remedy to this issue. But if you do not know what is going on, which documents will you ask to see?"[9]

Another frequent prescription to counter technocratic tendencies is to link government networks with broader policy networks of NGOs and corporations. The point here is not simply to put technocratic government officials into greater contact with activists from different constituencies. It is also to change the context of their decision making. Even if the outcome of their deliberations with one another is a set of codes of conduct or best practices, compilations without any formal authority, the technical consensus represented may be worrisome. It is unlikely that the formulators of these codes have been challenged by consumers, environmentalists, or labor, on the one hand, or by corporate and financial interests, on the other. By re-politicizing the decision-making process, at least to a degree, regulators have learned to question their own professional consensus and deliberate over the best collective solution, taking a much wider range of interests into account.

These charges of technocracy and lack of transparency are from the global perspective, mounted largely by international lawyers who seek to ensure the fairness and responsiveness of any system of global governance. Secret colloquies of technocrats, in this view, contrast unfavorably with the open, one-state–one-vote negotiations and voting systems of many actual or envisioned international organizations. Again, concerns about inequalities of power are a critical part of this equation; shifting authority to technocrats means privileging the views of those nations that *have* technocrats—inevitably the most developed nations. Yet as the next section demonstrates, these concerns resonate also with weaker and nonexpert constituencies within nations.

Distortion of National Political Processes

Click on the website of the U.S. public interest organization Public Citizen.[10] The left side lists buttons identifying the issue areas that are of specific concern to the organization. They include "Fast Track, WTO, NAFTA, China," and "Harmonization." Click on harmonization and read on. Here is the definition of what harmonization is and why the American public should be concerned about it: "Harmonization is the name given to the effort by industry to replace the variety of product standards and other regulatory policies adopted by nations in favor of uniform global standards."[11]

Public Citizen blames international trade regimes such as NAFTA and the WTO for a major boost in harmonization efforts, arguing that they "require or encourage" national governments either to harmonize standards or recognize foreign government standards as equivalent to their own.[12] This substantive commitment is implemented through the establishment of "an ever-increasing number of committees and working groups to implement the harmonization mandate."[13]

The problem with all these efforts, from Public Citizen's perspective, is that most of these working groups are industry-dominated, do not provide an opportunity for input by interested individuals or potentially affected communities, and generally conduct their operations behind closed doors. Yet, under current trade rules, these standard-setting processes can directly affect our national, state, and local policies.[14]

An immediate solution is to alert the public to what is happening. And indeed, Public Citizen publishes "Harmonization Alert," a newsletter available in print and on line that "seeks to promote open and accountable policy-making relating to public health, natural resources, consumer safety, and economic justice standards in an era of globalization."[15] It posts notice of proposed changes to U.S. regulations, comment periods, and important meeting dates and times. The aim is to increase the transparency of the harmonization process and make "otherwise obscure information" available to the public, in the hope "that more citizens, groups and organizations will get involved and have an impact on global standard-setting."[16] Scholars such as Sidney Shapiro are also beginning to alert administrative lawyers to the worrisome side of harmonization efforts.[17]

Over the longer term, public activists must seek to extend U.S. domestic procedural guarantees to transgovernmental activity. Public Citizen paints a relatively rosy view of the requirements of U.S. administrative law, noting that "U.S. policy-making must be conducted 'on the record,' with a publicly accessible docket, under laws such as the federal Administrative Procedure Act." Other U.S. statutes, such as the Federal Advisory Committee Act, "[require] balanced representation on and open operations of government advisory committees."[18] On the international side, however, agency adherence to the U.S domestic procedures for notice, balance, openness, and public input has been spotty at best. U.S. federal agencies follow different procedures for involving the public in their international harmonization negotiations and make differing amounts of information available to the public at different stages.[19]

The natural response is thus to "apply the due process and participation requirements of existing U.S. laws, such as the Administrative Procedure Act, Freedom of Information Act, and Federal Advisory Committee Act, to all international harmonization activities."[20] In practice, this means requiring regulators seeking to develop U.S. positions at harmonization talks or considering proposals from foreign regulators to create a record of all their actions; this record would then be subject to notice-and-comment rule making, allowing all interested members of the public full input.[21] The resulting agency action would presumably also be subject to judicial review by U.S. courts.

At first glance, concern over harmonization arises primarily from the goal of harmonizing regulations, with the resulting danger of "leveling down" the protections for public health, the environment, consumer safety, and other areas, but it's also the process. The idea of regulators meeting behind closed doors, without input from a wide variety of interested public groups at a time when they can still have impact on the discussion and the outcome, is deeply worrying in itself. Knowing that they are just exchanging information about common problems or providing technical assistance to one another will trigger less immediate alarm than knowing that they are actively engaged in harmonizing national regulations. Yet to the extent that the deeper concern is that regulators in a particular issue area are operating on a technocratic, professional set of assumptions that do not take into account other perspectives, interests, and politics, transgovernmental regulatory interaction of any kind is likely to prompt demands for more public participation, or at least sufficient transparency to allow interested groups to decide for themselves whether they want to have input.

Unlike the old "clubs" of ministers, deputy ministers, or even working officials within international organizations such as the IMF, NATO, and GATT, today the individuals involved are domestic regulators, public servants who are charged with formulating and implementing rules on a host of issues that have an everyday impact on ordinary citizens and that are thus ordinarily subject to a host of rules designed to enhance public scrutiny. Their foreign activity is an extension of their domestic activity, rather than occurring in a separate and distinct "international" sphere created to address "international" problems. Critics thus argue that these officials should be subject to the same restraints abroad as at home.

Unrepresentative Input into Global Political Processes

Another group of critics is less worried about existing government networks as described here, but rather about the larger phenomenon of "global policy networks" or "global issue networks"—networks of all individuals, groups, and organizations, governmental and nongovernmental, interested in a particular set of issues. The UN Secretary General, a vice president of the World Bank, and numerous scholars have championed these networks as optimal mechanisms of global governance.[22] And, as just noted, these wider networks are often invoked as the solution to the problem of technocracy with pure government networks. Still, the problem that immediately arises is how to separate out the structures of government from the much more amorphous webs of governance.

According to Martin Shapiro, the shift from government to governance marks "a significant erosion of the boundaries separating what lies inside a government and its administration and what lies outside them."[23] The result is to advantage "experts and enthusiasts," the two groups outside government that have the greatest incentive and desire to participate in governance processes but who are not representative of the larger polity.[24] From this perspective, relatively neutral government officials who are aware of the larger social trade-offs surrounding decision making on a particular issue will produce more democratic outcomes than decisions shaped primarily by deeply interested private citizens—even those acting with substantial knowledge of the issue and the best of intentions.

Instead of celebrating governance without government, critics like Shapiro argue for exactly the opposite: bringing government back into governance. Networks of government officials should become more readily distinguishable from the plethora of private actors that surround them—even from private actors purportedly acting in the public interest. The merging and blurring of lines of authority are ultimately likely to blur the distinction between public legitimacy and private power.

From this perspective, the question is how to raise the profile of government networks as networks within broader policy networks. Identifiable government officials must be responsible for ultimate decisions on the same kinds of questions that they would decide in their home countries, as well as for new kinds of decisions about best practices, codes of conduct, and the coordination of resources in the service of common problems. Determining and making clear who has the authority to make final decisions will also help regularize input into those decisions, preserving the contributions of the myriad private actors currently involved, but also creating more established channels of participation.

Unrepresentative Input into National Judicial Decision Making

How troubling is it that judges draw on the decisions of foreign and international courts as part of their deliberations on how to decide a domestic case? As discussed in chapter 2, U.S. Supreme Court justices differ over this question, quite heatedly. Should we leave it to them to resolve? Should Congress take a hand? Should the solicitor general, as the President's top advocate, take a position in arguments before the Court?

According to a former justice of the Supreme Judicial Court of Massachusetts, Charles Fried, drawing on foreign decisions could change the course of American law. Fried writes thoughtfully on the difference between scholarship and adjudication, noting that rejection of comparative analysis on the part of scholars "would seem philistine indeed," but is not necessarily so on the part of judges.[25] Judges must hand down answers, constrained by a confined set of sources. Thus, Fried writes, in reference to the debate between Justice Breyer and Justice Scalia in the *Printz* case:

Justice Breyer's remarks on comparative constitutional law, if they had appeared in a law review article, would have been quite unremarkable. . . . As part of a judicial opinion, they were altogether remarkable. Why should that be? The reason is that if Justice Breyer's insertion into the case of comparative constitutional law materials had gone unchallenged, it would have been a step towards legitimizing their use as points of departure in constitutional argumentation.[26]

If Breyer had succeeded, Fried continues, his recommendation would have been "something more than just a proposal or a good idea. It would have introduced a whole new range of materials to the texts, precedents, and doctrines from which the Herculean task of constructing judgments in particular cases proceeds."[27] By way of example, Fried points to the significance of allowing judges to cite sources other than pure case law, such as scientific reports, policy analyses, and other non-legal materials. Expanding a judge's universe of information will expand the range of considerations she thinks is relevant to a decision. Expanding the range of considerations, in turn, makes it possible to make a wider range of arguments for or against a particular decision.

Thus, for instance, when Justice Ruth Bader Ginsburg faces a decision under U.S. law on the constitutionality of affirmative action, she finds it valuable to look to the Indian experience as well as the U.S. experience.[28] Knowing the Indian experience gives her a different perspective on the problems that U.S. institutions may encounter with affirmative action programs, it also gives her a wider sense of the available options. Yet is the Indian experience really relevant to the United States? The enormous differences between the two countries raise the possibility—indeed the likelihood—that the same policy initiatives will have completely different results. More fundamentally, though, does democracy imply the right to make our own mistakes?

To a group of professional academics, framing the question this way seems radically anti-intellectual, but to politicians, and the citizens they represent, the critical issue may be controlling the inputs into a particular political process—including judicial deliberation—so as to be able to control or at least manage the output. The problem, from this perspective, is not so much a lack of good ideas, which could be remedied by looking to other countries, but the underlying battle of interests that informs any policy choice. Allowing judges, regulators, and

even legislators to inject new options into any policy debate by reference to the experience of other countries, and even to legitimate them
based on that experience, makes the entire political process much
harder to manage.

Similar concerns have been expressed outside the United States.
Christopher McCrudden documents debates about the appropriateness
of drawing on foreign judicial decisions in Israel, Singapore, South
Africa, Australia, and Hong Kong.[29] A principal concern in these debates is arbitrariness in choosing when to pay attention to foreign law
and when to ignore it, as well as in deciding which foreign courts to pay
attention to. Yash Ghai reports from Hong Kong that "the approach to
the use of foreign cases is not very consistent; they are invoked when
they support the position preferred by the court, otherwise they are dis-
missed as irrelevant."[30] In some ways this critique is analogous to
Macey's charge that Japanese banking regulators used the Basel Accords to bolster their domestic legitimacy and hence autonomy; judges
can point selectively to foreign authorities to strengthen their arguments. Yet the response in the judicial context would be to require a
high court to set forth a certain philosophy and even methodology
about when and how it is appropriate to canvass foreign decisions,
which could in turn give rise to precisely the systematic expansion of
legitimate legal sources that Fried worries about.

The Ineradicability of Power

A final problem is the way in which government networks either replicate or even magnify asymmetries of power in the existing international system. Some government networks represent exclusive preserves of officials from the most economically developed, and hence
powerful, nations. The Basel Committee—with its membership of Belgium, Canada, France, Germany, Great Britain, Italy, Japan, Luxembourg, the Netherlands, Sweden, Switzerland, and the United States—
is again a prime example. Similarly, the Technical Committee of
IOSCO, where most of the important work is done, is composed of a
fairly predictable group of nations with well-developed securities mar-

kets.[31] If such networks are to form the infrastructure for a networked world order, they must be given incentives to expand their membership in meaningful ways, inviting in government officials from poorer, less powerful, and often marginalized countries as genuine participants rather than largely passive observers.

Supporters of government networks as mechanisms of global governance are well aware of this problem. Lord Howell celebrates the Commonwealth over institutions such as the OECD for its greater inclusiveness. The OECD, he writes, "lacks an obvious and centrally valuable feature of the Commonwealth—namely, its scope for bringing together and giving a common voice to both richer and poorer, developed and developing societies."[32] Greater inclusiveness also drives former Canadian Finance Minister Paul Martin's insistence on using the G-20 instead of the G-7. The "breadth of [the G-20's] membership is crucial," he writes, "for we have learned a fundamental truth about policies to promote development: they will work only if the developing countries and emerging markets help shape them, because inclusiveness lies at the heart of legitimacy and effectiveness." And the G-20 is inclusive. Nations at all phases of development are at the G-20 table—and no one side of it is dictating to another.[33]

If "global government networks" are in fact only partial government networks, they will ultimately fail. They cannot address the world's problems, or even what appear to be only regional problems, as members of an exclusive club. This point is problematic for the members of some current networks, at least to the extent that one of the major intuitive advantages of networking over more formal international institutions is the ability to engage selectively with other like-minded governments in pondering hard problems rather than enduring the tedious procedural formalities of global deliberation. If all government networks were to become mini-UNs in different substantive areas, little would be gained. Yet as the example of the Commonwealth and APEC demonstrate, it is possible to have much more inclusive government networks without formalizing procedures.

From the perspective of weaker countries, however, being included does not solve the problem of power. On the contrary, as discussed extensively in the last chapter, officials—regulators, judges, legislators—

are simply subject to the soft power of the strongest members of the network. Even training, information, and assistance that they seek out is likely to push them steadily toward convergence with both the substance and style of more developed countries in any particular subject area, from constitutional rights to utilities regulation. Having a voice in collective discussions is better than being silenced by exclusion, but it does not guarantee that you will be heard.

The substance and strength of this critique must be appreciated in context. First, as discussed in the last chapter, the same factors that press toward convergence can inform a considered position of divergence for any particular country. Second, countries may converge toward multiple standards, as in competition policy. Third, it is possible for groups of weaker countries to band together and form "counternetworks," as a group of Southern African countries have done in the area of securities regulation. Fourth, as is evident in the judicial arena, the most influential national government institutions are not always from the most powerful countries, but rather from countries that themselves have had reason to canvass the positions of their fellow nations and develop a nuanced synthesis.

A final question in terms of power relations is whether weaker countries have more influence in governance mechanisms based on information exchange, discussion, and deliberation than in those based on weighted voting. Formal international institutions, with their various voting systems, will continue to exist alongside government networks; powerful nations will continue to have uneasy relationships with such institutions. Strong nations will continue to dictate terms to weaker nations in international institutions. And, indeed, the more likely it is that vertical networks will exist to ensure direct enforcement by national officials of the agreements that result from those negotiations, the more careful strong nations will be about what they agree to.

In such a world, with a global lattice of government networks will weaker nations be better or worse off? Where possibilities of genuine learning exist, representatives of even the world's most powerful nations are likely to be surprised by what they do not know or have not thought of. Further, of course, as in the United States' relations with the European Union over forty-five years, and the U.S. Supreme

Court's relations with many newer constitutional courts, successful mentoring can often produce students who turn the tables on their teachers. And individual government officials could be strengthened through these networks in their efforts to improve the governance of their entire country, ultimately strengthening its global position. These are the kind of factors that must be weighed in assessing the balance of power in a disaggregated world order.

2. A MENU OF POTENTIAL SOLUTIONS

The critics of government networks are themselves a diverse lot, criticizing a diverse phenomenon for a variety of different faults. If one group sees government without politics, another worries that the "politics" sought to be introduced are likely to be selective and distorted. Still others, largely approving of government networks as a form of governance, charge them with too much selectivity in choosing their members. And all these perceived problems take on a different cast when the vantage point is a particular national polity versus a hypothetical global community.

Ultimately, policymakers who wish to respond seriously to these various problems will have to formulate a solution on a case-by-case basis, after conducting more systematic research to verify the substance and the scope of each problem across different government networks. Yet even at this level of generality, it is possible to put forward some broader proposals. The starting point should be simply to recognize government networks as a prime form of global governance, equivalent in importance and effectiveness to traditional international organizations.

If we think of national government officials as performing governmental functions at the global or regional level, then we must hold them to the same standards and expectations that we impose on domestic government officials. We must stop thinking of their relationships with their foreign counterparts as marginal or interstitial, or of their meetings as mere junkets or talking shops. When government officials interact across borders—whether judges, regulators, chief executives and their top ministers, or legislators—the forum may be informal, but the substance is governmental.

We can begin by reconceiving the responsibilities of all national officials as including both a national and a transgovernmental component, such that they must all perform a dual function. That simple conceptual shift will prompt debate about what those responsibilities should actually be and how their performance should be monitored. Second is to make transgovernmental activity as visible as possible to legislators, interest groups, and ordinary citizens. Third is to ensure that government networks link legislators across borders as much as they do regulators and judges, to ensure that all three branches of government, with their relative strengths and weaknesses, are represented. Fourth is to use government networks as the spines of larger policy networks, helping to mobilize transnational society but at the same time remaining identifiably distinct from nongovernmental actors. Fifth is a grab-bag of different domestic policy decisions and arrangements that express the views of particular polities on questions ranging from the legitimacy of consulting and citing foreign judicial decisions to the acceptability of autonomous rule-making capacity in regulatory networks.

Dual Function, Dual Accountability?

In a representative democracy, regulators, judges, and legislators are held accountable for the job they do within national borders. Diplomats, on the other hand, are held accountable for the state of the nation's foreign relations—a job that can only be done across borders. The first step toward ensuring that transgovernmental networks are subject to at least the same checks and balances as national officials acting within national territory is understanding that henceforth *all* domestic officials work both within and across borders. It must be assumed that they will come to know and interact with their foreign counterparts in the same way that they would know their state or provincial counterparts in domestic federal systems.

Further, understanding "domestic" issues in a regional or global context must become part of doing a good job. Increasingly, the optimal solutions to these issues will depend on what is happening abroad, and the solutions to foreign issues, in corresponding measure, by what is happening at home. Consulting with foreign counterparts would thus become part of basic competence in carrying out routine domestic functions. To take an example close to home, suppose that the members of Congress sitting on the Senate and House agriculture committees need to keep track not only of foreign agricultural subsidies and import barriers, but also of the movements of migrant agricultural workers from all over Latin America. This is hardly a far-fetched scenario. What would be unusual, however, is that rather than approach lawmaking in these areas unilaterally, the members of these committees would exchange information with their counterpart legislators in the relevant foreign countries, and even coordinate policy initiatives or explore potential synergies or bargains.

Full-fledged international agreements would still have to be struck by chief executives and ratified by the full legislatures as specified under domestic law, but the legislators themselves would be much more involved in the process *with their foreign counterparts*. Regulators of all kinds, from health to education to the environment, would conduct their own foreign relations, subject to some kind of domestic interagency process that accepted this phenomenon but nevertheless attempted to aggregate interests. Prosecutors, judges, and law enforcement agents of all kinds would work actively with their foreign counterparts on problems requiring multiple coordinated initiatives across borders.

This concept of dual function would make it far easier for organizations like Public Citizen to mobilize ordinary Americans to understand that their government officials may well be playing on a larger global or regional playing field and to monitor their activities. These officials may have two faces, internal and external, but they still have only one audience. It would also make it more possible for critics like Martin Shapiro to realistically insist that government officials be held separately accountable for their activities in larger "policy networks."

Dual function thus does not imply dual accountability. Yet in a full-fledged disaggregated world order, national government officials would simultaneously be representatives of their national government and participants in a larger global or regional institution. Here again is an essential difference between the conception of a disaggregated world order and various traditional conceptions that focus on international institutions. In the traditional view, two sets of government officials—one national and one international—perform the same functions at different levels of governance, like state and federal governments in federal systems. In a pure disaggregated view, one set of government officials operates at both the national and the global-regional levels, performing a set of interrelated functions, but these officials would have to represent both national and global interests, at least to the same degree that heads of state and foreign ministers now do in conducting international negotiations and delegating responsibility to formal international institutions.

What would this mean in practice? Since September 11, it has not been hard to convince Americans in even the smallest communities what citizens of other countries have felt for decades: it is impossible to shut ourselves off from the world. Parents who adopt a foreign child; merchants who import and export goods; immigrants who maintain ties to their home communities; migrants and the employers who depend on them; labor, human rights, and environmental activists; educators who must teach children from different cultures speaking different languages—no corner of once "local" life is immune. The ties that bind a society together, that can weave a community into being, are increasingly transnational.

These are the clichés of globalization. But by changing individual lives, they ultimately change the character of communities. More gradually still, they change the nature of polities—the constituencies that government officials must represent and serve. Foreign citizens need not vote to be represented. For instance, if Romania shuts down its adoption services; if wages rise in China; if India makes it easier to remit money earned abroad; if Mexico's standard of health declines; if fires destroying the rain forest increase levels of carbon dioxide globally—the impact will ultimately be felt in a U.S. community in a way that is likely to cause U.S. voters to demand a government response.

It is still a leap, however, from the point that U.S. government representatives, in every branch, must take account of international events, trends, and interests to represent their constituents adequately to the argument that they should also see themselves as representing a larger transnational or even global constituency. Under the U.S. Constitution, our senators and representatives represent their state or district to ensure that the voices of their particular constituents are heard in the larger debate, but they are also expected to understand and safeguard the larger public interests of the nation as a whole, of which their constituents are part. If that whole should founder, the parts cannot survive.

A similar integration of national and global interests would have to take place, although much less formal and complete. In a true world government, representatives would be elected to some kind of global legislature from every nation. They would represent the citizens from their nation in a collective effort to make rules and set policy for the world. Invariably, such global parliamentarians would have to sort out the respective weights of their national interest and the global public interest. The larger backdrop for this exercise would be the deep understanding on the part of all peoples and their leaders that without a collaborative effort to resolve collective problems, we would all be imperiled.

A networked world order rejects such a formal, top-down, and inevitably centralized approach to global governance. National governments and national government officials must remain the primary focus of political loyalty and the primary actors on the global stage. If, however, they are to be actors in national and global policymaking simultaneously, officials would have to be able to think at once in terms of the national and the global interest and to sort out the relative priorities of the two on a case-by-case basis. A national environmental regulator would have to be able to push for a set of global environmental restrictions that do not unduly burden her national constituents, while at the same time making the case for those restrictions to her constituents. And at times she might have to agree to restrictions that would be considerably tighter than her constituents wanted to get an agreement that advanced the collective interests of all nations.

In short, to avoid global government, national government officials will have to learn to think globally. Following the old Roman god of gates and doors, or beginnings and endings, they must become Janus-faced, with one face pointing forward and the other backwards. In this case, however, one face must look inward and the other outward, translating quickly and smoothly from the domestic to the international sphere.

Making Government Networks Visible

In a true world government, government activity would take place in formal, physical institutions sited in the "world's capitol," or perhaps capitols. These institutions would be the focus of monitors and lobbyists, as now occurs in Washington, London, Tokyo, New Delhi, Beijing, or Brussels. They would also physically define the "public sphere," within which actors must "regularly and routinely explain and justify their behavior."[34] John Rawls constructed an entire political philosophy on this principle, relying on the value of "public reason," but public reason cannot exist without public space, whether real or virtual.[35]

To create a public sphere for the operation of government networks, we must try to achieve two distinct goals. First is making clear where exactly processes of governance are taking place. The space must be the equivalent of a physical site, for symbolic and practical reasons. We must replace the image of shadowy networks making "offshore" decisions with an actual vision of regularized governance processes in accessible places.

Second, we must create a space in which individual citizens can figure out what is actually happening. The buzzword response to accountability concerns has been "transparency." Make everything open and accessible, at every level of governance. The decentralization of governance, however, makes this an increasingly less satisfying response. Consider, for instance, the plethora of networks in the European Union. Having access to minutes of countless meetings and records of complex decision processes threatens overload more than promising oversight.

A partial answer to both these problems may be to create virtual space. It is possible to centralize information on a website that is the global equivalent of the massive carved buildings that host national departments of justice, treasury, defense, and social services. At the same time, this website would be linked to as many different national websites in the particular issue area as possible. Thus a citizen of any country seeking to learn about policymaking in any particular area could start at either a national website or the global website, each of which would send her to the other.

This is not a fantasy. Examples already exist. The website of the IMF offers links to the websites of national central banks and finance ministries and provides relevant articles and policy positions relating to each country's relationship with the IMF.[36] The Canadian government has created an innovative inward- and outward-looking portal: citizens can access local (provincial) government sites and, via the Department of Foreign Affairs website, also obtain information on, and links to, other countries and international organizations, like the European Union, the OAS, or APEC.[37] On the EU website, the EUR-Lex project is a "first step" aimed at "bringing together the whole body of EU official acts for consultation." Citizens of member-states and other interested individuals can review the European Union's official journal; treaties; legislation (both acts that are in force and those in preparation); case law; parliamentary questions; and documents of public interest.[38] Clicking on "legislation in preparation" produces a page entitled "pre-lex," which allows a viewer to see a host of commission proposals, records of parliamentary activity, and council documents. It also offers a specific guide to "monitoring the decision-making process between institutions."

Virtual public spaces also are emerging around international judicial bodies. The website for the ICC, whose enabling statute entered into force on 1 July 2002, provides valuable information on the functions of the Court; the ratification status of individual countries who have signed the treaty; press releases; the work of the Preparatory Commission; as well as the text of the Rome Statute itself and related documents. The site also provides links to the International Law Commission; the International Court of Justice; the International Criminal Tribunals for Rwanda and the Former Yugoslavia; as well as to the United Nation's international law page.[39] It is not hard to imagine further links to national constitutional courts, particularly to their criminal law decisions.

Linking national governments in virtual space and providing a central forum for citizens and groups from all countries would at least help convince officials operating in transgovernmental networks that they are under scrutiny and that in at least some circumstances they must justify their actions. That requirement sets in motion the process of dialogue between the holders and the subjects of power that can both articulate and resolve problems. More broadly, the creation of even a virtual public sphere would be a principal mechanism for placing government networks in the context of broader policy frameworks, which is likely to mean a renewed exposure to the messy demands of interest-group politics. In this space, regulators could no longer advance specific, national preferences within groups of more-or-less like-minded colleagues; rather, they would have to defend their positions and proposals within the broader context of other competing interests, advanced by government officials from other sectors and a wide range of private actors, from corporations to NGOs. Winning arguments in this setting is more likely to require appeals to principle than statements of preference, appeals that in turn are likely to be couched in terms of both the national and the global public interest.

Legislative Networks

Legislative oversight is the standard response to administrative delegation in both parliamentary and presidential systems. Where administrative officials are increasingly making decisions in conjunction with their foreign counterparts, legislative oversight committees would do well to coordinate with their counterparts, as well. Regular meetings between directly elected representatives from different countries on issues of common concern will help broaden the horizons of individual legislators in ways that are likely to feed back to their constituents. Coordinating legislation through direct legislator interaction rather than through treaty implementation may also result in faster and more effective responses to transnational problems, although the ability to generate legislation independent of the executive obviously varies in different national political systems.

In some areas, national legislation has been used to facilitate the growth of government networks.[40] In others, such as human rights and the environment, national legislators are increasingly recognizing that they have common interests. Global Legislators for a Balanced Environment (GLOBE) was founded in 1989 and is essentially an environmental NGO composed of parliamentarians.[41] As discussed in chapter 3, governments in the European Union must increasingly submit their European policies to special parliamentary committees, who are themselves networking. The result, according to German international relations scholar Karl Kaiser, is the "reparliamentarization" of national policy.[42] Yet encouragement of legislative networks across the board would help ensure that the direct representatives of peoples around the world communicated and coordinated with each other in the same ways and to the same degree as do their fellow government officials. It would help address the perceived problems of both global technocracy and distortion of national political processes, as well as adding another category of accountable government actors into the mix of entities participating in policy networks. It might also help expand the membership of existing government networks.

Richard Falk and Andrew Strauss have called for a global parliament as the backbone of global democracy.[43] Such a body would be huge and unwieldy; its members would also be two removes from their purported constituents. They would not be elected to exercise the direct national power that leads voters both to value them and to monitor them closely, but rather to engage in vague global deliberations. Contrast the vision of Louise Doswald-Beck, former secretary general of the International Commission of Jurists: "When members of Parliament are able to consider, in relation to any issue, what solution is in the best interests of the international community and of their own states in the medium-to-long term, they are able to contribute more effectively to global policy-making."[44]

Legislative networks are beginning to emerge to monitor the activities of traditional international organizations such as the World Bank and the WTO. The Parliamentary Network on the World Bank held its first conference in May 2000 and its second in January 2001 in London, where it was hosted by a select committee of the House of Commons.[45] The network has no official connection to the World Bank; it is an independent initiative by parliamentarians who want to play a more active role in global governance. Similar efforts to organize parliamentarians to oversee the activities of the WTO are ongoing, spurred by a meeting of parliamentarians at the WTO Ministerial Conference in Doha, Qatar, in November 2001, which was organized by the Inter-Parliamentary Union.[46]

Addressing the assembled parliamentarians at Doha, WTO Director General Michael Moore expressed precisely the sentiment that should motivate the formation of legislative networks of all kinds: "Parliamentarians have a vital role to play in bringing international organizations and people closer together and holding us and governments accountable. . . . Can I suggest that we should assemble more often and that all the multilateral institutions that you have created, that you own, could do with your assistance and scrutiny."[47] Parliamentarians have an equally vital role to play in monitoring the activities of transgovernmental regulatory networks and in helping to establish both regulatory and judicial networks more formally in ways that will allow them to play a more active role in strengthening domestic governance in different countries. By constituting themselves as legislative networks, they can provide the same support for parliamentarians in different countries. They can also pursue their own initiatives in terms of tackling global problems cooperatively through coordinated national legislation.

Mobilizing Transnational Networks

Government networks deploy information as power in a variety of new and effective ways. They collect, distill, and disseminate credible information. One of the most important corollaries of this activity is the empowerment of ordinary citizens within and across borders. Where the principal activity of an international entity is the production of accurate and considered information that has the imprimatur of collective deliberation by officials from many of the world's governments, individuals and groups in domestic and transnational society can readily use this information to build and press their case domestically on a particular policy issue.

Even more valuable, from the perspective of domestic political activists of all sorts, is the ability to participate directly in global policy networks. Kofi Annan has encouraged the formation and use of such networks from his UN bully pulpit, calling for the "creation of global policy networks" to "bring together international institutions, civil society and private sector organizations, and national governments in pursuit of common goals."[48] More generally, Wolfgang Reinicke and Francis Deng have developed both the concept and practice of the global public interest, promoted and pursued through networks.[49] Reinicke describes global public policy networks as "loose alliances of government agencies, international organizations, corporations, and elements of civil society such as nongovernmental organizations, professional associations, or religious groups that join together to achieve what none can accomplish on its own."[50]

These are the kinds of networks that Martin Shapiro and others worry about. As has been suggested above, government networks can provide the spine of these broader networks in ways that make it easier to distinguish politically accountable actors from "experts and enthusiasts." At the same time, however, the self-conscious creation and support of government networks as global governance mechanisms can help mobilize a whole set of transnational actors around them—to interact with them, monitor their activities, provide input into their decision making, and receive information from them. Indeed, to the extent that these transnational networks of NGOs, individuals, corporations, international officials, churches, charities, and voluntary associations can use the information provided to advance their own causes and solve their particular problems in the pursuit of a larger conception of the global public interest, it is possible to imagine the strengthening of a kind of disaggregated global democracy based on individual and group self-governance.

A Grab-Bag of Domestic Solutions

A final set of measures to address perceived or actual problems with the activities of existing government networks should come from domestic polities. The citizens of different countries, and their government officials, are likely to have different degrees of concern about these activities. The U.S. debate over citing foreign judicial decisions has been replicated in some other countries, but by no means all, and it has a different resonance depending on the length and nature of a particular country's legal tradition. Similarly, the citizens of some countries might be content with the role of their regulators in global or regional regulatory networks, whereas the citizens of other countries might seek more monitoring of, or direct input into, those networks.

In the United States, the first step should be to collect information. Congressional committees should require all agencies to report their international or foreign activity and contacts—when, where, for what purpose, and with what result. This information should become a matter of routine public record. It would also be valuable to collect information on which interest groups currently gain access to transgovernmental activity and decision making. Should we find that particular interest groups—such as the securities dealers association rather than various shareholder groups, or mining interests over environmental groups—gain more access than others, we might require legislative action to right the balance. It might even be desirable to develop a judicial framework for reviewing the process or results of transgovernmental regulatory cooperation.[51]

A number of distinguished legal scholars are beginning to think hard about "global administrative law," specifically about ways to ensure that the same procedural safeguards and guarantees of public participation in administrative rule making that have been painstakingly worked out at the domestic level will operate at the global level.[52] The American Bar Association has recommended that all federal administrative agencies: (1) "invit[e] the public periodically to comment on new and ongoing significant harmonization activities and to attend public meetings concerning such activities; (2) refer . . . significant harmonization issues to advisory committees where appropriate and possible; and (3) establish . . . a public docket of documents and studies available under the Freedom of Information Act (FOIA) pertaining to each significant harmonization activity."[53]

An even more complicated question for any domestic polity is to contemplate the balance between national and global interests, on the assumption that all national officials would in fact be accountable not only to their domestic constituents for both domestic and international activity, but also to a hypothetical global constituency. How should individual officials strike this balance? Consider the question from the perspective of an individual regulator. She would have to think both nationally and globally, trying to harmonize laws, solve common problems, develop codes of best practices, assist foreign regulators and receive such assistance in turn in enforcing national regulations and in various other activities. What would be the actual U.S. interest in each specific substantive issue area, particularly when traded off against other U.S. interests, as would naturally happen in a domestic interagency process? How should she think about the global public interest, to the extent that the global securities, antitrust, environmental, or criminal regime must be greater than the sum of its national parts? These are not questions that any regulator can answer alone. Ultimately it will be up to us to devise a domestic, and ultimately a transgovernmental, process to formulate and address them.

Or consider again the debate over whether U.S. Supreme Court judges should be citing foreign court decisions to illuminate domestic legal issues. This is not a purely domestic debate. It has foreign policy implications—*judicial* foreign policy implications. As a nation that prides itself on its tradition of the rule of law and particularly its history of constitutional jurisprudence, should we not continue to play a leading role in developing a global jurisprudence? Are we prepared to cede that role to the Canadian, German, and South African Constitutional Courts, together with the European Court of Human Rights? Global governance includes global judicial governance; U.S. judges have an external as well as an internal role.

Our judges remain American judges, bound by our laws and Constitution; the vast majority of their cases arise on U.S. soil. Yet does knowing how many other countries decided the same issue matter to how a U.S. judge would decide? Should it matter? What if the judge recognizes that her decision citing other foreign courts is likely to be cited by them in turn as part of an emerging global jurisprudence—although not necessarily a consensus—on a particular issue?

For most judges, I suspect, the impact of canvassing foreign decisions on the actual outcome of a case would depend critically on how determinate or open the applicable U.S. law was. Where a judge found herself confronting a new issue, or where the courts below were quite split, then looking to approaches taken by fellow judges across borders could sway the outcome—though probably more due to the soundness of a particular approach itself than any notion of keeping pace with the global community.

Results that are dictated by idiosyncratic or culturally specific lines of decision might well be identifiable as such. For instance, if the judges of the U.S. Supreme Court thought that they were playing to a global as well as a national audience, they might readily acknowledge that U.S. First Amendment jurisprudence is on the extreme end of the global spectrum for protecting speech, an artifact of the particular history of this country and the political value traditionally placed on free speech. At the same time, however, the Court might well try to argue for the U.S. approach as compared to less speech-protective doctrines applied in other countries, to strengthen the impact of the decision in the global judicial human rights dialogue described in chapter 2.

In addition, judges thinking both globally and nationally might be more inclined to try to identify the underlying common principle at work in a range of different doctrinal approaches. They might come to see their national case law as only one manifestation of this principle. The result could be a global jurisprudence, at least in some areas, combining universality with pluralism—the liberal ideal. Judges would no longer be divided along "international" and "domestic" lines. They would all be participants simultaneously in national legal systems and the construction of a global legal system.

National polities have to decide for themselves the degree to which they find a problem with the transgovernmental activities of their government officials and the ways in which they choose to regulate those activities. In a full-fledged disaggregated world order, each nation would also have to work out guidelines for how their national officials should balance the national interest with a larger global public interest, given that all national officials would be simultaneously fulfilling a national and a global governance function. Yet guidelines for defining and implementing the global public interest can never be simply the aggregation of national decisions. All nations must come together to deliberate over general norms governing the operation of transgovernmental networks as mechanisms of global governance. In the final section of this chapter, I propose a set of norms that could provide a starting point for a larger debate.

3. GLOBAL NORMS REGULATING GOVERNMENT NETWORKS

Here, as in the second half of the last chapter, we turn to what could be if government networks were, alongside traditional international organizations, widely recognized and self-consciously constituted mechanisms of global governance. In such a world, it would be important to think through how national officials operating in a world still divided into sovereign states could nevertheless exercise a collective responsibility to advance the global public interest with the input and participation of as many states as possible. This conception of global responsibility turns not only on geography, but also psychology; it is not only a question of adding numbers of actors but of changing the thinking of all participants.

Even if participants in government networks around the world were satisfactorily accountable to their domestic constituents, what duty do they owe to other nations? It may seem an odd question, but if these networks were in fact primary structures of global governance, together with more formal international and supranational organizations, then they would have to be subject to global as well as national norms. They would be responsible for collectively formulating and implementing policies in the global public interest. Equally important, the participants in these networks would have to develop and implement norms governing their relations with one another. Such norms may seem unnecessary when the principal activity in which these participants engage is information exchange; however, harmonization and enforcement activity requires the development of global ground rules. Finally, these networks should operate on a presumption of inclusivity rather than exclusivity.

What are the potential sources of these norms? First, it is natural to project domestic constitutional principles, developed by visionaries and thinkers from Madison to Monnet. Political philosophers are also relevant, providing first principles that can be adapted to this particular global context. Finally, norms are emerging from contemporary practice that can be generalized, adding an inductive dimension to the project.

It is particularly important to note the informal character of these norms, like that of the government networks they regulate. Proposals for global constitutions are already on the table, most notably from scholars such as Ernst-Ulrich Petersmann, but an actual global constitution suggests a formal global government, even if in fragmentary form.[54] I seek to develop an informal alternative—a set of principles and norms that can operate independently of formal codification, even as the actors and activities they would regulate form and reform in shifting patterns of governance. Both visions seek to underpin world order, but they diverge with respect to world government.

Global Deliberative Equality

The foundational norm of global governance should be global deliberative equality. Michael Ignatieff derives this concept from the basic moral precept that "our species is one, and each of the individuals who compose it is entitled to equal moral consideration."[55] His account of the progress of the human rights movement since 1945 builds from this precept, which lies at the heart of human rights, to the recognition that "we live in a plural world of cultures that have a right to equal consideration in the argument about what we can and cannot, should and should not, do to human beings."[56]

This idea, that "all human beings belong at the table, in the essential conversation about how we should treat each other," does not posit utopian harmony. On the contrary, it assumes a world "of conflict, deliberation, argument, and contention," but to the extent that the process of global governance is, at bottom, a conversation, a collective deliberation about common problems and toward common global objectives, then all affected individuals, or their representatives, are entitled to participate.[57]

This presumption of inclusion lies at the heart of the "Montreal Consensus" that former Canadian Finance Minister Paul Martin has put forward to counter the "Washington Consensus": a combination of fiscal discipline, tax reform, exhange rate liberalization, and privatization supported by Washington-based institutions such as the IMF, the World Bank, and the U.S. Treasury Department in negotiating with highly indebted countries. The heart of the Montreal Consensus is a "more balanced vision of how developing countries and poor countries can share in the benefits of the global economy."[58] It arises from the perception that developing countries are not threatened by globalization per se as much as by being left out and left behind. The solution is not to reverse globalization itself, but rather to find ways to share the wealth and integration it brings. That, for Martin and the G-20, is the essence of global accountability.

A principle or even a presumption of inclusion does not mean that government institutions from all countries will become members of all government networks. Many networks will address problems common only to a group of countries, or a region. And even where the problems themselves are global, government networks such as the G-20 reflect a philosophy of representation rather than direct participation.

What such a principle should mean, however, is that all government networks adopt clear criteria for participation that will be fairly applied. These criteria can require a particular degree of economic or political development or a level of performance in terms of compliance with agreed principles. It is also certainly permissible for some nations to move faster or deeper than others in making particular commitments—just as the European Union has multispeed integration in which some nations adopt a common currency and others do not. As discussed in chapter 4, the World Intellectual Property Organization

(WIPO) has incorporated a network of some advanced industrial countries alongside its traditional global decision-making processes. Yet countries that want to join such networks and that meet the stated criteria must be allowed in, in some form or other. At the same time, deliberative equality, as an ideal, means that those countries that have decided to join a network receive an equal opportunity to participate in agenda setting, to advance their position, and to challenge the proposals or positions of others.[59]

More generally, as argued in the last chapter, government networks should be explicitly designed to engage, enmesh, and assist specific government institutions. One of the great values of this form of governance is the ability to bolster the court or regulatory agency or legislature of any country—to offer directly targeted technical assistance, political support where necessary, and an all-important sense of professionalism and belonging in a wider global community. That in itself is a form of global deliberative equality.

Legitimate Difference

The second principle of transnational governance should be the principle of legitimate difference. As Justice Benjamin Cardozo put it while sitting on the Second Circuit:

> We are not so provincial as to say that every solution of a problem is wrong because we deal with it otherwise at home. The courts are not free to enforce a foreign right at the pleasure of the judges, to suit the individual notion of expediency or fairness. They do not close their doors unless help would violate some fundamental principle of justice, some prevalent conception of good morals, some deep-rooted tradition of the common weal.[60]

In conflicts of law, the principle of legitimate difference is limited by the public policy exception, whereby a court will not apply a foreign law that would be applicable if it violates a fundamental principle of domestic public policy. The principle of legitimate difference assumes that the public policy exception would be applied only rarely, in cases involving the violation of truly fundamental values. In the U.S. context, fundamental equates with constitutional, in the sense that state courts cannot invoke the public policy exception to bar enforcement of another state's act unless that act arguably violates the Constitution itself.[61]

Transposed from the judicial to the regulatory context and from the U.S. to the global context, the principle of legitimate difference should be adopted as a foundational premise of transgovernmental cooperation. All regulators participating in cooperative ventures of various kinds with their foreign counterparts should begin from the premise that "difference" per se reflects a desirable diversity of ideas about how to order an economy or society. That "we deal with it otherwise at home" is not a reason for rejecting a foreign law or regulation or regulatory practice unless it can be shown to violate the rejecting country's constitutional rules and values.

The principle of legitimate difference applies most precisely to foreign laws and regulations, but a corollary of the principle is a presumption that foreign government officials should be accorded the same respect due to national officials unless a specific reason exists to suspect that they will chauvinistically privilege their own citizens. Several examples from the judicial context illustrate the point. In highly publicized antitrust litigation brought by Sir Freddie Laker against both U.S. and British airlines alleging that they conspired to drive his low-cost airline out of business, U.S. federal district judge Harold Green decided not to restrain the British parties from petitioning the British government for help.[62] Judge Green was presuming the same good faith on the part of the British executive as he would on the part of the U.S. executive in a parallel circumstance and assuming that the British executive would not automatically ally with its own citizen in a case involving a foreign citizen in a foreign court.

The U.S. Court of Appeals for the Seventh Circuit has also made this premise explicit in several cases. In the Amoco Cadiz case, it chose to treat the French executive branch exactly as it would treat the U.S. executive branch; it deferred to a French executive ruling by applying a U.S. legal doctrine that requires deference to U.S. agencies.[63] And more recently, in a case arising under federal trademark legislation,

Judge Easterbrook argued that foreign courts could interpret such statutes as well as U.S. courts, noting that an entire line of Supreme Court precedents "depend on the belief that foreign tribunals will interpret U.S. law honestly, just as the federal courts of the United States routinely interpret the laws of the states and other nations."[64]

Note that thus formulated, the principle of legitimate difference lies midway on the spectrum from comity to mutual recognition. Traditional comity prescribes deference to a foreign law or regulation unless a nation's balance of interests tips against deference. Legitimate difference raises the bar for rejecting a foreign law by requiring the balance of interests to include values of constitutional magnitude. "Mutual recognition," on the other hand, has become an organizing principle in regimes of regulatory cooperation, as an alternative to either national treatment or harmonization.[65]

As practiced between member states of the European Union, mutual recognition requires two countries to recognize and accept all of each other's laws and regulations in a specific issue area.[66] This state represents a step toward closer and enduring cooperation by effectively assuming that the constitutional test has been met and passed for an entire corpus of foreign laws and regulations. Thus legitimate difference offers an intermediate position that reflects the intent of regulatory officials who seek further cooperation with one another to move beyond mere comity, but that does not require them to establish or even to work toward mutual recognition.

In sum, legitimate difference is a principle that preserves diversity within a framework of a specified degree of convergence. It enshrines pluralism as a basis for, rather than a bar to, regulatory cooperation, leaving open the possibility of further convergence between legal systems in the form of mutual recognition or even harmonization, but not requiring it. At the same time, however, it does not try to stitch together or cover over differences concerning fundamental values, whether those involving basic human rights and liberties or the organizing principles for a social, political, or economic system. At a more practical level, the principle of legitimate difference would encourage the development of model codes or compilations of best practices in particular regulatory issue areas, letting the regulators in different countries figure out for themselves how best to adapt them to local circumstance.

It is also important, however, to be clear as to what a principle of legitimate difference will *not* do. It does not help individuals or government institutions figure out which nation should be the primary regulator in a particular issue area or with regard to a set of entities or transactions subject to regulation. Thus it cannot answer the question of which nation should be in the position of deciding whether to recognize which other nation's laws, regulations, or decisions based on legitimate difference. Nevertheless, it can serve as a *Grundnorm* of global governance for regulators exploring a wide variety of relationships with their transnational counterparts. If regulators are not prepared to go even this far, then they are unlikely to be able to push beyond paper cooperation.

Positive Comity

Comity is a long-standing principle of relations between nations. The classic definition for American lawyers is the formulation in *Hilton v. Guyot*: "neither a matter of obligation on the one hand, nor of mere courtesy and good will on the other . . . comity is the recognition which one nation allows within its territory to the legislative, executive, or judicial acts of another nation."[67] "Recognition" is essentially a passive affair, signaling deference to another nation's action.

Positive comity, on the other hand, mandates a move from deference to dialogue. It is a principle of affirmative cooperation between government agencies of different nations. As a principle of governance for transnational regulatory cooperation, it requires regulatory agencies to substitute consultation and active assistance for unilateral action and noninterference.

Positive comity has developed largely in the antitrust community, as an outgrowth of ongoing efforts of EU and U.S. antitrust officials to put their often very rocky relationship on firmer footing. For decades the U.S. policy of extraterritorial enforcement of U.S. antitrust laws based on the direct effect doctrine, even in various modified forms, was met by diplomatic protests, administrative refusals, and a growing number of foreign blocking statutes that restricted access to important evidence located abroad or sought to reverse U.S. judgments.[68] The U.S. government gradually began to change course, espousing principles of comity and restraint in congressional testimony and in its international antitrust guidelines.[69]

In addition, U.S. regulators began relying less on unilateral state action and more on agency cooperation. In the early 1980s, the United States entered into separate cooperation agreements with the governments of Australia (June 1982) and Canada (March 1984). In both agreements, the parties consented to cooperate in investigations and litigation by the other even when this enforcement affected its nationals or the other party sought information within its territory. In return, the parties agreed to exercise *negative* comity—to refrain from enforcing competition laws where such enforcement would unduly interfere with the sovereign interests of the other party.[70]

These agreements have led not only to greater cooperation between states,[71] but also to more effective enforcement of the antitrust statutes of both parties.[72] Several other countries, such as Germany and France (1984) as well as Australia and New Zealand (1990), have adopted similar bilateral arrangements addressing mutual assistance, including notification of activities, enforcement cooperation, and information exchange.[73]

In 1991, the United States executed an extensive antitrust cooperation agreement with the European Community.[74] The agreement contained provisions on notification of enforcement activities, as well as on information sharing and biannual meetings.[75] Most notably, the agreement was the first to include the principle of positive comity. Article V of the agreement provides that if party A believes that its "important interests" are being adversely affected by anticompetitive activities that violate party A's competition laws but occur within the territory of party B, party A may request that party B initiate enforcement activities.[76] Thus, government B, in deference to government A, is expected to consider enforcement steps that it might not otherwise have taken.[77]

This notion of positive comity is the converse of the traditional idea of deference, or negative comity. Unlike the earlier agreements concluded by the United States with Australia and Canada, the EC agreement focuses less on protecting the sovereign interests of one jurisdiction against the antitrust activities of the other and more on facilitating cooperative and even coordinated enforcement by antitrust authorities.[78] Where deference would tend toward less affirmative enforcement action, positive comity was designed to produce more affirmative enforcement.[79] While the EC—U.S. agreement reflects the increasing trend toward transnational cooperation in antitrust enforcement, the extent of enforcement coordination and information sharing contemplated by the agreement was unprecedented.[80]

In practice, the agreement has spurred an increase in the flow of information between the parties.[81] In addition, there has been increased enforcement of antitrust objectives, both quantitatively and qualitatively.[82] In coordinating their activities, the parties under the agreement work together to minimize the disruption to international trade that multiple uncoordinated investigations might otherwise cause.[83] Merit Janow, reviewing transatlantic cooperation in competition policy, concludes that "positive comity is an important doctrine and that it can go some way in ameliorating tensions associated with extraterritorial enforcement and in facilitating enforcement cooperation."[84] At the same time, she advocates taking a step further toward enhanced comity through "an integrated or work-sharing approach" between U.S. and EU competition authorities, whereby one or the other would be designated the "de facto lead agency" in any investigation.[85]

Can positive comity be translated from the antitrust context into a more general principle of governance? Two potential objections arise. First is the concern of many within the antitrust community that positive comity is a label with little content. In the words of one critic, "It is not realistic to expect one government to prosecute its citizens solely for the benefit of another."[86] The point here is that positive comity could only work where both governments involved already have a direct interest in prosecuting because the behavior in question directly affects them, in which case cooperation is likely to occur anyway.[87] Further, any desire to undertake an investigation on behalf of a foreign government risks a domestic backlash.[88]

The second objection is a converse concern that to the extent positive comity works, it assumes enormous trust and close continuing re-lations between particular national regulatory agencies—factors that cannot be generalized. Spencer Weber Waller points out that coopera-tion among agencies responsible for antitrust policy creates a commu-nity of competition officials who have been trained and socialized to speak, write, and think about competition issues in a similar way.[89] Thus if positive comity works anywhere, it should work here, but how can we adopt positive comity as a global principle of transnational reg-ulatory cooperation before a relatively high level of cooperation has al-ready been established?

The response to both these objections is a simplified and less strin-gent version of positive comity. As a general principle it need mean no more than an obligation to act rather than merely to respond. In any case in which nation A is contemplating regulatory action and in which nation B has a significant interest in the activity under scrutiny, either through the involvement of its nationals or through the com-mission of significant events within its territorial jurisdiction, the regu-latory agency of nation A, consistent with the dual function of regula-tory officials developed above, has a duty at the very least to notify and consult with the regulatory agency of nation B. Nation A's agency must further wait for a response from nation B before deciding what ac-tion to take, and must notify nation B's agency of any decision taken.

Even the critics of positive comity acknowledge that to the extent a commitment to positive comity facilitates increased communication and exchange of information between governments, it may have an impact at the margin.[90] This communication and exchange of informa-tion in turn lays the foundation for more enduring relationships that ultimately ripen into trust. Thus at a global level, a principle of positive comity, combined with the principle of legitimate difference, creates the basis for a pluralist community of regulators who are actively seek-ing coordination at least and collaboration at best.

Checks and Balances

Fourth, and for many perhaps first, it is necessary to take a leaf from Madison's book. If in fact government networks, or indeed any form of global governance, are to avoid Kant's nightmare of "soulless despotism," the power of every element of the world order system set forth in this book must be checked and balanced. A system of checks and balances is in fact emerging in many areas, from relations between national courts and supranational courts to the executive of one state challenging the regulatory agency of another in national court. Yet these fragments of evolving experience should be understood and analyzed in the context of an affirmative norm of friction and constructive ambiguity in relations among participants in government networks of every kind. The whole should resemble the U.S. Constitution in at least this much—a system of shared and separated powers designed more for liberty than efficiency.

Writing about American federalism, David Shapiro has portrayed it as "a dialogue about government."[91] The federal system set forth in the Constitution frames a perpetual debate in which "neither argument—the case for unrestrained national authority or the case against it—is rhetorically or normatively complete without the other."[92] It is the dialogue itself that is a source both of creative innovation and tempering caution. This description also applies to relations between national courts in EU member-countries and the ECJ, a dialogue that lies at the heart of the EU constitutional order. Their debates over both jurisdictional competence and substantive law are matters of pushing and pulling over lines demarcating authority that are constructed and revised by the participants themselves. Each side is checked less by a specific grant of power intended to act as a check or a balance than by the ability of each side to challenge or refine any assertion of power by the other.

In some sense, the entire concept of the disaggregation of the state makes a global system of checks and balances possible. Given the correct incentive structures, government institutions of the same type in different systems, national and international, and of different types can check each other both vertically and horizontally. National courts can resist the excessive assertion of supranational judicial power; supranational courts can review the performance of national courts. Similar relationships are emerging between regulatory agencies, supranational and national, in the European Union and can easily be imagined globally. It is even possible to imagine relations between committees of national legislators from different countries nestled within international or supranational institutions entering into a balancing relationship with national parliamentary committees of similar jurisdiction, such as the NATO parliamentary council interacting with defense and security committees of national parliaments.

It is both likely and desirable, however, that a strong asymmetry of power remain between national and supranational institutions, in the sense that national institutions should remain the rule and supranational institutions the exception. That is the principle of subsidiarity, discussed below. At the same time, national institutions can check each other across borders, either by refusing to cooperate, as when a Japanese court might thwart the judgment or even the jurisdiction of a U.S. court, or by actively working at cross-purposes. An example here would be an effort by an executive to use its national courts to block the executive of another country, as the British government apparently tried to do with the British courts in the Laker litigation.[93]

Overall, checks and balances must become an accepted part of a global political arrangement among government institutions. Here again, networks of legislators would be a valuable addition to global government networks—to provide a counterweight, where necessary, to networks of regulators or even judges. Thus, for instance, when a network of securities regulators is promulgating a code of best practices, it is not impossible to imagine a similar code issuing from a network of legislative committees from different nations concerned with the same issues. The determination of what a best practice is and whose interests it is most likely to serve would likely be different. Certainly such a possibility would provide a counterweight to the consensus of professional technocrats.

Subsidiarity

The final normative principle necessary to structure a global political process of disaggregated national and supranational institutions is subsidiarity. Subsidiarity is the European Union's version of Madisonian checks and balances. The term may be unfamiliar, but the concept is not. It expresses a principle that decisions are to be taken as closely as possible to the citizen.[94] Article V of the Consolidated Treaty Establishing the European Community defines the principle of subsidiarity as the criterion for determining the division of powers between the community and its member-states.[95]

Projected onto a global screen, the principle of subsidiarity would reinforce the basic axiom of global governance through government networks: even on a global scale, the vast majority of governance tasks should still be taken by national government officials. Within nation-states, of course, subsidiarity may argue for the exercise of power at a lower level still—at the local or provincial level. Yet once at the level of the national government, the burden of proof to devolve power up to a regional or global entity will require a demonstration that the specific functions needed cannot be adequately provided by national government institutions either coordinating their action or actively cooperating.

Finally, within international or supranational institutions themselves, questions of institutional design and allocation of power should depend upon a demonstration of the need for personnel and powers in addition to, or superior to, networks of national government officials. The nesting of such networks within the institution, as in the EU Council of Ministers, would be entirely consistent with the principle of subsidiarity. The real rub would come with the decision whether and when to create a separate global or regional bureaucracy.

It is not my purpose to argue that such a bureaucracy should never be created. The world would be a far poorer place without Kofi Annan. And even without his particular charisma, the secretariats of many international institutions, such as the United Nations, the WTO, and the OSCE, are critical not only to the functioning of those institutions but to the global direction and implementation of security, trade, and human rights policy. Further, institutions such as the IMF and the World Bank depend on a cadre of professionals who perceive their loyalties as flowing to the fund or the bank rather than to specific national governments. Similarly, it is certainly true that supranational judicial institutions, such as the ECJ, can often perform functions that networks of national judges could not in fact take on.

The value of subsidiarity is that it institutionalizes a system or a political process of global governance from the bottom up. International lawyers, diplomats, and global dreamers have long pictured a world much more united from the top down. Even as the need for governance goes global, the ideal location of that governance may well remain local. The principle of subsidiarity requires proponents of shifting power away from the citizen at least to make the case.

4. CONCLUSION

The point of this book has been to identify the phenomenon of the disaggregated state and to explore the resulting possibilities for a disaggregated world order. The tone has been largely optimistic, seeking to focus on what does exist and elaborate what could exist as a solution to the tri-lemma of global governance: the need to exercise authority at the global level without centralized power but with government officials feeling a responsibility to multiple constituencies rather than to private pressure groups. No form of government is perfect, however, least of all at the global level. And even if, as with Winston Churchill's view of democracy, global governance through government networks is the "least worst" alternative, it still poses many problems that must ultimately be addressed.

Indeed, the critics are already lined up, with a range of charges. First is the accusation that networks of government officials—particularly judges and regulators—constitute the triumph of technocracy over democracy. These networks operate in a perfectly depoliticized world, in which like-minded, and similarly trained, officials can reinforce their common perceptions and professional norms in reaching a consensus about how to address common problems, from rising interest rates to the enforcement of rights to environmental protection. Within the safe confines of a government network they are never bombarded by competing evidence, uncomfortable normative claims, or even simply additional information that forces them to broaden the analytical framework for decision. This criticism operates both at the global level, coming from international lawyers who seek to ensure an open and just world order, and at the domestic level, coming from consumer groups who claim that they are shut out of the formation of international regulatory standards through harmonization processes.

A typical response to this criticism is to open up the decision-making process of government networks to the many different types of pressure groups that participate in a democratic domestic political process. Yet this solution alarms another set of critics who insist that government authority be clearly exercised by government officials rather than being diffused among a vast array of public, semi-public, and private actors in a global policy network. This problem of an unrepresentative global political process has echoes in a specific debate taking place within a number of countries over the legitimacy of reaching outside a particular national legal system to consult and cite the decisions of foreign judges. A final, unavoidable problem is the way in which power is exercised in government networks by strong countries against weak countries, both through exclusion from certain networks or from powerful groups within them, and through inclusion in networks that serve as conduits for soft power.

A menu of general responses to these charges includes a concept of dual function for all government officials, meaning that their jobs automatically include both domestic and international activity. They must thus be accountable to their national constituents for both categories of activity. In a full-fledged disaggregated world order, they would actually exercise both national and global responsibility, which would require accountability to both national and global norms. Second, any system of responsible government action requires that the action itself be visible; hence government networks must make their activities as visible as possible. One way to do this is to give them virtual reality through the use of readily available websites. Third is to encourage the proliferation of legislative networks, to ensure that the directly elected representatives of various national citizenries are as active in the transgovernmental realm as regulators and judges. Fourth is to use government networks to mobilize a wide range of nongovernmental actors, either as parallel networks or as monitors and interlocutors for specific government networks. Fifth is a grab-bag of domestic policy solutions, whereby each national polity must decide for itself whether different kinds of transgovernmental activity pose a problem and, if so, what to do about it.

These problems and solutions largely address government networks as they currently exist. If, however, we were to establish the disaggregated world order described in the last two chapters, in which government networks are self-consciously constituted as mechanisms both of global governance and of improving the quality and sustainability of national governance, then these networks would also have to operate in accordance with a more general set of global norms.

I suggest five such norms—some to operate primarily in horizontal relations between national government officials and others to operate more generally in vertical relations between national government officials and their supranational counterparts. First is a norm of global deliberative equality, a presumption that all government networks should be open to any government officials who meet specified criteria or conditions of membership. Further, once admitted, these officials would be entitled both to listen and be heard. Second is a norm of legitimate difference—the requirement that in their various deliberations, members of government networks understand and act on the principle that "different" does not equal "wrong." Third is positive comity, the substitution of a norm of affirmative cooperation between nations in place of the traditional deference by one state to another state's action. Fourth is the globalization of the American principles of checks and balances: the guarantee of continual limitation of power through competition and overlapping jurisdiction. Fifth, and finally, is a principle borrowed more from Jean Monnet than James Madison: the principle of subsidiarity, or the location of government power at the lowest level practicable among local, regional, national, and supranational authorities.

Members of government networks must interact with their foreign counterparts sufficiently transparently to be monitored by ordinary voters; they must give reasons for their actions in terms intelligible to a larger public; and they must be able to formulate arguments in sufficiently general, principled, "other-regarding" ways to be able to win the day in a process of deliberative decision making. Operating in a world of generalizable principles, however, requires a baseline of acceptable normative behavior. The norms I have prescribed ensure wide participation in government networks, seek to preserve local, regional, and national autonomy to the extent possible, and guarantee a wide space for local variation, including local variation driven by local and national politics.

At the loftiest level, these principles could be understood as part of a global transgovernmental constitution—overarching values to steer the operation of government networks. Yet the content of these specific principles is less important in many ways than the simple fact that there be principles—benchmarks against which accountability can be measured. Understanding government networks as a form of government, and then holding them to the same standards and subject to the same strictures that we hold all government, will do the rest.

Conclusion

The only way most states can realize and express their
sovereignty is through participation in the regimes that
make up the substance of international life.
—Abram Chayes and Antonia Handler Chayes[1]

GLOBAL GOVERNANCE THROUGH GOVERNMENT NETWORKS IS GOOD PUBLIC
policy for the world and good national foreign policy for the United
States, the European Union, APEC members, and all developing countries seeking to participate in global regulatory processes and needing
to strengthen their capacity for domestic governance. Even in their
current form, government networks promote convergence, compliance
with international agreements, and improved cooperation among nations on a wide range of regulatory and judicial issues. A world order
self-consciously created out of horizontal and vertical government networks could go much further. It could create a genuine global rule of
law without centralized global institutions and could engage, socialize,
support, and constrain government officials of every type in every nation. In this future, we could see disaggregated government institutions—the members of government networks—as actual bearers of a
measure of sovereignty, strengthening them still further, but also sub-

jecting them to specific legal obligations. This would be a genuinely different world, with its own challenges and its own promise.

1. GOVERNMENT NETWORKS AND GLOBAL PUBLIC POLICY

Wolfgang Reinecke, like many others, argues that national governments are losing their ability to formulate and implement national public policy within territorial borders rendered increasingly porous by the forces of globalization, immigration, and the information revolution. He proposes that they "delegate tasks to other actors and institutions that are in a better position to implement global public policies—not only to public sector agencies like the World Bank and the IMF, but also business, labor, and nongovernmental organizations."[2] He offers this strategy as an alternative to "[f]orming a global government," which "would require states to abdicate their sovereignty not only in daily affairs but in a formal sense as well."[3] In other words, national governments have already lost their sovereignty, but they should compensate for that loss by delegating their responsibilities to a host of nonstate actors—international organizations, corporations, and NGOs.

This is precisely the globalization tri-lemma. National governments are losing power. They can only recreate this power at the global level by creating a global government, but that is "unrealistic,"[4] so the alternative is a hodgepodge of private sector and public international organizations, for profit and not for profit. It is exactly this hodgepodge that Reinecke calls governance instead of government, and it is exactly why another group of critics fear that the formulation of global public policy is being left to experts, enthusiasts, international bureaucrats, and transnational businesspeople—everyone, that is, but politically accountable government officials.

A self-conscious world order of government networks could address these problems. National government officials would retain primary power over public policy, but work together to formulate and implement it globally. They would delegate some power to supranational officials, but then work closely with those officials through vertical networks. And they would interact intensively with existing international organizations, corporations, NGOs, and other actors in transnational society, but in a way that makes it clear that government networks are the accountable core of these larger policy networks.

This conception of a networked world order rests on fundamentally different assumptions about both the international system and international law. The old model of the international system assumes unitary states that negotiate formal legal agreements with one another and implement them from the top down, with a great emphasis on verification and enforcement. The new model advanced here assumes disaggregated states in which national government officials interact intensively with one another and adopt codes of best practices and agree on coordinated solutions to common problems—agreements that have no legal force but that can be directly implemented by the officials who negotiated them. At the same time, in this new model, states still acting as unitary actors will realize that some problems cannot be effectively addressed without delegating actual sovereign power to a limited number of supranational government officials, such as judges and arbitrators in the WTO, NAFTA, and the ICC. In such cases, the international agreements negotiated will be more immediately and automatically effective than the majority of agreements negotiated in the old system because they will be directly enforced through vertical government networks.

In practice, of course, these two models of the international system will coexist. Government networks, both horizontal and vertical, will operate alongside and even within traditional international organizations. Reinecke describes these traditional organizations as the "institutions of interdependence," meaning the institutions created by unitary sovereign states to manage the "macroeconomic cooperation" required by the growing economic interdependence of the 1960s and 1970s.[5] He describes transgovernmental regulatory organizations such as the Financial Stability Forum as "institutions . . . of globalization," meaning "the integration of a cross-national dimension into the very nature of the organizational structure and strategic behavior of individual companies."[6] Linking these two types of institutions, as he notes, "would help avoid bureaucratic overlap and turf fights between international institutions and permit a more integrated approach to developing economies' dual challenge of national liberalization and global public policy."[7]

What transgovernmental networks can do that traditional international organizations cannot, however, is to counter and engage transnational corporate, civic, and criminal networks. They permit a loose, flexible structure that can bring in national officials from a wide range of different countries as needed to address specific problems. They can target problems at their roots, plug loopholes in national jurisdictions, and respond to goods, people, and ideas streaming across borders. Their members can educate, bolster, and regulate one another in essentially the same ways that make private transnational networks so effective. They are indeed the "institutions of globalization," and far better suited to global governance in an age of globalization and information.

2. NATIONAL SUPPORT FOR GOVERNMENT NETWORKS

The European Union is pioneering governance through government networks in its internal affairs. As the multiple examples relied on in this book emphasize—from the relations between national courts and the ECJ to the creation of European information agencies to help the networks of regulators across the European Union—the European Union is a vibrant laboratory for how to establish the necessary degree of collective cooperation among a diverse group of states while retaining the dominant locus of political power at the national level. It has limited supranational institutions, and though they are more powerful than any that currently exist at the global level, they cannot function without the active cooperation and participation of national government officials. Beyond the Court and the commission, the power in the European Union rests with networks of national ministers and lower-level officials, who make decisions at the European level and implement them at the national level.

The European Union has many features that make its distinctive form of government by network exportable to other regions and to the world at large. It remains a collection of distinct nations, even as it works to create the governing power and institutions at the supranational level necessary to solve common problems and advance common interests for all its members. We might thus expect the European Union to support the creation of global government networks. In fact, however, it is the United States that has led the way in supporting these networks at the global level. The SEC, the EPA, and even the U.S. House of Representatives have taken the lead in organizing global government networks. And the U.S. Department of Justice established the Global Competition Network as an alternative to efforts to develop global antitrust regulations through the WTO. Even the U.S. Supreme Court and lower federal courts, although latecomers to global transjudicial dialogue, are beginning to network actively with their foreign counterparts. The United States has also been an active member of APEC, which has insisted on and refined the network form of regional governance.

More recently, the United States has pushed the even more informal approach of "coalitions of the willing," both at the unitary state level of enlisting military allies and at the disaggregated state level of networking to combat terrorist financing, share intelligence on terrorist activity, and cooperate in bringing individual terrorists to justice. Promoting actual government networks in all these areas is a far better approach, as it would institutionalize the cooperation that already exists and create a framework for deepening future cooperation in virtually every area of domestic policy. At the same time, however, government networks are far more transparent than "coalitions of the willing"; if done right, they would have a permanent and visible existence, criteria for membership, and ground rules for their operation applicable to all. U.S. officials could and would play a leading role in many instances, as they do already in existing government networks, but they would have to share the stage with officials from many other countries and be prepared to listen and learn.

Over the longer term, government networks can tackle the domestic roots of international problems and can do so both multilaterally and in a way that empowers domestic government officials in countries around the world to help themselves. The exchange of information, development of collective standards, provision of training and technical assistance, ongoing monitoring and support, and active engagement in enforcement cooperation that does and can take place in government networks can give government officials in weak, poor, and transitional countries the boost they need. Their counterparts in more powerful countries, meanwhile, can reach beyond their borders to try to address problems that have an impact within their borders.

For maximum impact and effectiveness, however, the work of government networks cannot be done in the shadows. Existing networks breed suspicion and opposition in many quarters, leading to charges of technocracy, distortion of global and national political processes, elitism and inequality. The United States and other countries should champion them openly as mechanisms of global governance and be prepared to reform and improve them as necessary. They will almost certainly have to become more visible and engage more systematically with corporate and civic networks. They should include more and more effective networks of legislators as well as of regulators and judges. And their members are likely to be subject to more national oversight and regulation specifically aimed at integrating the national and international dimensions of their jobs.

To maximize the accountability of the participants in government networks, it would be possible to take a step further and give them a measure of individual, or rather institutional, sovereignty. In a world of disaggregated states, the sovereignty that has traditionally attached to unitary states should arguably also be disaggregated. Taking this step, however, requires a different conception of the very nature of sovereignty. As described in the next section, sovereignty understood as capacity rather than autonomy can easily attach to the component parts of states and includes responsibilities as well as rights.

3. DISAGGREGATED SOVEREIGNTY

Theorists, pundits, and policymakers all recognize that traditional conceptions of sovereignty are inadequate to capture the complexity of contemporary international relations. The result is a seemingly endless debate about the changing nature of sovereignty: what does it mean? Does it still exist? Is it useful? Everyone in this debate still assumes that sovereignty is an attribute borne by an entire state, acting as a unit. Yet if states are acting in the international system through their component government institutions—regulatory agencies, ministries, courts, legislatures—why shouldn't each of these institutions exercise a measure of sovereignty as specifically defined and tailored to their functions and capabilities?

This proposal may seem fanciful, or even frightening, if we think about sovereignty the old way—as the power to be left alone, to exclude, to counter any external meddling or interference. Consider, however, the "new sovereignty," defined by Abram and Antonia Chayes as the capacity to participate in international institutions of all types—in collective efforts to steer the international system and address global and regional problems together with their national and supranational counterparts.[8] This is a conception of sovereignty that would accord status and recognition to states in the international system to the extent that they are willing and able to engage with other states, and thus necessarily accept mutual obligations.

Chayes and Chayes, like Reinecke, begin from the proposition that the world has moved beyond interdependence. Interdependence refers to a general condition in which states are mutually dependent on and vulnerable to what other states do, but interdependence still assumes a baseline of separation, autonomy, and defined boundaries. States may be deeply dependent on each other's choices and decisions, but those choices and decisions still drive and shape the international system. For Chayes and Chayes, by contrast, the international system itself has become a "tightly woven fabric of international agreements, organizations and institutions that shape [states'] relations with one another and penetrate deeply into their internal economics and politics."[9]

If the background conditions for the international system are connection rather than separation, interaction rather than isolation, and institutions rather than free space, then sovereignty-as-autonomy makes no sense. The new sovereignty is status, membership, "connection to the rest of the world and the political ability to be an actor within it."[10]

However paradoxical it sounds, the measure of a state's capacity to act as an independent unit within the international system—the condition that "sovereignty" purports both to grant and describe—depends on the breadth and depth of its links to other states.

This conception of sovereignty fits neatly with a conception of a disaggregated world order. If the principal moving parts of that order are the agencies, institutions, and the officials within them who are collectively responsible for the legislative, executive, and judicial functions of government, then they must be able to exercise legislative, executive, and judicial sovereignty. They must be able to exercise at least some independent rights and be subject to some independent, or at least distinct, obligations. These rights and obligations may devolve from more unitary rights and obligations applicable to the unitary state, or they may evolve from the functional requirements of meaningful and effective transgovernmental relations. Nonetheless the sovereignty of "states" must become a more flexible and practical attribute.

If sovereignty is relational rather than insular, in the sense that it describes a capacity to engage rather than a right to resist, then its devolution onto ministers, legislators, and judges is not so difficult to imagine. The concept of judicial comity discussed in chapter 2 rests on judges' respect for each other's competence as members of the same profession and institutional enterprise across borders. It assumes that a fully "sovereign" court is entitled to its fair share of disputes when conflicts arise, can negotiate cooperative solutions in transnational disputes, and can participate in a transnational judicial dialogue about issues of common concern. Regulators would be similarly empowered to interact with their fellow regulators to engage in the full range of activities described in chapter 1. And legislators would be directly empowered to catch up.

If, however, disaggregated state institutions are already engaged in these activities, as is the argument of this book, what difference does it make if they are granted formal capacity to do what they are already doing? The principal advantage is that subjecting government institutions directly to international obligations could buttress clean institutions against corrupt ones and rights-respecting institutions against their more oppressive counterparts. Each government institution would have an independent obligation to interpret and implement international legal obligations, much as each branch of the U.S. government has an independent obligation to ensure that its actions conform to the Constitution. As in the domestic context, either the courts or the legislature would have the last word in case of disputed interpretations of international law so as to ensure the possibility of national unity where necessary. In many cases, however, international legal obligations concerning trade, the environment, judicial independence, human rights, arms control, and other areas would devolve directly on government institutions charged with responsibility for the issue area in question.

By becoming enrolled and enmeshed in global government networks, individual government institutions would affirm their judicial, legislative, or regulatory sovereignty. They would participate in the formulation and implementation of professional norms and the development of best practices on substantive issues. And they would be aware that they are performing before their constituents, their peers, and the global community at large, as bearers of rights and status in that community.

This idea is not as far-fetched as it may seem. Actual examples already exist or are being proposed. Eyal Benvenisti has raised the possibility of formally empowering substate units to enter into agreements.[11] The Princeton Principles on Universal Jurisdiction make the case for establishing clear rules and principles under international law that are directly aimed at national judges, as they are the actual subjects of the international law doctrine. The ambiguity that helps statesmen negotiate treaties is often disastrous for judges, who must actually apply the law.

At first glance, disaggregating the state and granting at least a measure of sovereignty to its component parts might appear to weaken the state. On the contrary, it will bolster the power of the state as the primary actor in the international system. Giving each government institution a measure of legitimate authority under international law, with accompanying duties, marks government officials as distinctive in larger policy networks and allows the state to extend its reach. If sovereignty were still understood as exclusive and impermeable rather than relational, strengthening the state would mean building higher walls to protect its domestic autonomy. Yet in a world in which sovereignty means the capacity to participate in cooperative regimes in the collective interest of all states, expanding the formal capacity of different state institutions to interact with their counterparts around the world means expanding state power.

In conclusion, consider the following thought experiment. Imagine beginning with a world of sovereign states and trying to design a feasible, effective, and just system of global governance. Imagine that the governments of many of those states are seeking to fight crime, collect taxes, guarantee civil rights and civil liberties, protect the environment, regulate financial markets, provide a measure of social security, ensure the safety of consumer products, and represent their citizens fairly and accurately. Now assume that for a host of reasons, national government officials cannot do their jobs solely within their borders. Assume further that some of the problems they seek to address have global dimensions, and that the creators and vectors of those problems are acting through transnational networks. At the same time, individuals, groups, and organizations that can help address those problems are also acting through transnational networks. Finally, assume that one of the things the citizens of all these countries want is a safer, fairer, cleaner world.

These national government officials would never cede power to a world government, although they would certainly recognize that, with respect to some specific problems, only genuinely powerful supranational institutions could overcome the collective action problems inherent in formulating and implementing global solutions. In most cases, however, they would seek to work together in a variety of ways, recognizing that they could only do their jobs properly at the national level by interacting—whether in cooperation and conflict—at the global level. Their ordinary government jobs—regulating, judging, legislating—would thus come to include both domestic and international activity. Over time, they would also come to recognize responsibilities not only to their national constituents but to broader global constituencies. If granted a measure of sovereignty to participate in collective decision making with one another, they would also have to live up to obligations to those broader constituencies.

In short, they would create a world order. It would encompass many of the elements of the present international system and build on the trends I have described, but would overlay and surround them with government networks of all kinds. It would be a world order created by, and composed of, disaggregated state institutions, allowing nation-states to evolve in ways that keep up with changes in the private sector and that expand state power. It would be an effective world order, in the sense of being able to translate paper principles into individual and organizational action. To be truly effective, however, it would also have to be a just world order, as inclusive, respectful, tolerant, and equal as possible.

It would be a world order in which human hope and despair, crime and charity, ideas and ideals are transmitted around the globe through networks of people and organizations. So, too, would it be in the power of governments to represent and regulate their people. Harnessing that capacity, and strengthening it, is the best hope for a new world order.

Introduction

1. MacCormick, "Beyond the Sovereign State," 18.

2. Naím, "Five Wars of Globalization," 29.

3. Flynn, "America The Vulnerable," 60.

4. Sanger, "The World: When Laws Don't Apply; Cracking Down on the Terror-Arms Trade," *New York Times*, 15 June 2003, Sect. 4, 4.

5. Chote, "A World in the Woods," *Financial Times*, 2 November 1998, 20.

6. The Financial Stability Forum was initiated by the finance ministers and central bank governors of the Group of Seven (G-7) industrial countries in February 1999, following a report on international cooperation and coordination in the area of financial market supervision and surveillance by the president of the Deutsche Bundesbank. In addition to representatives from the Basel Committee, IOSCO, and the International Association of Insurance Supervisors (IAIS), its members include senior representatives from national authorities responsible for financial stability in significant international financial centers; international financial institutions such as the Bank for International Settlements (BIS), the IMF, the Organization of Economic Cooperation and Development (OECD), and the World Bank; and committees of central bank experts. "A Guide to Committees, Groups and Clubs," on on the International Monetary Fund homepage (cited 7 July 2003); available from *http://imf.org/external/np/exr/facts/groups.htm#FSF*.

7. American readers may be skeptical of these reports due to the widespread and completely false statistic about how few members of Congress have a passport. In fact, 93 percent of all members hold passports and average two trips abroad a year. Indeed, 20 percent claim to speak a foreign language. Eric Schmitt and Elizabeth Becker, "In-

sular Congress Appears to be Myth," *New York Times*, 4 November 2000, sect. A, 9. What is true is that some members fear that their constituents will identify trips to meet their counterparts abroad with "junkets," but that is a matter of public education.

8. Nye, *Paradox of American Power*, 9.

9. Ibid., xvi.

10. Dehousse, "Regulation by Networks in the European Community, 259.

11. Ibid., 254.

12. Robert O. Keohane "Governance in a Partially Globalized World," presidential address, annual meeting of the American Political Science Association, 2000, *American Political Science Review* 95 (March 2001): 1.

13. Ibid., 5.

14. Ibid., 1.

15. Ibid., 12, quoting Abraham Lincoln, "The Gettysburg Address," 19 November 1863.

16. Annan, *We the Peoples*, 70; see also Reinicke and Deng, *Critical Choices* and Reinicke, "The Other World Wide Web."

17. Bolton, "Should We Take Global Governance Seriously?" 206.

18. Shapiro, "Administrative Law Unbounded, 369.

19. Ibid., 376.

20. Ibid., 374.

21. Testimony of Francis Bator before the Subcommittee on Foreign Economic Policy, Committee on Foreign Affairs, House of Representatives, 25 July 1972. *U.S. Foreign Economic Policy: Implications for the Organization of the Executive Branch*, 110–11, quoted in Robert O. Keohane and Joseph S. Nye, Jr., "Transgovernmental Relations and International Organizations," 39, 42.

22. Keohane and Nye, "Transgovernmental Relations," 43. They included in their definition the increased communication between governmental agencies and business carried on by separate departments with their counterpart bureaucracies abroad. Ibid., 41–42. By contrast, a meeting of heads-of-state at which new initiatives are taken was still the paradigm of the state-centric (inter-state) model. Ibid., 43–44.

23. Cooke, *The Federalist*, No. 42.

24. See, e.g., the process of international rule-making described in Chayes and Chayes, *The New Sovereignty*.

25. For a highly theoretical but comprehensive overview of the development of the idea of "policy networks" in U.S. and British political science, a concept that includes but is broader than my concept of government networks, see R.A.W. Rhodes, *Understanding Governance*, 32–45.

26. Fulton and Sperling, "The Network of Environmental Enforcement and Compliance Cooperation in North America and the Western Hemisphere," 111.

27. Rome Statute of the International Criminal Court, UN Doc. A/CONF.183/9, reprinted in *International Legal Materials* 37 (1998): 999. For a detailed discussion of complementarity in and prior to the Rome Statute, see El Zeidy, "The Principle of Complementarity: A New Mechanism to Implement International Criminal Law," 869.

28. "*Council Regulation (EC) No 1/2003 of 16 December 2002.*" See Europa home-

page (cited 23 June 2003); available from *http://europa.eu.int/comm/competition/citizen/ citizen_antitrust.html#role*.

29. Dehousse, "Regulation by Network."

30. See Raustiala, "The Architecture of International Cooperation: Transgovernmental Networks and The Future of International Law," 1.

31. In Council for a Community of Democracies homepage (cited 7 July 2003); available from *http://www.ccd21.org/*.

32. See Reinecke, "Global Public Policy," 137. Reinecke argues that public policy issues, traditionally confined within state borders, must be addressed at a global level.

33. Chayes and Chayes, *The New Sovereignty*, 107.

CHAPTER 1
Regulators: The New Diplomats

1. Remarks before the Council of Women's International Leaders, 16 November 1999, United Nations, New York, New York.

2. Lyman, "The Growing Influence of Domestic Factors," 76–80.

3. Ibid., 83–85; Andrews, "Listening in on the US-EU Legal Dialogue," 35 (observing that the "State Department has a very limited role to play on substantive aspects of transatlantic regulatory cooperation").

4. "A Guide to Fund Committees, Groups,and Clubs," on International Monetary Fund homepage (cited 3 June 2003); available from *http://www.imf.org/external/np/ exr/facts/groups.htm*.

5. One example of this is the Human Security Network, "a group of like-minded countries from all regions of the world that, at the level of Foreign Ministers, maintains dialogue on questions pertaining to human security." On the Human Security Network homepage (cited 3 June 2002); available from *http://www.humansecuritynetwork.org/ network-e.php*.

6. See Keohane and Nye, *Power and Interdependence*, 8.

7. Majone, "The European Community as a Regulatory State," 321–419.

8. Kagan, "Presidential Administration," 2245.

9. See Introduction, note 21.

10. See Introduction, note 22.

11. Keohane and Nye, "Transgovernmental Relations," 39, 42.

12. Ibid.

13. Ibid.

14. Ibid., 475.

15. Putnam, "Diplomacy and Domestic Policy: The Logic of Two-Level Games," 451.

16. See generally Rosenau and Czempiel, eds., *Governance without Government: Order and Change in World Politics*; James Rosenau, *Along the Domestic-International Frontier: Exploring Governance in a Turbulent World*; Thomas Friedman, *The Lexus and the Olive Tree: Understanding Globalization*. For an excellent review of much of the governance literature, see Gerry Stoker, "Governance as Theory: Five Propositions,"

17–28; For an influential discussion of multilevel governance within the EU, see Scharpf, "Community and Autonomy: Multi-Level Governance in the European Union," 219; Marks, Hooghe, and Blank, "An Actor-Centered Approach to Multi-Level Governance," 20; Horeth, *The Trilemma of Legitimacy: Multilevel Governance in the EU and the Problem of Democracy.*

17. Haas, "Introduction: Epistemic Communities and International Policy Coordination," 3. See also Haas, ed., "Knowledge, Power and International Policy Coordination"; Haas, *Saving the Mediterranean: The Politics of International Environmental Cooperation.*

18. The members of the Basel Committee come from Belgium, Canada, France, Germany, Italy, Japan, Luxembourg, the Netherlands, Spain, Sweden, Switzerland, United Kingdom, and United States. See Bank for International Settlements homepage, Basel, Switzerland (cited 3 June 2003); available from *http://www.bis.org/bcbs/aboutbcbs.htm.*

19. Porter, *States, Markets and Regimes in Global Finance,* 3; see also Zaring, "International Law by Other Means: The Twilight Existence of International Financial Regulatory Organization," 284. Since 1999, the Basel Committee has been working toward and receiving comments on a new Capital Accord with a more risk-sensitive framework, expected to be implemented in 2005. See Bank for International Settlements homepage, Basel, Switzerland (cited 20 December 2002); available at *http://www.bis.org/publ/bcbsca.htm.*

20. The Financial Stability Forum was initiated by the finance ministers and central bank governors of the G-7 industrial countries in February 1999, following a report on international cooperation and coordination in the area of financial market supervision and surveillance by the president of the Deutsche Bundesbank. In addition to representatives from the Basel Committee, IOSCO, and the IAIS, its members include senior representatives from national authorities responsible for financial stability in significant international financial centers; international financial institutions such as the BIS, the IMF, the OECD, and the World Bank; and committees of central bank experts. See "A Guide to Fund Committees, Groups, and Clubs: Financial Stability Forum," on International Monetary Fund homepage (cited 20 December 2002); available from *http://www.imf.org/external/np/exr/facts/groups.htm#FSF.* For a discussion of additional networks created by the Basel Committee, IOSCO, and the IAIS, such as the Joint Forum on Financial Conglomerates and the Year 2000 Network, see Slaughter, "Governing the Global Economy through Government Networks," 186-88.

21. Zaring, "International Law by Other Means," 281; See also Porter, *States, Markets and Regimes,* 4–5.

22. Picciotto, "Networks in International Economic Integration," 1039.

23. Jacobs, "Why Governments Must Work Together," 18. "Regulatory Co-Operation for an Interdependent World: Issues for Government," 18.

24. "Regulatory Co-Operation for an Interdependent World," 35.

25. Majone, "The European Community."

26. Dehousse, "Regulation by Networks in the European Community: The Role of European Agencies," 254.

27. Work on this subject, often in the context of the European Union, includes Cohen and Sabel, "Directly-Deliberative Polyarchy," 313; Joerges and Neyer, "From

Intergovernmental Bargaining to Deliberative Political Processes: The Constitutional-isation of Comitology," 273; Weiler, *The Constitution of Europe: "Do the New Clothes Have An Emperor?" and Other Essays on European Integration.* For an excellent range of arguments by many of the authors engaged in these debates through the 1990s, see the articles collected in Joerges and Vos, eds., *EU Committees: Social Regulation, Law and Politics.*

28. Pollack and Shaffer, eds., *Transatlantic Governance in the Global Economy.*

29. Vogel, *Benefits or Barriers?: Regulation in Transatlantic Trade,* 10; see also Bermann, "Regulatory Cooperation between the European Commission and U.S. Administrative Agencies." 936: "Because . . . the E.C.'s stage of economic and social development is roughly similar to that of the U.S., and because their political and cultural values are broadly comparable, the regulations adopted in the two capitals cover broadly the same range of issues, and, within that range of issues, often pursue the same general policy ends [footnote omitted]."

30. Ibid., chap. 1.

31. Ibid. These are the questions animating the case studies collected in this volume.

32. See Koh, "The 1994 Roscoe Found Lecture: Transnational Legal Process," 181; Chayes and Chayes, *The New Sovereignty: Compliance with International Regulatory Agreements.*

33. Zaring refers to these as international financial regulatory organizations. Zaring, "International Law by Other Means," 281.

34. Gardner, *Sterling-Dollar Diplomacy in Current Perspective: The Origins and the Prospects of Our International Economic Order.*

35. Keohane and Nye, Jr., "The Club Model of Multilateral Cooperation and Problems of Democratic Legitimacy."

36. Ibid., 3.

37. Ibid., 4.

38. For an excellent brief overview of the OECD's origins and current activities, see James Salzman, "Labor Rights, Globalization and Institutions: The Role and Influence of the Organization for Economic Cooperation and Development," 776–83. The OECD website is also a rich source of information. "What is OECD?," On the Organization for Economic Cooperation and Development homepage (cited 20 December 2003); available from *http://www.oecd.org/about/general/index.htm.*

39. See Cheek, "The Limits of Informal Regulatory Cooperation in International Affairs: A Review of the Global Intellectual Property Regime," 313–14 (describing how the Stockholm Group in TRIPS negotiations allowed "a group of ten industrialized countries to meet together informally and reach consensus on various issues"). See also Keohane and Nye, "Transgovernmental Relations," 54. Keohane and Nye describe the ways in which international organizations "facilitate face-to-face meetings among officials in 'domestic' agencies of different governments; suggesting that 'strategically minded secretariats' of international organizations could plan meetings with an eye to encouraging such contacts; and identifying several networks involving both transgovernmental and transnational contacts specifically created by international organizations."

40. Pollack and Shaffer, *Transatlantic Governance,* 14–17.

41. Speech by President Clinton to the Council on Foreign Relations, 14 September 1998, "Transcript: President's Speech on the Global Financial Crisis," on the United States Mission to Italy homepage (cited 4 June 2003); available from *http:// www.usembassy.it/file9801/alia/98091402.htm*. Clinton was echoing calls by British Prime Minister Tony Blair to build a "new Bretton Woods for the next millennium." "Global Finance. Don't Wait Up," *The Economist* 3 October 1998, U.S. edition, 83.

42. Garten, "Needed: A Fed For the World," *New York Times*, 23 September 1998, A29. Two British economists, John Eatwell and Lance Taylor, proposed a World Financial Authority. See "Global finance. Don't wait up," 83.

43. Chote, "A World in the Woods," *Financial Times*, 2 November 1998, 20.

44. "Global finance. Don't wait up," 83. President Clinton and other leaders of APEC announced the creation of the Group of 22, on a temporary basis, at their meeting in Vancouver in November 1997. It was to be a group of finance ministers and central bank governors to advance reform of the architecture of global finance. Its original members included finance ministers and central bank governors from the G-7 countries plus fifteen emerging market countries (Argentina, Australia, Brazil, Canada, China, France, Germany, Hong Kong SAR, India, Indonesia, Italy, Japan, Korea, Malaysia, Mexico, Poland, Russia, Singapore, South Africa, Thailand, the United Kingdom, and the United States). It subsequently evolved into the G-33 and then the G-20. See "A Guide to Fund Committees, Groups,and Clubs."

45. "APEC's Family Feud," *The Economist*, 21 November 1998, 41.

46. Jeffrey Sachs proposed the creation of a G-16, composed of the G-8 plus "eight counterparts from the developing world." The group would "not seek to dictate to the world, but to establish the parameters from a renewed and honest dialogue." Sachs, "Making it work," *The Economist*, 12 September 1998, U.S. edition, 23; Jeffrey Garten proposed a G-15 (the G-8 plus Seven) to monitor the actions of a new global central bank. Garten, "Needed: A Fed For the World."

47. Chote, "A World in the Woods," 20.

48. Keohane and Nye, "Transgovernmental Relations," 51.

49. For a detailed description of many of these arrangements, see Slaughter, "Governing the Global Economy."

50. "About Fincen/Overview," on the Financial Crimes Enforcement Network homepage (cited 31 May 2003); available from *http://www.fincen.gov/af_overview.html*.

51. "International/Training and Technical Assistance," on the Financial Crimes Enforcement Network homepage (cited 31 May 2003); available from *http://www. fincen.gov/int_wwoc.html*.

52. "International/Egmont Group/FIUs," on the Financial Crimes Enforcement Network homepage (cited 31 May 2003); available from *http://www.fincen.gov/ int_fius.html*.

53. The Egmont Group," on the Financial Crimes Enforcement Network homepage (cited 31 May 2003); available from *http://www.fincen.gov/int_egmont.html*.

54. The Conference on Interaction and Confidence-Building Measures in Asia includes Afghanistan, Azerbaijan, China, Egypt, India, Iran, Israel, Kazakhstan, Kyrgyzstan, Mongolia, Pakistan, Palestine, Russia, Tajikistan, Turkey, and Uzbekistan. Further information is available at "CICA: The Road to Security in Asia," on the Embassy

of Kazakhstan in the United States homepage (cited 4 June 2003); available from *http://www.homestead.com/prosites-kazakhembus/CICA_Security_in_Asia.html*.

55. Dehousse, "Regulation by Networks in the European Community," 259.

56. Ibid.

57. Jacobs, "Why Governments Must Work Together," 18; *Regulatory Co-Operation for an Interdependent* World, 15–38, 18.

58. Bergsten, "American and Europe: Clash of Titans?" 33.

59. Portnoy, "Convergence and Diversity in Antitrust Globalization," unpublished manuscript presented at the Program on International Politics, Economics, and Security (PIPES), University of Chicago, January 1999, 22.

60. Fulton and Sperling, "The Network of Environmental Enforcement and Complicance Cooperation in North America and the Western Hemisphere," 122–123.

61. See Raustiala, "The Architecture of International Cooperation: Transgovernmental Networks and The Future of International Law," 1.

62. Shadid and Donelly, "America Prepares Coalition Building/Diplomatic Realignment: New Enemy May Mean New Friends," *The Boston Globe*, 24 September 2001, A14.

63. Dorf and Sabel, "A Constitution of Democratic Experimentalism," 352–53 (describing "best-practice rules" as "processes that are at least as effective in achieving the regulatory objective as the best practice identified by the agency at any given time").

64. "The Basel Committee on Banking Supervision," on the Bank for International Settlements homepage (cited 1 June 2003); available from *http://www.bis.org/bcbs/aboutbcbs.htm*.

65. "International/Training and Technical Assistance," on the Financial Crimes Enforcement Network homepage (cited 18 May 2003); available from *http://www.fincen.gov/int_wwoc.html*.

66. Majone, "The New European Agencies: Regulation by Information," 272.

67. Ibid., 271–72.

68. See Waller, "The Internationalization of Antitrust Enforcement," 364.

69. Ibid.

70. See "Interpol: An Overview," on the Interpol homepage (cited 20 December 2002); available from *http://www.interpol.com/Public/Icpo/FactSheets/FS200101.asp*.

71. Ibid.

72. See "The Euro-Mediterranean Partnership (EMP)," on the Euro-Mediterranean Human Rights Network homepage (cited 20 December 2002); available from *http://www.euromedrights.net/english/barcelona-process/EMP/main.html*.

73. Raustiala, "The Architecture of International Cooperation."

74. Devuyst, "Transatlantic Competition Relations," 127–28.

75. "Securities and Exchange Commission Annual Report 2002," on the U.S. Securities and Exchange Commission homepage (cited 4 June 2003); available at *http://www.sec.gov/pdf/annrep02/ar02intaffs.pdf*, 22.

76. "Environmental Training Modules: International Catalogue," on the United States Environmental Protection Agency homepage (cited 4 June 2003); available at *http://www.epa.gov/international/techasst/training/traincatalog.html*.

77. Raustiala, "The Architecture of International Cooperation," 33.

78. Waller, "Comparative Competition Law as a Form of Empiricism," 457.

79. "The Basel Committee on Banking Supervision," on the Bank for International Settlements homepage (cited 1 June 2003); available at *http://www.bis.org/bcbs/aboutbcbs.htm*.

80. "IOSCO Working Committees," on the OICU-IOSCO homepage (cited 1 June 2003); available at *http://www.iosco.org/about/about.cfm?whereami=page3*.

81. Raustiala, "The Architecture of International Cooperation," 48.

82. Ibid., 23.

83. "International Criminal Investigative Training Assistance Program," on the Department of Justice homepage (cited 18 May 2003); available at *http://www.usdoj.gov/criminal/icitap/index.htm*.

84. Raustiala, "The Architecture of International Cooperation," 48.

85. "Statement for the Record of Louis J. Freeh, Director of the FBI on International Crime before the United States Senate Committee on Appropriations Subcommittee on Foreign Operations Washington, D.C (21 April 1998)," on the FBI Homepage (cited 20 December 2002); available at *http://www.fbi.gov/congress/congress98/intrcrime.htm*.

86. Public Citizen observes that this harmonization is driven by industry and may not always be in the best interests of the public. See "Harmonization," on the Public Citizen homepage (cited 20 December 2002); available at *http://www.citizen.org trade/harmoninzation/index.cfm*.

87. Ibid. Public Citizen also publishes a Harmonization Alert on their web page that "seeks to promote open and accountable policy-making relating to public health, natural resources, consumer safety, and economic justice standards in the era of globalization." See "Harmonizaton Alert," on the Public Citizen homepage (cited 20 December 2002); available at *http://www.citizen.org/documents/FinalMay-June2001Harm.PDF*.

88. Shapiro, "International Trade Agreements, Regulatory Protection, and Public Accountability," 436.

89. "Public Citizen: Harmonization Handbook," on the Public Citizen homepage (cited 1 June 2003); available at *http://www.citizen.org/publications/release.cfm?ID=5193*.

90. Shapiro, "International Trade Agreements," 437.

91. See Bermann, "Regulatory Cooperation with Counterpart Agencies Abroad: The FAA'S Aircraft Certification Experience," 669.

92. Nicolaïdis, "Mutual Recognition Regimes: Towards a Comparative Analysis," (Working Paper 8, Center For International Affairs, Harvard University, 1998), 33.

93. Ibid.

94. Ibid., 49.

95. Waller, "Antitrust Enforcement," 396.

96. Ibid.

97. Address by Charles James, "International Antitrust in the Bush Administration" (21 September 2001), cited in Raustiala, "The Architecture of International Cooperation," 40.

98. Priest, "A Four-Star Foreign Policy? U.S. Commanders Wield Rising Clout, Autonomy," *Washington Post*, 28 September 2000, A1.

CHAPTER 2
Judges: Constructing a Global Legal System

1. "The Use of American Precedents in Canadian Courts," *Maine Law Review* 46 (1994): 216.

2. *Knight v. Florida*, 528 U.S. 990, 120 S. Ct. 459, 464 (U.S. 1999) (Breyer, J. dissenting from denial of cert) (citing *Pratt v. Attorney General of Jamaica* [1994] 2 A.C. 1[Jamaica 1994]; *Sher Singh v. State of Punjab*, A.I.R. 1983 S.C. 465 (India 1983); *Catholic Commission for Justice and Peace in Zimbabwe v. Attorney General* 1 Zimb. L.R. 239 (S) (1993); *Soering v. United Kingdom*, 11 Eur. Ct. H.R. (ser. A) 439 (Eur. Ct. H.R. 1989); *Kindler v. Minister of Justice* 2 S.C.R. 779 (Canada 1991); In re: *Barrett v. Jamaica* (Nos. 207/1988 and 271/1988) (UN Human Rights Committee 1988).

3. Westbrook, "International Judicial Negotiation," 567.

4. Sandra Day O'Connor, keynote address, *American Society of International Law Proceedings* 96 (2002): 348; Stephen Breyer, keynote address, American Society of International Law, *American Society of International Law Proceedings* (2003) (forthcoming).

5. William Rehnquist, Remarks of the Chief Justice, Court of Appeals for the Federal Circuit Twentieth Anniversary Judicial Conference, 8 April 2002, on the Supreme Court of the United States homepage (cited 14 June 2003); available from *http://www.supremecourtus.gov/publicinfo/speeches/sp_04-08-02a.html.*

6. New York University, The Project on International Courts and Tribunals, on "The Project on International Courts and Tribunals" homepage (cited 20 December 2002); available from *http://www.pict-pcti.org/Home.html.*

7. *Smith Kline and French Laboratories Ltd. v. Bloch* (1984) E.C.C. 103, 106 (U.K.).

8. Jay Lawrence Westbrook, "International Judicial Negotiation" (June 2003 draft on file with author).

9. By way of illustration, consider a 1993 resolution by the French Institute of International Law calling upon national courts to become independent actors in the international arena and to apply international norms impartially, without deferring to their governments. More generally, see Thomas M. Franck and Gregory H. Fox, eds., *International Law Decisions in National Courts*, 383. This important study of the "synergy between national and international judiciaries" emphasizes above all the joint role that national and international courts play in monitoring and implementing international law rules.

10. Benvenisti, "Judges and Foreign Affairs: A Comment on the Institut de Droit International's Resolution on 'Activities of National Courts and the International Relations of their States,'" 424.

11. For an analysis of the emergence of a community of courts in international criminal law, see Burke-White, "A Community of Courts: Toward a System of International Criminal Law Enforcement," 1.

12. Smith, "The Supreme Court in Present-day Society," 134–35.

13. Ibid., 135.

14. L'Heureux-Dubé, "The Importance of Dialogue," 16.

15. Loveland, "The Criminalization of Racist Violence," 257 (citing comments by Lord Browne-Wilkinson).

16. Constitution of South Africa, Sect. 39

17. *The State v. T Makwanyane and M Mchunu*, Case No. CCT/3/94 (South Africa, 6 June 1995).

18. McCrudden, "A Common Law of Human Rights?: Transnational Judicial Conversations on Constitutional Rights," 506.

19. To take the most obvious example, the architects of the United States Constitution were steeped in the principles of the common law and in the political theories of the Age of Enlightenment. The legal ideas expounded in the Constitution in turn influenced the framing of the French Declaration of the Rights of Man and of the Citizen and in turn spread to other continents through imperial rule. Anthony, "The Overseas Trade in the American Bill of Rights," 541. On the reception and internalization of foreign law generally, see Glenn, "Persuasive Authority," 296.

20. McClean, "A Common Inheritance? An Examination of the Private International Law Tradition of the Commonwealth," 9–98.

21. This phenomenon is well documented. See Lester, "The Overseas Trade," 541.; Coing, "Europaisierung der Rechtswissenschaft," 937–41; Rapaczynski, "Bibliographical Essay: The Influence of U.S. Constitutionalism Abroad"; Ackerman, "The Rise of World Constitutionalism," 771; Glendon, *Rights Talk: The Impoverishment of Political Discourse*, 158.

22. See generally Watson, *Legal Transplants*; Watson, "Legal Change: Sources of Law and Legal Culture," 1121–46; Smith, "Legal Imperialism and Legal Parochialism," 39–54.

23. In addition to L'Heureux-Dubé, "The Importance of Dialogue," 16; Choudhry, "Globalization in Search of Justification: Toward a Theory of Comparative Constitutional Interpretation," 819. Note that this most recent burst of scholarship contrasts with scholarship at the end of the 1980s that focused more on "one-way" traffic from the United States outward. See the Constitution of South Africa, Sect. 39.

24. O'Connor, Keynote Address, *American Society of International Law Proceedings*.

25. On the LEXIS/NEXIS homepage [cited 16 June 2003]; available from *http://www.lexis-nexis.com*; on the Westlaw homepage (cited 16 June 2003); available from *http://web2.westlaw.com/signon/default.wl?newdoor=true*.

26. On the CODICES homepage (cited 14 June 2003); available from *http://www.codices.coe.int*.

27. In the CODICES homepage [cited June 14, 2003]; available from *http://codices.coe.int/cgi-bin/om_isapi.dll?clientID=292647&infobase=codices.nfo&softpage=Browse_Frame_Pg42*.

28. Ibid.

29. "About Lawasia," in The Law Association for Asia and the Pacific homepage (cited 9 June 2003); available from *http://www.lawasia.asn.au*.

30. See generally, Choudhry, "Globalization in Search of Justification."

31. Schauer, "The Politics and Incentives of Legal Transplantation," 256.

32. Ibid., 257.

33. Ibid., 258.

34. Ibid.; These patterns of influence operate not just among Commonwealth countries, but far more broadly as well. Schauer observes that "the phenomenon ap-

pears to be strong not only in countries with a British Commonwealth background but also in countries as culturally removed from the British Commonwealth as Vietnam." Ibid.

35. Compare Schauer, "Incentives of Legal Transplantations," 258.

36. Ibid.

37. L'Heureux-Dubé, "The Importance of Dialogue," 17.

38. Ibid.

39. In The Republic of China Constitutional Court Grand Justices Council Reporter [cited 1 June 2003]; available from *http://www.judicial.gov.tw/j4e/*

40. O'Connor, keynote address, *American Society of International Law Proceedings*, 350.

41. *Knight v. Florida*, 528 U.S. 990, 990 (U.S. 1999).

42. Ibid., 997.

43. *Thompson v. Oklahoma*, 487 U.S. 815, 869 (U.S. 1988).

44. *U.S. v. Printz*, 521 U.S. 898, 977 (U.S. 1997) (Breyer, J. dissenting).

45. Ibid., 921.

46. Ginsburg, "Affirmative Action as an International Human Rights Dialogue," 3.

47. Ginsburg, "Remarks for Ottawa Panel," 28 September 2000, 4 (on file with author).

48. Ibid., 5.

49. *United States v. Then*, 56 F. 3d 464, 468–69 (U.S. 1995). Judge Calabresi argued that U.S. courts should follow the lead of the German and the Italian constitutional courts in finding ways to signal the legislature that a particular statute is "heading toward unconstitutionality," rather than striking it down immediately or declaring it constitutional. In conclusion, he observed that the United States no longer holds a "monopoly on constitutional judicial review," having helped spawn a new generation of constitutional courts around the world. "Wise parents," he added, "do not hesitate to learn from their children." Ibid., 469.

50. *Knight v. Florida*, 528 U.S. 990, 120 S. Ct. 459, 464 (U.S. 1999) (Breyer, J. dissenting from denial of cert).

51. *S. v. Lawrence; S. v. Negal; S. v. Solberg*, (4) SA 1176, 1223 (South Africa 1997).

52. Ibid.

53. Abrahamson and Fischer, "All the World's a Courtroom: Judging in the New Millennium," 276.

54. Ibid., 285.

55. Ibid., 284.

56. L'Heureux-Dubé, "The Importance of Dialogue," 17.

57. Smith, "The Supreme Court," 135.

58. Schauer, "Incentives of Legal Transplantations," 258–59; see also L'Heureux-Dubé, "The Importance of Dialogue," 16.

59. Abrahamson and Fischer, "All the World's a Courtroom," 280.

60. Ibid., 283–84.

61. See, e.g., *Pratt v. Attorney General of Jamaica* (1994) 2 A.C. 1(Jamaica 1994); *Sher Singh v. State of Punjab*, A.I.R. 1983 S.C. 465 (India 1983); *Catholic Commission*

for Justice and Peace in Zimbabwe v. Attorney General 1 Zimb. L.R. 239 (S) (1993); *Soering v. United Kingdom*, 11 Eur. Ct. H.R. (ser. A) 439 (Eur. Ct. H.R. 1989); *Kindler v. Minister of Justice* 2 S.C.R. 779 (Canada 1991); In re: *Barrett v. Jamaica* (Nos. 207/1988 and 271/1988) (UN Human Rights Committee 1988); *Knight v. Florida*, 528 U.S. 990, 995 (1999).

62. L'Heureux-Dubé, "The Importance of Dialogue," 37.

63. The South African Constitutional Court clearly recognized this point. While acknowledging the value of comparative law approaches, the Court added the following caveat: "We must bear in mind that we are required to construe the South African Constitution, and not an international instrument or the constitution of some foreign country, and that this has to be done with due regard to our legal system, our history and circumstances, and the structure and language of our own Constitution." See *The State v. T Makwanyane and M Mchunu*, Case No. CCT/3/94 (South Africa, 6 June 1995), at 21.

64. The European Convention on Human Rights codifies a basic catalogue of civil and political rights and confirms the desire of its signatories to achieve "a common understanding and observance" of those rights. 4 Nov. 1950, 213 U.N.T.S. 222. Although originally ratified principally by the nations of Western Europe, as of 1997 more than forty nations from Iceland to Russia have signed on to the treaty and one or more of its various protocols. Chart of Signatures and Ratifications of European Treaties, 1 July 1996 Update, Direction des Affaires juridiques, Section des Traites.

65. *Chrysostomos and Others v. Turkey*, App. No. 15299/89, 68 Eur. Com. H.R. Dec. & Rep. 216, 242 (Eur. Com. H.R. 1991).

66. See generally Merrills, *The Development of International Law by the European Court of Human Rights*, 18; Kay, "The European Convention on Human Rights and the Authority of Law," 218.

67. Polakiewicz and Jacob-Foltzer, "The European Human Rights Convention in Domestic Law: The Impact of Strasbourg Case Law in States Where Direct Effect Is Given to the Convention (pt. 1)," 66.

68. *The State v. T Makwanyane and M Mchunu*, Case No. CCT/3/94 (South Africa 6 June 1995).

69. *Ncube, Tshuma and Ndhlovu v. The State* (1988) 2 S. Afr. L. Rep. 702 (citing *Tyrer v. United Kingdom*, 26 Eur. Ct. H.R. (ser. A) (1978), 2 Eur. Hum. Rts. Rep. 1 (1979–80); *Juvenile v. The State*, Judgment No. 64/89, Crim. App. No. 156/88 (citing *Tyrer* and *Campbell and Cosans v. United Kingdom*, 48 Eur. Ct. H.R. (ser. A) (1982), 4 Eur. Hum. Rts. Rep. 293 (1982). See Hannum, "Recent Case," 768.

70. H.C. 5100/94, *Public Committee Against Torture in Israel v. The State of Israel* (6 Sept. 1999), 38 *International Legal Materials*, 1471 (quoting *Ireland v. United Kingdom* 2 Eur. Hum. Rts. Rep. 25 [1978], 18).

71. *Pratt & Morgan v. The Attorney General for Jamaica*, Privy Council Appeal No. 10, 2 Nov. 1993, reprinted in 14 Hum. Rts. L.J. 338 (1993). For a discussion of the case see Buergenthal, "International Tribunals and National Courts: The Internationalization of Domestic Adjudication," 689–91. The *Soering* decision, ECHR, Judgment of 7 July 1989, 11 Hum. Rts. L.J. 335 (1990) found that extradition of a prisoner held in Great Britain to a state in the United States where he might face the death penalty vi-

olated Art. 3 of the European Convention. See Jarmul, "Effects of Decisions of Regional Human Rights Tribunals on National Courts," 281–83.

72. Merrills, Development of International Law, 19.

73. Attanasio, "Rapporteur's Overview and Conclusions: of Sovereignty, Globalization, and Courts," 383. Supranational human rights tribunals outside Europe are also beginning to develop an audience among national courts, but more slowly. In 1992, the Supreme Court of Argentina reversed a lower court decision as well as its own precedent in reliance on an advisory opinion of the Inter-American Human Rights Court. *Ekmekdijan v. Sofovich* (1992-III) J.A. 199 (1992) (plaintiff claimed that he was unlawfully denied the right to reply to a television program alleged to be morally offensive and damaging to him). For a discussion of the case, see Jarmul, "Effects of Decisions," 258-59.

74. The South African Constitution, Sect. 39, requires South African courts to "consider international law." Many of the new or revised constitutions of the emerging democracies in Eastern and Central Europe also incorporate international law into domestic legal rules. Vereschetin, "The Relationship between International Law and National Law," 40–41. Similarly, Justice M. D. Kirby of the Australian Supreme Court notes that in many common law countries domestic courts have historically referred to international treaties ratified by their country as a source of guidance in constitutional and statutory construction and in the development of common law principles. Kirby, "The Role of the Judge in Advancing Human Rights by Reference to International Human Rights Norms," 515.

Note, however, that such requirements do not require a national court to look to the decisions of other *courts* for guidance; they could equally well interpret the relevant treaties themselves. Kirby notes that the invocation of international treaties by common law courts has recently become "politically controversial," but cites "the development of an increasingly large jurisprudence around such treaties" as one of the factors that will make it difficult for judges and lawyers to ignore them. Kirby, "The Role of the Judge," 515.

75. Benvenisti, "The Influence of International Human Rights Law on the Israeli Legal System: Present and Future," 147–48, 151.

76. Buergenthal, "International Tribunals and National Courts," 700; Kirby, "The Role of the Judge," 515.

77. Smith, "The Supreme Court," 96, 133.

78. Ibid., 133–34.

79. Ibid., 134.

80. For the classic accounts of the construction of the EC legal system, often referred to as the "constitutionalization" of the Treaty of Rome, see Stein, "Lawyers, Judges, and the Making of a Transnational Constitution," 1; Weiler, "The Transformation of Europe," 2403; and Bebr, *Development of Judicial Control of The European Communities*. For accounts from ECJ judges themselves, see Everling, "The Member States of the European Community before their Court of Justice," 215; Mancini, "The Making of a Constitution for Europe," 595; and Koopmans, "The Birth of European Law at the Crossroads of Legal Traditions," 493.

81. See Case 26/62, N.V. *Algemene Transp. & Expeditie Onderneming Van Gend & Loos v. Nederlandse administratie der belastingen*, 1963 E.C.R. 1, 12 (Ct. of Justice of the

Eur. Comm. 1962) (landmark decision allowing a private Dutch importer to invoke certain common market provisions of the Treaty of Rome directly against the Dutch government); Case 6/64, *Flaminio Costa v. ENEL (Ente Nazionale Energia Elettrica) 1964 E.C.R.* 588 (asserting that where a treaty term conflicts with a subsequent national statute, the treaty must prevail). For a discussion of "direct effect" jurisprudence, see George Bermann et al., *European Community Law.*

82. This view is not uncontroverted. Some political scientists have argued that these national courts were in fact following the wishes of their respective governments, notwithstanding their governments' expressed opposition before the ECJ. The claim is that all Community member-states agreed to economic integration as being in their best interests in 1959. They understood, however, that they needed a mechanism to bind one another to the obligations undertaken in the original treaty. They thus established a court to hold each state to its respective word. See Garrett, "International Cooperation and Institutional Choice: The European Community's Internal Market," 533; Garrett and Weingast, "Ideas, Interests and Institutions: Constructing the EC's Internal Market," 173; Garrett, Kelemen, and Schulz, "The European Court of Justice, National Governments, and Legal Integration in the European Union," 149.

This rationalist reconstruction ignores the apparent intent of the member-states to establish a court whose judgments they could all too easily prevent or avoid; it also flies in the face of the actual history recounted above. For a debate on precisely this point, see Mattli and Slaughter, "Law and Politics in the European Union: A Reply to Garrett," 183; Garrett, "The Politics of Legal Integration in the European Union," 171.

83. Alter, *Establishing the Supremacy of European Law: The Making of an International Rule of Law in Europe,* 80–87; idem, "Who Are the 'Masters of the Treaty'?: European Governments and the European Court of Justice," 121.

84. See Ploetner, "Report on France: The Reception of the Direct Effect and Supremacy Doctrine by the French Supreme Courts," 41–75; and Alter, *Establishing the Supremacy,* 145–57, 173 (both discussing the Cour de Cassation's decision in the 1975 case, *Administration des Douanes v. Societe Cafes Jacques Vabre and J. Weigel et Compagnie S.a.r.l.,* (Cour de Cassation, France 1975) 2 Common Mrkt. L. Rep. 343 (1975).

85. *Secretary of State for Transport, ex parte. Factortame Ltd.* Case 213/89, R. V. (U.K. 1989) 3 Common Market L.R. 867 (1990) (ECJ preliminary ruling that the British courts could grant interim relief to the applicants by setting aside the national law forbidding such relief); *R. v. Secretary of State for Transport, ex p. Factortame Ltd.* No. 2, 1 A.C. 603 (U.K. House of Lords 1991) (House of Lords decision awarding interim relief against the Crown). For a full discussion of these decisions and their implications (dicta of the House of Lords clearly curtails parliamentary sovereignty by stating the duty of courts to resolve conflicts in favor of EC law over national law), see Craig, "Report on the United Kingdom," 200–203.

86. Joseph Weiler was among the first to claim that national judges were motivated by dreams of "judicial empowerment," by which he seems to have meant the heady experience of engaging in judicial review of national law for conformity with European law. Weiler, "The Transformation of Europe", 2426; see also Burley and Mattli, "Europe Before the Court: A Political Theory of Legal Integration," 63–64.

87. Karen Alter has pioneered this thesis in several important articles and a forthcoming book. See Alter, *Establishing the Supremacy*, 45–52; idem, "Explaining National Court Acceptance of European Court Jurisprudence: A Critical Evaluation of Theories of Legal Integration," 227–252.

88. See Mattli & Slaughter, "Law and Politics in the European Union."

89. See Ploetner, "Reports on France," 61 (arguing that the Cour de Cassation accepted the supremacy of EC law out of a desire not to disadvantage the French merchants who were a prime constituency).

90. For a concise but thorough account of the principal cases in this dialogue, see Kokott, "Report on Germany," in 77–131.

91. *Brunner v. The European Union Treaty, Bundesverfassungsgericht* (2. Senat) (Federal Constitutional Court, 2d Chamber) 12 Oct. 1993, 1 C.M.L.R. 57 (F.R.G.).

92. 1 C.M.L.R. at 79; 89 BVerfGE 155, at 175. The BvG also continues to recognize the ECJ's exclusive competence as interpreter of European law, in the sense that the BvG will not offer an alternative interpretation of a particular legal provision, but will only decide whether that provision as interpreted is *ultra vires*. The recognition of the the ECJ's interpretive competence was laid down in the BvG's *Vielleicht-Beschluß* ("Maybe Decision") of 1979. 52 BVerfGE 187 (1979).

93. Kokott, "Report on Germany," 109. The most recent event in this saga preserves the status quo established by the *Maastricht* decision. In the *Bananas* Case, 2 BvL 1/97 (7 June 2000), the Second Senate of the BvG rejected a claim that the *Maastricht* decision stands for the Court's resumption of active, interventionist human rights review in the Community, of the type in which it had engaged prior to the landmark decision in *Solange II*, 73 BVerfGE 339 (22 Oct. 1986).

94. See Weiler, "Epilogue: The European Courts of Justice: Beyond 'Beyond Doctrine' or the Legitimacy Crisis of European Constitutionalism," 367. The Belgian *Cour d'arbitrage*, for example, was asked to strike down the law of 26 November 1992, which approved the Maastricht treaty, 18 Oct. 1994, Case 76/94. The applicants, who were Belgian nationals, argued that their (national) constitutional right to vote in municipal elections was infringed by the new European citizenship provisions, which extended the franchise to citizens of another EU member-state. In an earlier decision (Case 12/94, 3 February 1994), the Court had held that Article 107 of the Belgian Constitution cannot be read as authorizing the legislator to disregard the Constitution indirectly by virtue of the assent to an international agreement. However, the Belgian Constitutional Court took a much more restrictive approach to the challenge against the Maastricht treaty, however: While the right to vote is "the fundamental political right of a representative democracy," the dilution of the impact of an individual vote through the enlarged franchise did not create a sufficient interest to grant the applicants standing before the Court. See also Bibriosa, "Report on Belgium," 320–29.

95. The Maastricht decision uses the term "community of states" to describe the EU (*staatenverbund*) rather than "confederation" (*staatenbund*), 1 C.M.L.R., at paragraphs 36–38; 1993 WL 965303 (BverfG [Ger]), at 48.

96. See Alec Stone Sweet, "Constitutional Dialogues in the European Community," 305–8; Weiler, "Epilogue: The European Courts of Justice," 368 ("Constitutionalism . . . constitutes the official vocabulary of the inter-court dialogues").

97. *Howe v. Goldcorp Investments, Ltd.*, 946 F.2d 944, 950 (1st Cir. 1991).

98. In *The Matter of the Application of Euromepa*, SA, 51 F.3d 1095, 1101 (2d Cir. 1995).

99. *Hilton v. Guyot*, 159 U.S. 113, 164 (U.S. 1895) ("Comity in the legal sense, is neither a matter of absolute obligation on the one hand nor of mere courtesy and good will on the other. But it is the recognition which one nation allows within its territory to the legislative, executive, or judicial acts of another nation, having due regard both to international duty and convenience, and to the rights of its own citizens or of other persons who are under the protection of its laws.")

100. For an extensive overview of the history and multiple meanings of comity, see Paul, "Comity in International Law," 1.

101. See *Hartford Fire Insurance Co v. California*, 509 U.S. 764, 817 (U.S. 1993) (Scalia, J., dissenting) (distinguishing "judicial comity" from "legislative or prescriptive comity"). As authority for this distinction, Justice Scalia also turned back to Joseph Story's *Commentaries on the Conflict of Laws*. Story did distinguish between "the comity of the courts" and "the comity of the nation," emphasizing that courts did not defer to foreign law as a matter of judicial courtesy, but rather based on an interpretive principle requiring courts to read legislative silence regarding the effect of foreign law as tacit adoption of such law unless repugnant to fundamental public policy. Story, *Commentaries on The Conflict of Laws*, §38. Taken in context, however, Story does not appear to be distinguishing between different types of comity so much as insisting that the principle of comity is not a judicial creation but rather a corollary of a general legal principle embedded in international and U.S. law.

Other commentators have distinguished between "political" and "judicial" comity, referring to the political considerations inherent in maintaining good relations between nations versus the more specific judicial concerns in developing and maintaining a system in which national courts safeguard the national interest in making and enforcing national laws on a reciprocal basis. Maier, "Extraterritorial Jurisdiction at a Crossroads: An Intersection between Public and Private International Law," 283. My concern is less to distinguish between "political" and "legal" than the concerns of the state as an aggregated whole versus the specific concerns of courts. For a more detailed discussion of this version of judicial comity than space allows here, see Slaughter, "Court to Court," 708.

102. *Roby v. Corporation of Lloyds*, 996 F.2d 1353, 1363 (2d Cir. 1993) (citing *Mitsubishi Motors Corp. v. Soler Chrysler-Plymouth, Inc.*, 473 U.S. 614 [U.S. 1985]) ("international comity dictates that American courts enforce forum selection clauses out of respect for the integrity and competence of foreign tribunals").

103. *Gulf Oil Corp v. Gilbert*, 330 U.S. 501, 509 (U.S. 1947) (applying the *forum non conveniens* doctrine to dismiss a New York case in favor of a Virginia forum), quoted in *Piper Aircraft v. Reyno*, 454 U.S. 235, 241 (U.S. 1981) (dismissing a case brought in the United States in favor of a Scottish forum).

104. In the *Laker Airways* litigation, a complex series of cases involving parallel proceedings between the United States and Great Britain and efforts by litigants on both sides to block the suit in the other forum, Lord Scarman argued that individuals have a right to pursue causes of action under foreign law because they have a right to pursue "the process of justice," 1984 WL 281712 (HL), 25.

105. *Kaepa, Inc. v. Achilles Corp.*, 76 F.3d 624, 625 (5th Cir. 1996).

106. Ibid. (quoting *Allendale Mut. Ins. Co. v. Bull Data Sys., Inc.*, 10 F.3d 425, 430–31 (7th Cir. 1993). The court faced the question of whether to apply a restrictive or liberal standard of comity, with the former allowing a foreign litigation to proceed unless it undermines U.S. jurisdiction or policy. The Fifth Circuit chose the latter standard, whereby it inquired into the burden imposed on U.S. litigants by the foreign suit.

107. Ibid.

108. *Philips Med. Sys. Int'l B.V. v. Bruteman*, 8 F.3d 600, 605 (7th Cir. 1993).

109. *Allendale*, 10 F.3d at 431.

110. Ibid.; see also *Philips*, 8 F.3d at 605 (because neither the State Department nor the Argentine Foreign Ministry had complained to the court, it was unlikely that relations between the two nations had been put at risk).

111. See, e.g., Swanson, "The Vexationusness of a Vexation Rule: International Comity And Antisuit Injunctions," 35–36; Haq, "Note, *Kaepa, Inc. v. Achilles Corp.*: Comity in International Judicial Relations," 365, 382.

112. *Euromepa S.A. v. R. Esmerian, Inc.*, 1104.

113. *Naumus Asia Co. v. Standard Charter Bank*, 1 H.K.L.R. 396, 407–8 (H.K. High Court 1990).

114. Ibid., 407.

115. Ibid.,420.

116. *Allendale Mut. Ins. v. Bull Data Systems*, 10 F.3d 425, 431 (7th Cir. 1993).

117. See, e.g., *Sperry Rand Corp. v. Sunbeam Corp.*, 285 F.2d 542 (7th Cir. 1960) (reversing a district court decision enjoining litigation in a German court, on the ground that since the litigation in Germany involved a trademark registered in Germany and a cause of action under German law, it could not be held "vexatious" to the defendant); *Ingersoll v. Granger* 833 F.2d 680, 687 (7th Cir. 1987) (affirming a district court decision staying further proceedings in U.S. court until a judgment is rendered in a Belgian appeals court on the same case because the latter had granted the appellant a full and fair opportunity to present its claims).

118. *The Bremen v. Zapata Off-Shore Co.*, 407 U.S. 1 (U.S. 1972).

119. Ibid., 9.

120. *Tolofson v. Jensen*, 3. S.C.R. 1022, 1070 (Canada 1994).

121. Tetley, "New Development in Private International Law: Tolofson v. Jensen and Gagnon v. Lucas," 659–66; Furuta, "International Parallel Litigation: Disposition of Duplicative Civil Proceedings in the United States and Japan," 1. The situation in Japan is complicated. Traditionally, although a Japanese court would automatically defer to another Japanese court already seised of jurisdiction in the same case, it would not extend the same courtesy to a foreign court. The Japanese Supreme Court has also identified jurisdiction as part of judicial sovereignty, which is deemed coextensive with national sovereignty. Judgment of 16 Oct. 1981 (*Malaysia Airline System Berhad v. Goto*), S. Ct., 35 Minshu (vol. 7) 1224, translated in *Japanese Annual of International Law* 26 (1983): 122.

More recently, however, at least one court has held that it would be possible to dismiss a suit brought by a Japanese plaintiff who had already been sued in the same case abroad if it is clear that the foreign court will reach a final and irrevocable judgment first and that Japanese courts will be able to recognize that judgment. *Miyakoshi Kiko*

K.K. v. Gould, Inc., *Interim Judgment*, 1348 Hanrei Jiho 91, 94-95 (Tokyo District Ct. 30 May 1989).

122. *St. Pierre v. South American Stores K.B.* 382 (U.K. 1936).

123. *Spiliada Maritime Corp. v. Cansulex Ltd* A.C. 460, 476 (U.K. 1987). This line of cases is interestingly discussed in Sze-Kwok Wai, "Internationalism Ascending: Commerce, Cooperation and Cosmopolitanism as Public Policy Goals in Private International Law," (S.J.D. Thesis, Harvard Law School, 30 May 1998).

124. *Phillips Med. Syst. V. Bruteman*, 8 F.3d 249.

125. Ibid., 428.

126. Ibid., 432.

127. Ibid., 430.

128. *Canadian Overseas Ores Ltd. v. Compania e Acero del Pacifico, SA*, 528 F. Supp. 1337, 1342–43 (S.D.N.Y. 1982), affirmed on other grounds, 727 F.2d 1274 (2d Cir. 1984).

129. See, e.g., *McDonnell Douglas Corp. v. Islamic Republic of Iran*, 758 F.2d 342 (8th Cir.), cert. denied, 414 U.S. 948 (U.S. 1985).

130. *Allstate Insurance Co. v. Administratia Asigurarilor de Stat*, 962 F. Supp. 420, 424 (S.D.N.Y. 1997).

131. *Sussman v. Bank of Israel*, 801 F. Supp. 1068, at 1078(S.D.N.Y. 1992).

132. *Murty v. Aga Khan*, 92 F.R.D. 478, 482 (E.D.N.Y. 1981).

133. 407 U.S. 1, 12.

134. Born, *International Civil Litigation in United States Courts*, 3d ed., 353.

135. See *In re Union Carbide*, 634 F. Supp. 842 (S.D.N.Y. 1986), affirmed as modified, 809 F.2d 195 (2d Cir. 1987); *Sequihua v. Texaco*, 847 F. Supp. 61 (S.D. Tx. 1994); *Dow Chemical v. Castro Alfaro*, 786 S.W.2d 674 (S. Ct. Tx. 1990).

136. In the most celebrated of these cases, a suit brought by Indian citizens killed or injured by a deadly chemical at the Union Carbide factory in India, the court considered arguments regarding the Indian court's ability "to deal effectively and expeditiously" with the case and found that it was indeed an adequate forum. *In re Union Carbide*, 634 F. Supp. 842, 848 (S.D.N.Y. 1986). See also *Torres v. Southern Peru Copper Corporation*, 965 F. Supp. 899 (1996), aff'd 113 F.3d 540 (5th Cir. 1997) (finding that Peru was an adequate forum for resolving the dispute and dismissing the case based on comity).

137. For example, *Mobil Tankers Co. v. Mene Grande Oil Co.*, 363 F.2d 611, 614 (3d Cir. 1966); *Peabody Holding Co. v. Costain Group plc*, 808 F. Supp. 1425 (E.D. Mo. 1992).

138. *Fiorenza v. United States Steel Int'l*, 311 F. Supp. 117, 120–21 (S.D.N.Y. 1969).

139. *Lockman Found. v. Evangelical Alliance Mission*, 930 F.2d 764, 768 (9th Cir. 1991).

140. *Macedo v. Boeing Co.*, 693 F.2d 683, 688 (7th Cir. 1982).

141. *Wolf v. Boeing Co.*, 810 F.2d 943 (Wash. App. Ct. 1991).

142. Flaschen and Silverman, "Cross-Border Insolvency Cooperation Protocols," 589. For a discussion of how practitioner input, through the Insolvency and Creditors' Rights Committee of the International Bar Association, has influenced these proceedings by developing a "Concordat" ready to be adopted as a cross-border Protocol in

these cases, see Leonard, "Managing Default by a Multinational Venture: Cooperation in Cross-Border Insolvencies," 543.

143. Ibid. These proceedings involved Maxwell Communications Corporation, Olympia & York, Commodore Business Machines, Everfresh Beverages, Nakash, Solve-Ex., and AIOC.

144. Unt, "International Relations and International Insolvency Cooperation: Liberalism, Institutionalism, and Transnational Legal Dialogue," 1037; Westbrook, "Theory and Pragmatism in Global Insolvencies: Choice of Law and Choice of Forum," 461. See *Maxwell Communication Corp. v. Barclays Bank* (*In re* Maxwell Communications Corp.), 170 B.R. 800 (Bankr. S.D.N.Y. 1994).

145. Flaschen and Silverman, "Cross-Border Insolvency," 590.

146. For a detailed description of these proceedings, see ibid., 594–99.

147. Ibid., 596 n. 71; cited in ibid., 596.

148. Ibid., 599 n. 86.

149. Ibid., at 599 n. 87.

150. Unt, "International Relations," 1038.

151. "The Supreme Court justices gathered in the East Conference Room yesterday to greet members of the European Court of Justice," *New York Times*, 19 April 2000, 1.

152. Rehnquist, Remarks of the Chief Justice, Court of Appeals for the Federal Circuit Twentieth Anniversary Judicial Conference.

153. See, e.g., VI Conferencia de Tribunales Constitucionales Europeos, Tribunales Constitucionales Europeos y Autonomas Territoriales (1985).

154. Charter of the Organization of the Supreme Courts of the Americas, Article II, §2.1.

155. Ibid., Article II §2.2.

156. "Remarks by the President of the Supreme Court of Justice on the Occasion of the Opening of Judicial Year 1999," on Supreme Court of Justice of Venezuela homepage (cited 14 June 2003); available from *http://www.tsj.gov.ve/informacion/miscelaneas/opening1999.html*.

157. Delegates from Australia, New Zealand, Ireland, India, the United States, Canada, and Great Britain attended the First Worldwide Common Law Judiciary Conference, 28 May–2 June 1995. See "Justices, Judges from Common Law Countries Meet in Williamsburg and Washington," *International Judicial Observer* 1 (1995): 1. The Second Worldwide Common Law Judiciary Conference was held in May in Washington, D.C., at which representatives of the countries of Israel, Singapore, and South Africa joined the seven countries who participated in the first conference.

158. Ibid., 1.

159. See Hon. Rait Maruste, "Chief Justice, National Court of Estonia, Estonia: Leading Central Europe in Judicial Reform," *International Judicial Observer* 2 (1996): 3.

160. See The Law Association for Asia and the Pacific homepage (cited 20 December 2002); available from *http://www.lawasia.asn.au*. LAWASIA member countries are: Afghanistan; Australia; Bangladesh; China; Fiji; Hong Kong; India; Iran; Japan; DPR of Korea (North Korea); Korea (South Korea); Macao; Malaysia; Nepal; New Zealand; Pakistan; Papua New Guinea; Philippines; Russian Federation; Singapore; Sri Lanka; Thailand; Western Samoa.

161. See "CEELI Update," ABA *International Law News*, Summer 1991, 7.

162. "European Justices Meet in Washington to Discuss Common Issues, Problems," *International Judicial Observer* 1 (January 1996): 2, 3.

163. Papers from the conference have subsequently been published in Franck and Fox, *International Law Decisions*, 373, 383. See also, Franck, "NYU Conference Discusses Impact of International Tribunals," 3.

164. See Apple, "British, U.S. Judges and Lawyers Meet, Discuss Shared Judicial, Legal Concerns," 1.

165. "Yale Law School Establishes Seminar on Global Constitutional Issues," *International Judicial Observer* 4 (1997): 2.

166. One example is the Brandeis Institute for International Judges, founded by the International Center for Ethics, Justice, and Public Life at Brandeis University. The institute held its first session in June 2002, with the "the aim of encouraging the development of the new international jurisprudence, one that is informed as much by the practical application of ethical and moral considerations as it is by legal ones." According to the institute's annual report for 2002, the institute provided "an opportunity for confidential discussion among judges sitting on international courts and tribunals" and thereby fostered reflection, learning, and judicial innovation." *Brandeis Institute for International Judges Report*, Brandeis University (2002): 3.

167. "Global Legal Information Network", on the Library of Congress of the United States of America Global Legal Information Network website (cited 14 June 2003); available from *http://lcweb2.loc.gov/law/GLINv1/glintro.htm*.

168. Mihm, "International Judicial Relations Committee Promotes Communication Coordination," 1.

169. Committee on International Judicial Relations, Weekly Bulletin, 10–14 June 2002 (on file with author); Committee on International Judicial Relations, Weekly Bulletin, 2–6 September 2002 (on file with author).

170. Stephen Breyer, "The Supreme Court and The New International Law," The American Society of International Law, Ninety-seventh Annual Meeting, Washington, D.C., 4 April 2003.

171. Conversation reported at Brandeis Institute for International Judges, 9–15 June 2002.

CHAPTER 3
Legislators: Lagging Behind

1. William Wallace, "Europe, the Necessary Partner," 18.

2. Falk and Strauss, "Toward Global Parliament," 212.

3. For a discussion of unitary democracy, in which interests are aligned, and adversary democracy, in which interests conflict, see Mansbridge, *Beyond Adversary Democracy*.

4. Ackerman, "The New Separation of Powers," 689.

5. For example, Congress authorized joining the WTO subject to reauthorization every fifth year. See Goldstein and Martin, "Legalization, Trade Liberalization, and Domestic Politics: A Cautionary Note," in 226; see also Jones and Clark, *The Modali-*

ties of European Union Governance: New Institutionalist Explanations of Agri-Environmental Policy (discussing the role of subparliamentary policy networks and alliances within the EP).

6. For a concise summary of the purpose and setup of the NAA, see "About the North Atlantic Assembly" at the opening of Cartwright et al., The State of the Alliance 1986–1987: North Atlantic Assembly Reports.

7. Brumter, The North Atlantic Assembly. See also Lunn, "NATO's Parliamentary Arm Helps Further the Aims of the Alliance," 8–11.

8. The NAA publishes policy recommendations annually. The October 1995 edition, for example, includes resolutions formed at the spring session in Budapest in May 1995. The report number appears as AM 331, SA (95) 17.

9. See, e.g., "NATO Parliamentary Assembly President Welcomes NATO Commitment on Enlargement," NATO-PA Press Release, 13 June 2001, on Nato Parliamentary homepage (cited 20 January 2003); available from http://www.nato-pa.int/archivedpub/press/p010613a.asp.

10. "Hungarian OSCE Observer Doubts that Elections Were 'Free and Fair,'" The British Broadcasting Corporation, 2 April 1998.

11. "OSCE Parliamentary Assembly," on OSCE homepage (cited 20 December 2002); available from http://www.osce.org/pa/election.

12. Aleksandr Potemkin, "Russians Abstain Over Belarus During Final Vote at OSCE S Session in Warsaw," ITAR-TASS News Agency, 10 July 1997.

13. "OSCE Parliamentary Assembly Session Ends in Romania," Xinhua General News Service, 10 July 2000.

14. Standing Committee of the OSCE Parlimentary Assembly Declaration, "Security through Solidarity," on OSCE homepage (cited 20 December 2002); available from http://www.osce.org/pa/documents/declarations/files/sintra_declaration_09oct01.pdf.

15. On Asean Inter-Parliamentary Organization (AIPO) homepage (cited 20 December 2002); available from http://www.aipo.org/Bg_and_History.htm.

16. "ASEAN Politicians Agree to Compile AFTA Laws," Straits Times Press, 8 July 1995.

17. "AIPO Moves Closer to Electronic Bulletin Board System," Xinhua News Agency, 20 September 1996. See also "AIPO Should Improve Its Role, Says Harmoko," ANTARA: Indonesian National News, 24 October 1997. "Asean MPs Plan Computer Links to Forge Closer Ties," Singapore Straits Times, 23 September 1995.

18. Derwin Pereira, "ASEAN Must Cooperate to Stabilize Financial Markets," Singapore Straits Times, 7 September 1997. In September 2002, AIPO members met to discuss additional mechanisms for implementing the Asian Free Trade Agreement and promoting development, but rejected an Indonesian proposal to create an ad hoc committee to monitor implementation. "ASEAN Parliamentary Group Session Closes in Vietnam," BBC Monitoring: Voice of Vietnam, 12 September 2002.

19. See "AIPO News Bulletin," on Asean Inter-Parliamentary Organization (AIPO) homepage (cited 20 January 2003); available from http://www.aipo.org/AIPO_news.htm. These so-called dialogue partners attend the annual AIPO General Assembly. The Twenty-third General Assembly, held in Vietnam in 2002, saw participation from inter alia Australia, the EP, New Zealand, and Russia.

20. Gorius Aurore and Rivais Rafaele, "The Presidents of 15 Parliaments Appeal for the Abolition of the Death Penalty," *Le Monde*, 25 June 2001.

21. Agence France Presse, 26 June 2001.

22. "Weldon In Russia to Push Legislative Exchange Group," Associated Press Political Service, 20 November 1997.

23. "Gingrich Seeks to Create Defense Study Group with Russian Duma," *Defense Daily*, 28 February 1996.

24. The study group has since drafted proposals on economic cooperation. See "Russian and US Parliaments Vote for Abolition of Artificial Barriers to Trade Relations," *Pravda*, 6 December 2002.

25. Free Congress Foundation, Press Releases 2000, "US, Russian Lawmakers Suggest Joint Missile Defense," 22 June 2000, on Free Congress Foundation homepage (cited 15 June 2003); available from *http://www.freecongress.org/media/2000/000622. asp*.

26. Ibid.

27. See "09/23/97-GCC9 Text: Statement on Gore-Chernomyrdin Commission," on the United States Mission to Italy homepage (cited 12 April 1998); available from *http://www.usis.it/wireless/wf970923/97092326.htm*.

28. Ibid.

29. "Russian and US Parliaments Vote for Abolition of Artificial Barriers to Trade Relations," on *Pravda* homepage (cited 6 December 2002); available from *http:// english.pravda.ru/diplomatic/2002/12/06/40449.html*.

30. "Weldon Reiterates Need for US-Russia Engagement," on United States House of Representatives homepage (cited 12 June 2003); available from *http://www. house.gov/curtweldon/april30russia.html*.

31. "Medea, PAEAC, Euro-Arab Parliamentary Dialogue, Damascus 1998," on Medea homepage (cited 20 December 2002); available from *http://www.medea.be/ site.html?page=11&lang=en&doc=1002*.

32. Zarjevski, *The People Have the Floor: A History of the Interparliamentary Union*. See also "Statutes of the Inter-Parliamentary Union," on the Inter-Parliamentary Union homepage (cited 15 June 2003); available from *http://www.ipu.org/strct-e/ statutes.htm*. Currently the IPU includes 144 members and 5 associate members, including EP and PACE. See the Inter-Parliamentary homepage (cited 19 January 2003); available from *http://www.ipu.org/english/membshp.htm*.

33. Bassiouni, "Former Yugoslavia: Investigating Violations of International Humanitarian Law and the Creation of an International Criminal Tribunal," 1194.

34. Guevara, "Puerto Rico: Manifestations of Colonialism," 304.

35. Gary Borg, "Global Meeting Condemns French Nuclear Testing," *Chicago Tribune*, 14 October 1995, 15.

36. Nadire Mater, "Global Relations: World Parliamentarians Talk Peace, Peacefully," *Interpress Service*, 19 April 1996.

37. Nirmal Mitra, "Pact With Parliamentary Union Hailed," *India Abroad*, 8 November 1996, 6.

38. See "U.S. Reluctantly Joining Nuclear Test Conference," *Newark Star-Ledger*, 7 August 1993.

39. The organization's "trip-and-speech" focus has occasionally made it vulnerable to criticism. Members of the PGA have been attacked by newspapers in Britain and Canada for using it as an opportunity to take off on junkets. See, e.g., "Honourable Member for Flying Visits," *The Times (London)*, 4 Feburary 1996; Iain Hunter, "Traveling MPs: On Polite Exchanges or News Making Junkets, Many MPs Go Continent Hopping For Free," *Ottawa Citizen*, 19 February 1992, A3.

40. See Douglas Farah and William Booth, "UN Effort to Return Aristide Grinds to a Halt," *Montreal Gazette*, 28 October 1993, A6.

41. See ibid. The organization does not shy from trips to international trouble spots. The PGA also lobbied Togo's president-for-life to engage in democratic reforms for the country. See John Walker, "Elections Don't Equal Democracy: African Countries Struggle with Reform," *Edmonton Journal*, 14 August 1992, A13.

42. See "Appendix B: Report of the Secretary General Pursuant to Paragraph 2 of Security Council Resolution 808," *Criminal Law Forum* 5 (1994): 601.

43. See "International Law and Human Rights Program," on The Parliamentarians for Global Action (PGA) homepage (cited January 19, 2003); available from *http://www.pgaction.org/prog_inte.asp*. Since September 2002, the PGA has also been accredited as an NGO participant at the open sessions of the ICC Assembly of State Parties. See "The Case For Establishing An International Criminal Court," 1. Parliamentarians for Global Action: Occasional Paper 3 (October 1992): 1.

44. Two British Members of Parliament attended this conference. See "Register of Members' Interests," *Independent*, 30 October 1994. See Santosus, "An International Criminal Court: Where Global Harmony Begins," 25, nn. 5, 6.

45. "Workshop on Clean Air and Clean Water," on Parliamentarians for Global Action (PGA) homepage (cited 16 June 2003); available from *http://www.pgaction. org/prog_sust_past.asp?id=126*.

46. The World Bank homepage (cited 16 June 2003); available from *http://www. worldbank.org/wbi/sdparliamentarians/index.html*.

47. "Sustainable Development and Population—Upcoming Events," on Parliamentarians for Global Action (PGA) homepage (cited 16 June 2003); available from *http://www.pgaction.org/prog_sust_upco.asp*.

48. Parliamentarians for Global Action (PGA) homepage (cited 15 June 2003); available from *http://www.pgaction.org/about.asp*.

49. "Nordic Council Gets Under Way," on Nordic Council homepage (cited 15 June 2003); available from *http://www.norden.org/webb/news/news.asp?id=2274& lang=6*.

50. "Presentation, About the Assembly," on Assembly of the Inter-parliamentary European Security and Defence Assembly (WEU) homepage (cited 15 June 2003); available from *http://www.assembly-weu.org/en/presentation/presentation.html*.

51. "SAARC Profile," on The South Asian Association for Regional Cooperation (SAARC) homepage (cited 15 June 2003); available from *http://www.saarc-sec. org/profile/content.htm*. The SAARC Regional Convention on the Suppression of Terrorism was signed in Kathmandu in November 1987 during the Third SAARC Summit and came into force on 22 August 1988 following ratification by all member-states. Chapter 7, "Legal Issues, Conventions and Agreements," on The South Asian Associ-

ation for Regional Cooperation (SAARC) homepage (cited 15 June 2003); available from *http://www.saarc-sec.org/profile/ch7.htm.*

The SAARC Convention on Narcotic Drugs and Psychotropic Substances which was signed in Malé during the Fifth SAARC Summit in November 1990 came into force on 15 September 1993, following ratification by all member-states. The SAARC Convention on Prevention of Trafficking of Women and Children for Prostitution was signed on 5 January 2002, at the Eleventh Summit in Kathmandu. The SAARC Convention on Regional Arrangements for the Promotion of Child Welfare in South Asia was signed on 5 January 2002 at the inauguration of the Eleventh Summit in Kathmandu."

52. South Asian Association for Regional Cooperation (SAARC) homepage (cited 20 December 2002); available from *http://www.saarc-sec.org/brief.htm.*

53. "SAARC Speakers' Conference Concludes," *Xinhua English Newswire*, 28 October 1997.

54. Edward Epstein, "Baltic States Teaming Up," *San Francisco Chronicle*, 14 May 1992.

55. "About the Baltic Assembly," on the Baltic Assembly homepage (cited 15 June 2003); available from *http://www.baltasam.org/about/index.htm.*

56. "History of Cooperation," on the Baltic Assembly homepage (cited 15 June 2003); available from *http://www.baltasam.org/partners/benelux_his.htm.*

57. "Baltic Assembly to Officially Seek Merger with Nordic Council," *Baltic News Service*, 4 June 2001.

58. "Joint Meeting of the Nordic Council and The Baltic Assembly," on the Baltic Assembly homepage (cited 15 June 2003); available from *http://www.baltasam.org/others/welcome_general.htm.*

59. See the Latin American Parliament homepage (cited 15 June 2003), available from *http://www.parlatino.org.br/index.php*; see also the African Parliamentary Union, homepage (cited 15 June 2003), available from *http://www.uafparl.org/about.html*; the Arab Inter-Parliamentary Union homepage (cited 15 June 2003), available from *http://www.arab-ipu.org/english/*; and the Andean Group homepage (cited 20 December 2002), available from *http://www.comunidadandina.org/endex.htm.*

60. Williams, "Sovereignty and Accountability in the European Union," 155–176.

61. Ibid., 172–175. The idea of joint commissions or assizes is compatible with the basic framework of the EP, most of the whose work is carried out in its seventeen standing committees, as well as in additional subcommittees and temporary committees. Joint parliamentary committees maintain ongoing relations with the parliaments of states linked to the European Union by association agreements; and interparliamentary delegations do the same with the parliaments of many other countries and international organizations. The model of committees and subcommittees narrows the substantive matters dealt with, and thus allows for better alignment of interests among parliamentarians from different countries.

62. Protocol on the role of national parliaments in the European Union, O.J. C 340/1, at 113–14 (1997). The Protocol sets a six-week period before the Community institutions make a decision on legislative proposals to allow for national parliaments' consultation procedures. The protocol also provides for COSAC to participate in in-

stitutional debates whenever the issues debated might have a direct bearing on the rights and freedoms of individuals.

63. "The Parliamentary Conference of the Americas Brings Together Nearly 800 Participants from 28 Countries in the Americas," *PR Newswire*, 18 September 1997.

64. "Parliamentary Conference of the Americas: An Unprecedented Success," *Canada NewsWire*, 21 September 1997.

65. Parliamentary Conference of the Americas (COPA) homepage (cited 15 June 2003); available from *http://www.copa.qc.ca/Anglais/#*.

66. NCSL staffer interviewed by author, 5 April 1996.

67. See ibid., 6.

68. Inter-Parliamentary Union (IPU) homepage (cited 15 June 2003); available from *http://www.ipu.org/iss-e/rprsdem.htm#BM2*.

69. African Parliamentary Union homepage (cited 15 June 2003); available from *http://www.uafparl.org/hom5.html*.

70. International Legislators Network homepage (cited 20 December 2002); formerly available from *http://www.legnet.org/about/index.html*.

71. "Programs," on Parliamentarians for Global Action (PGA) homepage (cited 16 June 2003); available from *http://www.pgaction.org/prog.asp*.

72. Ellen Yan, "Traveling Troubles: Delegations' Trips Criticized as Junkets Paid with Tax Funds," *Newsday*, 22 November 1998, A26.

CHAPTER 4
A Disaggregated World Order

1. Rischard, "A Novel Approach to Problem-Solving," 31.

2. Treaty of European Union, Title I, Article A, (7 February 1992).

3. See "Supervision of Financial Conglomerates (consultation documents)," in Bank for International Settlements homepage (cited 22 June 2003); available from *http://www.bis.org/publ/bcbs34.htm*. The members of the Joint Forum are Australia, Belgium, Canada, France, Germany, Italy, Japan, the Netherlands, Spain, Sweden, Switzerland, United Kingdom, and United States.

4. "US Objections Prompt Limited Global Pact on Financial Services," *Banking Policy Report* 14 (1995): 17.

5. See "Supervision of Financial Conglomerates (consultation documents)."

6. "Press Release, Recommendation on the Development of National Year 2000 Strategies, Joint Year 2000 Council," on Bank for International Settlements homepage (cited 22 June 2003); available from *http://www.bis.org/press/p980706.htm*.

7. The sponsoring committees of the council began by organizing a round table on the Year 2000 at the Bank for International Settlements on 8 April 1998. The decision to organize the council was taken at that meeting; all the efforts described in the text were underway by October 1998. See "Global Round Table on the Year 2000," on Bank for International Settlements homepage (cited 22 June 2003); available from *http://www.bis.org/press/p980409.htm#pgtop*.

8. Howell, "The Place of the Commonwealth in the International Order," 29–32.

9. Ibid., 31.

10. Ibid.

11. Ibid.

12. House of Commons, Foreign Affairs Committee, "The Future Role of the Commonwealth," xi.

13. Ibid., x–xi.

14. Ibid., xivii. The eight permanent countries include Great Britain, who is represented by the secretary of state.

15. Ibid., l–li.

16. Ibid., xviii.

17. Ibid., lx.

18. The Nordic Council and Nordic Council of Ministers have a very informative website (cited 22 June 2003); available from *http://www.norden.org*.

19. Ibid.

20. "2000 Detailed Agenda," on The Nordic Council and Nordic Council of Ministers homepage (cited 20 December 2002); available from *http://www.norden.org/session2000uk/agenda.htm*.

21. Ibid.

22. "Nordic Council: Facts on Nordic Co-operation," on The Nordic Council and Nordic Council of Ministers homepage (cited 22 June 2003); available from *http://www.norden.org/faktab/uk/nr_generel.pdf*.

23. "The doctrine of the separation of powers was adopted by the Convention of 1787 not to promote efficiency but to preclude the exercise of arbitrary power. The purpose was not to avoid friction, but, by means of the inevitable friction incident to the distribution of the governmental powers among three departments, to save the people from autocracy." *Myers v. United States*, 272 U.S. 52, 293, 47 S. Ct. 21, 85, 71 L. Ed. 160 (1926). Recognizing the limits imposed under the system, a Nordic think tank proposed electing a single spokesperson to represent Nordic views in international forums on areas where the Nordic countries are in complete agreement. See "Nordic Council Session 2000," on The Nordic Council and Nordic Council of Ministers homepage (cited 22 June 2003); available from *http://www.norden.org/session2000uk/index.html*.

24. Efforts to reverse such grants of authority include attempts by members of the Nordic Council of Ministers in the European Union to end EU support for shipping industries and to develop a Nordic standard for labeling fish products to serve as an alternate to EU standards. See "Swedish Investigator to Develop Nordic Shipping Policy," *Nordic Business Report*, 7 November 2001; "Nordic Fish Retailers Want to Create Nordic Rules for Fresh Fish," *Nordic Business Report*, 10 June 2002; Recommendation 24/2001, 6th Extraordinary Session of the Nordic Council, 26 June 2001, on The Nordic Council and Nordic Council of Ministers homepage (cited 22 June 2003); available from *http://www.norden.org/session2001/dokument/uk/rekliste_eng.pdf*.

25. "APEC Brochure 2001," on Asia-Pacific Economic Cooperation homepage (cited 22 June 2003); available from *http://www.apecsec.org.sg/apec_organization/brochure2001.html*.

26. Ibid.

27. Ibid.

28. Ibid.

29. Kahler, "Legalization as Strategy: The Asia-Pacific Case," 174. "APEC [has] remained resolutely nonlegal; its members have shown little willingness to formalize APEC by means of binding agreements on a defined set of substantive economic or trade issues, nor have its members thought to create a regional institution with rule-making, interpretative, enforcement, or adjudicative powers."

30. Goldstein and Martin, "Legalization, Trade Liberalization, and Domestic Politics: A Cautionary Note," 219–248.

31. Ibid.

32. APEC members are: Australia, Brunei Darussalam, Canada, Chile, China (People's Republic of), Hong Kong (granted membership rights separate from the People's Republic of China), Indonesia, Japan, Republic of Korea, Malaysia, Mexico, New Zealand, Papua New Guinea, Peru, the Philippines, Russia, Singapore, Chinese Taipei (also granted full membership rights distinct from China), Thailand, the United States, and Vietnam. See "Question and Answer," on Asia-Pacific Economic Cooperation homepage (cited 22 June 2003); available from *http://www.apecsec.org.sg/loadall.htm? http://www.apecsec.org.sg/govtproc/gphome.html.*

33. "APEC Brochure 2001."

34. Ibid.

35. Ibid. (Following the envisioning of a "community of Asia-Pacific economies" at the 1993 meeting on Blake Island, "APEC Ministers and Leaders further refined this vision and launched mechanisms to translate it into action.")

36. Ibid. ("APEC Leaders also welcomed the Ministers' decision to seek an EVSL agreement with non-APEC members at the World Trade Organization.")

37. Ibid.

38. See "OECD: About," on the Organization for Economic Cooperation and Development homepage (cited 23 June 2003); available from *http://www.oecd.org/EN/about/0,,EN-about-0-nodirectorate-no-no-no-0,00.html.*

39. See, e.g., James, "Twenty-First Century Pirates Of The Caribbean: How The Organization For Economic Cooperation And Development Robbed Fourteen Caricom Countries Of Their Tax And Economic Policy Sovereignty," 29–30; "Convention on Combating Bribery of Foreign Public Officials in International Business Transactions, OECD/DAFFE/IME/BR(97)16/FINAL 18 Dec. 1997," *International Legal Materials* 37 (1998): 1; S. Treaty Doc. No. 105–43, entered into force for the United States 15 Feb. 1999 ("OECD Convention").

40. See Global Corporate Governance Forum homepage (cited 22 June 2003); available from *http://www.gcgf.org/*; "The OECD Guidelines for Multinational Enterprises," on The Organization for Economic Cooperation and Development homepage (cited 22 June 2003); available from *http://www.oecd.org/pdf/M000015000/M00015419.pdf.*

41. Howell, "The Place of the Commonwealth in the International Order," 30.

42. For example, efforts have been made within the OECD's Development Assistance Committee to "untie" development assistance (to permit aid recipients to use aid to purchase goods or services from any country, as opposed to "tied" assistance, which

requires purchasing goods or services from the donor country) since 1969, but no agreement was reached within the OECD to untie official development assistance until 2001. This expression of the donor states' self-interest has been seen as a "mercantilist attitude" in parts of the developed world. See "OECD, Policy Brief: Untying Aid to the Least Developed Countries," *OECD Observer* (July 2001): 2, on The Organization for Economic Cooperation and Development homepage (cited 22 June 2003); available from *http://www.oecd.org/pdf/M00006000/M00006938.pdf*.

43. "Notes for an address by the Honourable Paul Martin to the Royal Institute of International Affairs," London, U.K., 24 January 2001, on Department of Finance Canada homepage (cited 22 June 2003); available from *http://www.fin.gc.ca/news01/01-009e.html*.

44. An international organization, then, is an organization between states in which they come together as the formal bearers of rights and holders of duties in the international system—the sovereigns recognized under international law—to create an organization. It is an organization in which they continue to hold the power, however, in the sense that they must all agree as sovereigns, although sometimes with systems of weighted voting, to any initiative the organization undertakes. A supranational organization, by contrast, is an organization in which the participating states have actually delegated power to a separate entity, such as a court, or a commission, or even a parliament, that can take decisions on its own and enforce them against the member-states.

This distinction matters because a true vertical network between a national government official and his or her counterpart in a global or regional organization requires that the counterpart have independent governing power, which can only really happen in a supranational rather than an international organization. Compare, for instance, the many cases in which international organizations have "secretariats" or "commissions," entities that exist to facilitate the work of the organization. As discussed below, these entities often improve the working of horizontal government networks—networks of environmental or finance or labor ministers—but they have no independent governing power. A supranational court, or a parliament, or a regulatory commission can have such power, and can exercise it in conjunction with its national counterparts.

45. Brower, "Structure, Legitimacy, and NAFTA's Investment Chapter," 62–72; see also Goldstein, "International Law and Domestic Institutions, Reconciling North American 'Unfair' Trade Laws," 541–564.

46. Bass, *Stay the Hand of Vengeance: The Politics of War Crimes Tribunals*.

47. United Nations Security Council Resolution 827, S/Res/827 (25 May 1993). See also Hochkammer, "The Yugoslav War Crimes Tribunal: The Compatibility of Peace, Politics, and International Law," 150–51.

48. United Nations Security Council Resolution 827, S/Res/827 (25 May 1993), Art. 9, Sec. 2.

49. *Prosecutor v. Dusko Tadic*, Decision on Defense Motion for Interlocutory Appeal on Jurisdiction, 2 October 1995, Case # IT-94-1-I, Paras. 56–58.

50. See Lessig, "Introduction (Feature: Making Sense of the Hague Tribunal)," 73 (although the Court may represent a statement of important principle, it is the most prominent example of a judicial institution being used for political ends in a peace-making process). For a contrary view, see Teitel, "Judgment at the Hague," 81 (the role of

the tribunal is to insure some measure of accountability during extraordinary periods of lawlessness and an international criminal tribunal is justified by the failings of national justice to respond to ethnic persecution). See also Vojin Dimitrijevic, "The War Crimes Tribunal in the Yugoslav Context," 89–90 (noting the danger of allowing criminals to go free when international law fails to fill a break down in a national judicial system).

51. Bassiouni, *The International Criminal Court: Observations and Issues Before the 1997–98 Preparatory Committee; and Administrative and Financial Implications.*

52. General Council of the Bar of South Africa, All-Party Support for International Criminal Court, (noting Arbour's argument to reduce the primacy of national courts envisaged in the Rome Statute and fully recognize "concurrent jurisdiction, with no primacy between national courts and the ICC at the stage of investigations"). Ed Vulliamy, "Why We Still Need a Nuremberg Court," *The Guardian*, 5 August 1997 (citing ICTY President Gabrielle Kirk McDonald, who insisted that the ICC should have "primacy" over national jurisdictions). Brown, "Primacy or Complementarity: Reconciling the Jurisdiction of National Courts and International Criminal Tribunals," 403 (citing Richard Goldstone's argument that an international tribunal is the "'only proper forum for trying those accused of playing leading roles in' . . . ethnic cleansing").

53. On the history of complementarity, see El Zeidy, "The Principle of Complementarity: A New Mechanism to Implement International Criminal Law," 869 (observing that the principle was first articulated in the 1943 draft statute for an international criminal court). For a negotiator's perspective on complementarity, see, e.g., Scheffer, "Fourteenth Waldemar A. Solf Lecture in International Law: A Negotiator's Perspective on the International Criminal Court," 1. For an extremely detailed analysis of the negotiations over complementarity at the Rome Conference, see Kim, "The Preconditions to the Exercise of the Jurisdiction of the International Criminal Court: With Focus on Article 12 of the Rome Statute," 47. For other debates over complementarity, see Bleich, "Cooperation with National Systems," 245 (noting that the series of articles relating to cooperation between the court and national jurisdictions refer to affirmative acts of judicial assistance by states in furtherance of the Court's jurisdiction and that these articles seek to maximize reliance upon voluntary cooperation with the Court by official government organs). The ILA Report to the Preparatory Committee on the ILC draft was perhaps the most sensitive to state sovereignty concerns: "While at least some members of the Committee (ILA) believe that supranationalism is inevitable . . . the Committee, as a whole, understands the legitimate concern states may have in preserving the integrity of their criminal justice systems, and indeed, their sovereignty as a whole." Wexler, "Committee Report on Jurisdiction, Definition of Crimes and Complementarity," 230.

54. For a discussion of the broader role of complementarity as a means of regulating the jurisdiction of national and international courts, see Burke-White, "A Community of Courts: Toward a System of International Criminal Law Enforcement," 92–93 (arguing that national courts should defer to international courts under the principle of complementarity in cases of global importance or where critical new legal precedents are being set.)

55. Council Regulation (EC) No 1/2003 of 16 December 2002. See Europa home-

page (cited 23 June 2003); available from *http://europa.eu.int/comm/competition/citizen/ citizen_antitrust.html#role* (describing a "radical reform" of competition law that involves the "competition authorities and courts of the Member States more directly in the application of the Community competition rules." See also, Press Release, Landmark Reform Simplifies and Strengthens Antitrust Enforcement, IP/02/1739 [26 Nov. 2002].

56. Once such network related to the WIPO is the Stockholm Group, which was "created in 1996 by a group of policy makers from industrialized countries who wanted an informal forum in which to discuss copyright protection for digital works and databases—two topics to be addressed at a WIPO Diplomatic Conference in December 1996." It has subsequently continued to meet regularly to discuss WIPO issues." Cheek, "The Limits of International Regulatory Cooperation in International Affairs: A Review of the Global Intellectual Property Regime," 313–14.

57. "North American Agreement on Environmental Cooperation," U.S.-Can.-Mex., 32 *International Legal Materials* 32 (14 September 1993): 1480.

58. The following discussion of the NAAEC relies on work by Fulton and Sperling, "The Network of Environmental Enforcement and Compliance Cooperation in North America and the Western Hemisphere." The authors are principal deupty general counsel and senior attorney-advisor, respectively, of the U.S. Environmental Protection Agency.

59. Ibid., 128.

60. North American Agreement on Environmental Cooperation, arts. 8,9.

61. Ibid., 5(1).

62. Ibid. arts. 5(2), 5(3).

63. See Fulton and Sperling, "The Network of Environmental Enforcement and Compliance Cooperation," 129.

64. Ibid., 131.

65. North American Agreement on Environmental Cooperation, art. 10(6).

66. Swan, "NAFTA and the Juridification of Economic Relations in the Western Hemisphere."

67. Alan C. Swan, letter to author, 25 July 1997. (On file with author.)

68. "Harmonization," which has been the main vector of Community intervention in national policies, is a legislative exercise that strives for a uniformity of substantive rules in EC member-states' laws. Dehousse, "Regulation by Networks in the European Community: The Role of European Agencies," 247–249.

69. Ibid.

70. Ibid., 249.

71. Ibid., 249–51.

72. Ibid., 254.

73. Ibid., 255. I borrow this term from Dehousse, who uses it to describe a new generation of agencies in the European Union. It is not commonly used to describe the secretariats of international organizations, but the appellation fits.

74. Ibid., 254.

75. Majone, "The New European Agencies: Regulation by Information," 262–63; Dehousse, "Regulation by Networks in the European Community," 255–57. Dehousse quotes the regulation establishing the Lisbon Drug Monitoring Centre as specifying

that " 'The Centre may not take any measure which in any way goes beyond the sphere of information and the processing thereof.' " Article 1(4) of Council Regulation EEC 302/93, OJ No. L 36/1, 12 February 1993, quoted in ibid., 256-57. Similarly, Council Regulation No. 1210/90, 7 May 1990, sets forth the task of the European Environmental Agency as follows: "To provide the member states and the Community with information; to collect, record and assess data on the state of the environment; to encourage harmonization of the methods of measurement; to promote the incorporation of European environmental information into international monitoring programs; to ensure data dissemination; to co-operate with other Community bodies and international institutions." Majone, "The New European Agencies," 263.

76. Majone, "The New European Agencies," 263.

77. Ibid., 267–68.

78. Ibid.

79. Ibid.

80. Dehousse, "Regulation by Networks in the European Community," 255.

81. Ibid.

82. Ibid.

83. The UN website describes the role of secretary general with reference to the UN Charter. The Charter, in turn, describes the Secretary-General as "chief administrative officer" of the organization, who shall act in that capacity and perform "such other functions as are entrusted" to him or her by the Security Council, General Assembly, Economic and Social Council and other United Nations organs. "The Role of the Secretary-General," on The United Nations homepage (cited 23 June 2003); available from *http://www.un.org/News/ossg/sg/pages/sg_office.html.*

84. Keohane and Nye, "The Club Model of Multilateral Cooperation and Problems of Democracy Legitimacy." (cited 23 June 2003); available from *http://www.ksg.harvard.edu/prg/nye/clubmodel.pdf.*

85. Cf. Fox, "Toward World Antitrust and Market Access," 1 (proposing five models to achieve a similar goal).

86. Cheek, "The Limits of International Regulatory Cooperation," 316 (noting that the Stockholm Group has been "reasonably successful" in strengthening the WIPO, despite the fact that intellectual property issues were being addressed by the "GATT process").

87. Article I of the OAS Charter reads: "The American States establish by this Charter the international organization that they have developed to achieve an order of peace and justice, to promote their solidarity, to strengthen their collaboration, and to defend their sovereignty, their territorial integrity, and their independence." Charter of the Organization of American States, entered into force 13 Dec. 1951, 2 U.S.T. 2394, reprinted in *International Legal Materials* 33 (1994): 989. Within the United Nations, the OAS is a regional agency.

88. "OAS Structure," on Organization of American States homepage (cited 22 June 2003): available from *http://www.oas.org.*

89. Compare Ruggie, "What Makes the World Hang Together? Neo-utilitarianism and the Social Constructivist Challenge," 1.

90. Chroust, "Did President Jackson Actually Threaten the Supreme Court with Nonenforcement of Its Injunction Against the State of Georgia?" 76.

CHAPTER 5
An Effective World Order

1. International Competition Policy Advisory Committee to the Attorney General and Assistant Attorney General for Antitrust, *Final Report* (Washington, D.C.: U.S. Government Printing Office, 2000), 190.

2. For a classic description of networks as a fundamental category of human interaction, as distinct from either hierarchies or markets, see Powell, "Neither Market nor Hierarchy." For a discussion of recent European scholarship on "policy networks," see Börzel, "Organizing Babylon—On the Different Conceptions of Policy Networks," 260 (discussing the work of scholars such as Renate Mayntz, Fritz Scharpf, Patrick Kenis, Volker Schneider, and Edgar Grande).

3. Nye, *The Paradox of American Power: Why the World's Only Superpower Can't Go It Alone*, 9. Nye first elaborated the concept of soft power in *Bound to Lead: The Changing Nature of American Power*, 188–201.

4. Nye, *The Paradox of American Power*, 9.

5. Keohane and Nye, "Power and Interdependence in the Information Age," 81–94.

6. In domestic politics, this brave new world is often labeled "democratic experimentalism." Dorf and Sabel, "A Constitution of Democratic Experimentalism," 322. Cohen and Sabel have described a polity built on this model as a "directly deliberative polyarchy." "Directly Deliberative Polyarchy," 313.

7. Raustiala, "The Architecture of International Cooperation: Transgovernmental Networks and The Future of International Law," 7.

8. Ibid.

9. Ibid.

10. Ibid., 32.

11. Ibid., 29, quoting Longstreth, "The SEC after Fifty Years: An Assessment of its Past and Future," 1610 (book review).

12. Raustiala, "The Architecture of International Cooperation," 30 n. 126, quoting Congressional testimony from former SEC Chair David Ruder in 1988.

13. See Faith T. Teo, "Memoranda of Understanding among Securities Regulators: Frameworks for Cooperation, Implications for Governance," Harvard Law School (1998): 45 (on file with author). The IOSCO blueprint for MOUs "provides that if an authority is not able to provide assistance absent a requirement of dual illegality, or if the authority cannot assure confidential treatment of information obtained pursuant to an MOU, that authority should consider recommending that appropriate amendments be made to its domestic legislation to enable the assistance to be given."

14. Raustiala, "The Architecture of International Cooperation," 32–33.

15. Ibid., 33.

16. Ibid., 45–46. For ongoing information about the courses offered in a given year and the foreign agencies that have participated in EPA training programs, see the EPA's website, "Environmental Training Modules: International Catalogue," on Environmental Protection Agency homepage (cited 5 July 2003); available from *http://www.epa.gov/international/techasst/training/traincatalog.html*.

17. Raustiala, "The Architecture of International Cooperation," 46.

18. Ibid.

19. Ibid., 44–45.

20. International Network of Environmental Compliance and Enforcement homepage (cited 4 July 2003); available from *http://www.inece.org*.

21. Fulton and Sperling, "The Network of Environmental Enforcement and Complicance Cooperation in North America and the Western Hemisphere," 120.

22. See, e.g., Joelson, *An International Antitrust Primer: A Guide to the Operation of the United States, European Union, and Other Key Competition Laws in the Global Economy*.

23. "G.E. and Honeywell Officially End Merger Agreement," *New York Times*, 3 October 2001, C4.

24. Waller, "The Internationalization of Antitrust Enforcement," 475.

25. The committee concluded in its 2000 report that "it appears that interest in [anticartel] enforcement is growing in many jurisdictions around the world and that U.S. experiences are receiving close scrutiny." International Competition Policy Advisory Committee to the Attorney General and Assistant Attorney General for Antitrust, *Final Report*, 190.

26. See, e.g., Raustiala, "The Architecture of International Cooperation," 35–43; Daniel K. Tarullo, "Norms and Institutions in Global Competition Policy," 478; Waller, "The Internationalization of Antitrust Enforcement"; Hachigian, "International Antitrust Enforcement," 22; Guzman, "Is International Antitrust Possible?" 1501.

27. International Competition Policy Advisory Committee to the Attorney General and Assistant Attorney General for Antitrust, *Final Report*, 191.

28. Address by Charles James, "International Antitrust in the Bush Administration" (21 September 2001) cited in Raustiala, "The Architecture of International Cooperation," 40.

29. "About the ICN," on International Competition Network homepage (cited 5 July 2003); available from *http://www.internationalcompetitionnetwork.org/aboutus.html*.

30. "International Competition Network: Members," on International Competition Network homepage (cited 5 July 2003); available from *http://www.international competitionnetwork.org/members.html*; "International Competition Network: Annual Conference," on International Competition Network homepage (cited 5 July 2003); available from *http://www.internationalcompetitionnetwork.org/aboutus.html*.

31. "International Competition Network, News Archive," on International Competition Network homepage (cited 5 July 2003); available from *http://www.international competitionnetwork.org/news/newsarchives.html*.

32. Ibid., 41.

33. "Report Concerning Internationalization of Competition Law Rules: Coordination and Convergence," *American Bar Association Sections of Antitrust Law and International Law and Practice* (January 2000): 19, 36–37, quoted in Raustiala, "The Architecture of International Cooperation," 43.

34. Raustiala, "The Architecture of International Cooperation," 61.

35. Ibid., 33, 39, and 44.

36. Ibid., 64.

37. Ibid.

38. Keohane and Nye, "Power and Interdependence in the Information Age," 89.

39. Ibid.

40. Ibid.

41. Andres Rigo, "Law Harmonization Resulting from the Policies of International Financial Institutions: The Case of the World Bank" (speech delivered at a conference on Globalization and the Evolution of Legal Systems, University of Ottawa, October 2000). See generally Shelton, *Commitment and Compliance: The Role of Non-Binding Norms in the International Legal System.*

42. Rigo, "Law Harmonization."

43. Ibid.

44. Ibid.

45. Ibid.

46. Ibid.

47. *Legal Framework for the Treatment of Foreign Investment: Survey of Existing Instruments,* vol. 1, (Washington, D.C.: The World Bank, 1992), 6.

48. See generally Dorf and Sabel, "A Constitution of Democratic Experimentalism," 267, 322.

49. Rigo, "Law Harmonization."

50. Ibid.

51. Ibid., quoting Reinicke, "Global Public Policy," 137; and Reinicke and Deng, *Critical Choices: The United Nations, Networks, and the Future of Global Governance.*

52. Raustiala also has a long discussion of the impact of government networks on treaty compliance, making many of the same points made here concerning capacity building. "The Architecture of International Cooperation," 76–83.

53. "Notes for an address by the Honourable Paul Martin, to the Royal Institute of International Affairs," Ottawa, 24 January 2001, on G-20 homepage (cited 1 July 2003); available from *http://www.fin.gc.ca/news01/01-008e.html.*

54. Ibid.

55. Ibid (emphasis added).

56. Chayes and Chayes, *The New Sovereignty: Compliance with International Regulatory Agreements,* 4.

57. Ibid., 4.

58. Raustiala, "The Architecture of International Cooperation," 79.

59. Ibid., 80–83.

60. Ibid., 83

61. Keohane and Nye, "Power and Interdependence in the Information Age," 81–82.

62. Majone, "From the Positive to the Regulatory State: Causes and Consequences of Changes in the Mode of Governance," 139–67.

63. Majone, "The New European Agencies: Regulation by Information," 265.

64. Ibid.

65. Notis Lebessis and John Paterson, "The Future of European Regulation: A Review of the Workshop," (Working Paper 1997, European Commission, Forward Studies Unit, 11 June 1997) (summarizing a workshop attended by Giandomenico Majone and Renaud Dehousse), on Europa homepage (cited 2 January 2003); formerly available from *http://europa.eu.int/comm/cdp/working-paper/future_of_european.pdf*

66. Commission of the European Communities, "European Governance: A White Paper," 25 July 2001, 21.

67. Dehousse, "Regulation by Networks in the European Community," 255.

68. Lebessis and Paterson, "The Future of European Regulation"; Dehousse, "Regulation by Networks," 255.

69. Commission of the European Communities, "European Governance: A White Paper," 21.

70. Dehousse, "Regulation by Networks," 255.

71. Ibid., 254.

72. Lebessis and Paterson, "The Future of European Regulation"; see also Majone, "The New European Agencies," 267–68.

73. Lebessis and Paterson, "The Future of European Regulation" (summary of Dehousse and Majone presentation at conference).

74. Ibid.

75. "North American Agreements on Environmental Cooperation (NAAEC)," 14 September 1993, U.S.-Can.-Mex., *International Legal Materials* 32: 1480 (1993).

76. NAAEC, arts. 14 and 15.

77. NAAEC, arts. 15(1) and (2).

78. Ibid., art. 15(4).

79. Ibid., art. 15(7).

80. See Markell, "The Commission for Environmental Cooperation's Citizen Submission Process," 571.

81. See Freeman, "Collaborative Governance in the Administrative State," 6 (arguing that a better model of regulation "views the administrative process as a problem-solving exercise in which parties share responsibility for all stages of the rule-making process, in which solutions are provisional").

82. Lebessis and Paterson, "The Future of European Regulation."

83. Ibid.

84. Ibid.

85. Commission of the European Communities, "European Governance: A White Paper," 19.

86. "The Global Compact: Overview," on The Global Compact homepage (cited 5 July 2003); available from *http://www.unglobalcompact.org/Portal/*.

87. "Secretary-General Proposes Global Compact on Human Rights, Labour, En-

vironment," Address to the World Economic Forum in Davos, Switzerland, 31 January 1999, UN Doc SG/SM/6881/Rev.1*, on United Nations homepage (cited 5 July 2003); available from *http://www.un.org/partners/business/davos.htm#speech.*

88. Ruggie, "Global_Governance.net: The Global Compact as Learning Network," 371.

89. Ibid.

90. Ibid.

91. Ibid.

92. Dorf and Sabel, "A Constitution of Democratic Experimentalism," 352.

93. Ibid., 348–49.

94. Ibid., 352.

95. Ladeur, "Towards a Legal Concept of the Network in European Standard-Setting," 157.

96. Ibid., 161.

97. Gerstenberg and Sabel, "Directly-Deliberative Polyarchy: An Institutional Ideal for Europe," 289–341. This combination of direct participation in problem solving combined with constant, structured information pooling and benchmarking lies at the heart of Dorf and Sabel's vision of democratic experimentalism. Dorf and Sabel, "A Constitution of Democratic Experimentalism," 267.

98. See Cohen and Sabel, "Directly Deliberative Polyarchy," 332–33.

99. See Majone, "The New European Agencies."

100. Aviram, "Regulation by Networks" (on file with author).

101. Ibid., 16–21.

102. "Convention on Combating Bribery of Foreign Public Officials in International Business Transactions, OECD/DAFFE/IME/BR(97)16/FINAL 18 Dec. 1997," *International Legal Materials* 37 (1998). The number of signatories is available at the Organization for Economic Cooperation and Development homepage (cited 5 July 2003); available from *http://www.oecd.org/pdf/M00017000/M00017037.pdf.*

103. Basic Principles on the Independence of the Judiciary, Seventh United Nations Congress on the Prevention of Crime and the Treatment of Offenders, Milan, 26 August–6 September 1985, UN Doc. A/CONF.121/22/Rev.1 at 59 (1985); "Center for the Independence of Judges and Lawyers," on International Commission of Jurists homepage (cited 5 July 2003); available from *http://www.icj.org/rubrique. php3?id_rubrique=40&lang=en.*

104. See generally Hechter, *Principles of Group Solidarity.*

105. I am indebted to my former students Timothy Wu and Kal Raustiala for many of the insights in the discussion that follows. Now law professors themselves, they wrote papers for a seminar I taught in 1997 on transgovernmental regulatory cooperation. Each paper explored different ways that regulatory networks exercise power and how they can be said to establish "order without law."

106. Timothy Wu, "Order Without International Law—The Compliance Inducing Capacity of Transgovernmental Networks" (May 1997) (on file with author).

107. Ellickson, *Order Without Law: How Neighbors Settle Disputes.*

108. Ellickson, *Order Without Law;* Bernstein, "Opting Out of the Legal System: Extralegal Contractual Relations in the Diamond Industry," 115; idem, "Merchant

Law in Merchant Court: Rethinking the Code's Search for Immanent Business Norms," 1765.

109. Olson, *The Logic of Collective Action: Public Goods and the Theory of Groups*, 65.

110. Olson, *The Logic of Collective Action*, 61, quoted in Wu, "Order Without International Law," 11.

111. Olson, *The Logic of Collective Action*, 62.

112. Sociologist Sally Engle Merry argues that effective social control is possible only in "close-knit and durable social networks" where there are "homogeneous norms and values." Merry, *Urban Danger: Life in a Neighborhood of Strangers* 196, quoted in Wu, "Order Without International Law," 23.

113. Ellickson, *Order Without Law*, 182, cited in Wu, "Order Without International Law," 12.

114. Wu, "Order Without International Law," 14–15.

115. Ibid., 2.

116. Ibid., 1.

117. Kapstein, *Governing the Global Economy: International Finance and the State*, 45.

118. See Ibid.; also Wu, "Order Without International Law," 29–33.

119. See International Organization of Securities Commissions (IOSCO) homepage (cited 23 December 2002); available from *http://www.iosco.org/gen-info.html*.

120. "The Basel Committee on Banking Supervision," on Bank for International Settlements homepage (cited 23 December 2003); available from *http://www.bis.org/bcbs/aboutbcbs.htm*.

121. Aviram, "Regulation by Networks," 18.

122. Ibid., 18 n. 63, citing Bernstein, "Opting Out of the Legal System," 129.

123. Slaughter and Helfer, "Toward a Theory of Effective Supranational Adjudication," 286.

124. Foreign Affairs Committee, *The Future of the Commonwealth*, vol. 1, 27 March 1996, xlviii.

125. Chayes and Chayes, *The New Sovereignty*, 27.

126. I owe this insight directly to Kal Raustiala, who made the connection to the Chayes and Chayes work as part of a larger paper he wrote examining the power of government networks to induce structural change in domestic bureaucracies. Raustiala, "Order Without Law: Disaggregated Sovereignty and Structural Replication in the International System," (May 1997) (on file with author).

127. "Backgrounder," on the G-20 homepage (cited 23 December 2002); available from *http://www.g20.org/docs/bkgrnd-e.html*.

128. "From G7 to G8," on G-8 Information Center homepage (cited 23 December 2002); available from *http://www.g7.utoronto.ca/g7/what_is_g7.html*.

129. "Parliamentary Supremacy and Judicial Independence, Latimer House Guidelines (1998)," on Commonwealth Parliamentary Association homepage (cited 2 January 2003); available from *http://www.cpahq.org/download/latmrhse.pdf*.

130. Howell, "The Place of the Commonwealth in the International Order."

131. Justice Richard Goldstone, personal conversation with author, Hamburg, Germany, 23 August 2001.

132. Fearon, "Deliberation as Discussion," 44.

133. Compare, in this regard, Abram Chayes' claim that "the requirement of justification suffuses the basic process of choice. There is continuous feedback between the knowledge that the government will be called upon to justify its action and the kind of action that can be chosen." Chayes, *The Cuban Missile Crisis: International Crises and the Role of Law*, 103.

134. Fearon, "Deliberation as Discussion," 62. The quote is from Fearon, but he is paraphrasing Manin, "On Legitimacy and Political Deliberation," 352.

135. Ibid., 45. Fearon states the grounds he identifies for favoring discussion as follows:

Reveal private information;

Lessen or overcome the impact of bounded rationality;

Force or encourage a particular mode of justifying demands or claims;

Help render the ultimate choice legitimate in the eyes of the group, so as to contribute to group solidarity or to improve the likely implementation of the decision;

Improve the moral or intellectual qualities of the participants;

Do the "right thing," independent of the consequences of discussion.

136. Ibid., 47,

137. Ibid., 55.

138. Ibid., 58.

139. Ibid., 54.

140. Risse, "'Let's Argue!': Communicative Action in World Politics," 1–39.

141. This account of how humans behave is a very basic summary, courtesy of Thomas Risse, of some of the theories of the great German philosopher Juergen Habermas, who has spent decades making room for reason in a world that all too often seems to hold only atomistic interest-driven individuals or suffocating social structures. Habermas, *Theorie des kommunikativen Handelns* (translated as *Theory of Communicative Action*). Habermas sees individuals as beings who not only seek to persuade others, but who are themselves open to persuasion. A speaker's willingness to change his own mind in light of what he hears, often in response to what he says, is the precondition for "true reasoning." Risse, "Let's Argue!," 9.

142. March and Olsen, *Rediscovering Institutions: The Organizational Basis of Politics*; "The Institutional Dynamics of International Political Orders," 52, no. 4 (DATE): 943–69.

143. March and Olsen, "Institutional Dynamics," 943.

144. Risse, "Let's Argue!," 2.

145. Ibid., 1–2.

146. Ibid., 15, 19.

147. Ibid., 19.

148. See Rigo, "Law Harmonization."

149. Risse, "Let's Argue!," 33.

150. Ibid., 28–31.

151. Lani Guinier, "Rethinking Power," Tanner Lectures on Human Values, (lectures given by Professor Guinier at Sanders Theater, Harvard University, November 4–5, 1998); idem, *The Miner's Canary: Enlisting Race, Resisting Power, Transforming Democracy*.

152. Hirschman, *A Propensity to Self-Subversion*, 235.

153. Ibid., 237.

154. Ibid., 239.

155. Ibid., 242–44.

156. Ibid., 246.

157. Ibid., 244.

158. "Merger Busting in Europe," *New York Times*, 21 June 2001.

159. Larson, "Network Dyads in Entrepreneurial Settings: A Study of the Governance of Exchange Relationships," 76, quoted in Rhodes, *Understanding Governance*, 51. Rhodes himself reaches a similar conclusion. Rhodes, "The New Governance: Governing without Government," 652–667.

160. Robert Keohane, "Studying Cooperation and Conflict: Intra-Rationalistic and Extra-Rationalistic Research Programs," (talk at a roundtable on conflict and cooperation, American Political Science Association annual meetings, San Francisco, CA, August 1996) (on file with author).

161. Hart, and Sacks, *The Legal Process: Basic Problems in the Making and Application of Law*, lxxi–lxxii.

162. Chayes and Chayes, *The New Sovereignty*, 22–28.

163. Chayes and Chayes developed their analytical framework with regard to international regulatory treaties; it applies equally well to transnational regulatory relations. In earlier work Abram Chayes elaborated the link between regulatory law and public policy, arguing that the resolution of regulatory issues necessarily involves broad debates over public policy and public values. Chayes, "The Role of the Judge in Public Law Litigation," 1302.

164. Cover, "The Supreme Court, 1982 Term—Forward: Nomos and Narrative," 15, cited for a similar proposition in Koh, "The 1994 Roscoe Pound Lecture: Transnational Legal Process," 181.

165. Koh, "The 1998 Frankel Lecture: Bringing International Law Home," 623.

CHAPTER 6
A Just World Order

1. "Notes for an address by the Honourable Paul Martin to the Royal Institute of International Affairs," London, United Kingdom, 24 January 2001, on Department of Finance Canada homepage (cited 22 June 2003); available from *http://www.fin.gc.ca/news01/01-009e.html*.

2. Shklar, "The Liberalism of Fear." I am indebted to Robert Keohane for helping me see this point and for phrasing it so felicitously in Shklar's language.

3. Perez, "Who Killed Sovereignty? Or: Changing Norms Concerning Sovereignty In International Law," 476.

4. Alston, "The Myopia of the Handmaidens: International Lawyers and Globalization," 441.

5. See Picciotto, "Networks in International Economic Integration: Fragmented States and the Dilemmas of Neo-liberalism," 1047.

6. Ibid., 1049.

7. Darringer, "Swaps, Banks, and Capital: an Analysis of Swap Risks and a Critical Assessment of the Basle Accord's Treatment of Swaps," 259; but see also Kapstein, "Shockproof," 2 (capital adequacy requirements saved financial markets from the potentially disastrous consequences of the Mexican peso crisis and the Barings collapse.)

8. Macey, "The 'Demand' for International Regulatory Cooperation: A Public-Choice Perspective," 159–60.

9. Weiler, "To Be a European Citizen: Eros and Civilization," 349.

10. On Public Citizen homepage (cited 1 July 2003); available from *http://www.citizen.org*.

11. "Harmonization," on Public Citizen homepage (cited 1 July 2003); available from *http://www.citizen.org/trade/harmonization*.

12. "What Is Harmonization?" on Public Citizen homepage (cited 1 July 2003); available from *http://www.citizen.org/trade/harmonization/articles.cfm?ID=4390*.

13. Ibid.

14. Ibid.

15. "Harmonization Alert," on Public Citizen homepage (cited 1 July 2003); available from *http://www.citizen.org/trade/harmonization/alerts/*.

16. "What is Harmonization?"

17. Shapiro, "International Trade Agreements, Regulatory Protection, and Public Accountability," 435–58.

18. Harmonization Background Paper, "Accountable Governance in the Era of Globalization: the WTO, NAFTA, and International Harmonization," on Public Citizen homepage (cited 1 July 2003); available from *http://www.citizen.org/publications/release.cfm?ID=5193*.

19. Ibid.

20. Ibid.

21. Ibid.

22. Kofi A. Annan, *We the Peoples: The Role of the United Nations in the 21st Century*, 70; Rischard, "A Novel Approach to Problem-Solving," 31; Reinicke, "The Other World Wide Web: Global Public Policy Networks," 44.

23. Shapiro, "Administrative Law Unbounded: Reflections on Government and Governance," 369.

24. Ibid., 376.

25. Fried, "Scholars and Judges: Reason and Power," 818.

26. Ibid.

27. Ibid., 820–21.

28. Ginsburg and Merritt, "Affirmative Action: an International Human Rights Dialogue," 273.

29. McCrudden, "A Common Law of Human Rights?: Transnational Judicial Conversations on Constitutional Rights," 507–8.

30. Ghai, "Sentinels of Liberty or Sheep in Wolf's Clothing? Judicial Politics and the Hong Kong Bill of Rights," 479, quoted in ibid., 507.

31. Members of the Technical Committee include: Australia, Canada, France, Germany, Hong Kong, Italy, Japan, the Netherlands, Switzerland, United Kingdom,

and the United States of America. On OICU-IOSCO homepage (cited 1 July 2003); available from *http://www.iosco.org/lists/display_committees.cfm?cmtid=3*.

32. Howell, "The Place of the Commonwealth in the International Order," 30.

33. "Notes for an address by the Honourable Paul Martin."

34. Risse, "'Let's Argue!': Communicative Action in World Politics," 31.

35. Rawls, *Political Liberalism*.

36. On International Monetary Fund homepage (cited 1 July 2003); available from *http://www.imf.org*.

37. On government of Canada homepage (cited 1 July 2003); available from *http://canada.gc.ca*.

38. On EUR-Lex, European Union Law homepage (cited 1 July 2003); available from *http://www.europa.eu.int/eur-lex/*.

39. "Rome Statute of the International Criminal Court," on United Nations homepage (cited 1 July 2003); available from *http://www.un.org/law/icc/*.

40. MOUs between the U.S. SEC and its foreign counterparts, for instance, have been directly encouraged and facilitated by several U.S. statutes passed expressly for the purpose. Faith T. Teo, "Memoranda of Understanding among Securities Regulators: Frameworks for Cooperation, Implications for Governance," Harvard Law School (1998): 29–43. (on file with author).

41. On Globe International homepage (cited 1 July 2003); available from *http://www.globeinternational.org*.

42. Kaiser, "Globalisierung als Problem der Demokratie," 3. See also the EU Institutional Reform Commissioner's website, "Commissioner for Regional Policy and Institutional Reform" on Europa homepage (cited 1 July 2003); available from *http://europa.eu.int/comm/commissioners/barnier/profil/index_en.htm*, for proposals regarding further ties between national parliamentarians among EU members.

43. Falk and Strauss, "Toward a Global Parliament," : 212 .

44. Louise Doswald-Beck, "The Influence of National Parliaments on Global Policy-Making," *Berlin*, 26, November 2001, quoted in Steve Charnovitz, "Trans-Parliamentary Associations in Global Functional Agencies," *Transnational Associations* 2 (2002): 88–91, 90 n. 20.

45. Charnovitz, "Trans-Parliamentary Associations in Global Functional Agencies," 88.

46. Ibid., 89.

47. Mike Moore, "Promoting Openness, Fairness and Predictability in International Trade for the Benefit of Humanity," speech to the Inter-Parliamentary Union meeting on international trade, 8 June 2001, on World Trade Organization homepage (cited 1 July 2003); available from *http://www.wto.org/french/news_f/spmm_f/spmm64_f.htm*.

48. Annan, *We the Peoples*, 70.

49. Reinicke and Deng, *Critical Choices: The United Nations, Networks, and the Future of Global Governance*.

50. Reinicke, "The Other World Wide Web."

51. See Koch, "Judicial Review and Global Federalism," 491.

52. See the "Symposium on Global Administrative Law"; see also Aman, "Administrative Law for a New Century."

53. "American Bar Association House of Delegates Recommendation no. 107C, Harmonization Recommendation (August 2001)," on American Bar Association homepage (cited 1 July 2003); available from *http://www.abanet.org/leadeship/2001/107c.pdf.*, para. (2).

54. Petersmann, "Constitutionalism and International Organizations," 398; idem, "Constitutionalism and International Adjudication: How to Constitutionalize the U.N. Dispute Settlement System?" 753.

55. Ignatieff, *Human Rights as Politics and Idolatry*, 4.

56. Ibid., 94.

57. Ibid., 94–95.

58. "Notes for an address by the Honourable Paul Martin, to the Royal Institute of International Affairs."

59. Cohen, "Deliberation and Democratic Legitimacy," 74.

60. *Loucks v. Standard Oil Co.*, 120 N.E. 198, 201 (N.Y. 1918).

61. The full faith and credit clause of the Constitution requires each state to recognize the acts of another. U.S. CONST. art.IV,§1,cl.1. It is a basic instrument of federalism, knitting the states into one larger polity.

62. *Laker Airways Ltd. v. Sabena, Belgian World Airlines* 731 F.2d 909 (D.C. Cir. 1984).

63. In re Matter of Oil Spill by the Amoco Cadiz Off the Coast of France on 16 March 1978, 954 F.2d 1279, 1312–13 (7th Cir. 1992) (per curiam). The Chevron doctrine was set forth in *Chevron U.S.A. Inc. v. Natural Resources Defense Council, Inc.*, 467 U.S. 837, 844 (1984) (holding that "a court may not substitute its own construction of a statutory provision for a reasonable interpretation made by the administrator of an agency. We have long recognized that considerable weight should be accorded to an executive department's construction of a statutory scheme it is entrusted to administer.").

64. *Omron Healthcare, Inc. v. Maclaren Exports Ltd.*, 28 F.3d 600, 604 (7th Cir. 1994).

65. Kalypso Nicolaïdis, "Mutual Recognition of Regulatory Regimes: Some Lessons and Prospects," (Jean Monnet Working Paper No. 97/7, New York University School of Law, Jean Monnet Center, 1997), on Jean Monnet Program homepage (cited 1 July 2003); available from *http://www.jeanmonnetprogram.org/papers/97/97-07.html.*

66. After the Cassis de Dijon decision of 1979, in which German authorities were forced to respect French liquor standards, the European Commission announced the "mutual trust" principle: if one state's rules allow a product to be marketed, all other states should have confidence in the first state's judgment and likewise allow the product to be marketed. Case 120/78, *Rewe-Zentral AG v. Bundesmonopolverwaltung fur Branntwein*, E.C.R. 649 (1979). This concept has contributed significantly to creating an integrated internal market. It has been read to require mutual recognition of educational diplomas, so that professionals from one EU country are now largely free to practice in another without repeating their education. Council Directive 75/362, 1975 O.J. (L 167/1); Council Directive 89/48, 1989 O.J. (L 19/16). Additionally, it has been applied to banking regulation, where branches of foreign banks are now supervised not by the host state, but by the authorities of the state of the head office, or home state. This approach reflects that each EU state accords a high degree of "mutual trust" to the

banking supervisory capabilities of the others. See Second Council Directive 89/646 on credit institutions, 1989 O.J. (L 386/1).

67. 159 U.S. 113, 163–64 (1895).

68. Beginning with *United States v. Aluminum Co. of America (Alcoa)*, the Sherman Act was held applicable to foreign conduct that had a direct, substantial, and foreseeable effect on U.S. trade and commerce. 148 F.2d 416, 440–45 (2d Cir. 1945). This direct effect jurisdiction quickly became a source of tension with other states that argued that the United States had no right to assert jurisdiction over persons that were neither present nor acting within United States territory. Governments whose nationals and interests were affected by U.S. antitrust law filed diplomatic protests and amicus briefs, refused requests for assistance, invoked national secrecy laws, and eventually began passing blocking laws specifically aimed at the frustration of U.S. antitrust enforcement. Waller, "National Laws and International Markets: Strategies of Cooperation and Harmonization in the Enforcement of Competition Law," 1113–1114; see also Paul, "Comity in International Law," 32; Griffin, "EC and U.S. Extraterritoriality: Activism and Cooperation," 377.

69. Waller, "The Internationalization of Antitrust Enforcement," 375. By 1988 the Department of Justice stated that it would only challenge foreign anticompetitive conduct that directly harmed United States consumers. Shank, "The Justice Department's Recent Antitrust Enforcement Policy: Toward A "Positive Comity" Solution to International Competition Problems?" 165.

70. Charles F. Rule, "European Communities-United States Agreement on the Application of their Competition Laws Introductory Note," 1487, 1488. The U.S. signed a comparable agreement with Germany in 1976. See Snell, "Controlling Restrictive Business Practices in Global Markets: Reflections on the Concepts of Sovereignty, Fairness, and Comity," 234.

71. No use of the Canadian federal blocking statute has been reported since the signing of the 1984 Agreement. See Waller, "The Internationalization of Antitrust Enforcement," 368.

72. In the past five years, cooperation between United States and Canadian antitrust agencies has led to prosecutions in the fax paper and plastic dinnerware industries. See Stark, "International Antitrust Cooperation in NAFTA: The International Antitrust Assistance Act of 1994," 171–72.

73. Nina Hachigian, "Essential Mutual Assistance in International Antitrust Enforcement," 138. Antitrust cooperation has also been developing on a multilateral scale. The OECD has established regular consultation conferences among national competition officials and has drafted a recommendation on antitrust cooperation, which encourages "notification, exchange of information, coordination of action, consultation and conciliation on a voluntary basis." See Waller, "The Internationalization of Antitrust Enforcement," 362–63 (quoting "Revised Recommendation of the Council Concerning Co-operation Between Member Countries on Anticompetitive Practices Affecting International Trade," *International Legal Materials* 35 (1996): 1315–17. More recently, a group of twelve experts called the International Antitrust Code Working Group proposed an International Antitrust Code to be adopted as a plurilateral trade agreement under GATT. Under the code, an international antitrust author-

ity would be established, consisting of a president and an international antitrust council to ensure observance of the code by contracting parties. See Shank, "The Justice Department's Recent Antitrust Enforcement Policy," 186.

74. See "Agreement Regarding the Application of their Competition Laws, 23 Sept. 1991, E.C.-U.S.," *International Legal Materials* 30 (1991): 1491.

75. Ibid., 1056–59.

76. See Griffin, "EC and U.S. Extraterritoriality," 376.

77. Atwood, "Positive Comity—Is It a Positive Step?" 84.

78. See Rule, "European Communities-United States Agreement," 1488.

79. See Atwood, "Positive Comity—Is It a Positive Step?" 84.

80. See Rule, "European Communities-United States Agreement," 1487.

81. Griffin, "EC/U.S. Antitrust Cooperation Agreement: Impact on Transnational Business," 1063.

82. See generally Klein and Bansal, "International Antitrust Enforcement in the Computer Industry," 179.

83. See Rule, "European Communities-United States Agreement," 1490. This increased efficiency has also proven attractive to businesses themselves. In *United States v. Microsoft Corp.*, after learning that both the Department of Justice and the European Commission were investigating their licensing practices, Microsoft agreed to waive its confidentiality rights under United States antitrust law to permit the two authorities to exchange confidential information. See Shank, "The Justice Department's Recent Antitrust Enforcement Policy," 179.

84. Janow, "Transatlantic Cooperation on Competition Policy," 51.

85. Ibid.

86. See Atwood, "Positive Comity—Is It a Positive Step?" 87.

87. Ibid.

88. Ibid., 88.

89. See Waller, "National Laws and International Markets," 1125.

90. See Atwood, "Positive Comity—Is It a Positive Step?" 88.

91. Shapiro, *Federalism: A Dialogue,* 108.

92. Ibid.

93. See chapter 2, note 104.

94. Bermann, "Taking Subsidiarity Seriously: Federalism in the European Community and the United States," 331.

95. Consolidated Version of the Treaty Establishing the European Community, Art. V, *Official Journal C 325 of 24 December 2002*. According to the relevant provisions of this article:

In areas which do not fall within its exclusive competence, the Community shall take action, in accordance with the principle of subsidiarity, only if and insofar as the objectives of the proposed action cannot be sufficiently achieved by the Member States and can therefore, by reason of the scale or effects of the proposed action, be better achieved by the Community. Any action by the Community shall not go beyond what is necessary to achieve the objectives of this Treaty.

CONCLUSION

1. Chayes and Chayes, *The New Sovereignty: Compliance with International Regulatory Agreements* 27.

2. Reinecke, "Global Public Policy," 132. See also idem, *Global Public Policy: Governing without Government?*

3. Ibid.

4. Ibid.

5. Ibid., 133, 127.

6. Ibid.

7. Ibid., 134.

8. Chayes and Chayes, *The New Sovereignty*, 4.

9. Ibid., 26. As noted above, Reinecke similarly emphasizes the extent to which globalization, unlike interdependence, penetrates the deep structure and strategic behavior of corporations and other actors in the international system.

10. Ibid.

11. Benvenisti, "Domestic Politics and International Resources: What Role for International Law?" 109.

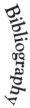

Abrahamson, Shirley S., and Michael J. Fischer. "All the World's a Courtroom: Judging in the New Millennium." *Hofstra Law Review* 26 (1997): 276.

Ackerman, Bruce. "The Rise of World Constitutionalism," *Virginia Law Review* 83 (1997): 771.

———. "The New Separation of Powers." *Harvard Law Review* 113 (2000): 633.

Alston, Philip. "The Myopia of the Handmaidens: International Lawyers and Globalization," supra, p. *European Journal of International Law* 8 (1997): 435.

Alter, Karen. "Explaining National Court Acceptance of European Court Jurisprudence: A Critical Evaluation of Theories of Legal Integration." In *The European Court and National Courts—Doctrine and Jurisprudence: Legal Change in Its Social Context*, edited by Anne-Marie Slaughter, Alec Stone Sweet, and J.H.H. Weiler. Evanston, Ill.: Northwestern University Press, 1998.

———. "Who Are the '"Masters of the Treaty"'?: European Governments and the European Court of Justice." *International Organization* 52 (1998): 121.

———. *Establishing the Supremacy of European Law: The Making of an International Rule of Law in Europe.* New York: Oxford University Press, 2001.

Aman, Alfred. "Administrative Law for a New Century." In *The Province of Administrative Law*, edited by Michael Taggart. Oxford: Hart Publishing, 1997.

Andrews, David R. "Listening in on the US-EU Legal Dialogue." In *Transatlantic Regulatory Cooperation, Legal Problems and Political Prospects*, edited by George A. Bermann, Matthais Herdegen, and Peter L. Lindseth. Oxford: Oxford University Press, 2000.

Annan, Kofi A. *We the Peoples: The Role of the United Nations in the 21st Century.* New York: United Nations, Department of Public Information, 2000.

"Appendix B: Report of the Secretary General Pursuant to Paragraph 2 of Security Council Resolution 808." *Criminal Law Forum* 5 (1994): 597.

Apple, James G. "British, U.S. Judges and Lawyers Meet, Discuss Shared Judicial, Legal Concerns," *International Judicial Observer* 2 (1996): 1.

Attanasio, John B. "Rapporteur's Overview and Conclusions: of Sovereignty, Globalization, and Courts." In *International Law Decisions in National Courts*, edited by Thomas M. Franck and Gregory H. Fox. Irvington-on-Hudson, N.Y.: Transnational Publishers, 1996.

Atwood, James R. "Positive Comity—Is It a Positive Step?" In *International Antitrust Law & Policy: Annual Proceedings of the Fordham Corporate Law Institute*, edited by Barry Hawk. Irvington-on-Hudson, N.Y.: Transnational Jurist Publications, 1993.

Bass, Gary Jonathan. *Stay the Hand of Vengeance: The Politics of War Crimes Tribunals*. Princeton, N.J.: Princeton University Press, 2000.

Bassiouni, M. Cherif. "Former Yugoslavia: Investigating Violations of International Humanitarian Law and the Creation of an International Criminal Tribunal." *Fordham International Law Journal* 18 (1995): 1191.

———, ed. *The International Criminal Court: Observations and Issues Before the 1997–98 Preparatory Committee; and Administrative and Financial Implications*. Chicago: International Human Rights Institute, DePaul University, 1997.

Bebr, Gerhard. *Development of Judicial Control of The European Communities*. Hingham, Mass.: Kluwer Boston Distributors, 1981.

Benvenisti, Eyal. "The Influence of International Human Rights Law on the Israeli Legal System: Present and Future." *Israel Law Review* 28 (1994): 147.

———. "Judges and Foreign Affairs: A Comment on the Institut de Droit International's Resolution on 'Activities of National Courts and the International Relations of their States.'" *European Journal of International Law* 5 (1994): 424.

———. "Domestic Politics and International Resources: What Role for International Law?" In *The Role of Law in International Politics*, edited by Michael Byers. New York: Oxford University Press, 2000.

Bergsten, C. Fred. "American and Europe: Clash of Titans?" *Foreign Affairs* 78 (1999): 20–33.

Bermann, George. "Regulatory Cooperation with Counterpart Agencies Abroad: The FAA's Aircraft Certification Experience." *Law and Policy of International Business* 24 (1993): 669.

———. "Taking Subsidiarity Seriously: Federalism in the European Community and the United States." *Columbia Law Review* 94 (1994): 331.

———. "Regulatory Cooperation between the European Commission and U.S. Administrative Agencies." *Administrative Law Journal* 9 (1996): 933.

Bermann, George, et al. *European Community Law*. St. Paul, Minn.: West Publishing Company, 1993.

Bernstein, Lisa. "Opting Out of the Legal System: Extralegal Contractual Relations in the Diamond Industry." *Journal of Legal Studies* 21 (1992): 115.

———. "Merchant Law in Merchant Court: Rethinking the Code's Search for Immanent Business Norms." *University of Pennsylvania Law Review* 144 (1996): 1765.

Bibriosa, Hervé. "Report on Belgium." In *The European Court and National Courts—Doctrine and Jurisprudence: Legal Change in Its Social Context* , edited by Anne-Marie Slaughter, Alec Stone Sweet, and J.H.H. Weiler. Evanston, Ill.: Northwestern University Press, 1998.

Bleich, Jeffrey. "Cooperation with National Systems." In *The International Criminal Court: Observations and Issues Before the 1997–98 Preparatory Committee; and Administrative and Financial Implications*, edited by M. Cherif Bassiouni. Chicago: International Human Rights Institute, DePaul University, 1997.

Bolton, John. "Should We Take Global Governance Seriously?" *Chicago Journal of International Law* 1 (2000): 205.

Born, Gary. *International Civil Litigation in United States Courts*, 3d ed. Boston: Kluwer Law International, 1996.

Börzel, Tanja A. "Organizing Babylon—On the Different Conceptions of Policy Networks." *Public Administration* 76 (1998): 253.

Brower, Charles H., II. "Structure, Legitimacy, and NAFTA's Investment Chapter." *Vanderbilt Journal of Transnational Law* 26 (2003): 37.

Brown, Bartram S. "Primacy or Complementarity: Reconciling the Jurisdiction of National Courts and International Criminal Tribunals." *Yale Journal of International Law* 23 (1998): 383.

Brumter, Christian. *The North Atlantic Assembly*. Boston: Martinus Nijhoff Publishers, 1986.

Buergenthal, Thomas. "International Tribunals and National Courts: The Internationalization of Domestic Adjudication." In *Recht Zwischen Umbruch Und Bewahrung: Festschrift Fur Rudolf Bernhardt*. New York: Springer-Verlag, 1995.

Burke-White, William W. "A Community of Courts: Toward a System of International Criminal Law Enforcement." *Michigan Journal of International Law* 24 (2002): 1.

Burley, Anne-Marie, and Walter Mattli. "Europe Before the Court: A Political Theory of Legal Integration." *International Organization* 47 (1993): 41.

Cartwright, John, et al. "About the North Atlantic Assembly." In *The State of the Alliance 1986–1987: North Atlantic Assembly Reports*. Boulder: Westview Press, 1987.

Chayes, Abram. *The Cuban Missile Crisis: International Crises and the Role of Law*. New York: Oxford University Press, 1974.

———. "The Role of the Judge in Public Law Litigation." *Harvard Law Review* 89 (1976): 1281.

Chayes, Abram, and Antonia H. Chayes. *The New Sovereignty: Compliance with International Regulatory Agreements*. Cambridge, Mass.: Harvard University Press, 1995.

Cheek, Marney L. "The Limits of Informal Regulatory Cooperation in International Affairs: A Review of the Global Intellectual Property Regime." *George Washington International Law Review* 33 (2001): 277.

Choudhry, Sujit. "Globalization in Search of Justification: Toward a Theory of Comparative Constitutional Interpretation." *Indiana Law Journal* 74 (1999): 819.

Chroust, Anton-Hermann. "Did President Jackson Actually Threaten the Supreme

Court with Nonenforcement of Its Injunction Against the State of Georgia?" *American Journal of Legal History* 4 (1960): 76.

Cohen, Joshua. "Deliberation and Democratic Legitimacy." In *The Good Polity: Normative Analysis of the State*, edited by Alan Hamlin and Philip Pettit. New York: Blackwell, 1989.

Cohen, Joshua, and Charles Sabel. "Directly Deliberative Polyarchy." *European Law Journal* 3 (1997): 313.

Coing, Helmut. "Europaisierung der Rechtswissenschaft." 15 *Neue Juristische Wochenschrift* (1990): 937.

Cooke, Jacob E., ed., *The Federalist*, No. 42 (James Madison). Middletown, Conn.: Wesleyan University Press, 1961.

Cover, Robert M. "The Supreme Court, 1982 Term—Forward: Nomos and Narrative." *Harvard Law Review* 97 (1983): 4.

Craig, P. P. "Report on the United Kingdom." In *The European Court and National Courts—Doctrine and Jurisprudence: Legal Change in Its Social Context*, edited by Anne-Marie Slaughter, Alec Stone Sweet, and J.H.H. Weiler. Evanston, Ill.: Northwestern University Press, 1998.

Darringer, Bruce. "Swaps, Banks, and Capital: an Analysis of Swap Risks and a Critical Assessment of the Basle Accord's Treatment of Swaps." *University of Pennsylvania Journal of International Business Law* 16 (1995): 259.

Dehousse, Renaud. "Regulation by Networks in the European Community: The Role of European Agencies." *Journal of European Public Policy* 4 (1997): 246–61.

Devuyst, Youri. "Transatlantic Competition Relations." In *Transatlantic Governance in the Global Economy*, edited by Mark A. Pollack and Gregory C. Shaffer. Lanham, Md.: Rowman and Littlefield, 2001.

Dimitrijevic, Vojin. "The War Crimes Tribunal in the Yugoslav Context." *Eastern European Constitutional Review* 5 (1996): 87.

Dorf, Michael C., and Charles F. Sabel. "A Constitution of Democratic Experimentalism." *Columbia Law Review* 98: (1998): 267.

Ellickson, Robert. *Order Without Law: How Neighbors Settle Disputes*. Cambridge, Mass.: Harvard University Press, 1991 (1994 printing).

El Zeidy, Mohamed M. "The Principle of Complementarity: A New Mechanism to Implement International Criminal Law." *Michigan International Law Journal* 23 (2002): 869

Everling, Ulrich. "The Member States of the European Community before their Court of Justice." *European Law Review* 9 (1984): 215.

Falk, Richard, and Andrew Strauss. "Toward Global Parliament." 80 *Foreign Affairs* (2001): 212.

Fearon, James D. "Deliberation as Discussion," In *Deliberative Democracy*, edited by Jon Elster. Cambridge: Cambridge University Press, 1998.

Flaschen, Evan D., and Ronald J. Silverman, "Cross-Border Insolvency Cooperation Protocols." *Texas International Law Journal* 33 (1998): 587.

Flynn, Stephen E. "America The Vulnerable." *Foreign Affairs* 81: (2002): 60–74.

Fox, Eleanor M. "Toward World Antitrust and Market Access." *American Journal of International Law* 91 (1997): 1.

Franck, Thomas M. "NYU Conference Discusses Impact of International Tribunals." *International Judicial Observer* 1 (1995): 3.

Franck, Thomas M., and Gregory H. Fox, eds., *International Law Decisions in National Courts*. New York: Transnational Publishers, 1996.

Freeman, Jody. "Collaborative Governance in the Administrative State." *UCLA Law Review* 45 (1997): 1.

Fried, Charles. "Scholars and Judges: Reason and Power." *Harvard Journal of Law and Public Policy* 23 (2000): 807.

Friedman, Thomas. *The Lexus and the Olive Tree: Understanding Globalization*. New York: Farrar, Straus and Giroux, 1999.

Fulton, Scott C., and Lawrence I. Sperling. "The Network of Environmental Enforcement and Compliance Cooperation in North America and the Western Hemisphere." *International Lawyer* 30 (1996): 111.

Furuta, Yoshimasa. "International Parallel Litigation: Disposition of Duplicative Civil Proceedings in the United States and Japan." *Pacific Rim Law and Policy Association* (November 1995): 1.

Gardner, Richard N. *Sterling-Dollar Diplomacy in Current Perspective: The Origins and the Prospects of Our International Economic Order*. New York: Columbia University Press, 1980.

Garrett, Geoffrey. "International Cooperation and Institutional Choice: The European Community's Internal Market." *International Organization* 46 (1992): 533.

———. "The Politics of Legal Integration in the European Union." *International Organization* 49 (1995): 171.

Garrett, Geoffrey, and Barry Weingast. "Ideas, Interests and Institutions: Constructing the EC's Internal Market." In *Ideas & Foreign Policy: Beliefs, Institutions and Political Change*, edited by Judith Goldstein and Robert O. Keohane. Ithaca: Cornell University Press, 1993.

Garrett, Geoffrey R., Daniel Kelemen, and Heiner Schulz. "The European Court of Justice, National Governments, and Legal Integration in the European Union." *International Organization* 52 (1998): 149.

Gerstenberg, Oliver and Charles F. Sabel, "Directly Deliberative Polyarchy: An Institutional Ideal for Europe." In *Good Governance in Europe's Integrated Market*, edited by Christian Jorges and Reanud Dehousse. Oxford: Oxford University Press, 2002.

Ghai, Yash. "Sentinels of Liberty or Sheep in Wolf's Clothing? Judicial Politics and the Hong Kong Bill of Rights." *Modern Law Review* 60 (1997): 459.

Ginsburg, Ruth Bader. "Affirmative Action as an International Human Rights Dialogue." *Brookings Review* 18 (2000): 2.

Ginsburg, Ruth Bader, and Deborah Jones Merritt, "Affirmative Action: An International Human Rights Dialogue." *Cardozo Law Review* 21 (1999): 253.

Glendon, Mary Ann. *Rights Talk: The Impoverishment of Political Discourse*. New York: Free Press, 1991.

Glenn, Patrick. "Persuasive Authority." *McGill Law Journal* 32 (1987): 261.

Goldstein, Judith. "International Law and Domestic Institutions, Reconciling North American 'Unfair' Trade Laws." *International Organization* 50 (1996): 541.

Goldstein, Judith, and Lisa Martin. "Legalization, Trade Liberalization, and Domestic Politics: A Cautionary Note." In *Legalization and World Politics*, edited by Judith Goldstein, Miles Kahler, Robert O. Keohane, and Anne-Marie Slaughter. Cambridge, Mass.: IO Foundation and Massachusetts Institute of Technology, 2001.

Griffin, Joseph P. "EC/U.S. Antitrust Cooperation Agreement: Impact on Transnational Business." *Law and Policy in International Business* 24 (1993): 1051.

———. "EC and U.S. Extraterritoriality: Activism and Cooperation." *Fordham International Law Journal* 17 (1994): 353.

Guevara, Arron. "Puerto Rico: Manifestations of Colonialism." *Revista Juridica Universidad de Puerto Rico* 26 (1992): 275.

Guinier, Lani. *The Miner's Canary: Enlisting Race, Resisting Power, Transforming Democracy*. Cambridge, Mass.: Harvard University Press, 2002.

Guzman, Andrew. "Is International Antitrust Possible?" *New York University Law Review* 73 (1998): 1501.

Haas, Peter M. *Saving the Mediterranean: The Politics of International Environmental Cooperation*. New York: Columbia University Press, 1990.

———. "Introduction: Epistemic Communities and International Policy Coordination." *International Organization* 46 (1992): 1.

———, ed. "Knowledge, Power and International Policy Coordination." *International Organization* 46 (Special Issue) (1992).

Habermas, Jurgen. *Theorie des kommunikativen Handelns*. Frankfurt am Main: Suhrkamp, 1981 (translated as *Theory of Communicative Action* [Boston: Beacon Press, 1984]).

Hachigian, Nina. "Essential Mutual Assistance in International Antitrust Enforcement." *International Lawyer* 29 (1995): 117.

———. "International Antitrust Enforcement." *Antitrust* 12 (1997): 22.

Hannum, Hurst. "Recent Case." *American Journal of International Law* 84 (1990): 768.

Haq, Arif S. "Note, *Kaepa, Inc. v. Achilles Corp.*: Comity in International Judicial Relations," *North Carolina Journal International Law and Commercial Regulations* 22 (1996): 365.

Hart, Henry M., Jr., and Albert M. Sacks. *The Legal Process: Basic Problems in the Making and Application of Law* (prepared for publication from the 1958 tentative edition by William N. Eskridge, Jr., and Philip P. Frickey). New York: Foundation Press, 1994.

Hechter, Michael. *Principles of Group Solidarity*. Berkeley: University of California Press, 1987.

Hirschman, Albert O. *A Propensity to Self-Subversion*. Cambridge, Mass.: Harvard University Press, 1995.

Hochkammer, Karl Arthur. "The Yugoslav War Crimes Tribunal: The Compatibility of Peace, Politics, and International Law." *Vanderbilt Journal of Transnational Law* 28 (1995): 119.

Horeth, Marcus. *The Trilemma of Legitimacy: Multilevel Governance in the EU and the Problem of Democracy*. Bonn: Zentrum fuer Europaeische Integrationsforschung, Rheinische Friedrich-Wilhelms-Universitaet Bonn, 1998.

House of Commons, Foreign Affairs Committee. "The Future Role of the Commonwealth." *House of Commons, Foreign Affairs Committee, First Report*. Vol. 1, (Session 1995–96): xi.

Howell, David. "The Place of the Commonwealth in the International Order." *The Round Table* 345 (1988): 29.

Ignatieff, Michael. *Human Rights as Politics and Idolatry*. Princeton, N.J.: Princeton University Press, 2001.

Jacobs, Scott H. "Why Governments Must Work Together." *The OECD Observer* 186 (February/March 1994): 15.

James, Vaughn E. "Twenty-First Century Pirates of the Caribbean: How the Organization for Economic Cooperation and Development Robbed Fourteen Caricom Countries of Their Tax and Economic Policy Sovereignty." *University of Miami Inter-American Law Review* 34 (2002).

Janow, Merit. "Transatlantic Cooperation on Competition Policy." In *Antitrust Goes Global*, edited by Simon J. Evenett, Alexander Lehmann, and Benn Steil. Washington, D.C.: The Brookings Institution, 2000.

Jarmul, Holly Dawn. "Effects of Decisions of Regional Human Rights Tribunals on National Courts." In *International Law Decisions in National Courts*, edited by Thomas M. Franck and Gregory H. Fox. New York: Transnational Publishers, 1996.

Joelson, Mark R. *An International Antitrust Primer: A Guide to the Operation of the United States, European Union, and Other Key Competition Laws in the Global Economy*. Kluwer Law International: The Hague, 2001.

Joerges, Christian, and Juergen Neyer. "From Intergovernmental Bargaining to Deliberative Political Processes: The Constitutionalisation of Comitology." *European Law Journal* 3 (1997): 273.

Joerges, Christian, and Ellen Vos, eds. *EU Committees: Social Regulation, Law and Politics*. Portland: Hart Publishers, 1999.

Jones, Alun, and Julian Clark. *The Modalities of European Union Governance: New Institutionalist Explanations of Agri-Environmental Policy*. New York: Oxford University Press, 2001.

Kagan, Elena. "Presidential Administration." *Harvard Law Review* 114 (2001): 2245.

Kahler, Miles. "Legalization as Strategy: The Asia-Pacific Case." In *Legalization and World Politics*, edited by Judith Goldstein, Miles Kahler, Robert O. Keohane, and Anne-Marie Slaughter. Cambridge, Mass.: IO Foundation and Massachusetts Institute of Technology, 2001.

Kaiser, Karl. "Globalisierung als Problem der Demokratie." *Internationale Politik* (April 1998): 3.

Kapstein, Ethan. *Governing the Global Economy: International Finance and the State*. Cambridge, Mass.: Harvard University Press, 1994.

———. "Shockproof." *Foreign Affairs* 74 (1996): 2.

Kay, Richard S. "The European Convention on Human Rights and the Authority of Law." *Connecticut Journal of International Law* 8 (1993): 217.

Keohane, Robert O., and Joseph S. Nye, Jr. "Transgovernmental Relations and International Organizations." *World Politics* 27 (1974): 39.

———. *Power and Interdependence: World Politics in Transition*. Boston: Little, Brown, 1977.

————. "Power and Interdependence in the Information Age," *Foreign Affairs* 77 (1998): 81.

————. "The Club Model of Multilateral Cooperation and Problems of Democratic Legitimacy." In *Efficiency, Equity, and Legitimacy: The Multilateral Trading System at the Millennium*, edited by Roger B. Porter, Pierre Sauvé, Arvind Subramanian, and Americo Beviglia Zampetti. Washington, D.C.: Brookings Institution Press, 2001.

Kim, Young Sok. "The Preconditions to the Exercise of the Jurisdiction of the International Criminal Court: With Focus on Article 12 of the Rome Statute." *Journal of International Law and Practice* 8 (1999): 47.

Kirby, M. D. "The Role of the Judge in Advancing Human Rights by Reference to International Human Rights Norms." *Australian Law Review* 62 (1988): 514.

Klein, Joel, and Preeta Bansal. "International Antitrust Enforcement in the Computer Industry." *Villanova Law Review* 41 (1996): 173.

Koch, Charles H., Jr. "Judicial Review and Global Federalism." *Administrative Law Review* 54 (2002): 491.

Koh, Harold Hongju. "The 1994 Roscoe Pound Lecture: Transnational Legal Process." *Nebraska Law Review* 75 (1996): 181.

————. "The 1998 Frankel Lecture: Bringing International Law Home." *Houston Law Review* 25 (1998): 623.

Kokott, Julianne. "Report on Germany." In *The European Court and National Courts—Doctrine and Jurisprudence: Legal Change in Its Social Context*, edited by Anne-Marie Slaughter, Alec Stone Sweet, and J.H.H. Weiler. Evanston, Ill.: Northwestern University Press, 1998.

Koopmans, Thijmen. "The Birth of European Law at the Crossroads of Legal Traditions." *American Journal of Comparative Law* 39 (1991): 493.

Ladeur, Karl Heinz. "Towards a Legal Concept of the Network in European Standard-Setting." In *Integrating Scientific Expertise into Regulatory Decision-Making: National Traditions and European Innovations*, edited by Christian Joerges, Karl-Heinz Ladeur, and Ellen Vos. Baden-Baden: Nomos, 1997.

Larson, Andrea. "Network Dyads in Entrepreneurial Settings: A Study of the Governance of Exchange Relationships." *Administrative Science Quarterly* 37 (1992): 76.

Leonard, Bruce. "Managing Default by a Multinational Venture: Cooperation in Cross-Border Insolvencies." *Texas International Law Journal* 33 (1998): 543.

Lessig, Lawrence. "Introduction (Feature: Making Sense of the Hague Tribunal)." *Eastern European Constitutional Review* 5 (1996): 73.

Lester, Anthony. "The Overseas Trade in the American Bill of Rights." *Columbia Law Review* 88 (1988): 537.

L'Heureux-Dubé, Claire. "The Importance of Dialogue: Globalization and the International Impact of the Rehnquist Court." *Tulsa Law Journal* 34 (1998): 15.

Longstreth, Bevis. "The SEC after Fifty Years: An Assessment of its Past and Future." *Columbia Law Review* 83 (1983): 1593.

Loveland, Ian. "The Criminalization of Racist Violence." In *A Special Relationship? American Influences on Public Law in the UK*, edited by Ian Loveland. Oxford: Clarendon Press, 1995.

Lunn, Simon. "NATO's Parliamentary Arm Helps Further the Aims of the Alliance." *NATO Review* 46 (1998): 8.

Lyman, Princeton N. "The Growing Influence of Domestic Factors." In *Multilateralism and US Foreign Policy: Ambivalent Engagement*, edited by Stewart Patrick and Shephard Forman. Boulder: Lynne Rienner Publishers, 2002.

MacCormick, Neil. "Beyond the Sovereign State." *Modern Law Review* 56 (1993).

Macey, Jonathan R. "The 'Demand' for International Regulatory Cooperation: A Public-Choice Perspective." In *Transatlantic Regulatory Co-Operation: Legal Problems and Political Prospects*, edited by George A. Bermann, Matthias Herdegen, and Peter L. Lindseth. Oxford: Oxford University Press, 2000.

Maier, Harold G. "Extraterritorial Jurisdiction at a Crossroads: An Intersection between Public and Private International Law." *American Journal of International Law* 76 (1982): 280.

Majone, Giandomenico. "The European Community as a Regulatory State." In *Collected Courses of the Academy of European Law*. Vol. 5, Bk. 1. Dordrecht, Netherlands: Kluwer, 1994.

———. "From the Positive to the Regulatory State: Causes and Consequences of Changes in the Mode of Governance." *Journal of Public Policy* 17 (1997): 139.

———. "The New European Agencies: Regulation by Information." *Journal of European Public Policy* 4 (1997): 262–75.

Mancini, G. Federico. "The Making of a Constitution for Europe." *Common Market Law Review* 26 (1989): 595.

Manin, Bernard. "On Legitimacy and Political Deliberation." *Political Theory* 15 (1987): 338.

Mansbridge, Jane. *Beyond Adversary Democracy*. Chicago: University of Chicago Press, 1983.

March, James G., and Johan P. Olsen. *Rediscovering Institutions: The Organizational Basis of Politics*. New York: Free Press 1989.

———. "The Institutional Dynamics of International Political Orders." *International Organization* 52 52, no. 4 (DATE):(1998).

Markell, David. L. "The Commission for Environmental Cooperation's Citizen Submission Process." *Georgetown International Law Review* 12 (2000): 545.

Marks, Gary, Lisbet Hooghe, and Kermit Blank. "An Actor-Centered Approach to Multi-Level Governance." *Journal of Regional and Federal Studies* 6 (1996): 20.

Mattli, Walter, and Anne-Marie Slaughter. "Law and Politics in the European Union: A Reply to Garrett." *International Organization* 49 (1995): 183.

McClean, David. "A Common Inheritance? An Examination of the Private International Law Tradition of the Commonwealth." In *Recueil des Cours 1996: Collected Courses of The Hague Academy of International Law*. The Hague: Academie de Droit International, 1997.

McCrudden, Christopher. "A Common Law of Human Rights?: Transnational Judicial Conversations on Constitutional Rights." *Oxford Journal of Legal Studies* 20 (2000): 499.

Merrills, J. G. *The Development of International Law by the European Court of Human Rights*. 2d ed. New York: St. Martin's Press, 1993.

Merry, Sally Engle. *Urban Danger: Life in a Neighborhood of Strangers*. Philadelphia: Temple University Press, 1981.

Mihm, Michael M. "International Judicial Relations Committee Promotes Communication Coordination." *International Judicial Observer* 1 (1995).

Naím, Moise. "Five Wars of Globalization." *Foreign Policy* (January/February 2003): 29–36

Nye, Joseph S., Jr. *Bound to Lead: The Changing Nature of American Power*. New York: Basic Books, 1990.

———. *The Paradox of American Power: Why the World's Only Superpower Can't Go It Alone*. New York: Oxford University Press, 2002.

Olson, Mancur, Jr., *The Logic of Collective Action: Public Goods and the Theory of Groups*. Cambridge, Mass., Harvard University Press, 1965.

Paul, Joel. "Comity in International Law. *Harvard International Law Journal* 32 (1991).

Perez, Antonio F. "Who Killed Sovereignty? Or: Changing Norms Concerning Sovereignty In International Law. *Wisconsin International Law Journal* 14 (1996): 463.

Petersmann, Ernst-Ulrich. "Constitutionalism and International Organizations. *Northwestern Journal of International Law and Business* 17 (1997): 398.

———. "Constitutionalism and International Adjudication: How to Constitutionalize the U.N. Dispute Settlement System?" *New York University Journal of International Law and Politics* 31 (1999): 753.

Picciotto, Sol. "Networks in International Economic Integration. *Northwestern Journal of Law and Business* 17 (1996–97): 1014.

Ploetner, Jens. "Report on France: The Reception of the Direct Effect and Supremacy Doctrine by the French Supreme Courts." In *The European Court and National Courts—Doctrine and Jurisprudence: Legal Change in Its Social Context*, edited by Anne-Marie Slaughter, Alec Stone Sweet, and J.H.H. Weiler. Evanston, Ill.: Northwestern University Press, 1998.

Polakiewicz, Joerg and Valerie Jacob-Foltzer. "The European Human Rights Convention in Domestic Law: The Impact of Strasbourg Case Law in States Where Direct Effect Is Given to the Convention (pt. 1)." *Human Rights Law Journal* 12 (1991): 65.

Pollack, Mark A., and Gregory C. Shaffer, eds. *Transatlantic Governance in the Global Economy*. Lanham, Md.: Rowman and Littlefield, 2001.

Porter, Tony. *States, Markets and Regimes in Global Finance*. New York: St. Martin's Press, 1993.

Powell, W. W. "Neither Market nor Hierarchy." In *Research in Organizational Behavior*, Vol. 12, edited by Barry Staw and L. L. Cummings. Greenwich, Conn.: JAI, 1979.

Putnam, Robert. "Diplomacy and Domestic Policy: The Logic of Two-Level Games." *International Organization* 43 (1988): 427.

Rapaczynski, Andrzej. "Bibliographical Essay: The Influence of U.S. Constitutionalism Abroad." In *Constitutionalism and Rights: The Influence of the United States Constitution Abroad*, edited by Louis Henkin and Albert J. Rosenthal. New York: Columbia University Press, 1990.

Raustiala, Kal. "The Architecture of International Cooperation: Transgovernmental

Networks and The Future of International Law." *Virginia Journal of International Law* 43 (2002): 1.

Rawls, John. *Political Liberalism.* New York: Columbia University Press, 1996.

"Regulatory Co-Operation for an Interdependent World: Issues for Government." In *Organisation for Economic Co-operation and Development, Regulatory Co-operation for an Interdependent World.* Paris, France: Organisation for Economic Co-operation and Development, 1994.

Reinicke, Wolfgang H. "Global Public Policy." *Foreign Affairs* 76 (1997): 137.

———. *Global Public Policy: Governing without Government?* Washington, D.C.: The Brookings Institution, 1998.

———. "The Other World Wide Web: Global Public Policy Networks." *Foreign Policy* (Winter 1999/2000): 44.

Reinicke, Wolfgang H., and Francis Deng, *Critical Choices: The United Nations, Networks, and the Future of Global Governance.* Ottawa: International Development Research Centre, 2000.

Rhodes, R.A.W. "The New Governance: Governing without Government." *Political Studies* 44 (1996): 652.

———. *Understanding Governance: Policy Networks, Governance, Reflexivity and Accountability.* Philadelphia: Open University Press, 1997.

Rischard, Jean-François. "A Novel Approach to Problem-Solving." *Global Agenda 2003—World Economic Forum* 1 (2003): 30.

Risse, Thomas. "'Let's Argue!': Communicative Action in World Politics." *International Organization* 54 (2000): 31.

Rosenau, James N. *Along the Domestic-International Frontier: Exploring Governance in a Turbulent World.* Cambridge: Cambridge University Press, 1997.

Rosenau, James N., and Ernst-Otto Czempiel, eds. *Governance without Government: Order and Change in World Politics.* Cambridge: Cambridge University Press, 1992.

Ruggie, John G. "What Makes the World Hang Together? Neo-utilitarianism and the Social Constructivist Challenge." In *Constructing the World Polity: Essays on International Institutionalism,* edited by John G. Ruggie. New York: Routledge, 1998.

———. "Global_Governance.net: The Global Compact as Learning Network." *Global Governance* 7 (2001): 371.

Rule, Charles F. "European Communities-United States Agreement on the Application of their Competition Laws Introductory Note." *International Legal Materials* 30 (1991): 1487.

Salzman, James. "Labor Rights, Globalization and Institutions: The Role and Influence of the Organization for Economic Cooperation and Development." *Michigan Journal of International Law* 21 (2000): 766–83.

Santosus, Bonnie. "An International Criminal Court: Where Global Harmony Begins." *Touro International Law Review* 5 (1995): 25.

Scharpf, Fritz W. "Community and Autonomy: Multi-Level Governance in the European Union." *Journal of European Public Policy* 1 (1994): 219.

Schauer, Frederick. "The Politics and Incentives of Legal Transplantation." In *Gover-*

nance in a Globalizing World, edited by Joseph S. Nye, Jr., and John D. Donahue. Washington, D.C.: The Brookings Institution, 2000.

Scheffer, David J. "Fourteenth Waldemar A. Solf Lecture in International Law: A Negotiator's Perspective on the International Criminal Court." *Military Law Review* 167 (2001): 1.

Shank, Robert D. "The Justice Department's Recent Antitrust Enforcement Policy: Toward A 'Positive Comity' Solution to International Competition Problems?" *Vanderbilt Journal of Transnational Law* 29 (1996): 155.

Shapiro, David L. *Federalism: A Dialogue.* Evanston, Ill.: Northwestern University Press, 1995.

Shapiro, Martin. "Administrative Law Unbounded: Reflections on Government and Governance." *Indiana Journal of Global Legal Studies* 8 (2001): 369.

Shapiro, Sidney A. "International Trade Agreements, Regulatory Protection, and Public Accountability." *Administrative Law Review* 54 (2002): 435.

Shelton, Dinah, ed., *Commitment and Compliance: The Role of Non-Binding Norms in the International Legal System.* New York: Oxford University Press, 2000.

Shklar, Judith. "The Liberalism of Fear." In *Political Thought and Political Thinkers,* edited by Stanley Hoffman. Chicago: University of Chicago Press, 1998.

Slaughter, Anne-Marie. "Court to Court," *American Journal of International Law* 92 (1998): 708.

———. "Governing the Global Economy through Government Networks." In *The Role of Law in International Politics,* edited by Michael Byers. New York: Oxford University Press, 2000.

Slaughter, Anne-Marie, and Laurence R. Helfer. "Toward a Theory of Effective Supranational Adjudication." *Yale Law Journal* 107 (1997): 273.

Smith, Carsten. "The Supreme Court in Present-day Society." In *The Supreme Court of Norway,* edited by Stephan Tschudi-Madsen. Oslo: H. Aschenhoug and Co., 1998.

Smith, T. B. "Legal Imperialism and Legal Parochialism." *Juridical Review* 10 (New Series) (1965): 39.

Snell, Steven L. "Controlling Restrictive Business Practices in Global Markets: Reflections on the Concepts of Sovereignty, Fairness, and Comity." *Stanford Journal of International Law* 33 (1997): 215.

Stark, Charles S. "International Antitrust Cooperation in NAFTA: The International Antitrust Assistance Act of 1994." *U.S.-Mexico Law Journal* 4 (1996): 169.

Stein, Eric. "Lawyers, Judges, and the Making of a Transnational Constitution." *American Journal of International Law* 75 (1981): 1.

Stoker, Gerry "Governance as Theory: Five Propositions." *International Social Science Journal* 155 (1998): 17–28.

Stone Sweet, Alec. "Constitutional Dialogues in the European Community." In *The European Court and National Courts—Doctrine and Jurisprudence: Legal Change in Its Social Context,* edited by Anne-Marie Slaughter, Alec Stone Sweet, and J.H.H. Weiler. Evanston, Ill.: Northwestern University Press, 1998.

Story, Joseph. *Commentaries on The Conflict of Laws.* Boston: Little, Brown, 1834.

Swann, Alan. "NAFTA and the Juridification of Economic Relations in the Western

Hemisphere." In *Perspectives of Air Law, Space Law, and International Business Law for the Next Century: Proceedings of an International Colloquium, Cologne, 7–9 June 1995 to Celebrate 70 years of the Institute of Air and Space Law and 20 Years of the Chair for International Business Law at the University of Cologne*, edited by Karl Heinz Bockstiegal. Köln: Carl Heymanns Verlag, 1996.

Swanson, Stephen R. "The Vexationusness of a Vexation Rule: International Comity And Antisuit Injunctions." *George Washington Journal of International Law and Economics* 30 (1996): 1.

"Symposium on Global Administrative Law." *Administrative Law Review* 54 (2002).

Tarullo, Daniel K. "Norms and Institutions in Global Competition Policy." *American Journal of International Law* 94 (2000): 478.

Teitel, Ruti. "Judgment at the Hague." *Eastern European Constitutional Review* 5 (1996): 81.

Tetley, William. "New Development in Private International Law: Tolofson v. Jensen and Gagnon v. Lucas." *American Journal of Comparative Law* 44 (1996): 647.

Unt, Lore. "International Relations and International Insolvency Cooperation: Liberalism, Institutionalism, and Transnational Legal Dialogue." *Law and Policy of International Business* 28 (1997): 1037.

"US Objections Prompt Limited Global Pact on Financial Services." *Banking Policy Report* 14 (1995): 17.

Vereschetin, Vladlen S. "The Relationship between International Law and National Law." *European Journal of International Law* 7 (1996): 29.

Vogel, David. *Benefits or Barriers?: Regulation in Transatlantic Trade*. Washington, D.C.: The Brookings Institution, 1997.

Wallace, William. "Europe, the Necessary Partner." *Foreign Affairs* 80 (2001): 16.

Waller, Spencer Weber. "Comparative Competition Law as a Form of Empiricism." *Brooklyn Journal of International Law* 23 (1997): 455.

———. "The Internationalization of Antitrust Enforcement." *Boston University Law Review* 77 (1997): 343.

———. "National Laws and International Markets: Strategies of Cooperation and Harmonization in the Enforcement of Competition Law." *Cardozo Law Review* 18 (1999): 1111.

Watson, Alan. *Legal Transplants*. Edinburgh: Scottish Academic Press, 1974.

———. "Legal Change: Sources of Law and Legal Culture." *University of Pennsylvania Law Review* 131 (1983): 1121.

Weiler, Joseph H. H. "The Transformation of Europe." *Yale Law Journal* 100 (1991): 2403.

———. "Epilogue: The European Courts of Justice: Beyond 'Beyond Doctrine' or the Legitimacy Crisis of European Constitutionalism." In *The European Court and National Courts—Doctrine and Jurisprudence: Legal Change in Its Social Context*, edited by Anne-Marie Slaughter, Alec Stone Sweet, and J.H.H. Weiler. Evanston, Ill.: Northwestern University Press, 1998.

———. *The Constitution of Europe: "Do the New Clothes Have An Emperor?" and Other Essays on European Integration*. New York: Cambridge University Press, 1999.

———. "To Be a European Citizen: Eros and Civilization." In *The Constitution of Eu-*

rope: "Do the New Clothes Have An Emperor?" and Other Essays on European Integration. New York: Cambridge University Press, 1999.

Westbrook, Jay Lawrence. "Theory and Pragmatism in Global Insolvencies: Choice of Law and Choice of Forum." American Banker Law Journal 65 (1991): 457.

——— "International Judicial Negotiation." Texas International Law Journal 38 (2003): 567.

Wexler, Leila Sadat. "Committee Report on Jurisdiction, Definition of Crimes and Complementarity." Denver Journal of International Law and Policy 25 (1997): 221.

Williams, Shirley. "Sovereignty and Accountability in the European Union." In The New European Community: Decisionmaking and Institutional Change, edited by Robert O. Keohane and Stanley Hoffmann. Boulder: Westview Press, 1991.

Zaring, David. "International Law by Other Means: The Twilight Existence of International Financial Regulatory Organizations." Texas International Law Journal 33 (1998): 281.

Zarjevski, Yefime. The People Have the Floor: A History of the Interparliamentary Union. Brookfield, Vt.: Gower, 1989.

Index